ANTICIPATIONS AND PURCHASES

An Analysis of Consumer Behavior

T0313907

NATIONAL BUREAU OF ECONOMIC RESEARCH
NUMBER 79, GENERAL SERIES

Anticipations and Purchases

AN ANALYSIS
OF CONSUMER BEHAVIOR

by

F. Thomas Juster

A STUDY BY THE

NATIONAL BUREAU OF ECONOMIC RESEARCH

PUBLISHED BY

PRINCETON UNIVERSITY PRESS

PRINCETON, NEW JERSEY

1964

Copyright © 1964 by National Bureau of Economic Research, Inc.
All Rights Reserved
L.C. Card No. 63-23396

Printed in the United States of America

NATIONAL BUREAU OF ECONOMIC RESEARCH
1964

OFFICERS

Albert J. Hettinger, Jr., *Chairman*
Arthur F. Burns, *President*
Frank W. Fetter, *Vice-President*
Donald B. Woodward, *Treasurer*
Solomon Fabricant, *Director of Research*
Geoffrey H. Moore, *Associate Director of Research*
Hal B. Lary, *Associate Director of Research*
William J. Carson, *Executive Director*

DIRECTORS AT LARGE

Robert B. Anderson, *New York City*
Wallace J. Campbell, *Nationwide Insurance*
Erwin D. Canham, *Christian Science Monitor*
Solomon Fabricant, *New York University*
Marion B. Folsom, *Eastman Kodak Company*
Crawford H. Greenewalt, *E. I. du Pont de Nemours & Company*
Gabriel Hauge, *Manufacturers Hanover Trust Company*
A. J. Hayes, *International Association of Machinists*
Albert J. Hettinger, Jr. *Lazard Frères and Company*
Nicholas Kelley, *Kelley Drye Newhall Maginnes & Warren*
H. W. Laidler, *League for Industrial Democracy*
Charles G. Mortimer, *General Foods Corporation*
George B. Roberts, *Larchmont, New York*
Harry Scherman, *Book-of-the-Month Club*
Boris Shishkin, *American Federation of Labor and Congress of Industrial Organizations*
George Soule, *South Kent, Connecticut*
Joseph H. Willits, *Langhorne, Pennsylvania*
Donald B. Woodward, *A. W. Jones and Company*

DIRECTORS BY UNIVERSITY APPOINTMENT

V. W. Bladen, *Toronto*
Francis M. Boddy, *Minnesota*
Arthur F. Burns, *Columbia*
Lester V. Chandler, *Princeton*
Melvin G. de Chazeau, *Cornell*
Frank W. Fetter, *Northwestern*
R. A. Gordon, *California*

Harold M. Groves, *Wisconsin*
Gottfried Haberler, *Harvard*
Maurice W. Lee, *North Carolina*
Lloyd G. Reynolds, *Yale*
Paul A. Samuelson, *Massachusetts Institute of Technology*
Theodore W. Schultz, *Chicago*

Willis J. Winn, *Pennsylvania*

DIRECTORS BY APPOINTMENT OF OTHER ORGANIZATIONS

Percival F. Brundage, *American Institute of Certified Public Accountants*
Nathaniel Goldfinger, *American Federation of Labor and Congress of Industrial Organizations*
Harold G. Halcrow, *American Farm Economic Association*
Murray Shields, *American Management Association*
Willard L. Thorp, *American Economic Association*
W. Allen Wallis, *American Statistical Association*
Harold F. Williamson, *Economic History Association*
Theodore O. Yntema, *Committee for Economic Development*

DIRECTORS EMERITI

Shepard Morgan, *Norfolk, Connecticut*
N. I. Stone, *New York City*
Jacob Viner, *Princeton, New Jersey*

RESEARCH STAFF

Moses Abramovitz
Gary S. Becker
William H. Brown, Jr.
Gerhard Bry
Arthur F. Burns
Phillip Cagan
Joseph W. Conard
Frank G. Dickinson
James S. Earley
Richard A. Easterlin
Solomon Fabricant
Albert Fishlow
Milton Friedman

Victor R. Fuchs
H. G. Georgiadis
Raymond W. Goldsmith
Challis A. Hall, Jr.
Millard Hastay
Daniel M. Holland
Thor Hultgren
F. Thomas Juster
C. Harry Kahn
Irving B. Kravis
Hal B. Lary
Robert E. Lipsey
Ruth P. Mack

Jacob Mincer
Ilse Mintz
Geoffrey H. Moore
Roger F. Murray
Ralph L. Nelson
G. Warren Nutter
Richard T. Selden
Lawrence H. Seltzer
Robert P. Shay
George J. Stigler
Norman B. Ture
Herbert B. Woolley
Victor Zarnowitz

RELATION OF THE DIRECTORS
TO THE WORK AND PUBLICATIONS
OF THE NATIONAL BUREAU OF ECONOMIC RESEARCH

1. The object of the National Bureau of Economic Research is to ascertain and to present to the public important economic facts and their interpretation in a scientific and impartial manner. The Board of Directors is charged with the responsibility of ensuring that the work of the National Bureau is carried on in strict conformity with this object.

2. To this end the Board of Directors shall appoint one or more Directors of Research.

3. The Director or Directors of Research shall submit to the members of the Board, or to its Executive Committee, for their formal adoption, all specific proposals concerning researches to be instituted.

4. No report shall be published until the Director or Directors of Research shall have submitted to the Board a summary drawing attention to the character of the data and their utilization in the report, the nature and treatment of the problems involved, the main conclusions, and such other information as in their opinion would serve to determine the suitability of the report for publication in accordance with the principles of the National Bureau.

5. A copy of any manuscript proposed for publication shall also be submitted to each member of the Board. For each manuscript to be so submitted a special committee shall be appointed by the President, or at his designation by the Executive Director, consisting of three Directors selected as nearly as may be one from each general division of the Board. The names of the special manuscript committee shall be stated to each Director when the summary and report described in paragraph (4) are sent to him. It shall be the duty of each member of the committee to read the manuscript. If each member of the special committee signifies his approval within thirty days, the manuscript may be published. If each member of the special committee has not signified his approval within thirty days of the transmittal of the report and manuscript, the Director of Research shall then notify each member of the Board, requesting approval or disapproval of publication, and thirty additional days shall be granted for this purpose. The manuscript shall then not be published unless at least a majority of the entire Board and a two-thirds majority of those members of the Board who shall have voted on the proposal within the time fixed for the receipt of votes on the publication proposed shall have approved.

6. No manuscript may be published, though approved by each member of the special committee, until forty-five days have elapsed from the transmittal of the summary and report. The interval is allowed for the receipt of any memorandum of dissent or reservation, together with a brief statement of his reasons, that any member may wish to express; and such memorandum of dissent or reservation shall be published with the manuscript if he so desires. Publication does not, however, imply that each member of the Board has read the manuscript, or that either members of the Board in general, or of the special committee, have passed upon its validity in every detail.

7. A copy of this resolution shall, unless otherwise determined by the Board, be printed in each copy of every National Bureau book.

(Resolution adopted October 25, 1926,
as revised February 6, 1933, and February 24, 1941)

Contents

vii

CONTENTS

CONTENTS

Tables

Charts

Preface

THIS study was originally designed as a companion piece to my *Consumer Expectations, Plans, and Purchases: A Progress Report*, Occasional Paper 70, published under the auspices of the National Bureau in 1959. The logical sequel to a "progress report" is presumably a "final report." The sophisticated reader will not be surprised to learn, however, that this monograph is somewhere between the two, and that in the course of investigation more questions were raised than answered.

The first complete draft of this manuscript was circulated to a National Bureau staff reading committee, as well as to a few of the people engaged in research on consumer anticipations, in May 1960. On the basis of comments received, especially from the staff reading committee of Milton Friedman, Jacob Mincer, Ruth Mack, and Phillip Cagan, I decided that it would be desirable to rewrite the entire manuscript. Its current orientation owes a great deal to Friedman. I am greatly indebted to Mincer for a host of ingenious suggestions relating to the concrete formulation of hypotheses and the construction of appropriate empirical tests.

Others at the National Bureau have given generously of their time at various stages of the project, especially Gary Becker, Zvi Griliches, and Geoffrey Moore. And I am indebted to Eva Mueller, Mona Dingle, Milton Moss, Robert Ferber, Nelson Foote, and Lee Wiggins for very useful comments on parts of the manuscript. Many others have made informal but valuable contributions, notably Albert Hart and Marshall Kolin. I wish also to thank the reading committee of the National Bureau's Board of Directors: George B. Roberts, Paul A. Samuelson, and Theodore O. Yntema.

Among the research assistants who worked on the project, special thanks are due Linda Fulton, Bette Fishbein, and Susan Fromm. During earlier stages of the investigation I was ably assisted by Jean Namias, George Stein, Stanley Besen, and Ann Picker. The charts were drawn by H. Irving Forman; the manuscript was edited by Ester Moskowitz.

Financial support for the project was provided by grants from the Relm Foundation, Ann Arbor, Michigan; Consumers Union of the U.S., Mount Vernon, N.Y.; and by other funds of the National Bureau.

I also wish to acknowledge my gratitude to the 25,000 odd anonymou "volunteers" who provided the basic date for the study. These families, who were Consumers Union member-subscribers in April 1958, have been subjected to a variety of impositions ranging from excessively long questionnaries to an (inadvertant) failure to include either a return envelope or postage on one mailing. The patience and cooperativeness of our panel members, in the face of these obstacles, has been most generous.

A Guide for Readers

Some sections of the manuscript will be of interest primarily to specialists, while other parts should be both accessible and of interest to the non-specialist. Most of chapter 3, all of 4, the second parts of 5 and 6, and Appendix B fall into the first category; Chapters 1, 2, the first parts of 3, 5 and 6, and Appendix C, fall into the second. Chapter 7 and Appendix A are predominantly statistical; standard multivariate regression techniques are used for the most part.

ANTICIPATIONS AND PURCHASES
An Analysis of Consumer Behavior

CHAPTER 1

Introduction and Summary

SINCE the end of the Second World War it has been increasingly clear that variations in consumer expenditures often play an active rather than a passive role in the generation of business cycles. Variations in consumer demand appear to be relatively, and perhaps absolutely, stronger in the durable goods component of consumer spending, especially automobiles, than in nondurable goods or services. And it is argued by many that changes in the factor variously called "consumer anticipations," or "attitudes," or "expectations" are importantly related to independent variations in expenditures, and that changes in consumer anticipations are capable of being measured and predicted. This monograph is concerned with the use of survey data on consumer anticipations as an aid to prediction of durable goods purchases.

Concentration on the problem of prediction—as opposed to explanation—bypasses a subject of considerable importance. Even if consumer surveys are able to provide an accurate measure of the current state of consumer anticipations, it does not necessarily follow that they will also be able to explain the way in which anticipations are formed. But for making predictions, it is unnecessary to decide whether anticipatory variables are in some sense basic determinants of consumer behavior, or whether they are themselves wholly predictable from purely objective (i.e., historical) factors like income levels, or past rates of income change, and so on. I am, of course, concerned with whether or not surveys of consumer anticipations can improve predictions of purchase behavior *relative to predictions that use only objective variables obtainable at the same date.* Analysis of the empirical relations between durable goods purchases and objective variables like past changes in income or liquid assets is thus important here because it provides a bench mark against which to assess the predictive value of anticipatory variables.

Cross-Section vs. Time Series Analysis

Although the basic objective of the study is improved prediction of changes over time, the data comprise a cross section of households covering a single time period. Cross sections provide substantially greater flexibility than time series in that they contain an almost complete spectrum of possible differences in household circumstances as well as potentially unlimited numbers of observations. This makes it possible to investigate the simultaneous influence of a large number of factors; more important, perhaps, complex interrelations among explanatory variables can be examined.

However, the use of cross-section data to illuminate the behavior of time series presents its own difficulties. An analysis of factors associated with behavior differences among households at a single point in time does not necessarily yield valid inferences about factors responsible for differences in behavior over time. To illustrate: cross-section data will ordinarily show that households with incomes of $5,000 per year act differently than households with incomes of $4,000 per year. Can it be inferred that households with an income of $4,000 in one period and $5,000 in a subsequent period will show the same difference in behavior? Probably not. In a cross section, behavior differences among households with different incomes are mainly a reflection of long-run adjustment to a particular income position: for many—perhaps the majority—of households, income has been at the same level for some time in the past and is expected to remain there for some time into the future. But the behavior of households whose current income represents a change from the past is bound to reflect recent arrival at a new income status, the fact of income change rather than income stability, and, perhaps, the influence of concurrent changes in the income of neighbors.

It is true that many of these differences, e.g., the first two just noted, can be handled by an appropriate selection of households from a cross section or by inclusion of enough variables in the analysis. But the third kind of difference, which exists because a given change over time never takes place in a vacuum and frequently takes place in conjunction with similar changes in other households, cannot really be handled by any data that currently exist.[1]

Another obvious difference between cross-section and time-series analysis lies in the relative importance assigned to certain variables. Imagine a community with constant population, birth rate, death rate, and marriage rate, but with income varying through time. In a cross-section analysis it would probably be found that the most important factors associated with purchases of durable goods are the demographic structure of the household and its current and past income level. At a given income level,

---

[1] In principle, even this problem could be managed with cross-section data covering a number of consecutive years for identical households. Then one could talk about the effects of an income change for household A during a period when community income was also changing, and compute the effect on A's behavior of a change in A's income, community income unchanged, or of a change in community income, A's income unchanged. Daniel Suits of the University of Michigan has been working in this area, both in the development of statistical techniques and in fitting empirical relationships. I am not aware of any published results.

newly married couples with young children typically buy more durables than older couples whose children have married. But in such a community, demographic structure would clearly be of little or no importance to an explanation of time series changes in purchases because it is invariant over time.[2]

Another reason for caution in using single-time cross sections to illuminate time series problems is the "personality correlation" problem,[3] the difficulty encountered in isolating real behavior relationships from cross-section data. Observed differences among families may reflect mainly differences in the characteristics of the families themselves rather than in objective circumstances like financial status. To illustrate: the existence of personal debt must have a tendency to inhibit purchases, other things equal: a family with large debt would surely be less apt to buy than if the *same* family had a smaller debt but all other relevant circumstances were the same. Yet cross-section data from the Survey of Consumer Finances[4] indicate that relatively high levels of debt in a given period tend to be associated with relatively large purchases during a subsequent period. Does this mean that debt encourages purchases? Certainly not.

The empirical results presumably reflect the tendency of families with large debts to be spending-oriented and of families with low debts to be saving-oriented. By definition, spenders buy more than savers. But the empirical data do not indicate what the effect would be if all households— spenders and savers alike—had an increased level of debt and other factors remained the same. The answer to the latter question cannot be obtained because the empirical tests are dominated by personality differences that are in turn correlated with debt level. An independent test is needed to distinguish "spenders" from "savers," so that the effect of debt on households with the same personality traits can be investigated. For example, one might test for the effect on purchases of debt differences at two points in time for identical households, thus holding personality constant.

---

[2] Even in this extreme case demographic structure might be highly relevant for predicting changes over time. It cannot be assumed that the aggregate pattern of spending or saving is independent of the distribution of income change among households. If income increases were generally concentrated in younger households, the effect on purchases would be quite different than if the same aggregate income increases were concentrated in older households. Here, even when the distribution of powerful cross-section variables remains absolutely invariant over time, it would still be necessary to include these variables in an analysis concerned solely with movements over time.

[3] See James Tobin, "Consumer Debt and Spending: Some Evidence from Analysis of a Survey," *Consumer Instalment Credit: Conference on Regulation,* Board of Governors of the Federal Reserve System, 1957, Part II, Vol. 1.

[4] *Ibid.*

As already noted, tests of the simultaneous influence of a large number of variables constitute one of the basic advantages of cross-section over times-series data; even more important, perhaps, complex interrelationships among variables can be tested with much greater precision in a cross section of households. In my view, it is quite likely that the relation between consumer behavior and many of the potential explanatory variables is statistically complex rather than simple; i.e., the appropriate relations are likely to involve some form of nonlinearity. For example, income change may well exert more influence on the purchases of the young than the old; debt may inhibit purchases for the old but not the young; optimism may exert a more than proportional influence if it pervades all facets of household expectations than if it is mixed with some pessimism; fears of depression probably affect the behavior of wage earners more than that of salary earners; and so forth.

These nonlinearities and interactions can generally be isolated only from cross-section data. Moreover, they can be integrated into forecasting models only if survey data are regularly available. If it becomes necessary to know, not average income change for the entire population but income change for the population under forty-five years old, not average consumer debt but debt for households in which the chief wage earner is over forty-five, etc., the customary time series materials clearly become inadequate and need to be supplemented by survey data. It is self-evident that the existence of substantively important relations between consumer behavior and consumer anticipations can only be exploited by survey data.

An investigation of differences among households in a cross section is thus essential, in my view, to the construction of an appropriate model for the prediction of time series changes. Some aspects of the relation between cross-section differences and time series movements, in connection with the problems of predicting consumer purchases from surveys of consumer buying intentions, have been examined by Arthur Okun.[5] Okun shows that the accuracy of purchase predictions over time, based on surveys of buying intentions, depends on three factors: the size of the cross-section difference in purchase rates between households who reported buying intentions (intenders) and those who did not (nonintenders), the time series correlation between the proportion of intenders in the population and the purchase rates of both intenders and nonintenders, and the amount of variation over time in the proportion of intenders in the population.[6]

[5] See "The Value of Anticipations Data in Forecasting National Product," *The Quality and Economic Significance of Anticipations Data*, Princeton University Press for National Bureau of Economic Research, 1960.

[6] These relations are discussed at greater length in Chapter 3.

Cross-section data must be used to examine the first of these three factors, that is, differences in purchase rates between intenders and nonintenders.[7]

Nature of Sample and Data

Most of the data presented in this paper are drawn from a reinterview of some 24,000 households, which were (or still are) member-subscribers to Consumers Union of U.S., Inc. (CU), the product-testing and rating organization. The background of these surveys is discussed in Appendix C, and is summarized below.

In April 1958 questionnaries were mailed to some 33,000 CU households that had volunteered to participate in a survey designed to investigate consumer spending and saving behavior. Since I was especially interested in analysis of buying intentions, I split the sample into five randomly selected subgroups; each subgroup was sent a question about intentions to buy that varied with respect to planning period and certainty specification. Over 26,000 returns were received; more than 24,000 of these respondents agreed to further interviews with the understanding that reference numbers would be attached to future questionnaires to permit a matching of responses from identical households.

A follow-up survey was mailed to these 24,000 households in October 1958, six months after the date of the original survey; about 20,000 returns were obtained. Additional reinterview surveys were taken in April 1959 and in April 1960. Some 16,000 responses were received in April 1959,

---

[7] A finding that no difference exists would be conclusive evidence that buying intentions have no predictive value over time; on the other hand, the opposite finding would not in itself demonstrate that intentions are necessarily useful for predicting purchases. The existence of intender-nonintender differences in purchase rates constitutes a necessary but not a sufficient condition for demonstrating the proposition that intentions have predictive value over time.

This analysis of the relation between cross-section differences and time series prediction may be applied generally. For example, one could examine the effects of optimism or age on purchases by classifying the sample into optimist-pessimist or young-old groups. If a larger fraction of "optimists" buy than "pessimists," other things being equal, it can be shown that a time series measuring changes in population optimism will be positively correlated with purchases, provided that the fraction of the sample expressing optimism is independent of the fraction of optimists or pessimists that buy, and provided that the fraction of optimists varies over time (see Chapter 3). Similarly with age, income, or any other variable.

There would be no disagreement with the formal statement of this conclusion. There is disagreement, however, about the adequacy of the empirical (cross-section) tests that have been used to determine whether or not particular variables have net predictive value in time series. (See the comment by Eva Mueller following Okun's article in *Anticipations Data;* see also George Katona, *The Powerful Consumer*, New York, 1960, pp. 254–256.)

and about 8,500 in April 1960.[8]   Responses from the first three surveys—April 1958, October 1958, and April 1959—form the empirical basis for this monograph.[9]

The Consumers Union Panel, as it might now be called in view of the number of reinterviews available, is unique in many respects.   In the first place, the sample size is large enough to permit detailed stratification by relevent household characteristics while still retaining relatively large cell sizes.   Secondly, the sample comprises families whose educational level and cooperativeness are such that they apparently can give accurate responses to mail questionnaires; it is evident that many respondents consulted records for data they could not reproduce from memory.

These families are obviously not a random selection from the population as a whole, nor even from the population of CU subscribers.[10]   But because of their social and economic status their behavior may well throw considerable light on the causes of fluctuations in durable goods purchases for the population as a whole.   Broadly speaking, these fairly young, middle- or upper-middle-income families with college backgrounds own homes and comparatively large stocks of durables.   At present, households like these account for a relatively small but steadily increasing fraction of total United States families; and such families are responsible for a relatively heavy share of the fluctuations in durable goods buying that are the main focus of research on consumer discretionary expenditures.[11]

Further, the factors that are associated with fluctuations in the purchases of this group are possibly easier to disentangle, since these families have a greater-than-average ability to articulate their preferences, attitudes, and expectations.   In sum, my view is that a study of behavior patterns in

[8] These two surveys were conducted under the auspices of the Columbia University Expectational Economics Center, directed by Albert G. Hart.   The last questionnaire contained substantially more quantitative detail with respect to income, assets, debt, and durable goods stocks than previous ones; the comparatively low response rate was apparently due to the time-consuming nature of the questionnaire rather than to the sensitivity of respondents to providing information, judging from the (unsolicited) comments that accompanied many of the returned questionnaires.

[9] The bulk of the empirical analysis in this monograph is based on the 20,000 October 1958 responses and the matching April 1958 data, although in Chapters 2 and 3 the 16,000 April 1959 responses (and the matching October 1958 and April 1958 data) are used extensively.

[10] For a thorough discussion of the characteristics of the CU sample, see Appendix C, below, and F. Thomas Juster, "The Predictive Value of Consumers Union Spending-Intentions Data," *The Quality and Economic Significance of Anticipations Data*, Princeton for NBER, 1960.

[11] The cyclical pattern of expenditures on durables is somewhat more pronounced in the CU sample than in the population as a whole.   This can be seen in my *Consumer Expectations, Plans, and Purchases: A Progress Report*, Occasional Paper 70, New York, NBER, 1959, Tables 1 and 2.

this sample tells a great deal about the factors that can be used to predict or explain differences in the spending behavior of consumers generally. I would judge that these data have provided definitive answers to some of the unsettled questions concerning the relation between consumer antici-pations and purchases and have added materially to the forecasting value of anticipations data. At the very least the CU data have provided a fertile field for the exploration, development, and refinement of hypotheses about these relations.

Summary of Findings

A basic objective of this study is analysis and evaluation of consumer inten-tions to buy durable goods. The empirical results are presented in Chap-ter 2. For each of thirteen consumer durable products (ranging from new automobiles to garbage disposal units) the subsequent purchase rates of households who reported buying intentions (intenders) and of those who did not (nonintenders) are summarized. Purchase rates are calcu-lated for both six and twelve months subsequent to the intentions survey, and for seven alternative intender-nonintender classifications based on differences in the type of intentions question asked. The data show that:

1. Intenders always have higher purchase rates than nonintenders: this generalization holds for each of the thirteen products, for both time peri-ods, and for all seven intender-nonintender classifications.

2. For a given product and time period, the purchase rates of both intenders and nonintenders are systematically related to the proportion of intenders in the alternative classifications: the larger the proportion of intenders, the smaller the purchase rates of both intenders and nonintenders.

3. For a given product and time period, the *difference* between intender and nonintender purchase rates is systematically related to the proportion of intenders: the larger the proportion of intenders, the smaller the dif-ference between intender and nonintender purchase rates.

4. Of the alternative intender-nonintender classifications tested, one is consistently superior to the other six in predicting differences in purchases among a cross section of households. This superior classification is experi-mental, and has never been used by any of the surveys that currently report consumer buying intentions.

The data presented in Chapter 2 suggest the hypothesis that buying intentions are essentially statements about subjective purchase probability: those reporting that they "intend to buy A" are simply saying that their probability of purchasing A is at least as high as the minimum probability implied by the intentions question; those reporting that they "do not intend to buy A," that their purchase probability is less than the minimum implied by the question. Further, the data suggest that the distribution of purchase probabilities in the population is a continuous, rather than a discrete, function: households are located at every probability level between zero and unity, rather than at two or three distinct points.

Given this interpretation of buying intentions, a number of generalizations are developed in Chapter 3. These involve the relations among mean purchase probability in the sample, mean probability among intenders, mean probability among nonintenders, the minimum probability associated with the respective intentions questions, and the proportions of the sample reporting intentions to buy when asked the respective intentions questions. Although none of these variables except the last are directly observable from a survey of buying intentions, data from a follow-up or reinterview survey yield information about the purchase rate in the sample as a whole, among intenders, and among nonintenders; and these constitute estimates of mean purchase probability in the respective groups.

The observed data are generally consistent with the probability hypothesis: intenders always have higher purchase rates than nonintenders; for any given commodity, the difference between intender and nonintender purchase rates is larger the smaller the fraction of intenders; and the variance of intender-nonintender purchase rate differences among the several intentions questions is greater for commodities purchased by relatively few households in the sample. But these are comparatively weak empirical tests, since the hypothesis was developed from certain of these same observed relationships. Other empirical tests, based on indirect implications of the model, are constructed; the observed data are shown to be generally consistent with these implications. In neither case, however, can it be argued that the tests do more than suggest that the model is empirically plausible. I see no way, given the available data, to devise a convincing test of the basic hypothesis; such a test would require a survey specifically designed for the purpose.

Sampling variation aside, the probability hypothesis implies that current surveys of buying intentions are likely to yield poor predictions of purchases on some occasions, although it does not follow that they will necessarily do so. The objective of a survey is to predict the population purchase rate during some future period. The best estimate of this purchase rate is presumably mean (*ex ante*) purchase probability in the population. But existing surveys yield an estimate of the proportion of intenders, that is, the proportion of the population with purchase probabilities above some unknown cut-off point. It cannot be assumed that, over time, the proportion of intenders is perfectly correlated with mean purchase probability; even if it were, a linear relation cannot be assumed. And forecasts of the population purchase rate based on the proportion of intenders in a survey make precisely these assumptions. One test of the accuracy with which surveys of intentions can predict purchases shows that only about one-third of the time series variance in the latter can be explained by the former. In addition, a series that constitutes a reasonable but necessarily crude proxy for purchase probability among non-intenders is able to explain a substantial part of the residual variance—the variance in purchases not explained by intentions.

Finally, it can be shown empirically that the accuracy of predictions based on dichotomous (yes-no) survey questions can be substantially improved. Aside from sampling errors, such surveys might yield poor predictions for either of two reasons: (1) the survey does not obtain enough information about *ex ante* probability because respondents are asked a dichotomous question; (2) the *ex post* purchases of respondents differ from their *ex ante* purchase probability because of events that were unforeseen or imperfectly foreseen at the survey date. Improvements in survey design can reduce errors in the first category; those in the second category cannot be avoided unless the incidence of unforeseen events can itself be predicted. Using the most extreme set of assumptions, the data suggest that even complete elimination of the influence of unforeseen events still leaves a good deal of residual error in predictions based on dichotomies. It follows that the potential improvement from better survey design is quantitatively important.

Chapter 4 explores some characteristics of the probability distributions for a number of different commodities and for different groups of households. The observed differences in purchase rates (hence, estimated mean probability) among those reporting intentions to buy automobiles, refrigerators, clothes dryers, etc., suggest that the minimum probability associated with any given question about buying intentions is not likely to be the same for all commodities. In contrast, the minimum probability for a given intentions question and commodity appears to be independent of household characteristics such as income, age, etc.; ownership of an item may be a possible exception.

It is also shown that, given the commodity and the intentions question, the distribution of probabilities below the cut-off point (i.e., among non-intenders) is systematically related to household characteristics such as income, age, etc. Generally speaking, the higher the mean probability for any class of households, the higher the mean probability among non-intenders in that class. There is no evidence that this generalization holds for intenders. By implication, therefore, the variation in mean probability among classes of households is a function of two factors: (1) differences among the classes in the proportion of intenders, and (2) differences in mean probability among nonintenders. I regard this as an additional a priori indication that the change over time in the proportion of intenders is unlikely to be a consistently good proxy for change in mean *ex ante* probability. Further, the data suggest that differences in the level of buying intentions among groups of households are seriously inadequate as a predictor of differences in purchase rates among these same groups.

Chapter 5 is concerned with the relation between alternative measures of aggregate buying intentions, aggregate purchases, and a limited number of explanatory variables other than intentions. It is shown that the strong association between aggregate intentions to buy durable goods and aggregate purchases of durables, again based on analysis of differences among households for a given time period, cannot be attributed to the common influence of other variables, such as income, life-cycle status, or intentions to purchase houses. The variance in durable goods purchases explained by intentions is far in excess of the maximum that can be explained by income or life-cycle status, and the intentions-purchases relation is about as close among households that did not report house-buying intentions as among those that did. In short, buying intentions for durable goods are not a proxy for other variables that we have been able to measure.

In this chapter also, I examine alternative statistical procedures for combining responses to "standard" and "contingent" buying intentions questions, i.e., questions with, respectively, a relatively high and a relatively low probability cut-off. For the most part, the questions are such that standard intenders are likely to be more homogeneous with respect to actual purchase probability than are standard nonintenders. As a consequence, purchase rates among standard nonintenders are correlated with variables such as income, age, or education, while purchase rates of standard intenders do not appear to be related in this way. By the same token, it appears that purchase rates are more closely associated with contingent buying intentions among standard nonintenders than among standard intenders.

Chapter 6 is given over to a detailed investigation of consumer attitudes (or expectations) and their interrelations with buying intentions and purchases of durables. The first part of this chapter examines some of the problems involved in the construction of an index of consumer attitudes.

The data suggest that the relation between purchases and attitudes may be nonlinear; households with very optimistic (very pessimistic) responses to a set of questions appear to purchase relatively more (less) than would be consistent with the assumption of linearity. Further, households with a moderately optimistic set of attitudes do not show a significantly different purchase rate than those with a moderately pessimistic set. In short, optimistic households apparently purchase more than pessimistic ones, other things being equal, entirely because of the behavior of the relatively small number of households with extreme views rather than because of a consistent relation between the degree of optimism and the purchase rate.

The last part of Chapter 6 is concerned with the relation among unexpected developments, buying intentions, and purchases. The investigation fails to turn up any convincing evidence that the difference between actual and expected change in family income has a systematic influence on the relation between intentions and purchases. There may, however, be a nonlinear relation among these variables. Households were classified into three groups: those that experienced unexpectedly favorable developments with respect to changes in both family income and in general business conditions, designated (F); those that experienced unexpectedly unfavorable developments with respect to both, designated (U); and those whose experience was mixed, designated (N). Within the F group, the association between contingent (probable-possible) buying intentions and purchases tends to be *stronger* than in the other groups; within the U group, in contrast, the association between standard (definite) buying intentions and purchases tends to be *weaker* than in the other groups. All the results in Chapter 6 are best regarded as suggestive of possible relations, since some of the available evidence does not support the findings summarized above.

The last chapter summarizes the results of a multivariate regression analysis of durable goods purchases on fifteen independent variables. Seven of these—designated as initial-data variables—are responses to questions about income, assets, expectations, etc., that were included on the buying intentions survey. Five are responses to questions included on the follow-up survey; these are designated as intervening variables, since they measure the degree to which households are affected by events that were wholly or partly unforeseen. The remaining three variables are responses to questions about buying intentions. In addition, results are presented from a regression of so-called standard buying intentions (one of the three intentions variables) on initial-data and intervening variables. Regressions are computed for nine separate groups of house-

13

holds, classified by life-cycle status and characteristics of the buying-intentions variable.

The hypotheses tested are mainly implications of the proposition that buying intentions represent probability judgments on the part of respondents. In general terms, the hypotheses—and their analytical bases—are as follows:

1. Among alternative buying-intentions variables, that constructed from an intentions question with a relatively high cut-off probability should have a relatively large net regression coefficient. According to the probability model, the regression coefficient of intentions measures the difference in mean purchase probability between intenders and nonintenders. In the Consumers Union survey, the higher the cut-off probability associated with a given intentions question, the larger the difference in mean probability between intenders and nonintenders; hence, the higher the probability cut-off, the larger should be the regression coefficient of intentions.

2. Since the association between purchase probability and actual purchases is weakened by the impact of unforeseen events, initial-data variables ought to be more closely related to buying intentions—which are a proxy for purchase probability—than to purchases. Conversely, intervening variables ought to be more closely related to purchases than to intentions, since they represent events that were not perfectly foreseen at the survey date.

3. In a stepwise multiple regression of purchases on initial-data variables, intervening variables, and buying intentions, variables in the first two categories ought to be associated with purchases when buying intentions are ignored. Holding intentions constant, however, the influence of initial-data variables on purchases should be reduced or eliminated because these variables are redundant to purchase probability or to its proxy, buying intentions. On the other hand, intentions should have little or no influence on the net association between purchases and intervening variables, since the latter have no systematic relation to intentions except insofar as they are foreseen.

4. Among comparable variables that partly reflect initial-data considerations and partly reflect intervening events, the variable with the larger initial-data component should have the stronger net relation to buying intentions; and that with the larger intervening-event component, the stronger net relation to purchases.

5. Anticipatory variables should be more closely associated with both purchases and buying intentions for families with relatively young heads;

for variables that reflect current financial position, in contrast, the association with purchases or intentions should be stronger for families with relatively older heads. This constitutes a test of the hypothesis that consumption decisions are more closely associated with wealth, defined to include the value of discounted future income, than with current income.

The data are generally consistent with all of these propositions, especially the first three: the regression coefficients for the buying-intentions variables are almost completely in accord with the predicted rankings based on probability cut-offs; the partial correlations of both objective and anticipatory initial-data variables are consistently higher with buying intentions than with purchases, while for intervening variables, the partial correlations are consistently higher with purchases; and initial-data variables explain (net of other variables) about twice as much of the variation in purchases before intentions are held constant as after, while intervening variables explain approximately the same amount before as after.

Conclusions

The findings of this study suggest that surveys of consumer anticipations should be able to make a significant contribution to the prediction of durable goods purchases. However, there is a good deal of evidence that existing surveys do not fully exploit these possibilities and that the potential improvement is of considerable magnitude. The most important finding is that consumer buying intentions essentially reflect judgments by respondents about their probability of purchasing a particular commodity. It follows as a matter of course that surveys should attempt to estimate mean purchase probability in the population, not the proportion with sufficiently high probabilities to report that they "intend to buy." It may be, of course, that such a survey is impractical because of cost considerations or because sufficiently precise responses cannot be obtained. Since there is no a priori way to find out, I conclude that considerable experimentation with survey design is called for.

Secondly, the evidence strongly suggests that certain kinds of anticipatory variables—those that implicitly (or explicitly) require respondents to make judgments about the combined influence of the basic causal factors—are much more likely to be useful predictors of household behavior than are the specific anticipations or facts that form the basis for such judgments. Buying intentions are clearly in this category, since they presumably reflect the combined influence of current and prospective financial and other factors on purchase probability. The other survey variables most closely related to purchases—"Is this a good or bad time for you to buy durables?" and "Which items in your current durables inventory are in need of replacement?"—also reflect judgments about combined or joint influence. None of the straightforward variables that measure current financial position or expectations about change proved to be of much use in predicting differences among households. I conclude that households are, in many cases, better equipped to make complicated estimates of joint influence than are statisticians working with computers: each household is free to assign the appropriate weight to each of the relevant variables, or to assign a weight of zero if the variable is irrelevant to a particular decision; in contrast, computers (implicitly) use the same set of weights for all households in the sample.

Finally, the results seem to me highly relevant to anticipations surveys other than those dealing with the behavior of consumers. Broadly speaking, I have argued that consumer surveys of "plans" or "intentions" require respondents to make rather complicated judgments about purchase probabilities; the data suggest that respondents can and do make such judgments. If so, the same logic should apply with even greater force to surveys of business anticipations regarding sales, inventories, and so on, since business anticipations must surely have a more rational structure, on the average, than the anticipations of consumer units.

Surveys of business firms, especially those concerned with intentions to invest in plant and equipment, have yielded relatively accurate predictions for the most part. However, business surveys have been comparatively unsuccessful in some important respects, e.g., in producing an accurate forecast of how business investment plans are revised in the light of unforeseen changes in sales or other operating variables. It is not unreasonable to suppose that the extent of these revisions is partly a function of the probability attached to the original sales forecast, or that the probability attached to "investment intentions" is neither unity nor invariant over time. These and related possibilities are worthy of systematic exploration.

CHAPTER 2

An Empirical Analysis of Buying Intentions and Subsequent Purchases

Introduction

THE Consumers Union reinterview survey was specifically designed for an analysis of purchase rates of households that had reported buying intentions. Not only are data on intentions and purchases available for a large number of individual products, but the survey contains alternative sets of questions about intentions. The original sample was randomly divided into five subsamples; households in each subsample were sent questionnaires identical in all respects except for the question(s) dealing with buying intentions. This design served two purposes: the feasibility of designing an "optimal" intentions question could be judged, and the performance of experimental intentions questions could be compared with that of questions similar to those currently in use on other surveys. Given this design,

TABLE 1

INTENTIONS QUESTIONS USED IN CONSUMERS UNION REINTERVIEW SURVEY, APRIL, 1958

Subsample Designation	Intentions Question Designation	Intentions Question
A	A_1	Which of the following products do you definitely plan to buy over the next 12 months or so?
	A_2	Which . . . products will you probably or possibly buy over the next 12 months or so?
B	B_1	Which . . . products do you plan to buy within 6 months?
	B_2	Which . . . products do you plan to buy later?
C	C_1	Which . . . products do you plan to buy over the next 12 months or so?
	C_2	Which . . . products do you plan to buy over the next 12 months or so if your family income during this period were to be 10 to 15 per cent *higher* than you now expect?
	C_3	Which . . . products do you plan to buy over the next 12 months or so if your family income during this period were to be 10 to 15 per cent *lower* than you now expect?
D	D_1	Which . . . products do you plan to buy over the next 12 months or so?
E	E_1	Which . . . products do you plan to buy before next October?
	E_2	Which . . . products do you plan to buy between October and a year from now?

SOURCE: Consumer Purchases Study, NBER.

purchase rates for all households should vary only at random among the five subsamples. But purchase rates for intenders and nonintenders should vary systematically among the subsamples, depending on the characteristics of the particular set of intentions questions asked.

The five sets of intentions questions are listed in Table 1. Of these, data are presented and analyzed for all but the E_1, E_2, and C_3 questions. The E_2 question was systematically misinterpreted by a large fraction of respondents, and has never been fully processed;[1] E_1 turned out to be almost identical to B_1, as anticipated. The C_3 question was left blank by a very heavy majority of respondents, and my suspicion is that many did so because they found the question irrelevant to their own circumstances and therefore uninteresting. In addition, so few households reported intentions to buy that the cell sizes are quite small and the data behave erratically.

Analysis of Intentions Questions

Before turning to the empirical results, it will be useful to examine the structure of the intentions questions.[2] It must be borne in mind that the

---

[1] See Juster, *Consumer Expectations, Plans, and Purchases: A Progress Report*, New York, NBER, 1959. Many respondents appear to have misread the phrase in E_2 "and a year from *now*" as saying "and a year from *then*."

[2] On the questionnaire schedule, a number of commodities were listed below the question(s); as many columns as needed, with a brief heading that repeated the key words in the intentions question and a box for each commodity, formed the body of what was essentially a table. Respondents simply marked X to indicate that they intended to buy a particular item. One of the five sets of questions, and the format, is shown below.

RECENT PURCHASES AND BUYING PLANS

Which of the following products have you bought in the *past 12 months or so?* (Column A) Which of the following products do you plan to buy over the *next 12 months or so*, and how certain are you of these plans? (Columns B *and* C)

Product	Have Bought A	Definitely Will Buy B	Probably or Possibly Will Buy C
Air conditioner, room			
Automobile, new			
Less than $2,500			
$2,500–$3,499			
$3,500 and over			
Automobile, used			
Camera, movie			
Carpets and rugs (over $100 cost)			
Clothes dryer			
Dishwasher			

.   .   .   .

18

interpretation of the question is left entirely to the respondent, a necessity in any mail survey but generally also in personal interview surveys. The A_1 and A_2 questions are very similar to those used in the Survey of Consumer Finances (SCF) conducted by the University of Michigan's Survey Research Center and sponsored by the Federal Reserve Board until 1959. The time dimension specified by A_1 and A_2—next twelve months *or so*—is slightly more open ended than that specified by the SCF questions, which generally ask about prospective purchases during a calendar year in a survey taken early in the same year.

The B_1 question is similar to one of those asked on the quarterly survey of buying intentions currently conducted by the United States Bureau of the Census; the only apparent difference is that the Census question reads "expect to buy" instead of "plan to buy." The meaning of the B_2 question is difficult to judge. (This question was included mainly for comparability with a previous survey of the Consumers Union sample.) Taking the question literally (Which . . . products do you plan to buy later?), any respondent under forty-five years of age would presumably check almost every product on the list. Most respondents did not do so; they apparently thought (sensibly enough!) that "later" must mean something like a couple of years but not indefinitely, and appear to have checked those commodities they had given some thought to purchasing or would like to buy if they could afford to do so.

The C_1 and C_2 questions are experimental, while the D_1 question is much the same as another of those now asked on the Census survey. Note that the C_1 and D_1 questions, taken by themselves, appear to be absolutely identical; the wording of both is exactly the same. I have previously shown that the distribution of yes and no responses is not identical for C_1 and D_1, and that the differences are systematic rather than random.[3] The reason is, presumably, that the set of three questions given the C subgroup tends to reduce the dispersion among respondents in the interpretation of the phrase "plan to buy." The C_1 question must be interpreted as meaning "What do you plan to buy *if your income is as expected?*," since C_2 and C_3 specifically ask about "buying plans if family income were to be higher (lower) than expected." But D_1 simply asks about plans to buy. While it is true that the most reasonable interpretation of D_1 is "What do you plan to buy, *given* your expectations?," some respondents are bound to interpret the question differently. And since D_1 respondents have only two choices—to check or not to check the box under the plan-

---

[3] See Juster, *Consumer Expectations.*

to-buy column—the dispersion of what yes respondents actually had in mind must be greater in D_1 than in C_1.[4]

Another illuminating comparison involves D_1 and the combination of A_1 and A_2. D_1 asks about plans to buy "over the next twelve months or so"; A_1 asks respondents what they *definitely* will buy, A_2 what they *probably* or *possibly* will buy, also "over the next twelve months or so." Thus the only difference is that D_1 says nothing at all about the certainty that is supposed to accompany a yes response while A_1 and A_2 are explicit on this score.[5] The results show that the average respondent interprets the question "do you plan to buy?" when "plan" is not subject to any qualification, as implying a higher degree of certainty than the more specific question "will you definitely, probably, or possibly buy?"; substantially fewer respondents reported yes to the D_1 question than to the combination of A_1 or A_2.

Empirical Findings

The basic empirical results are summarized below in Table 2. Respondents have been divided into dichotomous (yes-no) classes based on the alternative intentions questions. Excluding the E_1, E_2, and C_3 questions for reasons already noted, seven dichotomous classifications can be constructed. The A subsample, for instance, yields two such classifications: A household either reports that it "definitely will buy"—a yes response to A_1—or does not so report—a no response to A_1; alternatively, a household either reports that it definitely, probably, or possibly will buy—a yes response to *either* A_1 or A_2—or does not so report—a no response to *both* A_1 and A_2.

In limiting the presentation of data to dichotomous distributions, it is clear that potentially useful information is ignored: Again using the A subsample for illustration, a classification into these three groups (definitely yes, probably-possibly yes, neither) is quite likely to be more useful than either of the dichotomous groupings shown in Table 2. However,

[4] The data indicate that the proportion of respondents giving a more liberal interpretation to D_1 than to C_1, that is, those who would say yes if asked D_1 but no if asked C_1, must have been larger than the proportion giving a more restrictive interpretation, since on balance relatively more households reported buying intentions on D_1. There is no way to tell how large the gross differences are, since the data show only net differences (proportion interpreting D_1 more liberally than C_1 minus proportion interpreting D_1 as more restrictive than C_1).

[5] That is, A_1 and A_2 have explicit qualifying adjectives—"definitely" (A_1) and "probably or possibly" (A_2). I do not imply that all respondents interpret these adjectives in the same way. In fact, one of the conclusions of this study is that these verbal proxies for degree of certainty may be a major source of error in using intentions data for prediction.

the dichotomous groupings bring out some interesting points, and more refined groupings are examined in Chapter 3.

ORGANIZATION OF BASIC DATA

The basic data table is divided into thirteen sections, one for each of the commodities analyzed.[6] The stub lists the seven intender-nonintender (yes-no) classifications available from the data. The classifications are designated by the nomenclature used above to denote the intentions questions. The classification labeled A_1, for example, divides the A subsample into those reporting that they "definitely will buy over the next twelve months or so," i.e., those answering yes to the A_1 intentions question, and those replying no. Similarly, the classification labeled A_1 or A_2 divides the A sample into those reporting either that they "definitely will buy over the next twelve months or so," or that they "probably or possibly will buy . . ." i.e., those answering yes to either the A_1 or A_2 intentions questions, and those not so reporting.

The seven dichotomous classifications are listed in order of the proportions of intenders typical for the thirteen commodities. These proportions are generally ordered in the same way for all of the commodities, although there are exceptions. A larger proportion of households reported intentions to buy food freezers when asked A_1 rather than B_1, for example, although the reverse is true for the other twelve items.

The first eight columns contain the raw data on purchases and buying intentions. Columns 1 and 2 show the number of purchasers, per hundred respondents, for the sample as a whole during the six months and twelve months, respectively, following the intentions survey. Column 3 shows the total number of intenders, again per hundred respondents, while columns 4 and 5 show the number of intenders who purchased within six and twelve months, respectively. Columns 6, 7, and 8 contain comparable data for nonintenders—total number per hundred, and of these, the number purchasing within six and twelve months.

The remaining eight columns contain statistics based on these data. Columns 9 and 10 show purchase rates among intenders and nonintenders, respectively, for the six-month period; columns 11 and 12 list the same statistic for the twelve-month period. Columns 13 and 14 show the pro-

---

[6] A few of the items listed on the survey schedule are not shown, either because they were purchased by so few households as to make the data behave erratically (house air-conditioning systems, home heating systems, color television sets) or because of doubt whether their classification as a "major" purchase was appropriate (movie camera). A good deal of evidence, both a priori and empirical, suggests that buying intentions have predictive value mainly with respect to relatively large-unit-cost items.

TABLE 2

BASIC DATA, RELATING INTENTIONS TO BUY AND SUBSEQUENT PURCHASES, BY SPECIFIED COMMODITY AND INTENTIONS QUESTION

BUYING INTENTIONS QUESTION	Total Purchases Within		INTENDERS	Purchasing Within		NONINTENDERS	Purchasing Within		PER CENT OF INTENDERS (r) AND NONINTENDERS (s) WHO PURCHASED WITHIN				Intenders' Purchases as Percentage of Total Purchases Within		Simple Correlation Between Intentions and Purchases Within	
			All						6 Mos.		12 Mos.					
	6 Mos. (1)	12 Mos. (2)	All (3)	6 Mos. (4)	12 Mos. (5)	All (6)	6 Mos. (7)	12 Mos. (8)	r (9)	s (10)	r (11)	s (12)	6 Mos. (13)	12 Mos. (14)	6 Mos. (15)	12 Mos. (16)
			(number per 100 respondents)													
AUTOMOBILE																
A₁	19.1	33.2	8.1	4.5	6.1	91.9	14.5	27.1	56.6	15.8	75.5	29.5	24	18	.283	.267
B₁	19.8	33.0	10.8	6.2	7.8	89.2	13.6	25.2	57.7	15.2	72.7	28.2	32	24	.332	.293
C₁	20.6	34.7	23.2	10.7	15.2	76.8	9.9	19.5	46.1	12.9	65.7	25.4	52	44	.346	.358
D₁	19.4	33.1	24.4	9.5	14.3	75.6	9.9	18.7	39.0	13.1	58.7	24.8	49	43	.281	.310
A₁ or A₂	19.1	33.2	31.0	10.8	17.1	69.0	8.3	16.1	34.9	12.1	55.3	23.4	57	52	.268	.313
C₂	20.6	34.7	43.5	14.5	23.2	56.5	6.3	11.6	33.4	11.1	53.4	20.5	70	67	.274	.313
B₁ or B₂	19.8	33.0	49.4	13.3	21.3	50.6	6.6	11.7	26.9	13.0	43.1	23.2	67	64	.173	.212
FURNITURE																
A₁	18.7	31.9	13.5	6.6	8.8	86.5	12.0	23.1	49.3	13.9	65.3	26.7	36	28	.310	.283
B₁	19.4	32.3	15.7	6.8	9.6	84.3	12.6	22.7	43.1	15.0	61.0	26.9	35	30	.259	.266
C₁	19.5	32.4	29.5	11.9	16.9	70.5	7.5	15.5	40.5	10.7	57.3	22.0	61	52	.344	.344
D₁	19.0	31.4	26.7	9.6	14.4	73.3	9.4	17.0	35.9	12.8	53.9	23.2	50	46	.259	.293
A₁ or A₂	18.7	31.9	31.9	10.5	15.6	68.1	8.2	16.3	33.0	12.0	48.9	23.9	56	49	.251	.249
C₂	19.5	32.4	45.8	13.9	21.6	56.2	5.7	11.2	30.4	10.2	47.1	19.9	72	67	.253	.290
B₁ or B₂	19.4	32.3	38.0	11.3	17.9	62.0	8.1	14.3	29.7	13.0	47.0	23.1	58	55	.205	.249
CARPETS AND RUGS																
A₁	7.6	14.1	5.7	2.1	3.1	94.3	5.5	10.9	37.6	5.8	54.4	11.6	28	22	.277	.285
B₁	7.2	14.3	7.7	2.0	3.5	92.3	5.2	10.8	25.8	5.6	45.4	11.7	28	24	.207	.257

C_1	7.7	13.6	14.5	3.7	5.4	85.5	4.0	8.2	25.5	4.7	37.2	9.6	48	40	.276	.283
D_1	7.2	14.0	13.3	2.4	4.6	86.7	4.8	9.4	18.1	5.5	34.5	10.8	33	33	.164	.232
A_1 or A_2	7.6	14.1	17.1	3.4	6.1	82.9	4.1	8.0	20.1	5.0	35.7	9.6	45	43	.214	.283
C_2	7.7	13.6	26.2	4.7	7.5	73.8	3.1	6.1	17.8	4.2	28.6	8.3	60	55	.224	.261
B_1 or B_2	7.2	14.3	26.0	3.8	7.5	74.0	3.4	6.8	14.5	4.6	29.0	9.2	52	53	.167	.249

HIGH-FIDELITY EQUIPMENT

A_1	6.5	13.9	4.3	1.3	2.1	95.7	5.2	11.8	30.4	5.4	48.3	12.3	20	15	.207	.210
B_1	7.0	13.6	6.9	2.3	3.6	93.1	4.7	10.0	34.0	5.0	52.6	10.7	34	27	.277	.310
C_1	6.1	13.5	11.7	2.6	5.0	88.3	3.5	8.5	22.1	4.0	43.1	9.6	42	37	.234	.315
D_1	8.3	15.2	14.0	3.4	5.6	86.0	4.9	9.6	24.5	5.7	40.0	11.2	41	37	.245	.277
A_1 or A_2	6.5	13.9	17.0	2.4	5.3	83.0	4.0	8.5	14.4	4.8	31.0	10.2	38	38	.144	.225
C_2	6.1	13.5	25.9	3.4	6.8	74.1	2.7	6.6	13.0	3.7	26.4	8.9	56	51	.170	.224
B_1 or B_2	7.0	13.6	25.6	3.5	6.9	74.4	3.5	6.8	13.7	4.7	27.0	9.1	50	51	.155	.228

RANGE

A_1	5.2	8.9	2.5	1.2	1.4	97.5	4.0	7.5	47.8	4.1	56.8	7.7	23	16	.308	.268
B_1	4.6	8.4	3.2	1.2	1.8	96.8	3.4	6.5	36.4	3.5	56.8	6.7	26	22	.268	.318
C_1	4.1	6.8	5.5	1.7	2.5	94.5	2.5	4.3	31.1	2.6	46.3	4.6	41	37	.360	.378
D_1	5.7	9.6	6.3	1.7	2.8	93.7	4.0	6.7	26.6	3.3	45.3	7.2	30	30	.235	.315
A_1 or A_2	5.2	8.9	8.4	2.2	3.1	91.6	3.0	5.9	25.7	3.3	36.5	6.4	42	34	.282	.313
C_2	4.1	6.8	9.3	2.0	3.2	90.7	2.1	3.6	21.5	2.3	34.1	4.0	48	46	.282	.348
B_1 or B_2	4.6	8.4	13.0	2.0	3.6	87.0	2.5	4.8	15.6	2.9	27.5	5.5	44	42	.202	.266

REFRIGERATOR

A_1	5.6	8.3	2.5	1.3	1.5	97.5	4.3	6.8	50.8	4.4	60.0	7.0	23	18	.313	.300
B_1	5.1	8.7	3.3	1.3	1.7	96.7	3.8	6.9	38.2	3.9	52.8	7.1	25	20	.277	.277
C_1	5.3	8.6	7.6	2.3	3.4	92.4	3.0	5.2	30.1	3.2	44.3	5.6	43	39	.290	.366
D_1	5.4	8.2	5.8	1.9	2.7	94.2	3.5	5.6	32.6	3.7	47.4	6.0	35	34	.298	.352
A_1 or A_2	5.6	8.3	10.6	2.6	3.4	89.4	2.9	4.9	24.9	3.3	32.5	5.5	47	42	.288	.302
C_2	5.3	8.6	13.4	3.1	4.6	86.6	2.2	4.1	23.1	2.5	34.0	4.7	58	53	.313	.356
B_1 or B_2	5.1	8.7	15.1	2.4	4.1	84.9	2.6	4.5	16.1	3.1	27.3	5.3	48	47	.212	.279

(continued)

23

TABLE 2 (continued)

BUYING INTENTIONS QUESTION	Total Purchases Within		INTENDERS Purchasing Within			NONTENDERS Purchasing Within			PER CENT OF INTENDERS (r) AND NONINTENDERS (s) WHO PURCHASED WITHIN				Intenders' Purchases as Percentage of Total Purchases Within		Simple Correlation Between Intentions and Purchases Within	
									6 Mos.		12 Mos.					
	6 Mos. (1)	12 Mos. (2)	All (3)	6 Mos. (4)	12 Mos. (5)	All (6)	6 Mos. (7)	12 Mos. (8)	r (9)	s (10)	r (11)	s (12)	6 Mos. (13)	12 Mos. (14)	6 Mos. (15)	12 Mos. (16)
			(number per 100 respondents)													
WASHING MACHINE																
A_1	7.5	12.4	3.3	1.3	1.6	96.7	6.1	10.7	40.9	6.3	48.9	11.1	18	13	.234	.205
B_1	7.0	12.2	5.0	1.9	2.6	95.0	5.1	9.7	37.8	5.4	51.5	10.2	27	21	.277	.272
C_1	6.6	11.1	8.2	2.8	3.8	91.8	3.8	7.3	34.5	4.1	46.2	8.0	43	34	.338	.333
D_1	6.9	12.9	9.9	2.7	4.4	90.1	4.2	9.0	26.9	4.7	44.1	10.0	39	35	.261	.303
A_1 or A_2	7.5	12.4	11.9	2.8	4.4	88.1	4.8	8.0	23.3	5.4	37.4	9.1	37	36	.221	.277
C_2	6.6	11.1	13.5	3.4	5.1	86.5	3.2	6.1	25.5	3.7	37.5	9.0	52	46	.300	.332
B_1 or B_2	7.0	12.2	14.7	3.5	5.4	85.3	3.5	6.8	23.6	4.1	36.7	8.0	50	44	.270	.310
TELEVISION SET																
A_1	5.3	10.9	2.5	0.5	1.0	97.5	4.8	9.8	19.7	4.9	40.9	10.1	9	10	.100	.154
B_1	5.7	11.9	4.1	1.0	2.1	95.9	4.7	9.8	24.5	4.9	50.9	10.2	17	17	.164	.249
C_1	5.9	12.3	8.1	2.2	3.7	91.9	3.8	8.6	26.8	4.1	45.4	9.4	37	30	.261	.298
D_1	5.8	11.8	9.2	1.9	3.4	90.8	3.9	8.5	20.7	4.3	36.5	9.4	33	30	.200	.234
A_1 or A_2	5.3	10.9	11.6	1.4	3.4	88.4	3.8	7.3	11.8	4.3	29.2	8.3	26	31	.109	.214
C_2	5.9	12.3	15.0	2.4	5.0	85.0	3.5	7.3	16.3	4.1	33.5	8.6	42	41	.184	.270
B_1 or B_2	5.7	11.9	13.8	2.3	4.4	86.2	3.4	7.5	16.5	4.0	32.0	8.7	40	37	.184	.249
AIR CONDITIONER																
A_1	5.4	6.3	2.1	1.0	1.0	97.9	4.4	5.3	46.3	4.5	48.2	5.4	18	16	.257	.251
B_1	3.4	3.9	3.9	0.8	0.8	96.1	2.7	3.2	20.0	2.8	21.0	3.3	23	21	.167	.176

	1	2	3	4	5	6	7	8	9	10	11	12	13	14	15	16
C_1	3.9	4.9	5.3	1.4	1.5	94.7	2.6	3.3	25.8	2.7	28.1	3.5	35	31	.268	.255
D_1	4.8	5.5	7.1	1.8	2.0	92.9	3.0	3.4	25.6	3.2	27.5	3.7	38	36	.290	.267
A_1 or A_2	5.4	6.3	11.8	2.7	3.0	88.2	2.6	3.2	23.0	3.0	25.6	3.6	50	48	.286	.291
C_2	3.9	4.9	14.3	1.8	2.0	85.7	2.0	2.7	12.8	2.4	14.3	3.2	47	42	.187	.179
B_1 or B_2	3.4	3.9	14.0	1.5	1.7	86.0	1.9	2.2	10.8	2.2	12.4	2.5	44	44	.164	.176

CLOTHES DRYER

	1	2	3	4	5	6	7	8	9	10	11	12	13	14	15	16
A_1	4.6	8.1	2.8	0.8	1.4	97.2	3.9	6.9	28.4	4.0	48.7	7.1	17	17	.190	.251
B_1	4.2	7.4	3.6	1.2	1.6	96.4	3.0	5.9	33.7	3.1	44.9	6.1	29	22	.285	.276
C_1	4.5	8.2	7.9	1.8	2.7	92.1	2.7	5.4	22.2	2.9	34.4	5.9	39	33	.251	.279
D_1	4.4	7.6	7.2	1.4	2.3	92.8	3.0	5.3	19.6	3.2	32.3	5.7	32	30	.210	.259
A_1 or A_2	4.6	8.1	11.4	2.0	3.5	88.6	2.7	4.8	17.7	3.0	30.7	5.4	44	43	.224	.296
C_2	4.5	8.2	18.0	2.2	4.2	82.0	2.2	3.9	12.3	2.7	23.2	4.8	50	51	.179	.257
B_1 or B_2	4.2	7.4	17.2	2.1	3.7	82.8	2.1	3.7	12.2	2.5	21.6	4.5	50	50	.182	.247

DISHWASHER

	1	2	3	4	5	6	7	8	9	10	11	12	13	14	15	16
A_1	2.6	5.0	1.9	0.7	1.0	98.1	1.9	4.0	39.2	1.9	52.9	4.1	29	20	.322	.305
B_1	2.3	5.0	2.3	0.6	1.0	97.7	1.7	4.0	27.4	1.7	45.1	4.1	27	21	.257	.283
C_1	2.5	4.4	4.0	0.9	1.3	96.0	1.5	3.0	22.9	1.6	33.4	3.1	37	31	.265	.298
D_1	3.3	5.9	4.5	1.2	1.9	95.5	2.1	3.9	26.3	2.2	42.5	4.1	36	32	.279	.338
A_1 or A_2	2.6	5.0	7.5	1.3	2.0	92.5	1.3	3.0	17.2	1.4	26.3	3.3	50	39	.259	.277
C_2	2.5	4.4	10.8	1.2	1.9	89.2	1.3	2.4	10.7	1.5	17.7	2.7	44	44	.187	.228
B_1 or B_2	2.3	5.0	11.8	1.1	2.2	88.2	1.6	2.8	9.4	1.3	18.5	3.2	48	44	.176	.226

FOOD FREEZER

	1	2	3	4	5	6	7	8	9	10	11	12	13	14	15	16
A_1	2.7	4.3	1.6	0.5	0.7	98.4	2.0	3.6	31.7	2.2	41.5	3.7	19	15	.230	.234
B_1	2.6	4.8	1.4	0.4	0.5	98.6	2.0	4.1	28.2	2.0	33.3	4.2	17	12	.200	.161
C_1	2.7	4.3	3.7	0.9	1.2	96.3	1.8	3.1	23.9	1.9	33.0	3.2	32	28	.256	.277
D_1	2.6	4.4	5.0	0.9	1.4	95.0	1.7	2.9	18.0	1.8	28.8	3.1	35	33	.217	.272
A_1 or A_2	2.7	4.3	8.3	1.2	1.9	91.7	1.5	2.5	14.8	1.6	22.7	2.7	42	44	.221	.272
C_2	2.7	4.3	12.5	1.2	1.8	87.5	1.6	2.5	9.4	1.8	14.4	2.9	43	41	.155	.187
B_1 or B_2	2.6	4.8	13.3	1.0	1.8	86.7	1.6	3.0	7.7	1.8	13.8	3.5	39	38	.126	.164

(continued)

25

TABLE 2 (concluded)

BUYING INTENTIONS QUESTION	Total Purchases Within		INTENDERS			NONINTENDERS			PER CENT OF INTENDERS (r) AND NONINTENDERS (s) WHO PURCHASED WITHIN				Intenders' Purchases as Percentage of Total Purchases Within		Simple Correlation Between Intentions and Purchases Within	
				Purchasing Within			Purchasing Within		6 Mos.		12 Mos.					
	6 Mos.	12 Mos.	All	6 Mos.	12 Mos.	All	6 Mos.	12 Mos.	r	s	r	s	6 Mos.	12 Mos.	6 Mos.	12 Mos.
	(1)	(2)	(3)	(4)	(5)	(6)	(7)	(8)	(9)	(10)	(11)	(12)	(13)	(14)	(15)	(16)
			(number per 100 respondents)													
GARBAGE DISPOSAL UNIT																
A$_1$	2.3	4.5	1.5	0.4	0.6	98.5	1.9	3.8	27.5	1.9	40.0	3.9	18	13	.210	.212
B$_1$	2.0	4.2	2.3	0.6	1.1	97.7	1.5	2.9	25.4	1.5	49.2	3.0	29	26	.251	.344
C$_1$	2.1	3.9	3.1	0.8	1.1	96.9	1.3	2.7	25.3	1.3	36.0	2.8	38	29	.286	.297
D$_1$	2.2	4.0	3.7	0.6	1.2	96.3	1.5	2.8	17.1	1.6	31.7	2.9	29	29	.210	.277
A$_1$ or A$_2$	2.3	4.5	5.1	0.8	1.3	94.9	1.5	3.2	14.9	1.6	25.3	3.4	33	29	.176	.232
C$_2$	2.1	3.9	7.0	0.9	1.4	93.0	1.2	2.5	13.0	1.3	20.7	2.7	44	37	.207	.236
B$_1$ or B$_2$	2.0	4.2	8.9	0.7	1.6	91.1	1.3	1.7	7.9	1.4	18.2	1.9	35	38	.130	.232

SOURCE: Basic data from Consumer Purchases Study, NBER. All data in columns 1 through 8 are rounded. Consequently, the figures shown in the remaining columns may not be reproducible from those in columns 1–8 when the procedure indicated in the text is followed.

(concluded)

portion of total purchases accounted for by intenders during the six- and twelve-month periods, and the last two columns show the simple correlation between intentions and purchases for the respective purchase periods. In making the latter calculation, households were assigned values of unity or zero, depending on whether they reported intentions or purchases (= unity) or did not do so (= zero).

It may be useful to spell out some of the definitional relations among these data. Column 1 is necessarily equal to the sum of columns 4 and 7, since total purchases must comprise purchases by intenders and nonintenders; similarly, column 2 is the sum of columns 5 and 8. And columns 3 and 6 must always add to 100, since they simply constitute different ways of breaking up the respective samples into intenders and nonintenders. The numbers of intenders and nonintenders who did not purchase within either six or twelve months after the survey (data not shown) are the respective differences (columns 3 minus 4 or 5) and (columns 6 minus 7 or 8).

The last eight columns are easily obtainable from the others. Column 9 is simply column 4 divided by column 3, column 10 is 7 divided by 6, column 11 is 5 divided by 3, and column 12 is 8 divided by 6. Purchase rates for intenders and nonintenders during the period from seven to twelve months after the survey can readily be calculated from the differences between columns 9 and 11 (intenders) or between 10 and 12 (nonintenders); the same figure can also be obtained by dividing column 3 into the difference between column 4 and 5 (intenders), or by dividing column 6 into the difference between 7 and 8 (nonintenders). Column 13 is simply column 4 divided by 1, while column 14 is 5 divided by 2. The derivation of the last two columns is not so obvious, but it can be shown[7]

---

[7] Following the terminology used by Okun (see Chapter 1), define:

p_i as the proportion of the ith sample reporting intentions to buy A at the beginning of the forecast period, where i denotes a particular yes-no question about buying intentions and A denotes a particular commodity;

x_i as the proportion of the ith sample purchasing commodity A during the forecast period;

r_i as the proportion of ith sample intenders ("yes" responders) who purchase during the forecast period;

s_i as the proportion of ith sample nonintenders ("no" responders) who purchase during the forecast period.

In addition, let

N_i denote the ith sample size;

$P_i(1,0)$ denote a (yes, no) response to the ith intentions question;

$X_i(1,0)$ denote a (yes, no) observation of purchase in the ith sample.

Dropping the subscripts for convenience,

$$R^2_{P,X} = \frac{[\text{Cov } (P,X)]^2}{\sigma^2_P \sigma^2_X}$$

27

that column 15 must be equal to the square root of

$$\frac{\text{col. 3 (100 − col. 3)}}{\text{col. 1 (100 − col. 1)}} \text{ times (col. 9 − col. 10)}^2$$

while column 16 must be equal to the same expression, substituting columns 2 for 1, 11 for 9, and 12 for 10.[8]

But

1.0 $$\text{Cov }(P,X) = \frac{\sum_1^n PX}{N} - \overline{PX}$$

Since $\overline{P} = p$, and $\overline{X} = x$, equations 1.0 can be written as

1.1 $$\text{Cov }(P,X) = \frac{\sum_1^n PX}{N} - px$$
$$= pr - px$$
$$= p(r - x)$$

In addition,

2.0 $$\sigma_P{}^2 = p(1 - p),$$

and

3.0 $$\sigma_X{}^2 = x(1 - x);$$

hence

4.0 $$R^2{}_{P,X} = \frac{p^2(r - x)^2}{p(1 - p)x(1 - x)}$$

By definition,

5.0 $$x = r(p) + s(1 - p)$$

Manipulating equation 5.0 to obtain an expression for $r - x$ and substituting into the numerator of equation 4.0, we get

4.1 $$R^2{}_{P,X} = \frac{p^2(1 - p)^2(r - s)^2}{p(1 - p)x(1 - x)} = \frac{p(1 - p)(r - s)^2}{x(1 - x)}$$

which is the description given above in the text.

[8] The sign of the correlation coefficient is determined by the algebraic difference between intender and nonintender purchase rates, i.e., by column 9 minus column 10. If these purchase rates are equal the correlation will be zero, a sensible enough result: for if nonintenders purchase with the same frequency as intenders, it obviously makes no difference whether households are classified as one or the other. In fact, column 9 always exceeds column 10; hence, all the correlations are positive.

In order for the correlation to be unity, it can be shown that column 9 must equal 100 per cent and column 10, zero per cent; that is, it must be true that all intenders purchase and that none of the nonintenders purchase. If this is the case, columns 3 and 1 must be equal, because intenders and purchasers are identical households, column 9 minus column 10 must equal unity, and the whole expression will equal unity.

Finally, if column 9 is less than unity, as is always the case, column 3 can never be

Analysis of Findings

The empirical relations among these data exhibit some notable regularities. As I have pointed out, the classification by intentions question in the stub of Table 2 has been ordered so that the proportion of intenders (column 3) increases steadily as it is read from top to bottom. The pattern is not perfectly consistent for all thirteen commodities, but deviations appear only when two adjacent classifications have approximately equal proportions of intenders in any case. Columns 1 and 2 should be random with respect to the different subsamples and intentions questions, since both represent purchase rates for the group as a whole and the subsamples were selected by a random process. The data in these columns clearly follow the expected random pattern; for example, automobile purchase rates among the seven subgroups of households asked alternative intentions questions vary only from 33.0 per cent (B_1) to 34.7 per cent (C_1).[9]

Although total purchases show only random variation among the seven subgroups, both the number and proportion of intenders and nonintenders who purchase any given commodity are systematically related to the proportion of intenders: the larger the proportion of intenders in the sample—column 3—the greater the number of purchases made by intenders—columns 4 and 5—but the smaller the proportion of intenders who purchase—columns 9 and 11. Correspondingly, the smaller the proportion of nonintenders—column 6—the fewer the number of purchases by nonintenders—columns 7 and 8; but in contrast to the pattern for intenders, the smaller the proportion of nonintenders in the sample the *smaller* the proportion of nonintenders who purchase—columns 10 and 12. It follows that the proportion of total purchases accounted for by intenders—columns 13 and 14—is higher the larger the proportion of intenders in the sample.[10]   Finally, the purchase rate of intenders is always

---

enough higher than column 1 to make the whole expression equal unity. At the extreme, assume that column 9 ($= r$) is less than unity but that column 10 ($= s$) is still zero; that is, all purchases are still made by intenders, but some intenders do not purchase. In that case it can be shown that the correlation between P and X is equal to the square root of $\dfrac{(r - x)}{(1 - x)}$, which must be less than unity if r is less than unity. In fact, all the correlations are quite small, as is to be expected with cross-section data of this kind.

[9] Purchase rates among the seven subgroups differ significantly (0.05 level) from each other in only two of twenty-six possible comparisons.

[10] To illustrate: perthous and households in the A_1 sample, 191 and 332 purchased an automobile within six and twelve months, respectively; only 81 reported intentions to buy an automobile. Of the 81 intenders, 45 purchased within six months, 61 within twelve months. Thus, almost 57 per cent of the A_1 intenders bought within

higher than that of nonintenders, given the commodity, for any of the intentions questions and in either of the two purchase periods, as well as in any part of these periods.[11]

The above generalizations apply equally well to both six- and twelve-month purchase periods and can be observed in the data for all thirteen commodities tested, although data for a few products behave erratically (air conditioners and television sets in particular). The consistency of these relationships is indicated by Table 3, which shows rank correlations between the proportion of intenders in the sample and each of the relevant columns. Ranks are used rather than absolute values because the relationships are generally nonlinear, as discussed at greater length in Chapter 3.

These relations have a tendency to be somewhat more consistent for the twelve-month purchase period than for the shorter period. The reason may simply be that absolute differences among the groups tend to be greater for the longer period; hence, the ranks for six months' purchases may be affected by purely sampling variability to a somewhat greater degree. However, the strength of these relations apparently is not determined by any particular characteristic of the commodities examined. The thirteen items include those with very high unit cost (automobiles) and much lower unit cost (garbage disposal units); they include items with very high ownership ratios (auto, range, refrigerator) and very low ownership ratios (dishwasher, food freezer, air conditioner). Yet the rank correlations and a careful inspection of the basic data themselves fail to show that either of these characteristics is associated with systematically

---

six months, while about 75 per cent bought within twelve months. And of the 919 A_1 nonintenders per thousand households, 145 bought within six months and 271 within twelve months, amounting to roughly 16 and 30 per cent, respectively, of the A_1 nonintenders. Finally, 45 of the 191 households (per thousand) in A_1 who purchased an automobile within six months were intenders (about 24 per cent), while only 61 of 332 purchases within twelve months (roughly 18 per cent) were made by intenders. In contrast, per thousand (B_1 or B_2) households, 494 reported intentions to buy an automobile, although about the same number as in A_1 actually purchased within either six or twelve months—198 and 330, respectively. Of the 494 intenders, 133 bought within six months, 213 within twelve months; thus 27 and 43 per cent, respectively, of the (B_1 or B_2) intenders purchased within six and twelve months. And of the 506 nonintenders in this group, 66 and 117 purchased within six and twelve months, respectively, amounting to 13 and 23 per cent. Finally, 133 of the 198 (B_1 or B_2) households (per thousand) who purchased automobiles within six months were intenders, as were 213 of the 330 who purchased within a year; these correspond to about 67 and 64 per cent, respectively. (Details may not add to totals due to rounding.)

[11] Data for the period from seven to twelve months after the survey can be obtained by simply subtracting six-month from twelve-month data in all but the last four columns (13 through 16) of Table 2.

TABLE 3
RANK CORRELATIONS BETWEEN INTENDERS AND PURCHASERS, BY COMMODITY

	RANK CORRELATIONS BETWEEN PROPORTION OF HOUSEHOLDS THAT REPORTED BUYING INTENTIONS (COLUMN 3 IN TABLE 2) AND PROPORTION OF					
	Intenders Buying Within		*Nonintenders Buying Within*		*Total Purchases by Intenders Within*	
	6 Months	12 Months	6 Months	12 Months	6 Months	12 Months
COMMODITY	(col. 9)	(col. 11)	(col. 10)	(col. 12)	(col. 13)	(col. 14)
Automobile	−0.96	−1.00	−.71	−.96	+.96	+0.93
Furniture	−0.93	−0.93	−.71	−.79	+.86	+0.96
Carpets and rugs	−0.86	−0.89	−.96	−.94	+.96	+1.00
High-fidelity equipment	−0.93	−0.93	−.61	−.82	+.86	+0.98
Range	−1.00	−0.97	−.53	−.64	+.93	+0.86
Refrigerator	−1.00	−0.96	−.93	−.93	+.96	+0.96
Washing machine	−0.89	−0.96	−.68	−.78	+.89	+0.96
Television set	−0.64	−0.75	−.72	−.83	+.86	+0.96
Air conditioner	−0.75	−0.75	−.68	−.64	+.86	+0.86
Clothes dryer	−0.89	−0.93	−.89	−.93	+.99	+1.00
Dishwasher	−0.96	−0.93	−.75	−.86	+.82	+0.99
Food freezer	−0.96	−0.96	−.80	−.61	+.89	+0.86
Garbage disposal unit	−1.00	−0.96	−.45	−.75	+.69	+0.96

SOURCE: Estimated from basic data in Table 2.
NOTE: Correlation coefficients higher than 0.86 are statistically significant at the 0.01 level; those higher than 0.74 are significantly different from zero at the 0.05 level.

weaker or stronger relationships between the proportion of intenders and the other variables.

There are, of course, systematic differences in the data that do relate to characteristics of the commodities. For example, items owned by most of the sample generally tend to have higher purchase rates, not only in the sample as a whole, which is to be expected, but among both intenders and nonintenders for any given intentions question. Items like automobiles, furniture, and refrigerators tend to have six-month purchase rates among intenders that range from upward of 40 per cent down to roughly 25 per cent, depending on the intentions question; for the twelve-month period, purchase rates for these kinds of items range from upward of 60 per cent down to roughly 35 per cent. For commodities with low ownership ratios, in contrast, purchase rates for intenders rarely exceed 30 per cent for the six-month period and occasionally drop to as low as 10 per cent, again depending on the intentions question; for the twelve-month period, purchase rates for these items rarely exceed 45 per cent and frequently go down to 20 per cent or lower. The same pattern is apparent in the purchase rates of nonintenders for commodities with differing ownership ratios, except that the contrast is even sharper.

In addition, the data show clearly that, among commodities for a given intentions question, purchase rates for both intenders and nonintenders tend to be correlated with purchase rates for the sample as a whole; this is hardly surprising, since purchase rates for the sample must be a weighted average of those for intenders and nonintenders. But the correlation is typically much stronger for nonintenders than for intenders, and the difference cannot be attributed to the fact that nonintenders make most of the purchases. This would explain why the purchase rates of A_1 or B_1

TABLE 4

RANK CORRELATIONS BETWEEN SAMPLE PURCHASE RATES FOR THIRTEEN
COMMODITIES AND PURCHASE RATES OF INTENDERS AND NONINTENDERS

| | RANK CORRELATION COEFFICIENT BETWEEN SAMPLE PURCHASE RATES AND THOSE FOR | | | | *Median Per Cent of Purchases Made by Intenders Within* | |
| | *Intenders Purchasing Within* | | *Nonintenders Purchasing Within* | | | |
INTENTIONS QUESTION	6 Months (1)	12 Months (2)	6 Months (3)	12 Months (4)	6 Months (5)	12 Months (6)
A_1	.57	.63	0.97	0.99	20	16
B_1	.59	.74	1.00	0.99	27	22
C_1	.30	.71	0.98	0.99	41	34
D_1	.61	.71	1.00	1.00	35	33
A_1 or A_2	.58	.88	0.94	0.98	45	42
C_2	.86	.90	0.98	0.98	50	46
B_1 or B_2	.78	.75	0.97	0.97	48	44

SOURCE: Estimated from basic data in Table 2.

nonintenders are more closely related to sample purchase rates than those of A_1 or B_1 intenders; in both cases nonintenders typically account for more than three-fourths of total purchases and comprise over four-fifths of all households. Thus, differences in sample purchase rates (among commodities) must show up as roughly equivalent differences in nonintender purchase rates. But for the C_2 and the (B_1 or B_2) intentions questions, the association between nonintender and sample purchase rates is also much closer than that between intender and sample rates, even though intenders typically account for about half of total purchases. This relationship can be seen (Table 4) from the rank correlations, for each of the seven intentions questions, between sample and both intender and nonintender purchase rates.

All of the relationships described above are consistent with the proposition that responses to questions about buying intentions are essentially a reflection of the respondents' subjective probability of purchase for particular products. The more restrictive the phrasing of a question about buying intentions, either because the specified time period is relatively short or because certainty specifications are explicitly stated in the question, the higher must be the respondent's purchase probability for a yes answer to be forthcoming. Similarly, the less restrictive the phrasing of the question, the lower the purchase probability that might be associated with yes responses. This hypothesis is elaborated and tested in Chapter 3. For present purposes, it is sufficient to note that the probability interpretation suggests one of the criteria for optimality in a buying-intentions question: any household reporting that it "intends to buy" should have a higher subjective purchase probability than a household reporting that it "does not intend to buy." In effect, an optimal intentions question should at least eliminate overlap or misclassification, in that every intender should have a higher purchase probability than every nonintender.[12]

The Efficiency of Alternative Intentions Questions

In the remainder of this chapter, alternative intentions questions are examined with a view to determining which is the best predictor of subsequent behavior. The last two columns of Table 2 showed the simple correlation between responses to the alternative intentions questions and purchases during six- and twelve-month periods after the survey. For prediction, it is clear that the best intentions question is simply the one which has the highest correlation with subsequent purchases.

It is worth noting that the intentions question that best predicts future purchases is not necessarily more efficient than the available alternatives in the sense that there must be less misclassification between intenders and nonintenders with respect to purchase probabilities. An intentions question for which every intender has a higher purchase probability than every nonintender can be a much poorer predictor of future purchases, using the maximum-correlation criterion, than an alternative question for which some intenders had lower probabilities than some nonintenders. The latter question may identify many more prospective purchasers than the former; and the variation in purchases is what needs to be explained. For example, in the illustration below the two households reporting intentions on question 1 very likely have higher subjective probabilities of purchase

---

[12] It does not follow that observed purchase rates are bound to be higher for intenders than for nonintenders in every conceivable group of households: unforeseen events influence (*ex post*) purchases but not (*ex ante*) purchase probability.

than any of the 98 nonintenders, while it is perfectly possible that at least some of the 40 question-2 intenders have lower probabilities than some of the 60 nonintenders.[13] Of course a question that is similar to 2 but

QUESTION 1				QUESTION 2			
Intentions	Purchases			Intentions	Purchases		
to Buy	Yes	No	Total	to Buy	Yes	No	Total
Yes	2	0	2	Yes	15	25	40
No	18	80	98	No	5	55	60
Total	20	80	100	Total	20	80	100
$r_{P,X}$	.29				.36		

which successfully reclassifies households—so that every intender has a higher purchase probability than every nonintender—will predict even better than 2; but that may not be an available alternative. As the illustration suggests, the proportion of intenders in the sample is relevant to the question of predictive accuracy.

The data in Table 2 (columns 15 and 16) indicate that all of the observed correlations—between any of the intentions variables and purchases of any commodity—are positive, although all are relatively small in absolute terms; none of the observed correlations exceeds 0.40. As noted above and elaborated in Chapter 3, this is to be expected.

Using the maximum-correlation criterion it is evident that, among the alternatives shown in Table 2, intentions question C_1 is noticeably better than any of the others. C_1 shows the highest correlation of any intentions question with purchases (six-month period) for seven of the thirteen commodities, and the second highest for three others; for purchases during the twelve-month period, C_1 shows the highest correlation in eight cases, and the second highest in three of the remaining five. No other intentions question is even remotely as good a predictor, as shown in Table 5: if a question had the highest correlation among all seven questions for each of the thirteen items, its average rank would be 1.0; if the lowest correlation for all items, the average rank would be 7.0. The average proportion of the variance in purchases explained by each of the intentions questions is also shown; this average is taken as the median squared correlation among the thirteen commodities.

Several points should be noted. First, of the intentions questions currently used by the major consumer surveys (A_1, A_2, B_1, D_1) there is rela-

---

[13] The reader will recall that the squared correlation coefficient between buying intentions and purchases is equal to:

$$(r - s)^2 \frac{p(1 - p)}{x(1 - x)},$$

where the variables are as defined earlier.

TABLE 5

AVERAGE RANKING AND PROPORTION OF EXPLAINED VARIANCE IN PURCHASES,
THIRTEEN COMMODITIES

Intentions Questions	Purchases Within Six Months		Purchases Within Twelve Months	
	Mean Rank	Median r^2	Mean Rank	Median r^2
A_1	3.2	.066	5.1	.063
B_1	3.8	.067	4.5	.076
C_1	1.8	.072	1.6	.089
D_1	3.6	.060	3.4	.077
A_1 or A_2	4.8	.050	4.0	.077
C_2	4.4	.043	3.7	.068
B_1 or B_2	6.3	.031	5.8	.061

SOURCE: Estimated from basic data in Table 2.

tively little difference in predictive performance. For predicting purchases six months ahead, A_1 (definitely intend to buy within a year) and B_1 (plan to buy within six months) are slightly superior to D_1 or to the combination of A_1 and A_2. But for predicting purchases twelve months in advance, A_1 is clearly the worst of the three; and there is little to choose among B_1, D_1, or the A_1, A_2 combination.[14] The C_1 question is significantly better than any of these for predicting purchases either six or twelve months ahead. Although the differences in explained variance are small in absolute terms, the correlation between purchases and C_1 intentions is significantly higher in 51 of 104 cases—0.05 probability level—than the

---

[14] The phrase "for predicting purchases six or twelve months in advance" refers to the prediction of differences in behavior among households during the respective periods. That is to say, the preceding correlations measure the degree of accuracy with which the incidence of future purchase or nonpurchase among a group of households is predicted by one question or another. It does not follow that predictions about change in population purchase rates over time must necessarily be more accurately foreshadowed by the question that best distinguishes differences among households, but it is quite likely that this is the case. If the cross-section correlation between intentions question A and purchases is higher than that between question B and purchases, and if the time series variance in the proportion of A intenders in the population is at least as high as that of B intenders, the time series correlation between the proportion of A intenders and purchases must exceed that between the proportion of B intenders and purchases; if the time series variance in the proportion of A intenders is lower than that of B, the time series correlation between A and purchases may not be higher than that of B and purchases (see Chapter 3, where this relation is discussed).

To the extent that data are available, they indicate that the intentions questions that show (above) relatively high cross-section correlations tend to have relatively high time series variances in the proportion of intenders as well. This statement would certainly apply to a comparison among A_1, A_1 or A_2, B_1, C_1, and D_1; A_1 and B_1 tend to have cross-section correlations that are lower or about the same as the others, and both are known to have a smaller time series variance than (A_1, A_2) or D_1. No time series data on C_1 are available, but the time series variance of C_1 would presumably be much like that of D_1.

correlation between purchases and other intentions questions.[15]   In only one of 104 cases is the C_1 correlation significantly lower.   Further, although the differences in explained variance seem small, an r^2 of 0.08 does represent an improvement of 33 per cent over an r^2 of 0.06.   If this can be translated into an improvement in the accuracy of time series predictions, the gain is far from small.

Next, the time dimension specified in the intentions question seems to have no bearing at all on the purchase period for which any given question is most useful as a predictor.   As noted, the A_1 question is almost identical to B_1 for predicting six months ahead, but worse than B_1 for predicting

TABLE 6

ACCURACY OF PREDICTION OF INTENTIONS QUESTIONS, SIX MONTHS AND
TWELVE MONTHS FORWARD

(number of commodities for which $r_{P,X}$ is higher)

Intentions Question	$r_{P,X}$ Higher for 6 Months Ahead than for 12 Months	$r_{P,X}$ Higher for 12 Months Ahead than for 6 Months
A_1	7	6
B_1	5ᵃ	8
C_1	3ᵃ	10
D_1	1	12
A_1 or A_2	1	12
C_2	1	12
B_1 or B_2	0	13
Total	18	73

SOURCE: Estimated from basic data in Table 2.
ᵃ Six-month and twelve-month correlations were equal in one of these cases.

twelve months ahead.   Yet A_1 asks about prospective purchases over a twelve-month period, B_1 about prospective purchases over a six-month period!   In fact, the relation that stands out here has to do solely with the proportion of intenders associated with a particular question.   The data (Table 6) indicate that the smaller the proportion of intenders (because the question asks about purchases for a relatively short time period, or specifies a high degree of certainty, or does both), the better the question predicts six months ahead and the worse it predicts twelve months ahead. Further, it is interesting to note that all of the intentions questions on the CU survey, with the single exception of A_1, tend to predict more accurately for a twelve months' forward period than for six months ahead.   Although

[15] The 104 cases consist of four comparisons—C_1 with, respectively, A_1, A_1 or A_2, B_1, and D_1—for each of thirteen commodities in each of two time periods.

the twelve-month correlations are generally higher than the six-month ones it does not follow, of course, that the correlation between intentions and purchases is higher for the "second" six months—the period from seven to twelve months after the survey—than for the first six months. The correlation between intentions reported at the survey date and purchases during the second six months, while always positive, is higher than the first-six-months correlation in only five of ninety-one cases; but combining the first and second six-month periods generally seems (empirically) to yield better cross-section predictions than those observed for the six-month period immediately following the intentions survey.[16]

There also appear to be some differences in the relative predictive accuracy of these questions with respect to type of commodity, especially for twelve-month predictions. Excluding automobiles, which comprise a unique category, the remaining items can be divided into groups characterized by relatively high or low ownership ratios.[17] Although the C_1 intentions question predicts both categories more accurately than any other question during both purchase periods, it predicts twelve-month purchases of items with high ownership ratios much more accurately than the other questions but has only a small advantage over D_1 or (A_1, A_2) for predicting twelve months' purchases of items in the low-ownership group.[18] And the question next best to C_1 for predicting purchases of high-ownership items is C_2, which is basically C_1 plus an additional question (see Table 1).

[16] Even though purchases during the second six-month period are positively correlated with buying intentions reported at the survey date, it need not follow that predictions for twelve months ahead are better than those for six months ahead. To the degree that intenders buy during the second six months, the twelve-months-ahead correlations will be higher than the six-month ones; but to the degree that nonintenders buy during the second six months, the twelve-month correlations will be lower. It happens that the first of these factors generally outweighs the second.

Further, it does not necessarily follow that predictions about change in purchase rates over time must also be better for a twelve-month forecast period than for six months ahead, given the fact that cross-section predictions are better for the longer period. This would be the case only if (1) no unforeseen events took place at all, or (2) those unforeseen events with time series variance had the same or a lesser variance when averaged over twelve-month periods than over six-month ones.

[17] Air conditioners, clothes dryers, dishwashers, food freezers, garbage disposal units, and high-fidelity equipment are regarded as low-ownership items; carpets and rugs, furniture, ranges, refrigerators, television sets, and washing machines are designated as the high-ownership group.

[18] For the six items in the high-ownership category, C_1 explains from 8.0 to 14.3 per cent of the variance in twelve-months purchases; the average for the six is 11.2 per cent. The next best question, aside from C_2, is D_1, which explains from 5.4 to 12.4 per cent of the variance in twelve-month purchases, averaging 8.6 per cent. Thus C_1 is almost 30 per cent better than its closest competitor in this particular category. C_1 is also substantially more accurate in predicting automobile purchase twelve months ahead, being about 30 per cent better than its closest competitor.

Finally, it is easily shown that not only is C_1 a more efficient intentions question in that it consistently shows higher correlations than the alternative questions, but it is also more efficient in the sense of having a lesser degree of overlap or misclassification, given the subjective purchase probabilities of intenders and nonintenders. I have already noted that the question with the highest cross-section correlation need not necessarily have the least overlap if the proportions of intenders and nonintenders are quite different among the questions. If the proportions are the same, however, maximum correlation implies minimum misclassification; in fact, differences in correlation are entirely due to differences in the extent of misclassification.[19] If the proportions of intenders for the alternative questions are even roughly the same, as is clearly the case here, it can be shown that differences in the correlation coefficients, assuming the complete absence of misclassification, will tend to be smaller than those observed between C_1 and the other intentions questions.[20] Hence, the observed differences in the correlations of purchases with C_1 and purchases with the alternative intentions questions must be due in some part to the fact that

[19] If, among households asked intentions question A, 10 per cent report intentions, and if an identical proportion of households report intentions for question B, any difference in the correlation between purchases and A intentions or purchases and B intentions must be due entirely to differences in the observed purchase rates of intenders and nonintenders. In note 7, I developed the proposition that the correlation between intentions (P) and purchases (X) can be expressed as

$$r^2{}_{P_i,X_i} = p_i(1 - p_i)(r_i - s_i)^2/x_i(1 - x_i),$$

where the subscript refers to the ith sample. If both the ith sample (those asked intentions question A) and the jth sample (those asked intentions question B) show the same proportion of intenders, then $p_i = p_j$. Neglecting sampling errors and assuming that i and j are both random samples, $x_i = x_j$. Thus, if $r^2{}_{(P,X)_i}$ and $r^2{}_{(P,X)_j}$ differ, it must be that $r_i - s_i$ and $r_j - s_j$ are not equal; the sample with the larger such magnitude will have the higher correlation. But the r and s quantities are simply the purchase rates for intenders and nonintenders, respectively. If these purchase rates are closer together in one sample than in the other, it must be because the mean purchase probabilities of intenders and nonintenders are also closer together; hence, one question must misclassify to a greater extent than the other.

[20] An illustrative tabulation, which assumes that households have specified purchase probabilities, that they purchase in accord with the average of these probabilities, and that they answer an array of intentions questions with either yes or no depending on their purchase probability and on the characteristics of the question, yields the following results (for each intentions question, it is assumed that every intender has a higher purchase probability than every nonintender; that is, each intentions question splits the sample cleanly between high- and low-probability households; hence, there is no misclassification at all):

Proportion of intenders in sample	.01	.02	.04	.06	.10	.20	.50
Squared correlation between intentions and purchases	.045	.065	.096	.103	.106	.101	.074

Note that the correlation falls off very sharply when there are very few or very many intenders relative to the number of purchasers—the mean purchase rate in the above illustration was assumed to be 18.7 per cent, roughly the observed six months' purchase rate for automobiles in the CU data. But in the range from $p = 0.04$ to

C_1 misclassifies households to a lesser extent than do the alternative questions.

The findings just discussed have some obvious implications for survey design. These are discussed at length in Chapter 3, which is mainly concerned with the probability interpretation of buying intentions questions. At this point, the reader should note again one rather striking fact. Of the alternative dichotomous (yes-no) questions about buying intentions for specific commodities, one variant—C_1—consistently predicts better than any of the others. The structure of this variant is rather interesting.[21] Respondents were asked three questions about intentions to buy a list of durables: (1) "Which . . . do you plan to buy . . . ? (2) Which would you buy . . . if your family income were to be 10–15 per cent higher than you now expect?"; and (3) "Which . . . would you buy . . . if your income were . . . lower than you now expect?" The second of these questions implicitly includes the first, in that respondents would presumably report a greater amount of prospective expenditure (though not necessarily the same items plus some additional ones) if their income were to be higher than expected than if it were not. And the entire set of questions clearly imply that responses to the first question should be contingent on the family income behaving about as currently anticipated, since replies to the other two questions are specifically contingent on the assumption that income diverges from current expectations.

This set of questions has two aspects that set it apart from the others. First, the questions are extremely cumbersome, especially for a mail questionnaire. In trying to design a reasonably compact format, I finally decided to include, along with the list of commodities, nothing but the box head

Plan to Buy

———————

A   B   C

This was the only description directly above the columns in which checkmarks were to be made. The reader was asked to "please fill in all three columns after reading questions A, B, and C above." It was hoped that respondents would thus be forced to read all three questions carefully,

---

$p = 0.20$, differences among the correlations are relatively small despite the sizable variation in the proportion of intenders.

Another illustrative calculation based on similar assumptions but with a lower purchase rate assumed for the sample—one of 8 per cent—indicates that the correlations fall off very sharply when the proportion of intenders goes below 0.02 or rises above 0.10. These calculations are basically arbitrary, of course, but the general principle seems valid.

[21] I am pleased to record my debt to Ruth P. Mack, who suggested the question and persuaded me that it constituted an interesting gamble.

and hence be forced to decide before answering any of the questions whether to classify prospective purchases as being contingent on unusually favorable income developments or, more importantly perhaps, not being so contingent. In effect, a reasonably specific set of guidelines were provided as to the meaning of the words "plan to buy"; in the context of the format used on the C questionnaire, a plan to buy should have been construed as a purchase that would be made if everything were to work out neither more nor less favorably than anticipated. But using the appropriate guidelines must have required a fair amount of thought by the respondent, and could not have represented a "top of the head" reaction to a question about prospective purchases.

Secondly, the question encouraged respondents to think about prospective purchases in terms of contingencies and probabilities. After all, respondents cannot rationally say what they would buy "if income were to be higher than [they] now expect" until they first decide what they expect income to be. And I would think it plausible that many respondents were encouraged to make judgments about contingencies other than family income in answering the question, since the phrasing clearly implies that contingencies as a class of events should be reflected in responses. For example, I would suppose that respondents to the C questionnaire gave more attention than other respondents to the condition of their durables stock before deciding about purchase intentions. The phrase "what would you buy if income were to be higher than you now expect" suggests that responses to intentions questions should also depend on what would be done if, e.g., a major repair bill came along on the family car, thus leading to a greater awareness that the probability of a major repair bill is a relevant consideration in deciding whether or not to report car-buying intentions.

Since the C_1 intentions question shows markedly better predictions, I infer that survey respondents should be asked questions that explicitly suggest the complicated nature of a probability judgment, rather than questions with undefined phrases that the respondent must interpret as best he can. Further, I infer that buying intentions questions should be asked *after* the respondent has been questioned about his financial situation, expectations, durables stock position, and so forth, since any realistic judgment about purchase probability clearly must depend on such considerations.

Comparisons with Random Population Samples

It may be objected that the superior predictive performance of the C_1 question in these cross sections, and the inferences drawn, mainly reflect special characteristics of a sample of Consumers Union subscribers and, hence, are not relevant to surveys of a representative sample of the population. There is no way, given the data now available, to evaluate this possibility directly. All of the indirect evidence that I have seen suggests that households in the CU sample are no different from a random selection of all households except for measurable differences in financial, demographic, and educational status—households in the CU sample are known to be considerably richer, somewhat younger, and much more highly educated than the population at large. But the data also indicate that household characteristics like these either are unrelated to purchase rates among intenders and nonintenders for the alternative intentions questions, or are systematically related in the same way for all the questions. Thus, *differences* in the predictive performance of the intentions question do not seem related in any way to financial, demographic, or educational factors. Further, the above data contain several intentions questions that are essentially identical to those asked of random population samples. The observed purchase rates for intenders and nonintenders in the CU data, given comparable intentions questions and allowing for the influence of factors like income, etc., do not appear to differ significantly from those of random population samples. The purchase rates for the CU and population samples as a whole are of course quite different, as are the proportions of intenders, given comparable commodities and intentions questions. But there is no evidence that the *interpretation* of comparable intentions questions, or the behavior of households with a *given* response to a particular intentions question, differs for the CU sample and the population.

This can be seen in Table 7, where purchase rates for intenders and nonintenders in a random sample of the United States population are compared with those for the sample of Consumers Union member-subscribers analyzed above.

Although purchase rates in the CU sample tend to be higher than in the population both for intenders and nonintenders, the main disparity is in nonintender purchase rates. As I show in the next two chapters, differences in family income and life-cycle status have a pronounced relation to nonintender purchase rates but appear to have little or no relation to those of intenders. Thus, all of the important differences between the population and the CU sample can be readily explained by known differences in income (which is higher in the CU sample) and life-cycle status (more younger marrieds in the CU sample). Hence, there is no evidence that households in the CU sample differ from the population in their interpretation of intentions questions, and it can reasonably be argued that relationships found in this sample can be extrapolated to the population.

TABLE 7
CONSUMERS UNION SAMPLE PURCHASE RATES OF INTENDERS AND NONINTENDERS
COMPARED WITH PURCHASE RATES IN A RANDOM SAMPLE OF THE U.S. POPULATION

	Purchase Rate Observed in Reinterview Survey (per cent)	
Intentions Question	U.S. Population	Consumers Union Sample
Automobile		
1. Plan to buy new car within 12 months	(1952)	(1958)[a]
Yes, bought new or used within 12 months	55	59
No, bought new or used within 12 months	19	25
2. Definitely plan to buy new car within 12 months	(1948)	(1958)[a]
Yes, bought new or used within 12 months	67	76
No, bought new or used within 12 months	13	30
3. Definitely, probably, possibly will buy new car within 12 months	(1948)	(1958)[a]
Yes, bought new or used within 12 months	48	55
No, bought new or used within 12 months	12	23
4. Definitely, probably, possibly will buy new car within 12 months	(1948)	(1958)
Yes, bought new within 12 months	49	55[b]
No, bought new within 12 months	5	23[b]
5. Plan to buy new or used car within 6 months or within 12 months	(1959)	(1958)
Plan in 6 months, bought new or used in 12 months	71	73
Plan in 12 months, bought new or used in 12 months	65	59
No, bought new or used in 12 months	23	25
6. Plan to buy new or used car within 3 months	(1959)	(1958)
Yes, bought new or used within 3 months	46	n.a.
No, bought new or used within 3 months	7	n.a.
7. Plan to buy new or used car within 6 months	(1959)	(1958)
Yes, bought new or used within 6 months	50	58
No, bought new or used within 6 months	13	15
Refrigerator		
8. Definitely plan to buy within 12 months	(1948)	(1958)
Yes, bought within 12 months	50	60
No, bought within 12 months	6	7
9. Definitely, probably, possibly will buy within 12 months	(1948)	(1958)
Yes, bought within 12 months	38	32
No, bought within 12 months	4	6
Furniture		
10. Definitely plan to buy within 12 months	(1948)	(1958)
Yes, bought within 12 months	57	65
No, bought within 12 months	10	27
11. Definitely, probably, possibly will buy within 12 months	(1948)	(1958)
Yes, bought within 12 months	48	49
No, bought within 12 months	9	24

SOURCE: Consumers Union data from Table 2, above. Population data as follows. Line 1: Irving Schweiger, "Forecasting Short-term Consumer Demand From Consumer Anticipations," *Journal of Business*, April 1956, pp. 90–100. Lines 2, 3, 8, 9, 10, and 11: John B. Lansing and Stephen B. Withey, "Consumer Anticipations: Their Use in Forecasting Consumer Behavior," *Short-Term Economic Forecasting*, Princeton for NBER, 1955, pp. 381–453. Lines 5, 6, and 7: *Federal Reserve Bulletin*, September 1960, pp. 973–1003. Line 4: Peter De Janosi, "Factors Influencing the Demand for New Automobiles," *Journal of Marketing*, April 1959, pp. 412–418.

[a] Plans to buy new or used; about three-fourths are new.

[b] Bought new or used car, hence proportion identical to that shown in Question 3.

CHAPTER 3

Buying Intentions and Purchase Probability: I

Introduction

THE empirical analysis in Chapter 2 demonstrated the existence of a very systematic relation between the proportions of households reporting intentions to buy a particular commodity, given alternative questions about buying intentions, and the subsequent purchase rates of households classified as intenders and nonintenders by the alternative questions. Using the terminology developed above, let:

p_i be the fraction of the ith subsample reporting intentions to buy at the beginning of the forecast period, where the ith subsample was asked a particular question or set of questions about intentions to buy;

x_i be the fraction of the ith sample purchasing during the forecast period, i.e., the period over which purchase behavior is to be analyzed;

r_i be the fraction of intenders in the ith subsample who bought during the forecast period;

s_i be the fraction of nonintenders in the ith subsample who bought during the forecast period.

The following empirical generalizations are observable in the data. First, the fraction of intenders who buy—r_i—is always greater than the fraction of nonintenders who buy—s_i—whatever the forecast period examined or the alternative definitions of intender and nonintender. Hence, the responses on a survey of buying intentions have behavioral significance; on the average, the subsequent purchase rates of yes and no responders do differ. Secondly, the proportion of intenders—p_i—is negatively correlated with the fraction of both intenders and nonintenders who purchase; intentions questions with relatively high values of p tend to have relatively low values of both r and s. Thirdly, the proportion of intenders is negatively correlated with $r_i - s_i$, that is, with the algebraic difference in purchase rates between intenders and nonintenders.[1] The first two generalizations have already been discussed at length in Chapter 2; the third is documented by Table 8.

The Probability Hypothesis

All three generalizations are consistent with the intuitively plausible hypothesis that responses to questions about buying intentions are essentially a reflection of the respondent's subjective estimate of his purchase

---

[1] The second and third generalizations apply only to a comparison among alternative intentions questions for a given commodity.

TABLE 8

DIFFERENCE IN PURCHASE RATES OF INTENDERS (r) AND NONINTENDERS (s), SELECTED INTENTIONS QUESTIONS AND PURCHASE PERIODS

Buying Intentions Question	Auto	Furniture	Carpets and Rugs	Hi-Fi Components	Range	Refrigerator	Washing Machine	TV	Air Conditioner	Clothes Dryer	Dishwasher	Food Freezer	Garbage Disposal Unit
SIX MONTHS SUBSEQUENT TO SURVEY													
A₁	40.8	35.4	31.8	25.0	43.7	46.4	34.6	14.8	41.8	24.4	37.3	29.5	25.6
B₁	42.5	28.1	20.2	29.0	32.9	34.3	32.4	19.6	17.2	30.6	25.7	26.2	23.9
C₁	33.2	29.8	20.8	18.1	28.5	26.9	30.4	22.7	23.1	19.3	21.3	22.0	24.0
D₁	25.9	23.1	12.6	18.8	22.3	28.9	22.2	16.4	22.4	16.4	24.1	16.2	15.5
A₁ or A₂	22.8	21.0	15.1	9.6	22.4	21.6	17.9	7.5	20.0	14.7	15.8	13.2	13.3
C₂	22.3	20.2	13.6	9.3	19.2	20.6	21.8	12.2	10.4	9.6	9.2	7.6	11.7
B₁ or B₂	13.9	16.7	9.9	9.0	12.7	13.0	19.5	12.5	8.6	9.7	8.1	5.9	6.5
TWELVE MONTHS SUBSEQUENT TO SURVEY													
A₁	46.0	38.6	42.8	36.0	49.1	53.0	37.8	30.8	42.8	41.6	48.8	37.8	36.1
B₁	44.5	34.1	33.7	41.9	50.1	45.7	40.9	40.7	17.7	38.8	41.0	29.1	46.2
C₁	40.3	35.3	27.6	33.5	41.7	38.7	38.2	36.0	24.6	28.5	31.3	29.8	33.2
D₁	33.9	30.7	23.7	28.8	38.1	41.4	34.1	27.1	23.8	26.6	38.4	25.7	28.8
A₁ or A₂	31.9	25.0	26.1	20.8	30.1	27.0	28.3	20.9	22.0	25.3	23.0	20.0	21.9
C₂	32.9	27.2	20.3	17.5	30.1	29.3	28.5	24.9	11.1	18.4	15.0	11.5	18.0
B₁ or B₂	19.9	23.9	19.8	17.9	22.0	22.0	28.7	23.3	9.9	17.1	15.3	10.3	16.3

SOURCE: Derived from columns 9 through 12 of Table 2. For buying intentions questions, see Table 1.

probability, designated Q. More precisely, the statement "I intend [plan] to buy X within Y months" simply means that the respondent judges that his probability of purchasing X within Y months is high enough for him to consider yes a more accurate answer than no, given the particular question asked.[2] Moreover, I read the data as suggesting that households have a rather precise notion as to their purchase probability, given the commodity and the time period, and further suggesting that the distribution of purchase probabilities among households is a continuous function. The hypothesis that responses to questions about buying intentions reflect judgments about the respondent's subjective probability of purchase is essentially a priori—I can think of no other reasonable meaning that might be attached to the statement that "I intend to buy X within Y months." The other two parts of the probability hypothesis—that respondents have relatively precise quantitative notions of their purchase probability and that the probability function is continuous—are inferences from the data.

Some Alternative Hypotheses

Not only are the data broadly consistent with these hypotheses but they also clearly contradict some alternative hypotheses. It could be argued, for example, that households have only the very roughest of notions about purchase probability, and that any more refined classification than a simple division into "high-" or "low-probability" groups would be meaningless. But if that were so it would be observed that either (1) the proportion of intenders who purchase is about the same for all intentions variants and is independent of the proportion of the sample classified as intenders, or (2) the proportion of intenders in the sample is about the same for most or all of the intentions variants. The data, however, do not show either of these characteristics; rather, they indicate quite clearly that a change in the intentions question will alter both the proportion of

[2] A yes answer does not necessarily imply a purchase probability equal to 0.5 or more, although the data are not inconsistent with this proposition. All questions about buying intentions in this and other surveys use imprecise language that will be interpreted differently by different respondents. For example, the probabilities associated with the statement "I plan to purchase a car within a year" may range all the way from perfect subjective certainty ($Q = 1$) to something very much less ($Q = 0.25$). The reason is that the meaning of the words "plan" or "intend" is imprecise. To some people "plan" implies that they have thought about purchasing and might buy within the year; to others "plan" may convey a much more rigorous interpretation: that they have figured out next year's budget, they will purchase a car unless an unexpectedly adverse (and important) event happens, and they have already shopped around or will in the near future.

intenders and the purchase rates of intenders and nonintenders in a way consistent with the probability model.

Another possibility is that the universe distribution is not continuous but basically trichotomous, comprising those who *really* expect to buy, those who do not, and those for whom contingencies determine the answer.[3] But if that were true the purchase rates for definite intenders and definite nonintenders ought to approach 1.0 and zero, respectively, substantially higher (lower) than those observed in the data.[4]

Analysis of the Probability Model

The probability hypothesis is worth elaborating before its consistency with the data is examined more thoroughly. Let me begin by assuming that all households know the subjective probability that they will purchase a particular product during some specified future period of time—the forecast period. These probabilities are distributed in some way between zero (perfect certainty of nonpurchase) and unity (perfect certainty of purchase). The mean of this *ex-ante* probability distribution—designated x'—is the expected value of the population purchase rate during the forecast period. Evidently, x' constitutes the best estimate of the population purchase rate that can be obtained from survey data of this sort.[5]

The distribution of purchase probabilities must be highly skewed for any product purchased by a small fraction of the population, since most households must have probabilities close to zero for mean probability in the population to be relatively small. For an item purchased by a large majority of the population during the forecast period, the distribution must be skewed in the opposite direction, since most households are bound in that case to have relatively high probabilities. The distribu-

---

[3] Trichotomous distributions of this sort undoubtedly do exist. Suppose, for example, a survey were made of "expected births during the next six months." Everyone with a wife more than three months' pregnant would evidently say yes, everyone with a wife either two months pregnant or not pregnant at all would answer no, and a few people would say that "it depends." The birth rate would be close to 1.0 for the yes group, close to zero for the no group, and around 0.5 for those reporting that "it depends." And the responses would be the same whether the survey asked about "definite" or "probable" births. But if the survey had been concerned with expected births during the next two years, the data would begin to take on the character of a continuous distribution.

[4] Wholly unanticipated developments might account for some departure from these expected purchase rates, as will be discussed below; but it seems implausible to me that such events are frequent enough to account for the observed results.

[5] Although mean probability (x') in the sample is the best estimate of population purchases (x), it does not necessarily follow that x' will be an accurate predictor of x. For example, important and unforeseen events may result in an actual value of x greater or smaller than x' for any given forecast period; hence, the time series correlation between the two cannot be determined a priori.

tion is likely to be symmetrical for an item purchased by about half the population, although it could resemble either a normal (bell-shaped) function, a relatively peaked or relatively flat function, or possibly a U-shaped function.

An Illustrative Distribution Function

Given some distribution of purchase probabilities, what would be observed from an analysis of data obtained by a survey of intentions to buy and a follow-up survey of actual purchases? Given the characteristics (planning period and certainty dimension) of the buying-intentions question asked in the survey, all households with subjective purchase probabilities (Q) greater than the minimum probability associated with the question—designated C_i—would report that they intended to buy; all others would report the reverse. It will not necessarily be true that every household reporting an intention to buy has a higher purchase probability than every other household, since the minimum probability implied by the question may itself vary among households. It is obvious, however, that mean probability for intenders will exceed that for nonintenders except under extreme assumptions.[6]

Alteration of the certainty dimension (definite, probable, etc.) or time horizon (six months, twelve months, etc.) of the intentions question would result in a different distribution of intenders and nonintenders, since C_i must vary with the certainty dimension of the question and Q with time horizon. The lower the degree of certainty implied by the ith survey question, holding the time horizon constant, the lower the cut-off probability as judged by the typical respondent. Similarly, the longer the time horizon of the question, holding degree of certainty constant, the higher the Q of the typical respondent. For if a respondent thinks the chances are one in four that he will buy within six months, he will typically

---

[6] If all households interpret the ith intentions question as having the same cut-off point, all intenders must have a higher probability than all nonintenders; hence mean probability—q—is necessarily greater for intenders than for nonintenders. If C_i varies among households, q for intenders will exceed that for nonintenders except in the extreme case where Q and C_i are perfectly correlated, that is, where households with high values of Q systematically interpret the question as having a high cut-off probability, and vice versa. Otherwise, it must be true that q is greater for intenders than for nonintenders even if C_i varies: In any subgroup of households that interpret the ith question as having the same C, mean probability for intenders will exceed that for nonintenders. The means for all such subgroups combined will evidently have the same property, since in each subgroup q for intenders, although different among the groups, must be greater than q for nonintenders. Thus it is only necessary to find some variation in Q among households with a common interpretation of C_i in order to demonstrate the above proposition.

judge the chances better than one in four that he will buy within a year, and better still that he will buy within two years.

Further, it can be shown that not only C_i but also the mean probabilities for intenders and nonintenders will be related to the specifications of the buying-intentions question, with the mean probability for both groups being higher the higher the cut-off probability. These relations are

CHART 1

Illustrative Distribution of Households by Subjective Purchase Probability

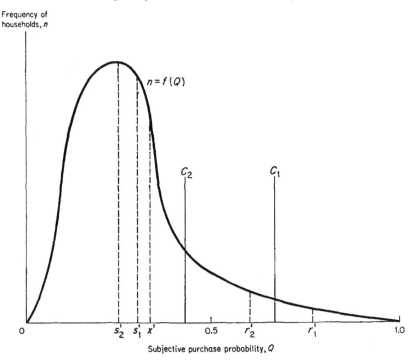

illustrated in Chart 1. For ease of exposition I assume that C_i is the same for all households, although this assumption is not essential to most of the results. The probability distribution relating to a specified forecast period (say, one year) is shown as a skewed function, $n = f(Q)$, with most households having relatively low values of Q. If a sample of 100 households is asked whether they "definitely" intend to buy within a year, all those with purchase probabilities higher than the C implied by the question—C_1 in Chart 1—will answer yes; the rest of the sample will answer no. If asked whether they might "possibly" buy within a year, a larger number will respond affirmatively, since this question must be interpreted as having a lower cut-off probability, designated as C_2.[7] Thus, numbers of households (N) equal to, respectively,

$$N_1 = \int_{C_1}^1 f(Q)dq,$$

and

$$N_2 = \int_{C_2}^1 f(Q)dq$$

will report that they definitely" or probably" will buy within a year. Similarly, numbers of households equal to, respectively,

$$100 - N_1 = \int_0^{C_1} f(Q)dq,$$

and

$$100 - N_2 = \int_0^{C_2} f(Q)dq$$

will report that they do not intend to buy within a year when asked about definite or possible purchases. The relative frequencies of definite intenders and nonintenders correspond to the areas under the distribution function from C_1 to 1.0 and from zero to C_1, respectively. When these households are asked about possible rather than definite purchases, the areas from C_2 to 1.0 and zero to C_2 represent the respective numbers of intenders and nonintenders.

The mean of the distribution function, x', is roughly 0.25 on the scale in Chart 1. The mean probability among intenders and nonintenders depends on the cut-off probability. When C_1 is the cut-off, the magnitude designated r'_1 is the mean probability for intenders; that designated s'_1, the mean probability for nonintenders. When C_2 is the cut-off point, both means are necessarily lower—r'_2 for intenders and s'_2 for nonintenders: lowering the cut-off probability shifts the highest probability segment of the original nonintender group into the intender classification; mean probability for the "shifters" is necessarily lower than for (original) intenders and higher than for (original) nonintenders.

A number of generalizations can be derived from Chart 1. First, mean probability for intenders is always higher than for nonintenders; hence, the algebraic difference between the two is necessarily positive. This generalization holds for any cut-off probability C_i and, therefore, for any

---

[7] Anyone who responds affirmatively to the first question will obviously respond affirmatively to the second, but the reverse is not necessarily true. It follows that the maximum probability among "marginal" intenders—those who respond no to definite but yes to possible purchase, must be less than the minimum probability for those who respond yes to both questions.

survey question about intentions to buy. Secondly, both r'_i and s'_i must be positively related to C_i, although the relationship is generally nonlinear. Since the proportion of intenders in the sample—p_i—depends on and is negatively correlated with C_i, both r'_i and s'_i must be negatively related to p_i. Third, the algebraic quantity $(r' - s')_i$ also appears to be positively correlated with C_i, negatively, with p_i. This result is entirely due to the shape of the distribution function in Chart 1, and is neither true for all possible distribution functions nor even necessarily true for all functions similar to the one shown above.[8] The relation between $r_i - s_i$ and p_i is discussed at greater length in the appendix to this chapter.[9]

Finally, $(r' - s')_i$ as a function of C_i generates a relatively large variance as C_i moves from zero to unity. This is readily seen by moving the cut-off point to extreme positions. When the cut-off probability is very high, p will approach zero, r' will approach unity, and s' will approach x'. When the cut-off probability is very low, p will approach unity, r' will approach x', and s' will approach zero. Thus, the variance of $(r' - s')_i$—as a function of C_i—depends largely on whether $1 - x'$ and x' are close together or far apart. Since the distribution function in Chart 1 has a mean x' of about 0.25, $(r' - s')_i$ will have a relatively large variance.

Some Alternative Distribution Functions

It is useful to observe how these relations would be altered by different assumptions about the shape of the distribution function. Chart 2 contains three types of functions: the top panel has a skewed function much like that in Chart 1. The function in the middle panel is also skewed, but the skew is in the opposite direction. The bottom panel shows a rectangular distribution function. If the same questions about intentions to buy,

[8] For the function $n = f(Q)$ in Chart 1, variations in the cut-off probability that are confined to the region around C_1 and C_2 cause large movements in r' relative to s'. The distribution function in Chart 1 happens to have a relatively small density and a flat slope in the probability region around these cut-off points. Consequently, a change in C has a relatively large impact on the mean probability for households with probabilities higher than C_i, that is, on r'_i. The peak frequencies for the function in Chart 1, and the vast bulk of the total frequencies, are below both cut-off points; therefore a change in C has a relatively small influence on the mean probability for households with probabilities lower than C_i, that is, on s'_i.

[9] The conclusions in the appendix are as follows: the relation between $(r' - s')_i$ and p_i is rather complicated, and appears to depend on the absolute size of both p_i and x'. Given the general shape of the distribution function, $(r' - s')_i$ seems to be negatively correlated with p_i throughout the entire range of p_i (from zero to 100 per cent) provided that x' is sufficiently small. The correlation between the two seems to be positive throughout the entire range of p_i provided that x' is sufficiently large. For intermediate values of x' the correlation seems to depend on the size of p_i, being negative when p_i is small and positive when p_i is large.

CHART 2

Alternative Distributions of Households
by Subjective Purchase Probability

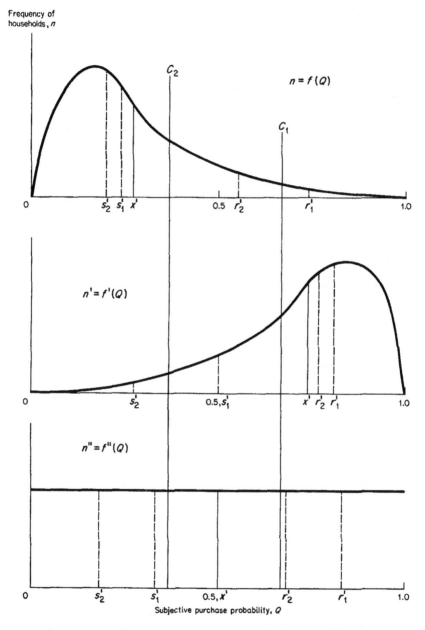

involving the same cut-off points, were asked about commodities characterized by these three distributions, the following relations would be
observed.

For all three functions r'_i is necessarily greater than s'_i; hence, $(r' - s')_i$
is always positive. In the top panel, r'_i, s'_i, and $(r' - s')_i$ are all positively correlated with C_i and, therefore, negatively with p_i. Given a
lower cut-off probability, p will increase; and the mean probabilities for
intenders and nonintenders (necessarily) and the difference between the
two (generally) will decline. For the middle panel—$n' = f'(Q)$—r'_i and
s'_i are also positively correlated with C_i and negatively with p_i, as before;
but $(r' - s')_i$ appears to have exactly the reverse relationship—negative
correlation with C_i, positive with p_i. This is clearly true when C_i is such
that p_i is relatively large, but does not necessarily follow for all values of
C_i and p_i. In the rectangular distribution—$n'' = f''(Q)$—r'_i and s'_i are
again positively correlated with C_i and negatively with p_i, but there is no
correlation at all between $(r' - s')_i$ and p_i, because $(r' - s')_i$ is a constant,
equal to 0.5. Finally, $(r' - s')_i$—as a function of C_i or p_i—has a relatively
large variance in the two skewed distributions but none in the rectangular
one: the appropriate generalization here is that the more skewed the distribution function, the greater the variance in $(r' - s')_i$.[10]

A Mathematical Note

It is interesting to note that almost all the above analytical generalizations
can be obtained with a minimum of assumptions about the distribution
function. Let

x' = mean purchase probability in the sample, $0 \leq x' \leq 1$

p = fraction of the sample reporting intentions to buy, $0 \leq p \leq 1$

$1 - p$ = fraction not reporting intentions to buy

r' = mean purchase probability among intenders, $0 \leq r' \leq 1$

s' = mean purchase probability among nonintenders, $0 \leq s' \leq 1$

By definition,

1.0 $\qquad\qquad\qquad x' = r'p + s'(1 - p)$

1.1 $\qquad\qquad\qquad x' = p(r' - s') + s'$

Since x' is a weighted average of r' and s' and intenders must have

---

[10] If the distribution function were a normal curve the relations in the rectangular
function would generally hold, except that $(r' - s')_i$ would not be a constant. The
quantity $(r' - s')_i$ would be (linearly) uncorrelated with p_i and would have a relatively
small variance; there would be positive correlation between $(r' - s')_i$ and p_i in the
region where p_i was relatively large; negative correlation between the two, where p_i
was relatively small.

higher mean probabilities than nonintenders, it follows that:

$$r' > x' > s'$$
$$r' > s'$$

Further, since x' is the mean of a frequency distribution comprising the points (r',p) and $[s',(1 - p)]$, the variance of the distribution—V—can be written in any one of the following ways:

2.0 $\qquad\qquad V = pr'^2 + (1 - p)s'^2 - x'^2$

2.1 $\qquad\qquad V = p(1 - p)(r' - s')^2$

2.2 $\qquad\qquad V = (r' - x')(x' - s')$

If both x' (the mean probability) and V (the variance) are assumed to be constants, the following relations can be derived. Rewriting equation 2.2:

2.2 $\qquad\qquad r' = [V/(x' - s')] + x'$

Hence,

2.21 $\qquad\qquad \dfrac{dr'}{ds'} = V/(x' - s')^2$

and $\dfrac{dr'}{ds'} > 0$. Rewriting equation 1.1,

1.1 $\qquad\qquad p = \dfrac{x' - s'}{r' - s'}$

Therefore,

1.11 $\qquad\qquad \dfrac{dp}{dr'} = \dfrac{-2p}{(r' - s')}$

and $\dfrac{dp}{dr'} < 0$, since $r' > s'$. In addition,

1.12 $\qquad\qquad \dfrac{dp}{ds'} = 2[(x' - r')/(r' - s')^2]$

Hence,

$$\dfrac{dp}{ds} < 0$$

Finally, rewriting equation 2.1

2.1 $\qquad\qquad (r' - s')^2 = V/p(1 - p)$

Therefore,

2.11 $\qquad\qquad \dfrac{d(r' - s')}{dp} = \dfrac{-V(1 - 2p)}{2p^2(1 - p)^2(r' - s')}$

53

Hence,

$$\frac{d(r' - s')}{dp} \begin{cases} < 0 \text{ when } p < 0.5 \\ = 0 \text{ when } p = 0.5 \\ > 0 \text{ when } p > 0.5 \end{cases}$$

Relation 2.21 says that r' and s' are positively correlated although not necessarily in a linear fashion. Relations 1.11 and 1.12 say that both r' and s' are negatively correlated with p. All these generalizations hold for any type of distribution function and for any value of p, and are identical to the comparable relations derived from Chart 2. Relation 2.11 contradicts one of the generalizations discussed above, however, since it specifies that the association between $r' - s'$ and p depends entirely on whether $p \gtreqless 0.5$. In Charts 1 and 2, the illustrative negative correlation between $r' - s'$ and p is, in fact, associated with a value of p less than 0.5 [illustrative function $n = f(Q)$], while the illustrative positive correlation between the two is associated with a value of p greater than 0.5 [$n' = f'(Q)$, in Chart 2]. The contradiction is real, however, since it was argued above that $r' - s'$ is negatively correlated with p throughout the entire range of p provided that x' is sufficiently small (see note 9). The geometrical analysis is based on the assumption that the entire distribution is fixed and given, but relation 2.11 is based on the much weaker assumption that the mean and variance of the distribution are fixed. The difference in assumption is sufficient to account for the difference in conclusions.[11]

Empirical Tests of the Model

The empirical data contained in Chapter 2 and in Table 8 are obviously related to these analytical constructs. The mean purchase probability in the ith sample (x'_i) is evidently a forecast of the proportion of the ith sample that will actually purchase (x_i). Similarly, the mean probabilities for intenders (r'_i) and nonintenders (s'_i) are forecasts of the purchase rates for intenders (r_i) and nonintenders (s_i). Alternatively, the *ex post* x_i is an

---

[11] The estimate of the variance underlying relation 2.11 is based on two points. If these two points are drawn from a "true" distribution that is actually continuous (for example, from any of the distributions shown in Charts 1 and 2), the variance computed from combinations of observed points $(r',p)_i$ and $[s',(1-p)]_i$ will not be the same for every i. An estimate of the variance computed in this way will be relatively large when p takes on intermediate values, relatively small when p is either very large or very small. At the extreme, i.e., when p is either zero or one, the variance estimated from two such points will be zero, since the mean will be the same as either r'_i or s'_i. For the variance to be constant, as specified in relation 2.11, the (implicit) distribution must itself shift as p changes. As a consequence, this relation will never hold exactly if the distribution function is continuous, and will hold approximately only within moderate ranges of p.

estimate of what the *ex ante* x'_i must have been; r_i, of what r'_i must have been; and s_i, of what s'_i must have been.   Interpreted in this way columns 9 and 11 of Table 2 contain alternative estimates of r'_i corresponding to different cut-off points and proportions of intenders, while columns 10 and 12 have a complementary set of estimates of s'_i.   The data do not contain any direct empirical estimates for C_i, although column 3 of Table 2 shows the proportion of households with probabilities between (the unknown) C_i and 1.0, that is, p_i.

THE PROBLEM OF BIAS

It is important to note that reconstruction of the *ex ante* probability distribution may not be possible from the observed data, which consist of purchase rates (estimates of *ex ante* mean probability) for a number of complementary chunks drawn from the underlying distribution.   Two kinds of bias must be reckoned with in assuming that the observed purchase rates for intenders or nonintenders are valid estimates of mean *ex ante* probability in the appropriate segment of the distribution.   The first is essentially a regression bias between *ex ante* and *ex post* magnitudes; the second and probably more important bias arises because the cut-off probability for any given buying-intentions question is not likely to be invariant among households.

Unforeseen events will influence the relation between the observed r_i and s_i points in Table 2 and the corresponding *ex ante* values of r'_i and s'_i. Many households report a very low or zero *ex ante* purchase probability, given the commodity and the forecast period.   But some of these will encounter conditions that are wholly unanticipated, e.g., a severe accident, fully covered by insurance, with a new automobile; others will disregard likely contingencies, e.g., the necessity of replacing an old washing machine should it break down.   In a survey of buying intentions, both these types of households would report that they do not intend to purchase, but in a follow-up survey many would have actually purchased.   On the other side, any number of unexpected contingencies could result in postponement of a prospective purchase that had an *ex ante* probability of close to 1.0.   All households in this situation would have reported buying intentions, but many would not have been observed to purchase.

Unanticipated events of this sort (those whose probability of occurrence is not taken account of in the estimate of subjective purchase probability) will influence the relation between the *ex post* rate of purchase and the *ex ante* mean probability for a group of households even if such events are distributed at random among the population.   Unfavorable surprises will have a systematically stronger influence on the difference between expected and observed behavior the higher the mean *ex ante* probability for any group of households, while favorable surprises will have a systematically stronger influence on this difference the lower the mean *ex ante* probability. As a consequence r tends to underestimate r' while s tends to overestimate s'; there seems to be no inherent reason for x to be a biased estimate of x'. And these considerations imply a progressively more serious upward bias in estimates of s'_i based on s_i as C_i decreases.[12] The bias in estimates of r'_i obtained from r_i is just the reverse; here, the empirical estimates are too low as C_i approaches 1.0, gradually becoming unbiased as C_i approaches zero.

The second source of bias is illustrated by Chart 3, which shows the effect on r' and s' of variation in the cut-off probability among households. Assume that a distribution of purchase probabilities among households, $n = f(Q)$, is given. Whether the cut-off probability for the ith intentions question varies or not, every household with a purchase probability higher than (its estimate of)C_i will report an intention to buy, and every household with a purchase probability lower than (its estimate of) C_i will report no intention to buy. By definition, all intenders must be located to the right of their own estimated C_i; all nonintenders, to the left. If C_i is invariant among households, every intender must have a higher purchase probability than every nonintender; and C_i can be represented by a vertical line, as in Charts 1 and 2. But if C_i varies among households, these cut-off points themselves constitute a distribution, and purchase probability will be lower for some intenders than for some nonintenders.

In Chart 3, C'_1 and C'_2 illustrate the distribution of *purchase* probabilities among households that reported buying intentions when asked questions 1 and 2, on the assumption that cut-off probabilities for these questions are not the same for all households in the sample. The distribution of *cut-off* probabilities for intenders and nonintenders cannot be wholly inferred from the shape of C'_1 or C'_2. In Chart 3, for example, households with a purchase probability of 0.7 might or might not have reported buying intentions, since some intenders have purchase probabilities as high as 0.7 and so do some nonintenders. Some of these 0.7-probability households must have cut-off probabilities equal to or less than 0.7 (other-

---

[12] The bias in estimates of s' obtained from s is presumably more serious the greater the possibility of unexpected breakdowns or major repair bills, which in turn are related to the number of households that own the item. Therefore, the s function for widely owned items such as automobiles, ranges, washing machines, etc., ought to deviate more from the true s' function than the s function for less widely owned items such as dishwashers, clothes dryers, etc.

wise none of the group would have reported buying intentions) and some must have cut-off probabilities higher than 0.7 (otherwise all would have reported intentions). But the actual cut-off probabilities among either intenders or nonintenders are unknown.[13]

CHART 3

Illustrative Distribution of Households
Having Variable Cut-Off Probability

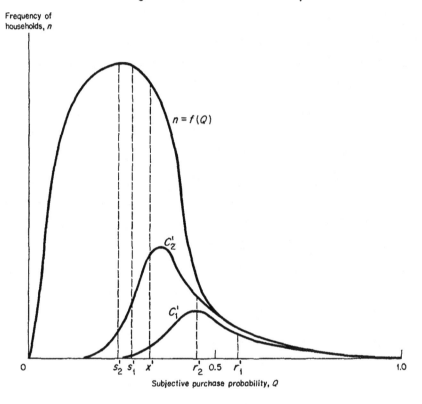

It is readily demonstrated that any variation in cut-off probabilities will necessarily result in values of r', hence also r, that are smaller than

[13] In general, the distribution of cut-off probabilities is likely to show less variance than the distribution of purchase probabilities among intenders. Cut-off probabilities for intenders at the low end of the probability range must be about the same as their purchase probabilities; such households would not have reported intentions to buy if their C_i were above Q, and their Q is so low that C_i cannot be very far below it. On the other hand, the cut-off probabilities for intenders at the high end of the range could be anywhere below their purchase probabilities. It seems intuitively plausible that the distribution of cut-off probabilities among both intenders and nonintenders approximates a normal distribution.

if the cut-off probability were invariant, given the same proportion of the sample reporting buying intentions. In Chart 3, for example, the area under C'_1 is the proportion of households reporting intentions on question 1, and r'_1 is the mean purchase probability for these households. If cut-off probabilities were invariant C'_1 would consist of a vertical line from the horizontal axis to the distribution function, and would then coincide with the function itself. If such were the case and if a given proportion of households reported intentions, r'_1 would necessarily be further to the right than shown. On similar reasoning, s'_1 would be further to the left than it is on Chart 3. It follows that r_i would be larger and s_i smaller if the cut-off probability were invariant, other things equal; consequently, $r_i - s_i$ and the correlation between intentions and purchases would also be larger. Finally, it is evident that the previous assumption of invariance in C_i among households is simply a limiting case of the general proposition that C_i constitutes a distribution—the limiting case being one in which the distribution is peaked to such an extent that it can be represented by a single vertical line with zero variance.[14]

If household cut-off probabilities for an intentions question do vary, it becomes much more difficult to make an accurate estimate of the distribution of *ex ante* purchase probabilities from data on the observed purchase rates for intenders and nonintenders. For intentions questions 1 and 2 in Chart 3, the mean probabilities for intenders are r'_1 and r'_2; for nonintenders, s'_1 and s'_2. The mean probability for the entire sample is x'. Clearly, the relations among r'_i, s'_i, p_i, and x' depend not only on the distribution function—$n = f(Q)$—but also on the distribution of cut-off points among intenders—$C_i = f(D)$—where D represents whatever variables are associated with the distribution of cut-off probabilities for the ith intentions question. The latter function cannot be observed at all in the empirical data. Hence, it is necessary to make the extreme assump-

---

[14] It is implicit in this analysis that the distribution of purchase probabilities among intenders—the C'_1 and C'_2 functions in Chart 3—will not overlap for a set of $i \ldots j$ intentions questions if either the certainty or the time specifications of the question are altered, but may overlap if both are altered simultaneously in different directions. For example, the distribution of purchase probabilities among a group of households reporting intentions to buy within six months must be wholly contained within a similar distribution among a group reporting intentions to buy within twelve months. Any household reporting an intention to buy within six months must necessarily report that it intends to buy within twelve months unless the questions are misunderstood; and any household reporting that it did not intend to buy within twelve months can hardly report that it intends to buy within six months. Similar reasoning applies to intentions questions about definite plans to buy within X months and possible purchases within X months. On a priori grounds, however, it is not possible to tell whether the distributions would overlap for households "planning to buy within six months" or "definitely planning to buy within twelve months."

tion of invariance in the cut-off probabilities in using the (*ex post*) r_i, s_i, p_i, and x variables to estimate the (*ex ante*) distribution function. And if the distribution of cut-off probabilities has greater variance for some intentions questions than for others, as seems likely, estimation of the distribution function from the observed points becomes even more troublesome.

A TEST OF PLAUSIBILITY

The probability model described above can be subjected to several kinds of tests. If (1) the distribution function can be specified and if it can be assumed that (2) regression bias is negligible and that (3) the cut-off probability for any given intentions question is invariant among households, an estimate of the cut-off probability (C_i), and the variance of the distribution (T_i) can be obtained from p_i, r_i, and x.[15] Since the data provide alternative measures of buying intentions ($i \ldots j$) and corresponding measures of r and p, it is possible to estimate the respective cut-off points $C_{i \ldots j}$ and variances $T_{i \ldots j}$. That is, given the distribution function, the observed data (r_1, p_1, x), (r_2, p_2, x), etc., will yield estimates of (C_1, T_1), (C_2, T_2), etc. If the correct distribution function has been specified, all the $T_{i \ldots j}$ will be the same; and the $C_{i \ldots j}$ will follow a consistent pattern related to the specifications of the buying intentions questions.

A test of this kind seems to me of limited usefulness. There is good reason to suppose that none of the necessary assumptions hold, and I would judge that the difference between assumption and reality is quantitatively important. A number of functions that fit the data reasonably well could be located. But the "best" function may well be different for one commodity than for another, and I do not see any practical way of deciding which, among several that provide reasonably good fits, is the "true" function.

The basic hypothesis is obviously not contradicted by the data. Thus, it is known from the start that the observed results, in a very general sense, could have been generated by responses that reflect a continuous distribution of purchase probabilities. In Tables 9 and 10 the data have been rearranged to show the distribution of households by two alternative classifications based on the variant questions about buying intentions. Table 9 summarizes the fraction of households (in parentheses), and the proportion of these purchasing, that reported definite, probable-possible, or no intentions to buy specific items. Panel A contains data for each of the three

[15] The variable s_i is redundant to the calculation because it is determined completely by r_i, p_i, and x.

available categories (definite, probable-possible, none). The fraction of households in each category corresponds to areas of the distribution function between the respective (but unknown) cut-off probabilities—C_d (minimum probability for definite intenders), C_p (minimum for probable-

TABLE 9

PERCENTAGE DISTRIBUTION OF HOUSEHOLDS BY SPECIFIED CERTAINTY OF THEIR BUYING INTENTIONS, AND THE PROPORTION OF EACH GROUP PURCHASING WITHIN SIX MONTHS OF INTENTIONS SURVEY

	A. All Households Purchase Probabilities:			B. Intenders Purchase Probabilities:			C. Nonintenders Purchase Probabilities:		
	$\geqq C_d$	$<C_d, \geqq C_p$	$<C_p, \geqq 0$	$\geqq C_d$	$\geqq C_p$	$\geqq 0$	$<C_d$	$<C_p$	<0
Automobile	56.6	27.2	12.1	56.6	34.9	19.1	15.8	12.1	0.0
	(8.1)	(22.9)	(69.0)	(8.1)	(31.0)	(100.0)	(91.9)	(69.0)	(0.0)
Furniture	49.3	21.0	12.0	49.3	33.0	18.7	13.9	12.0	0.0
	(13.5)	(18.4)	(68.1)	(13.5)	(31.9)	(100.0)	(86.5)	(68.1)	(0.0)
Carpets and rugs	37.6	11.4	5.0	37.6	20.1	7.6	5.8	5.0	0.0
	(5.7)	(11.4)	(82.9)	(5.7)	(17.1)	(100.0)	(94.3)	(82.9)	(0.0)
Washing machine	40.9	16.4	5.4	40.9	23.3	7.5	6.3	5.4	0.0
	(3.3)	(8.6)	(88.1)	(3.3)	(11.9)	(100.0)	(96.7)	(88.1)	(0.0)
High-fidelity equipment	30.4	9.0	4.8	30.4	14.4	6.5	5.4	4.8	0.0
	(4.3)	(12.7)	(83.0)	(4.3)	(17.0)	(100.0)	(95.7)	(83.0)	(0.0)
Refrigerator	50.8	17.0	3.3	50.8	24.9	5.6	4.4	3.3	0.0
	(2.5)	(8.1)	(89.4)	(2.5)	(10.6)	(100.0)	(97.5)	(89.4)	(0.0)
Range	47.8	16.1	3.3	47.8	25.7	5.2	4.1	3.3	0.0
	(2.5)	(5.9)	(91.6)	(2.5)	(8.4)	(100.0)	(97.5)	(91.6)	(0.0)
Clothes dryer	28.4	14.2	3.0	28.4	17.7	4.6	4.0	3.0	0.0
	(2.8)	(8.6)	(88.6)	(2.8)	(11.4)	(100.0)	(97.2)	(88.6)	(0.0)
Television set	19.7	9.7	4.3	19.7	11.8	5.3	4.9	4.3	0.0
	(2.5)	(9.1)	(88.4)	(2.5)	(11.6)	(100.0)	(97.5)	(88.4)	(0.0)
Air conditioner	46.3	18.0	3.0	46.3	23.0	5.4	4.5	3.0	0.0
	(2.1)	(9.7)	(88.2)	(2.1)	(11.8)	(100.0)	(97.9)	(88.2)	(0.0)
Food freezer	31.7	10.9	1.6	31.7	14.8	2.7	2.2	1.6	0.0
	(1.6)	(6.7)	(91.7)	(1.6)	(8.3)	(100.0)	(98.4)	(97.7)	(0.0)
Dishwasher	39.2	9.5	1.4	39.2	17.2	2.6	1.9	1.4	0.0
	(1.9)	(5.6)	(92.5)	(1.9)	(7.5)	(100.0)	(98.1)	(92.5)	(0.0)
Garbage disposal unit	27.5	9.6	1.6	27.5	14.9	2.3	1.9	1.6	0.0
	(1.5)	(3.6)	(94.9)	(1.5)	(5.1)	(100.0)	(98.5)	(94.9)	(0.0)

SOURCE: All data obtained directly from Table 2, except for the middle column in Panel A, which was calculated from columns 3 and 4 of Table 2.

NOTE: Figures in parentheses are proportions of households with specified purchase probabilities; that is, reporting specified intentions. Upper figure in each cell is proportion of these who actually purchased. See accompanying text for explanation of symbols.

possible intenders), and C_n (minimum for nonintenders). C_n of course equals zero, but the other cut-off points are not observable. The proportions purchasing are estimates of mean probability in the distribution function *between* these cut-off points. Panel B shows the proportion of households *above* the various cut-off points and the respective proportions purchasing; these correspond to estimates of areas under the distribution function and mean probabilities *above* the respective cut-off points, that is, of p_i and r'_i. Panel C contains companion figures for the proportion of households (areas), and the proportion purchasing (mean probabilities) *below* the same cut-off points. These are estimates of $(1 - p)_i$ and s'_i, respectively.

Table 10 follows the same format except that time, rather than explicit certainty specification, is used as the basis for classification. More observations are possible here because households were asked about intentions to buy within six months, within twelve months, "later," or not at all. Hence, panel A has estimates of the area under the distribution function and the corresponding mean probability based on the fraction of households (areas), and the proportions purchasing (mean probabilities), that intended to buy within six months, seven to twelve months, twelve months to later, and not at all. The corresponding estimates of r'_i and s'_i in panels B and C are based on the proportion purchasing among households intending or not intending to buy within six months, twelve months, later, or not at all. The cut-off probability for six-month intenders is designated as C_6; for twelve-month intenders, C_{12}; for later intenders, C_{30}; and for nonintenders, C_n.[16]

The last column of panel B in each table shows the proportion of households with probabilities higher than zero, i.e., the entire sample, and their estimated mean probability, i.e., the observed proportion of the sample

---

[16] Some of the calculated mean probabilities in panel A of Table 10 are based on reponses from different samples of households. In such cases, sampling variation will occasionally result in logically implausible observations. In Table 10, for example, several of the calculated mean probabilities turn out to be negative.

The calculation of mean probability estimates based on purchase rates from different samples is as follows. Assume that 5 per cent of one sample report that they intend to buy within six months and that 10 per cent of a second sample report that they intend to buy within twelve months. Further assume that 50 per cent of the first sample and 20 per cent of the second actually purchase. The estimated proportion purchasing among those who plan to buy within the period from six to twelve months after the survey data is $[(0.10 \times 0.20) - (0.05 \times 0.50)] \div 0.05 = -0.10$. This negative proportion (minus 10 per cent) is logically absurd, since those who reported intentions to buy within twelve months must consist of those intending to buy within six months plus those intending to buy in the period from seven to twelve months after the survey date. Since 50 per cent of the six-month intenders were assumed to buy, and 5 per cent of this sample were assumed to be six-month intenders, at least 2.5 per cent of the entire sample will buy even if no one but six-month intenders actually purchases. But in the illustration only 20 per cent of the twelve-month intenders (based on a different sample) were assumed to purchase; since 10 per cent of this sample are assumed to be intenders, only 2.0 per cent of the entire sample would appear to have purchased if no one but intenders actually purchases. Thus the arithmetic implies that negative purchases are made by those who would have been seven-to-twelve-month intenders and that their mean probability must therefore have been negative.

TABLE 10

PERCENTAGE DISTRIBUTION OF HOUSEHOLDS BY INTENDED TIME OF PURCHASE, AND THE PROPORTION OF EACH GROUP PURCHASING WITHIN SIX MONTHS OF INTENTIONS SURVEY

	A. All Households—Purchase Probabilities:				B. Intenders—Purchase Probabilities:				C. Nonintenders—Purchase Probabilities:			
	$\geq C_6$	$<C_6, \geq C_{12}$	$<C_{12}, \geq C_{30}$	$<C_{30}, \geq 0$	$\geq C_6$	$\geq C_{12}$	$\geq C_{30}$	≥ 0	$<C_6$	$<C_{12}$	$<C_{30}$	<0
Automobile	57.7 (10.8)	24.2 (13.6)	15.1 (25.0)	13.0 (50.6)	57.7 (10.8)	39.0 (24.4)	26.9 (49.4)	19.6[a] (100.0)	15.2 (89.2)	13.1 (75.6)	13.0 (50.6)	0.0 (0.0)
Furniture	43.1 (15.7)	25.6 (11.0)	15.0 (11.3)	13.0 (62.0)	43.1 (15.7)	35.9 (26.7)	29.7 (38.0)	19.2 (100.0)	15.0 (84.3)	12.8 (73.3)	13.0 (62.0)	0.0 (0.0)
Carpets and rugs	25.8 (7.7)	7.5 (5.6)	10.7 (12.7)	4.6 (74.0)	25.8 (7.7)	18.1 (13.3)	14.5 (26.0)	7.2 (100.0)	5.6 (92.3)	5.5 (86.7)	4.6 (74.0)	0.0 (0.0)
Washing machine	37.8 (5.0)	15.8 (4.9)	16.8 (4.8)	4.1 (85.3)	37.8 (5.0)	26.9 (9.9)	23.6 (14.7)	7.0 (100.0)	5.4 (95.0)	4.7 (90.1)	4.1 (85.3)	0.0 (0.0)
High-fidelity equipment	34.0 (6.9)	15.3 (7.1)	0.7 (11.6)	4.6 (74.4)	34.0 (6.9)	24.5 (14.0)	13.7 (25.6)	7.6 (100.0)	5.0 (95.0)	5.7 (86.0)	4.6 (74.4)	0.0 (0.0)
Refrigerator	38.2 (3.3)	25.2 (2.5)	5.8 (9.3)	3.1 (84.9)	38.2 (3.3)	32.6 (5.8)	16.1 (15.1)	5.2 (100.0)	3.9 (93.1)	3.7 (94.2)	3.1 (84.9)	0.0 (0.0)
Range	36.4 (3.2)	16.5 (3.1)	5.3 (6.7)	2.9 (87.0)	36.4 (3.2)	26.6 (6.3)	15.6 (13.0)	5.0 (100.0)	3.5 (96.8)	4.3 (93.7)	2.9 (87.0)	0.0 (0.0)
Clothes dryer	33.7 (3.6)	5.5 (3.6)	6.9 (6.7)	2.5 (82.8)	33.7 (3.6)	19.6 (7.2)	12.2 (17.2)	4.3 (100.0)	3.1 (96.4)	3.2 (92.8)	2.5 (82.8)	0.0 (0.0)
Television set	24.5 (4.1)	17.6 (5.1)	8.1 (10.0)	4.0 (86.2)	24.5 (4.1)	20.7 (9.2)	16.5 (13.8)	5.8 (100.0)	4.9 (95.9)	4.3 (90.8)	4.0 (86.2)	0.0 (0.0)
Air conditioner	20.0 (3.9)	32.4 (3.2)	−4.4 (4.6)	2.2 (86.0)	20.0 (3.9)	25.6 (7.1)	10.8 (14.0)	4.1 (100.0)	2.8 (96.1)	3.2 (92.9)	2.2 (86.0)	0.0 (0.0)
Food freezer	28.2 (1.4)	14.0 (3.6)	1.5 (6.9)	1.8 (86.7)	28.2 (1.4)	18.0 (5.0)	7.7 (13.3)	2.6 (100.0)	2.0 (98.6)	1.8 (95.0)	1.8 (86.7)	0.0 (0.0)
Dishwasher	27.4 (2.3)	25.2 (2.2)	−1.0 (8.3)	1.3 (88.2)	27.4 (2.3)	26.3 (5.0)	9.4 (11.8)	2.8 (100.0)	1.7 (97.7)	2.2 (95.5)	1.3 (88.2)	0.0 (0.0)
Garbage disposal unit	25.4 (2.3)	3.5 (1.4)	1.4 (7.3)	1.4 (91.1)	25.4 (2.3)	17.1 (3.7)	7.9 (8.9)	2.1 (100.0)	1.5 (97.7)	1.6 (96.3)	1.4 (91.1)	0.0 (0.0)

SOURCE: Same as Table 9, except that data in the two middle columns of Panel A have been estimated from columns 3 and 4 of Table 2.

NOTE: Figures in parentheses are proportions of households with specified purchase probabilities, that is, reporting intentions to buy within a specified number of months; upper figure in each cell is proportion of these who actually purchased. See accompanying text for explanation of symbols.

[a] This column differs from the comparable one in Table 9 because it was derived from a different sample. The proportion of the sample that purchased each item in this table is an average for samples B and D. The comparable column in Table 9 is based on sample A.

purchasing. The largest proportion purchasing any one item during the six-month period is for automobiles (19.1 per cent). Hence, all of the distribution functions must be skewed even more than the function $n = f(Q)$ shown in Chart 2, since the mean there was about 0.25. The proportion of households in each category of panel A also documents the proposition that all the distribution functions are very highly skewed, and that the vast majority of these households have very low probabilities.

In the discussion of the model, I specified the relation between a set of $i \ldots j$ buying intentions questions and the corresponding purchase rates for intenders and nonintenders, given a probability function like the one at the top of Chart 2. To repeat: (1) r_i is always greater than s_i; (2) r_i and s_i are both positively related to C_i and, hence, negatively related to p_i; (3) $(r - s)_i$ should be positively related to C_i, negatively to p_i; (4) the variance of $(r - s)_{i \ldots j}$ as a function of $C_{i \ldots j}$ or $p_{i \ldots j}$ is greater the more highly skewed the distribution. The first two generalizations hold regardless of the shape of the distribution function, and are clearly true for the data in panels B and C of both Tables 9 and 10. The third is also clearly observable. The quantity r falls much more rapidly than s as C_i decreases (and p_i increases); hence, $(r - s)_i$ falls as C_i decreases (and p_i increases). The fourth essentially says that the variance in $(r - s)_{i \ldots j}$ should be greater for commodities with relatively small values of x, since the smaller is x' the more highly skewed is the distribution. This relationship is difficult to judge from the data in Tables 9 and 10; but the rank correlations between commodity purchase rates and the variance of the $r_i - s_i$ values are -0.32 and -0.68 for the six- and twelve-month purchase periods, respectively, in Table 9. In Table 10, the comparable rank correlations are, respectively, -0.15 and -0.55.[17] Thus all of the empirical observations are consistent with predictions of the probability model, although the model is specified in very general terms.

An analysis complementary to the above is contained in an appendix to this chapter; here some cumulative functions based on Chart 1 are developed. These functions are the precise *ex ante* counterparts to the observed r_i, s_i, p_i, and x_i points; observed data for several commodities are plotted and illustrative functions are fitted to the observed points. The appendix tests are necessarily impressionistic, as are those just described; both essentially document the proposition that the existence of a probability distribution is empirically plausible.

---

[17] Strictly speaking the comparison of variance in $r_i - s_i$ with x is valid only if households assign the same cut-off point, given the intentions question, to all commodities; data in Chapter 4 suggest that this is unlikely to be the case.

A TEST OF AN ALTERNATIVE MODEL

I turn now to some quite different (and rather indirect) tests of the hypothesis. Table 9 contains data for intentions variants that differ as to certainty dimension (definite intenders, probable-possible intenders, etc.), but each variant has the same planning period. Table 10 contains data for intentions variants that differ as to length of the planning period (six-month intenders, twelve-month intenders, etc.) but have the same certainty dimension. Each table shows the fraction of households reporting intentions to buy for the $i \ldots j$ intentions variants and the fraction that purchased within six months of the survey date. What is the most fruitful interpretation of responses to survey questions that differ as to planning period but not as to certainty dimension? Are such statements essentially judgments about the probable *timing* of purchases or do they reflect a judgment about purchase probability relating to *any* future period of time? In the analysis above, these data were treated as if they were probability statements. It seems more natural to interpret these data as judgments about probable timing. The available data permit a test of these two interpretations. The results, in my view, provide strong support for the proposition that households do seem to make the kind of probability judgment that is the central theme of this chapter.[18]

The alternative interpretations can be illustrated by the intentions data for groups B and D. Households in group B were asked whether they "intended to buy within the next six months"; D, whether they "intended to buy within the next twelve months." More households reported buying intentions in group D than B, as must be the case. In fact, twelve-month intenders can usefully be thought of as comprising two subgroups—those who would, if asked, have reported that they intended to buy within six months and those who would not have been willing to make this judgment. Those reporting intentions to buy within six months are designated as p_6; those reporting intentions to buy within a year, p_{12}; and $p_{12} - p_6$ is designated as p_{6-12} (obviously $p_6 + p_{6-12} \equiv p_{12}$).

What are the empirical implications of the two interpretations? If statements about intentions to buy within varying time periods reflect probable timing—*when* the household expects to make a particular

[18] It should be noted that the probability model does not depend on whether or not statements about intentions to buy within different forward periods actually represent judgments about the probability of purchase, unrelated to the timing of purchases. Nothing in the model requires that a probability interpretation be placed on responses to these particular questions, although the model gains in empirical plausibility if a probability interpretation turns out to be consistent with the empirical results.

purchase—the p_6 group ought to show a relatively heavy purchase rate in the six months subsequent to the survey (Period I) and a relatively lower purchase rate during the period from six to twelve months after the survey (Period II). The Period II purchase rate for the p_6 group would be zero if these statements were interpreted as reflecting perfect certainty about timing, but this extreme assumption is not necessary. The timing interpretation requires only that the purchase rate be lower in Period II than in period I for the p_6 group. Households in the p_{6-12} group, on the other hand, are saying that they expect to buy in Period II rather than in Period I. Some may end up buying in Period I, but the purchase rate in II will surely be higher.

The probability interpretation essentially says that the p_6 group has a higher cut-off and mean probability than the p_{6-12} group. The p_{12} group must have the same cut-off point as the p_{6-12} group, and its mean probability must be a weighted average of the means for its two subgroups. The probability model can be interpreted as specifying that these relations be independent of the forecast period. In short, one (plausible) version of the probability interpretation suggests that the only difference between six- and twelve-month intenders is that the former are more likely to purchase during any arbitrarily specified period. But in that case purchase rates ought to be higher for the p_6 than for the p_{6-12} group in Period I and, also, in Periods II, III, . . . , n.

All told there are four sets of intentions questions that permit comparisons of the sort just described. The B sample was asked about plans to buy within six months. The A sample was asked about definite plans to buy within twelve months and also about probable or possible purchases within twelve months. Both the C and D samples were asked about plans to buy within twelve months. Hence, the purchase rate of six-month planners—r_6—can be compared with rates for four groups of twelve-month planners. The timing interpretation predicts that the six-month intenders will have a higher purchase rate during Period I and a lower purchase rate during Period II than any of the four groups of twelve-month intenders. That is, for Period I

$$r_6 > r_{12} > r_{6-12};$$

and for Period II

$$r_6 < r_{12} < r_{6-12}$$

The probability interpretation, on the other hand, predicts that for intentions questions with the same certainty dimension purchase probability is inversely correlated with the planning period, i.e., those planning to buy within n months have a higher purchase probability than those planning to buy within $n + 1$ months, irrespective of the forecast period. That is, for both periods, I and II,

$$r_6 > r_{12} > r_{6-12}$$

For intentions questions with the same planning period, the probability interpretation argues that the more restrictive the certainty dimension the higher the purchase probability of the group reporting intentions. For intentions questions that vary both as to planning period and certainty dimension, the probability model can be interpreted as requiring that the lower the fraction of households reporting intentions, the higher

TABLE 11

PREDICTED DIFFERENCES IN INTENDERS' PURCHASE RATES FOR PERIODS I AND II

Period I		Period II	
Probability Interpretation	Timing Interpretation	Probability Interpretation	Timing Interpretation
$B_1 < A_1$	$B_1 > A_1$	$B_1 < A_1$	$B_1 < A_1$
$B_1 > A_1 + A_2$	$B_1 > A_1 + A_2$	$B_1 > A_1 + A_2$	$B_1 < A_1 + A_3$
$B_1 > C_1$	$B_1 > C_1$	$B_1 > C_1$	$B_1 < C_1$
$B_1 > D_1$	$B_1 > D_1$	$B_1 > D_1$	$B_1 < D_1$

NOTE: The intentions questions are as follows:
A_1 Definite intentions to buy within twelve months
$A_1 + A_2$ Definite, probable, or possible intentions to buy within twelve months
C_1 Intentions to buy within twelve months (if income is as expected)
D_1 Intentions to buy within twelve months
B_1 Intentions to buy within six months

the purchase probability of intenders. Since all these relations hold for any forecast period, the intentions variants ought to show the same pattern for Periods I, II, III, etc.

Given the characteristics of the six-month intentions question and the four twelve-month questions, the probability interpretation predicts that definite twelve-month intenders will buy more than six-month intenders during all forecast periods because the fraction of intenders is lower for the definite twelve-month variant. The probability interpretation predicts a priori (compare the questions) that six-month intenders will purchase more than the other three groups of twelve-month intenders in both periods; in addition, the fraction of intenders is lower for the six-month group than for these three twelve-month groups.

The survey data yield four pairs of observed purchase rates, for each of thirteen commodities, in which the probability and timing interpretations predict a different relation between purchase rates for six- and twelve-month intenders. One of the pairs involves Period I purchase rates; the other three, Period II purchase rates. In the remaining four comparisons the two interpretations predict the same outcome. The possible

TABLE 12

TEST OF PROBABILITY AND TIMING INTERPRETATIONS OF CONSUMERS UNION SURVEY DATA

(proportions of intenders who purchased)

	Intentions Specified by Variant				
	A_1	B_1	A_1 or A_2	C_1	D_1
PERIOD I: WITHIN SIX MONTHS OF SURVEY DATE					
Automobile	56.6	57.7	34.9	46.1	39.0
Air conditioner	46.3	20.1	23.0	25.8	25.6
Clothes dryer	28.4	33.7	17.7	22.2	19.6
Dishwasher	39.2	27.4	17.2	22.9	26.3
Food freezer	31.7	28.2	14.8	23.9	18.0
Range	47.8	36.4	25.7	31.1	26.6
Refrigerator	50.8	38.2	24.9	30.1	32.6
Television set	19.7	24.5	11.8	26.8	20.7
Washing machine	40.9	37.8	23.3	34.5	26.9
Carpets and rugs	37.6	25.8	20.1	25.5	18.1
Furniture	49.3	43.1	33.0	40.5	35.9
Garbage disposal unit	27.5	25.4	14.9	25.3	17.1
High-fidelity equipment	30.4	34.0	14.4	22.1	24.5
PERIOD II: WITHIN SEVEN TO TWELVE MONTHS OF SURVEY DATE					
Automobile	18.9	15.0	20.4	19.6	19.7
Air conditioner	1.9	1.0	2.6	2.3	1.9
Clothes dryer	20.3	11.2	13.0	12.2	12.7
Dishwasher	13.7	17.7	9.1	11.5	16.2
Food freezer	9.8	5.1	7.9	9.1	10.8
Range	9.0	20.4	10.8	15.2	18.7
Refrigerator	9.2	14.6	7.6	14.2	14.8
Television set	21.2	26.4	17.4	18.6	18.2
Washing machine	8.0	13.3	14.1	11.7	17.2
Carpets and rugs	16.8	19.6	15.6	11.7	16.4
Furniture	16.0	17.9	15.9	16.8	18.0
Garbage disposal unit	12.5	23.8	10.4	10.7	14.6
High-fidelity equipment	17.9	18.6	16.6	21.0	15.5

SOURCE: Period I data from column 9 of Table 2. Period II data are the respective differences between columns 11 and 9 of Table 2.

comparisons are summarized in Table 11, along with the outcomes predicted by the two interpretations; the observed purchase rates are summarized in Table 12.

The evidence generally supports the probability interpretation of responses to questions about intentions to buy within different time periods. Of the fifty-two differences that discriminate between the alternative interpretations, seventeen are so small (two percentage points or less) that they can be ignored; of the remaining thirty-five, twenty-four are consistent with the probability interpretation, hence inconsistent with the timing interpretation. And of the differences that are statistically more reliable, ten of thirteen significant at the 0.10 level and six of the seven differences significant at the 0.05 level[19] are consistent with the probability hypothesis.

Intentions Data and Purchase Predictions

The accuracy of purchase predictions based on surveys of buying intentions evidently depends on the time series correlation between p, the proportion of intenders in the population, and x, the proportion of purchasers in the population. It has been demonstrated by Arthur Okun that p and x will be positively correlated over time if the purchase rate of intenders exceeds that of nonintenders, that is, if r exceeds s; more precisely, Okun shows that p and x will be positively correlated if $\bar{R}$ exceeds $\bar{S}$, where the latter variables are the respective means of the random variables r and s. The time series correlation between x and p turns out to be positively associated with the algebraic difference between $\bar{R}$ and $\bar{S}$ and with the time series variance in p.[20] These relations hold completely provided that the time series movements in both r and s are independent of those in p; otherwise, the relation may be weaker or stronger than indicated by the above analysis.[21]

---

[19] All deviant cases where the differences are fairly reliable involve purchase rates for automobiles. The majority of these purchases (in this sample) consist of new cars. Since Period I extends from April 1958 to October 1958 and Period II from October 1958 to March 1959, April planners waiting for new models would tend to show up as twelve-month planners and Period II purchasers; hence, buying intentions for new automobiles may have a strong element of probable timing.

[20] Formally, Okun shows that

$$M_{xp} = (\bar{r} - \bar{s})M_{yp} + pM_{rp} + (1 - p)M_{sp} + M_{rpp} - M_{spp},$$

where M designates the respective variances or covariances. All the terms to the right of $(\bar{r} - \bar{s})M_{pp}$ are zero if both r and s are independent of p. If such is the case the estimated slope of the time series regression of x on p (M_{xp}/M_{pp}) is $(\bar{r} - \bar{s})$. In addition, the squared time series correlation between x and p turns out to be:

$$r^2_{xp} = (\bar{r} - \bar{s})^2 \frac{M_{pp}}{M_{xx}}$$

Thus, the size of the time series correlation between x and p depends on the size of $\bar{r} - \bar{s}$ and of M_{pp} and is positively associated with both.

[21] For example, if p were to be positively correlated with r and/or s, the time series correlation between p and x would be larger than indicated by the $r - s$ difference; if the time series relation of p with r and/or s happens to be negative, the correlation between p and x will be smaller than suggested by the $r - s$ difference. To illustrate

It is intuitively obvious, and easily demonstrated, that if both r and s are completely invariant over time, p will be a perfect linear predictor of x. Start with the definitional equation,

$$x = p(r - s) + s$$

If both r and s are wholly invariant, they can be replaced by the constants k and K, respectively. Then the above equation can be written $x = K + kp$, and x is a completely determined linear function of p with intercept of K $(= s)$ and slope of k $(= r - s)$. To the extent that either purchase rate (r or s) varies, either randomly or systematically, p will be an imperfect predictor of x.

THE IMPORTANCE OF NONINTENDERS FOR PREDICTION

Given that r and s are not, and should not be expected to be, invariant over time, what can be inferred about the predictive ability of alternative intentions surveys? First, the proportion of total purchases accounted for by intenders appears to be highly relevant in determining which intentions surveys or questions are likely to be better time series predictors of purchases. Intentions questions characterized by small proportions of intenders relative to purchasers, hence, by low ratios of purchases by intenders to total purchases, will necessarily yield poor predictions of population purchases unless changes in the proportion of intenders (p) happen to be correlated with changes in the purchase rate of nonintenders (s). Given the definitional relation among these variables, intentions questions with relatively high cut-off probabilities will necessarily be associated with relatively small values of p, and it has been shown above that such questions will have relatively large values of r, s, and $r - s$, and values of s that are very close to x; but in that event most of the time series variance in x is a consequence not of changes in $(r - s)p$, the first term on the right-hand side of the definitional equation, but of changes in s, the second term. Whether p is an accurate predictor of x thus will depend largely on the correlation between p and s; and there is no a priori reason

---

the common sense interpretation of these statements, assume that p and s are negatively correlated over time. If so, when p increases the product $s(1 - p)$ will decrease. If the latter falls, it is quite possible that x will also fall, since by definition,

$$x = rp + s(1 - p),$$

and the second term on the right-hand side of this identity is generally much larger than the first term. But in that case, an increase in buying intentions (p) would be associated with a fall in purchases (x), and the time series correlation between p and x would be negative.

to suppose that these two variables (the proportion of intenders in the population and the purchase rate of nonintenders) will be strongly related. In effect, an intentions question with a relatively high probability cut-off is likely to be a very good time series predictor of purchases *by intenders* (because the purchase rate among intenders, r, is likely to be comparatively stable over time), but a poor predictor of total purchases: most purchases are made by nonintenders; therefore, most of the time series variance in x, the population purchase rate, is a consequence of changes in s, the purchase rate of nonintenders; and p, the proportion of intenders in the population, may be either not closely related or unrelated to s.

On the other hand, an intentions question with a relatively low probability cut-off will necessarily be characterized by a relatively high value of p. Such questions have been observed to have relatively low values of r, s, and $r - s$, and values of s that are substantially below x. In this case p may be both a worse predictor of purchases by intenders (because r is likely to be less stable over time than in the previous case) and a better predictor of total purchases. In sum, time series changes in s are likely to dominate time series changes in x whenever p is small relative to x, simply because a large part of the variation in x will then be a direct consequence of variation in s; as a consequence, the time series correlation between p and x will depend largely on the size of the correlation between p and s. If p is not so small, less of the variation in x will be a direct consequence of variation in s, and the time series correlation between p and x is less heavily dependent on the p, s correlation.[22]

PREDICTION OF DIFFERENCES IN COMMODITY PURCHASE RATES

Table 2 contained estimates of the proportion of total purchases made by intenders for each of the alternative intentions questions. The estimates,

[22] Another way of looking at this proposition is to note that if (1) r is essentially invariant over time, and (2) r is so large relative to s that $r - s$ can also be taken as invariant, time series changes in s will tend to show up as forecast errors in predicting x from p. Since

$$x = p(r - s) + s,$$

a linear regression of x on p will yield

$$x = a + bp + u,$$

where a is an estimate of $\bar{s}$, b of $(\bar{r} - \bar{s})$, and u is the error term. If p tends to be quite small because of the characteristics of the intentions question and if s and p are independent, the nonintender purchase rate during any specific period—s_j—is approximately $\bar{s} + uj$. Moreover, when p is small in absolute terms it will also tend to have little time series variance. Hence, the approximate variance of x will be u, and the correlation between x and p will be very small. On the same reasoning, the higher the level of p, the larger its variance, the smaller the error variance, and the larger the correlation between p and x, other things equal.

TABLE 13

PROPORTION OF TOTAL PURCHASES BY INTENDERS RELATED TO PURCHASE RATES FOR INTENDERS, NONINTENDERS, AND TOTAL SAMPLE

| | *Intentions Question A_1*
(definitely intend to buy) | | | | *Intentions Questions A_1 or A_2*
(definitely, probably, possibly will buy) | | | | |
	Intenders' Purchases as Per Cent of Total	p	x	r	s	Intenders' Purchases as Per Cent of Total	p	x	r	s
	PURCHASES WITHIN SIX MONTHS									
Automobile	24	.081	.191	.566	.158	57	.310	.191	.349	.121
Furniture	36	.135	.187	.493	.139	56	.319	.187	.330	.120
Carpets and rugs	28	.057	.076	.376	.058	45	.171	.076	.201	.050
High-fidelity equipment	20	.043	.065	.304	.054	38	.170	.065	.144	.048
Range	23	.025	.052	.478	.041	42	.084	.052	.257	.033
Refrigerator	23	.025	.056	.508	.044	47	.106	.056	.249	.033
Washing machine	18	.033	.075	.409	.063	37	.119	.075	.233	.054
Television set	9	.025	.053	.197	.049	26	.116	.053	.118	.043
Air conditioner	18	.021	.054	.463	.045	50	.118	.054	.230	.030
Clothes dryer	17	.028	.046	.284	.040	44	.114	.046	.177	.030
Dishwasher	29	.019	.026	.392	.019	50	.075	.026	.172	.014
Food freezer	19	.016	.027	.317	.022	42	.083	.027	.148	.016
Garbage disposal unit	18	.015	.023	.275	.019	33	.051	.023	.149	.016
Squared correlation coefficients	$r^2_{px} = .847, r^2_{sx} \sim 1.0$					$r^2_{px} = .949, r^2_{sx} \sim 1.0$				
	PURCHASES WITHIN TWELVE MONTHS									
Automobile	18	.081	.332	.775	.295	52	.310	.332	.553	.234
Furniture	28	.135	.319	.653	.267	49	.319	.319	.489	.239
Carpets and rugs	22	.057	.141	.544	.116	43	.171	.141	.357	.096
High-fidelity equipment	15	.043	.139	.483	.123	38	.170	.139	.310	.102
Range	16	.025	.089	.568	.077	34	.084	.089	.365	.064
Refrigerator	18	.025	.083	.600	.070	42	.106	.083	.325	.055
Washing machine	13	.033	.124	.489	.111	36	.119	.124	.374	.091
Television set	10	.025	.109	.409	.101	31	.116	.109	.292	.083
Air conditioner	16	.021	.063	.482	.054	48	.118	.063	.256	.036
Clothes dryer	17	.028	.081	.487	.071	43	.114	.081	.307	.054
Dishwasher	20	.019	.050	.529	.041	39	.075	.050	.263	.033
Food freezer	15	.016	.043	.415	.037	44	.083	.043	.227	.027
Garbage disposal unit	13	.015	.045	.400	.039	29	.051	.045	.253	.034
Squared correlation coefficients	$r^2_{px} = .852, r^2_{sx} \sim 1.0$					$r^2_{px} = .955, r^2_{sx} \sim 1.0$				

SOURCE: Table 2. See accompanying text for explanation of symbols.

for two of these intentions questions and all thirteen commodities, are shown in Table 13, along with purchase rates for intenders, nonintenders, and the sample as a whole. Although time series data on p and x for the alternative intentions questions are not available in the CU data, comparisons among commodities with different purchase rates constitute an interesting proxy.

71

For both six- and twelve-month purchase periods, the correlation between p and x is noticeably stronger for the intentions question characterized by a relatively high ratio of p to x—hence, also, a high ratio of purchases by intenders to total purchases; the correlation between s and x approximates unity.[23]   Data for the other intentions questions are also consistent with the generalization that the (p,x) correlation is stronger for questions with relatively low cut-off probabilities, with the exception of the two questions that have extremely low cut-off points—C_2 and (B_1 or B_2).   The tabulation, below, of r^2_{px} values computed from the same kind of data as in Table 13, documents this proposition.[24]

Intentions Question	r^2_{px} Among Commodities for Purchases Within	
	6 Months	12 Months
A_1	.847	.852
B_1	.876	.876
C_1	.926	.932
D_1	.956	.965
A_1 or A_2	.949	.955

The evidence in Table 13 illuminates one of the major difficulties in using the current buying intentions surveys to predict purchases of durables. Those who report that they "definitely will buy during the next twelve months" account for only between 20 and 30 per cent of total purchases during the six months following the survey, and for an even smaller proportion during the twelve months following.   Even those who report that they "definitely, probably, or possibly will buy during the next twelve months" generally account for only 40 to 50 per cent of total purchases during the six months following the survey and, again, for a smaller proportion during the twelve months.   Clearly, the majority of durable goods purchases are made by households that are generally classified as nonintenders by consumer surveys.   As a consequence, the accuracy of purchase predictions based on intentions surveys depends

---

[23] All these correlations have a strong upward bias because s is a major component of x, and x has an extremely large variance among commodities.   More precisely, the correlations have a strong upward bias as a measure of the success that would be enjoyed in making short-run predictions of x from p.   An appropriate analogy is that, although the correlation between income and consumption over the period 1900 to 1960 must be close to 1.0, predictions of the change in consumption between two adjacent years are likely to be quite poor if based solely on income.   Since consumption is a large part of income, any substantial variance in consumption must be strongly associated with a corresponding variance in income.

[24] This proposition does not depend on the comparative "efficiencies" of the intentions question, as the term is used in Chapter 2.   It is clear, for example, that the C_1 is a more efficient question than A_1 or A_2 combined in terms of its ability to discriminate between buyers and nonbuyers of particular commodities; but the (p,x) correlation among commodities is somewhat stronger for the combination of A_1 or A_2.

largely on whether or not changes in the proportion of intenders can successfully predict changes in the purchase rate of nonintenders, i.e., on whether or not p and s are strongly correlated over time.

From the data in Table 13 it appears that the probability cut-off point for definite, probable, or possible intenders is quite low, ranging from somewhere around 0.25 for automobiles to about 0.10 for garbage disposal units.[25] One possible conclusion is that estimates of the frequency distribution in the low-probability region are at least as critical as estimates of the distribution in the high-probability region, since at least half of the total purchase probabilities (hence, expected purchases) are contained in the former region.[26] It is also possible, however, that the low-probability region really contains a very small part of the total *ex ante* probabilities (hence, of expected purchases) and that these data give a misleading impression.

If the cut-off probabilities for any given intentions question are highly variable among households, a substantial number of relatively high-probability households will be classified as nonintenders. Since an estimate of the relative importance of low-probability households depends on the proportions and observed purchase rates of intenders and non-intenders, misclassification of households due to the inefficiency of the survey question could account for the relatively high proportion of purchases made by nonintenders. Alternatively, contingencies may be quantitatively important enough to produce this result. As already noted, my estimates are based on the observed r_i and s_i points. But r_i is too low as an estimate of r'_i (the mean probability in the distribution above C_i), and s_i is too high as an estimate of s'_i (the mean probability in the region

---

[25] The cut-off probability, C_i, must be lower than r'_i, the mean probability in the segment of the distribution located above C_i; how much lower depends on the shape of the distribution. No direct estimates of either C_i or r'_i are available, but r_i, the proportion of intenders who purchase, constitutes a downwardly biased estimate of r'_i. It does not seem unreasonable to assume that

$$C_i = r_i - 0.25r_i,$$

which is the basis for the statement in the text.

[26] Part of the data in Table 13 forms the empirical basis for estimating the cummulative expected purchases function—the middle panel of Chart 6—developed in the appendix to this chapter. The above data indicate that 19.1 per cent of the sample purchased an automobile, 8.1 per cent reported definite intentions to buy, and 31.0 reported either definite, probable, or possible intentions to buy. Further, 56.6 per cent of the definite intenders purchased, accounting for 24 per cent of total purchases; and 34.9 per cent of the definite-probable-possible intenders purchased, accounting for 57 per cent of total purchases. If the cut-off probabilities are assumed to be equal to $r_i - 0.25r_i$—see note 25, above—observed points on the appendix function 2.2 are: $C_i = 0.42$, $Br/Nr = .081 \times .566 = .046$; $C_i = 0.26$; $Br/Nr = .310 \times .349 = .108$; and $C_i = 0, Br/Nr = .191$.

below C_i). Thus, if the bias between *ex ante* and *ex post* values is sufficiently powerful, a similar analysis based on r'_i and s'_i might yield substantially different results.

IMPLICATIONS OF THE PROBABILITY MODEL FOR PREDICTION

For predicting future purchases of durables the probability model simply says that the best estimate of x, the proportion of households that will purchase during the forecast period, is x', the mean of the distribution function. All current surveys of buying intentions are designed to provide an estimate of the proportion of households in the high-probability segment of the distribution above some unknown but presumably stable cut-off point C_i. Even if the C implicit in the language of the intentions question is in fact invariant over time—and the evidence suggests that it is[27]—the mean of the distribution (x'_i) need not have a simple or fixed relation to p_i, the proportion of the population with purchase probabilities above C_i. Certain kinds of distributions do have the property that p is a unique function of x'; most do not.

These relations are worth examining more carefully, since they lie at the root of the forecasting problem. In Chart 4 two distribution functions are shown, one relating to period t_0—$n_0 = f_0(Q)$—and the other relating to period t_1—$n_1 = f_1(Q)$. If a survey of buying intentions is taken in t_0, a fraction p_0 will report intentions, a fraction $1 - p_0$ that they do not intend to buy. The buying intentions question is assumed to have an invariant (among households) cut-off probability of C_0, so that

$$p_0 = \left[\int_{C_0}^1 f_0(Q)dq \right] \div \left[\int_0^1 f_0(Q)dq \right]$$
$$1 - p_0 = \left[\int_0^{C_0} f_0(Q)dq \right] \div \left[\int_0^1 f_0(Q)dq \right]$$

A similar survey taken in t_1, using the same intentions question, will show different results if the distribution of households is assumed to have shifted. If the cut-off probability of the intentions question is also invariant over time so that $C_0 = C_1$, p_1 intenders and $1 - p_1$ nonintenders will be observed, where

$$p_1 = \left[\int_{C_0}^1 f_1(Q)dq \right] \div \left[\int_0^1 f_1(Q)dq \right]$$
$$1 - p_1 = \left[\int_0^{C_0} f_1(Q)dq \right] \div \left[\int_0^1 f_1(Q)dq \right]$$

[27] Reinterview data from the Federal Reserve Board–Census Bureau survey indicates very little time series variance in the purchase rate of households reporting intentions to buy within six months. There is also no apparent correlation between the purchase rate for intenders and the population purchase rate.

As the functions in Chart 4 are drawn, p_1 is somewhat higher than p_0, although the percentage change p_1/p_0 appears to be quite small. However, the mean of the t_0 distribution (x'_0) appears to differ from the t_1 mean (x'_1) by something like 50 per cent, that is, $x'_1/x'_0 \sim 1.50$. In order to forecast the change in purchases it is necessary to predict the

CHART 4

**Illustrative Time Series Changes
in Probability Distribution**

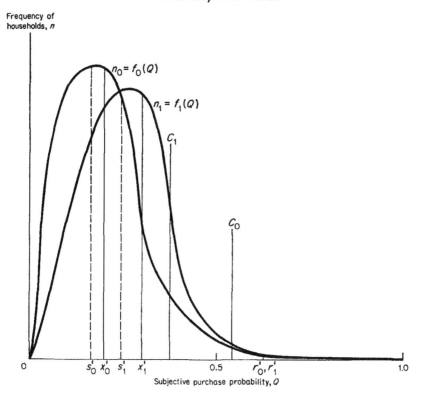

Subjective purchase probability, Q

ratio x_1/x_0. The best estimate of this ratio is clearly x'_1/x'_0; p_1/p_0 may turn out to be the same or very close to x'_1/x'_0; but it may also turn out to be quite different.

The relationship between p_1/p_0 and x'_1/x'_0 is easily shown to depend on the level, as well as the change, of mean probabilities for intenders (r'_0, r'_1) and nonintenders (s'_0, s'_1). As I have noted before, mean probability in the sample as a whole is a weighted average of the means for intenders and nonintenders, since

$$x'_0 = r'_0 p_0 + s'_0 (1 - p_0)$$
$$x'_1 = r'_1 p_1 + s'_1 (1 - p_1)$$

Hence the change in mean probability between t_0 and t_1 is

$$\frac{x'_1}{x'_0} = \frac{r'_1 p_1 + s'_1 (1 - p_1)}{r'_0 p_0 + s'_0 (1 - p_0)}$$

The ratio p_1/p_0 will equal x'_1/x'_0 only if $r'_1 = r'_0$ and if $s'_0 = s'_1 = 0$; otherwise, the two ratios will be the same only by chance. The point is not that the ratio p_1/p_0 will necessarily yield a bad forecast of x'_1/x'_0, but that there is no obvious reason why it should yield a good forecast. From Chart 4 it is abundantly clear that one could construct distribution functions for periods t_0 and t_1, with means of x'_0 and x'_1, and either a very high ratio of p_1/p_0 or a very low one. Further, one might get quite different results simply by varying the intentions question; in Chart 4 a question with a lower cut-off probability than C_0—say, C_1—would be a better predictor because the new p_1/p_0 ratio would be higher than the one shown above. But a question with a higher cut-off probability—say, C_2—would apparently give worse results.

The above argument can be stated more succinctly in general form. Prediction of durable goods purchases from consumer surveys requires that the survey yield an estimate of x', the mean purchase probability in the population. If x' is a linear function of p_i, an estimate of p_i will be a perfect substitute for x' in linear regressions. If x' is a unique but non-linear function of p_i, an estimate of p_i will be a perfect substitute for x' provided that the functional relation between p_i and x' can be established. But if x' cannot be determined solely from p_i, the latter will be an inferior substitute, one that cannot reliably predict purchases. One final point is worth noting. All surveys are necessarily limited in sample size. The problem of sampling error is maximized for a survey that concentrates on measuring p, especially if, as is typically the case, intentions questions with relatively high cut-off probabilities are used.

In addition to these analytical considerations, the question of stability over time in the distribution function is of considerable importance. It may well be true that the proportion of households with probabilities above some relatively high value, say 0.50, is much less variable over time than the proportion with probabilities between 0.10 and 0.20.[28] Since a

---

[28] Very little empirical evidence is available on this point. One interesting scrap of data (unpublished, from a confidential market research study) suggests that, for the commodity under study, the entire shift in the probability distribution between two

large majority of households appear to have quite low purchase probabilities for most items, variations in the number of households in the probability region below 0.25 may be a more important source of changes in population mean probability than variations in the number of households in the region above 0.50 or 0.75.

An Exploratory Time Series Test

For the most part, the propositions just discussed cannot be tested directly with existing time series data on consumer intentions to buy. Empirical evidence does suggest that a relatively large share of the time series variance in purchases is due to variation over time in the purchases of nonintenders, rather than intenders. There is no survey evidence that bears directly on the predictability of these critically important movements in nonintenders' purchase rates. But the probability hypothesis suggests a possible proxy for nonintender purchase rates—more precisely, for the variation in mean *ex-ante* purchase probability among nonintenders. Empirically, the proxy variable performs extremely well; it explains a substantial part of the variance in over-all purchase rates that cannot be accounted for by changes in the proportion of intenders. I regard these results as suggestive but inconclusive, for two reasons. First, there are only eleven time series observations on which the relevant test can be run. Second, and more important, quantitative assumptions are necessary to conduct the test; while the precise assumptions used below are plausible and consistent with the probability hypothesis, other equally plausible and consistent quantitative assumptions could also have been made—with results considerably less striking than the ones presented below.

---

time periods took place in what must have been a very low probability range. During the same two periods the purchase rate changed by some 20 per cent. The pattern was roughly as follows:

Proportion of Sample Reporting Intentions to Buy	Period 1	Period 2
Within a year	2%	2%
Within a few years	4	4
Interested, no plans	10	14
Not interested	84	80

Here the only shift was between households "not interested," presumably with probabilities of zero or close to it, and those "interested, no plans," presumably with probabilities somewhat higher than zero but very low in absolute terms. A very crude calculation indicates that mean probability in the latter group is quite likely to have been less than 0.10, assuming that the observed change in purchases had been due solely to the increased frequency in that group.

The basic data are the surveys of consumer intentions to buy automobiles, conducted since January 1959 by the U.S. Bureau of the Census. Other intentions surveys cover a longer time span but the detailed classifications of intenders needed to implement the test would require retabulation and possibly even recoding of the survey schedules. For data on automobile purchases, I rely on Ward's Automotive Reports. An alternative purchase series is available—the Census survey of buying intentions also asks about past purchases—but the Ward's series seems to be regarded as the more accurate estimate of automobile sales to consumer units; in addition, use of the Ward's data insures that the intentions and purchases series are completely independent.

Because the intentions data have a strong seasonal pattern, I rely exclusively on comparisons of change from year to year.[29] The variable to be predicted is the change in the proportion of households purchasing a new automobile during successive twelve-month purchase periods. The explanatory variables are the change in the (weighted) proportion of households reporting intentions to buy a car at the beginning of each purchase period, the corresponding change in the (weighted) proportion of households reporting that they "don't know" or are "uncertain" about car buying intentions, and the change in the (weighted) proportion of nonintenders adjusted by an index of change in the proportion of "don't know" households.

The weights are essentially estimates of mean purchase probability for the various classes of households. Those reporting that they definitely intend to buy a new car within six months are assigned a weight of 0.7—roughly, the observed purchase rate among such households during the twelve months subsequent to an intentions survey. Those reporting that they might buy a new car within six months are assigned a weight of 0.5, those reporting that they intend to (definitely will, probably will, or might) buy a new car within twelve months (but not within six months) are assigned a weight of 0.3, and those reporting that they intend to buy a *used* car within twelve months, a weight of 0.2. Summing up the weighted proportions of households reporting these various types of intentions yields

---

[29] The seasonal pattern in car buying intentions does not match the seasonal in consumer purchases of new automobiles. For the Census data, intentions to buy new cars are much higher in the October survey than in any of the other (January, April, and July) surveys; intentions to buy new cars may also be seasonally high in January. Purchases are at their peak in the spring. Of course, the seasonal in intentions should lead that in purchases.

Attempts to make a seasonal adjustment of intentions based on the limited number of available observations have convinced me that the risks of so doing are greater than those in comparisons of year-to-year change.

a series designated as p'. Households reporting either that they "don't know" about automobile purchases within six months or within twelve months are each assigned a weight of 0.1; this series is designated as d. The two "don't know" categories have some overlap, but it is by no means complete. For example, a household might well report that they "don't know" about purchases within a six month period but "might" or "probably will" buy within twelve months. The probability weight is assumed to be invariant over time for all these groups; hence any change in expected purchases must be a consequence of changes in the proportion of households reporting intentions to buy or reporting "don't know."

For the nonintender series—designated as z—I use a probability weight of 0.05.[30] For nonintenders, however, I do not make the assumption that the probability weight is constant over time and that changes in the proportion of households measure changes in expected purchases. Rather, I assume that mean probability among nonintenders will vary over time, and that it varies directly with the change in the fraction of households reporting "don't know." In general terms, the argument is that an increase (decrease) in the proportion of "don't know" households is symptomatic of a general increase (decrease) in purchase probability among all households in the low probability regions of the distribution. One could, of course, use movements in other intender classes as being symptomatic of movements in purchase probability among nonintenders. It seems plausible to me, however, that movements in the intender class with the lowest purchase probability are more likely to reflect movements in average probability among nonintenders simply because these two classes are adjacent in the probability distribution. In effect, I am assuming that the p, s correlation is likely to be stronger the lower the probability interval defined by any given p. Concretely, I not only assume that the chance in the proportion of "don't know" responses is symptomatic of a general increase (decrease) in mean probability among nonintenders, but is the best estimate of the amount of the increase (decrease). Other assumptions are equally plausible.

The basic data are shown in Tables 14 and 15. Table 14 has the propor-

[30] Nonintenders will not precisely equal the total sample minus all the groups discussed above. The Census data contain one classification comprising households reporting intentions to buy either new or used cars within twelve months. I have defined nonintenders as the total sample less the sum of this comprehensive category and of households reporting that they "don't know" about their twelve-month intentions.

Because I have included both six- and twelve-month "don't know" groups among the intenders, some households are counted twice; consequently, the sum of all intender groups, plus the nonintenders as defined in this note, slightly exceeds 100 per cent.

tions of households in the buying categories of intention, don't know, and nonintention; Table 15 contains the weighted constructs designated above as p', d, and z. As noted above, the existence of seasonal variation in the buying-intentions data requires either seasonal adjustment of the data or analysis based on differences between successive periods twelve months

TABLE 14

BASIC DATA FOR ANALYSIS OF TIME SERIES RELATIONS BETWEEN PURCHASES OF NEW AUTOMOBILES AND INTENTIONS TO BUY AUTOMOBILES
(per cent of households reporting)

Survey Date	Definitely Intend to Buy a New Car Within 6 Mos. (1)	Might Buy a New Car Within 6 Mos. (2)	Intend to Buy a New Car Within 7–12 Mos. (3)	Intend to Buy a Used Car Within 12 Mos. (4)	*Don't Know About Buying Plans* Within 6 Mos. (5)	Within 12 Mos. (6)	No Plans to Buy Within 12 Mos. (7)
Jan. 1959	1.2	1.9	3.6	8.5	3.4	6.9	76.0
April 1959	0.9	1.8	3.9	7.2	3.0	6.4	77.8
July 1959	1.2	2.0	3 8	7.8	3.1	6.5	76.4
Oct. 1959	1.8	2.9	4.9	9.3	2.8	5.6	73.2
Jan. 1960	1.3	2.2	3.9	8.4	3.6	7.8	73.5
April 1960	1.5	1.8	3.7	7.2	3.0	7.5	75.4
July 1960	1.2	1.9	3.8	7.2	2.8	7.1	76.1
Oct. 1960	1.5	2.2	4.2	8.0	2.8	7.1	74.3
Jan. 1961	1.4	2.1	3.9	8.3	2.7	7.4	74.7
April 1961	1.1	2.0	3.7	7.7	2.9	7.6	75.8
July 1961	1.4	2.0	4.2	7.9	2.9	7.3	75.3
Oct. 1961	1.6	2.1	4.4	8.2	3.1	8.0	73.5
Jan. 1962	1.5	2.2	4.1	8.2	3.0	7.7	74.2
April 1962	1.5	1.9	4.3	9.2	3.3	7.9	73.2
July 1962	1.4	2.0	4 0	8.1	2.9	7.6	75.0
Oct. 1962	1.8	2.3	5.0	8.3	3.2	8.0	72.5
Jan. 1963	1.5	2.4	3.9	8.7	3.2	8.1	73.3
April 1963	1.8	2.3	4.0	8.0	3.5	8.6	73.2

SOURCE: All data are from Table 1 in *Consumer Buying Intentions*, Department of Commerce, U.S. Bureau of Census, Current Population Reports, Series P-65, No. 2, May 22, 1963. The first six columns are shown directly in Table 1; the last column is equal to 100 per cent minus the sum of those with twelve-month intentions to buy new or used cars plus those who "don't know" about twelve-month intentions.

apart. I have selected the latter course; hence Δx is defined as the difference in the new automobile purchase rate between successive twelve-month periods, e.g., as the difference in the purchase rate for the periods January 1, 1960 to December 31, 1960 and January 1, 1959 to December 31, 1959; or between the periods April 1, 1960 to March 31, 1961, and April 1, 1959 to March 31, 1960, etc. The buying intentions series are treated similarly; hence, the intentions variables used in the empirical analysis are $\Delta p'$, Δd, and Δz; these measure differences in the respective

TABLE 15

WEIGHTED PERCENTAGES OF HOUSEHOLDS INTENDING TO BUY AND PURCHASING AUTOMOBILES

Time Period[a]	Intenders[b] (p')	Don't Know[c] (d)	Nonintenders[d] (z)	Total $(p' + d + z)$	Purchasers[e] (x)
1 Jan. 1959–31 Dec. 1959	4.57	1.03	3.80	9.40	11.84
1 April 1959–31 Mar. 1960	4.14	.94	3.89	8.97	12.14
1 July 1959–30 June 1960	4.54	.96	3.82	9.32	12.27
1 Oct. 1959–30 Sept. 1960	6 04	.84	3.66	10.54	12.21
1 Jan. 1960–31 Dec. 1960	4.92	1.14	4.02	10.08	12.61
1 April 1960–31 Mar. 1961	4.50	1.05	4.06	9.61	11.91
1 July 1960–30 June 1961	4.37	.99	3.76	9.12	11.39
1 Oct. 1960–30 Sept. 1961	5.01	.99	4.16	10.16	11.03
1 Jan. 1961–31 Dec. 1961	4.86	1.01	3.44	9.31	11.07
1 April 1961–31 Mar. 1962	4.42	1.05	4.06	9.53	11.65
1 July 1961–30 June 1962	4.82	1.02	3.86	9.70	12.22
1 Oct. 1961–30 Sept. 1962	5.13	1.11	4.60	10.84	12.45
1 Jan. 1962–31 Dec. 1962	5.02	1.07	3.67	9.76	12.96
1 April 1962–31 Mar. 1963	5.13	1.12	4.26	10.51	13.20
1 July 1962–30 June 1963	4.80	1.05	3.93	9.78	13.30
1 Oct. 1962–30 Sept. 1963	5.57	1.12	4.60	11.29	n.a.
1 Jan. 1963–31 Dec. 1963	5.16	1.13	3.84	10.13	n.a.
1 April 1963–31 Mar. 1964	5.21	1.21	4.56	10.98	n.a.

[a] Time period shown is period over which the purchase rate (x) is measured. The intentions surveys are taken during the first mentioned month of each period, usually in the third week.

[b] Derived from data in Table 14: percentages in the first four columns multiplied by weights of 0.7, 0.5, 0.3 and 0.2, respectively, then summed. See above text for further description of procedures.

[c] Derived from data in Table 14: percentages in the fifth and sixth columns multiplied by weight of 0.1, then summed. See above text for further description of procedures.

[d] Derived from Table 14: percentages in the last column of Table 14 are first multiplied by weight of 0.05, then adjusted by the average of two link relative indexes obtained from the fifth and sixth columns in Table 14. To illustrate: for data in columns five and six the link relatives between January 1959 and January 1960 are 105.9 and 113.0 respectively; the average of these two indexes is 109.4. Thus, the January 1960 observation in the z column (4.02) is the January 1960 figure from the seventh column of Table 14 (73.5) $\times$ 0.0547; (the 0.0547 figure is equal to 0.05 $\times$ 109.4). Similarly, the January 1961 z observation is equal to the January 1961 figure from the last column of Table 14 (74.7) $\times$ (0.0547 $\times$ 84.3 = 0.0461); the 84.3 figure is the average of the link relatives between January 1961 and January 1960 for the fifth and sixth columns in Table 14. See above text for further description.

[e] Derived from Table 1-B in *The Predictive Value of Consumer Buying Intentions: A Study of Aggregate Time Series*, April 1963, an unpublished manuscript by Theodore Flechsig of the Federal Reserve Board. Flechsig's data on sales come directly from *Ward's Automotive Reports*. He has converted total sales figures to proportions of households for a six-month time period, and I have simply added together his respective six-month figures to obtain a twelve-month series. The last few figures shown in this column represent figures calculated in the same manner as the rest except that they were not yet available at the time Flechsig's manuscript was circulated, hence are not contained in his Table 1-B.

intentions series based on surveys taken twelve months apart. As a consequence, only eleven (overlapping) observations are available for an investigation of the relation between purchases and buying intentions.

Table 15 provides the basic data for an examination of two related problems. First, is the time series variation in automobile purchase rates due mainly to variation in intenders', as opposed to nonintenders', purchases? If so, time series variation in purchases will be due mainly to changes in the proportion of intenders; if not, variation in purchases will be due mainly to changes in mean probability among nonintenders. If it is assumed that mean purchase probability for the various intender groups is as specified above (ranging from 0.7 for those with definite new car intentions within six months to 0.2 for those intending to buy used cars within twelve months) and is constant over time,[31] the change in total purchases (Δx) can be separated into the change in intenders' purchases ($\Delta p'$) and a residual, $\Delta x - \Delta p'$. Δx is an *ex-post* magnitude, and $\Delta p'$ is *ex-ante* by construction; $\Delta x - \Delta p'$ can be thought of as the sum of purchases that nonintenders expected to make—an unobserved but *ex-ante* magnitude—and of purchases that reflect the influence of unforeseen events. Although the relative importance of unforeseen events cannot be measured directly, there is no reason to expect that it will be the dominant element in the variance of $\Delta x - \Delta p'$.

The data indicate that the variance of $\Delta p'$—intenders purchases—is less than about one-fourth the size of the variance in $\Delta x - \Delta p'$. This empirical finding is not altered if intenders are defined to include households reporting that they "don't know" whether they will buy a car: the variance of $\Delta p' + \Delta d$ is almost exactly the same as that of $\Delta p'$ itself, and the variance of the new residual, $\Delta x - \Delta p' - \Delta d$, is still more than four times as large. I conclude that a major part of the time series variance in purchase rates consists of the variation in mean probability among nonintenders. It follows that the correlation between Δx and $\Delta p'$ will be relatively small unless changes in the proportion of intenders happen to be a good predictor of changes in nonintender mean probability, and hence nonintender purchase rates.

The second question concerns the correlation between intentions and purchases. The basic data are drawn from Table 15; the empirical results are summarized in Table 16.

---

[31] What evidence I have seen suggests that mean probability among intenders is in fact quite stable over time. But it is not even necessary that such be the case: an exact estimate of the total purchases made by intenders will have the same variance over time as my constructed estimate provided that mean probability among intenders is uncorrelated with the proportion of households reporting intentions.

Changes in weighted buying intentions ($\Delta p'$) explain about 40 per cent of the variance in purchase rate changes (eq. a in Table 16); the correlation is barely significant at the 0.05 level. By themselves, changes in the "don't know" (Δd) or nonintender (Δz) groups explain considerably less of the variance in purchase rate changes than does $\Delta p'$. However, the sum of $\Delta p'$ and Δd brings the explained variance up to almost 50 per cent (equation e), while summing all three expected purchases series $\Delta(p' + d + z)$ brings the explained variance up to roughly two-thirds of the total (equation f). The correlation between Δx and $\Delta(p' + d + z)$ is significantly different from zero at the 0.01 level, and is significantly *higher* than the correlation between Δx and $\Delta p'$ at the 0.05 level.

TABLE 16
TIME SERIES CORRELATIONS BETWEEN THE CHANGE IN NEW AUTOMOBILE
PURCHASE RATES AND THE CHANGE IN ALTERNATIVE MEASURES OF
AUTOMOBILE BUYING INTENTIONS

Equation Number	Equation	Squared Correlation Coefficient
(a)	$\Delta x = +.19 + 1.74\Delta p'$,	$r^2 = .39$[a]
(b)	$\Delta x = +.03 + 5.53\Delta d$,	$r^2 = .13$
(c)	$\Delta x = +.07 + 1.97\Delta z$,	$r^2 = .23$
(d)	$\Delta x = +.09 + 1.80\Delta(p' + d)$,	$r^2 = .47$[a]
(e)	$\Delta x = +.06 + 1.49\Delta(d + z)$,	$r^2 = .15$
(f)	$\Delta x = -.11 + 1.77\Delta(p' + d + z)$,	$r^2 = .67$[b]

SOURCE: Estimated from basic data in Table 15. See the notes to Table 15 or the text for explanation of symbols.
[a] F ratio significantly different from unity at 0.05 level.
[b] F ratio significantly different from unity at 0.01 level.

In effect, a substantial part of what may be regarded as the residual variance in actual purchases is explained by adding a very crude proxy for nonintenders' expected purchases to expected purchases by intenders: changes in expected purchases by intenders explains 39 per cent of the variance in total purchases; accounting for changes in expected purchases by the "don't know" and *nonintender households brings the explained variance up to 67 per cent.* Thus almost half of the residual variance (28 of 61 percentage points) is explained by this crude approximation for nonintender purchases.

An alternate way of investigating the same proposition with somewhat different assumptions involves correlating Δd—the change in the proportion of "don't know" households—with the purchase rate of nonintenders. The latter can be estimated by the following procedure.

1. Using the probability weights assigned above to the various intender groups, estimate the actual purchases of nonintenders by calculating $x - p' - d$ from Table 15.

2. Estimate the purchase *rate* of nonintenders by dividing the proportion of nonintenders into estimated purchases by nonintenders; that is, divide $x - p' - d$ by column 7 of Table 14. The resulting values can be thought of as estimates of mean *ex-ante* purchase probability among nonintenders.

Designating the nonintender purchase rate as s, and it's year-to-year change as Δs, we have

$$\Delta s = 0.04 + 2.67\Delta d, \, r^2 = 0.21$$

The correlation between Δs and Δd, while positive, is not significantly different from zero at conventional levels. This test thus implies a less strong association between changes in the purchase probability of nonintenders and changes in the proportion of "don't know" households than the set of regressions discussed earlier. It should be noted, however, that relative to the earlier regressions, the $\Delta s, \Delta d$ test has an added constraint as well as an extra degree of freedom.[32]

Another interesting piece of time series evidence concerns the explanatory power of the above intender series net of other variables that are associated with purchase rates. In the final chapter of this monograph I present cross-section data in which durable goods purchases are regressed on some fifteen independent variables. Some of the independent variables represent circumstances that were known at the survey date (designated as initial-data variables), while others represent circumstances that were wholly or partly unforseen at the survey date (designated as intervening variables). The probability hypothesis implies that initial-data variables should be more strongly related to buying intentions than to purchases, while the opposite relation should hold for intervening variables. Further, the hypothesis implies that intervening variables will make a larger contribution than initial-data variables to an explanation of the residual variance in purchases, buying intentions held constant. The argument is simply that the influence of initial-data variables will be accounted for by intentions because the values of such variables are known to the respondent

---

[32] The two procedures would show substantially similar results if the regression of Δx on $\Delta(p' + d)$ yielded a slope coefficient close to unity. This is the general nature of the constraint; the data show that the regression coefficient of $\Delta(p' + d)$ is considerably higher than unity (see Table 16). On the other hand, the $\Delta s, \Delta d$ correlation permits the regression coefficient of Δd to vary, while the first procedure forces the coefficients of Δd and $\Delta p'$ to equality. There are other differences as well in the two procedures, but these are the most important ones.

at the time intentions are reported; this is less true of intervening variables because they reflect wholly or partly unforseen events that influence actual purchases but not buying intentions or purchase probabilities.[33]

On this line of argument, changes in concurrent income, as compared with past income, should be *more* strongly associated with changes in purchases, *less* strongly associated with changes in buying intentions. Past income change is clearly an initial-data variable, while concurrent income is intervening to the extent that the change is not foreseen.

TABLE 17

Time Series Correlations Between the Change in New Automobile Purchase Rates, the Change in Automobile Buying Intentions, and the Change in Disposable Income

Equation	Dependent Variable	Independent Variable(s)	Multiple R^2 or Simple r^2	Partial r^2 for $\Delta(p' + d + z)$	Δy_{-1}	Δy
(g)	Δx	Δy_{-1}	.56[b]			
(h)	Δx	Δy	.86[b]			
(i)	$\Delta(p' + d + z)$	Δy_{-1}	.31			
(j)	$\Delta(p' + d + z)$	Δy	.43[a]			
(k)	Δx	$\Delta y_{-1}, \Delta y$	.90[b]		.30	.78[b]
(l)	$\Delta(p' + d + z)$	$\Delta y_{-1}, \Delta y$	.46		.06	.22
(m)	Δx	$\Delta(p' + d + z),$ Δy_{-1}	.79[b]	.53[a]	.38	
(n)	Δx	$\Delta(p' + d + z),$ Δy	.94[b]	.54[a]		.81[b]
(o)	Δx	$\Delta(p' + d + z),$ $\Delta y_{-1}, \Delta y$	.94[b]	.38	05	.71[b]

Source: Basic data for purchases and buying intentions are shown in Table 15; concurrent and past income changes calculated from the *Survey of Current Business*, U.S. Department of Commerce, various issues. See Table 15 and the above text for explanation of symbols.

[a] *F* ratio significantly different from unity at 0.05 level.

[b] *F* ratio significantly different from unity at 0.01 level.

Designating concurrent income change as Δy and past income change as Δy_{-1},[34] the results shown in Table 17 are obtained.

Concurrent income is more highly correlated with purchases than with buying intentions, it is more highly correlated with purchases than is past

[33] See Chapter 7, pp. 166–168, for a more detailed analysis.

[34] The symbol Δy_{-1} is defined as the difference in disposable income between the quarter immediately preceding the intentions survey and the comparable quarter one year earlier. The symbol Δy is defined as the average difference in disposable income between the first two quarters of a twelve-month purchase period and the comparable two quarters one year earlier; both differences are measured in billions of current dollars. Interestingly enough, when concurrent income change is measured further along in the purchase period, its correlation with the purchase rate is weakened, possibly because of a lag in the relation between the two. A similar pattern of results is shown in Flechsig's manuscript.

income, and it adds considerably more to the explanation of purchases net of buying intentions than does past income; all these results are in accord with predictions. Actually, a linear combination of change in buying intentions—$\Delta(p' + d + z)$—and concurrent income—Δy—explains almost all of the variance in purchase rates, and an F test indicates that both partial correlations are highly significant. The explanation of purchases is hardly improved at all when past income is added to concurrent income and buying intentions (compare equations n and o in Table 17). However, many of the predicted relations involving income changes and buying intentions do not appear. Concurrent income is somewhat more strongly (rather than less strongly) associated with intentions than is past income and concurrent income adds more than past income to an explanation of buying intentions (compare equations i, j, and l in Table 17).

The findings of this exploratory time series investigation are summarized in Chart 5. The upper panel shows first differences in the actual purchase rate of new automobiles, and in the rate of expected purchases by intenders, nonintenders plus don't know households, and the sum of the two. In almost every time period, it is evident that adding nonintenders' expected purchases (estimated as described above) to those of intenders improves the fit with actual purchases. The lower panel shows first differences in actual purchases plotted against regression estimates based on expected purchases and on the combination of expected purchases and concurrent income. The latter combination of variables evidently explains almost all of the variance in actual purchases.

Let me note once again that the above results cannot be viewed as conclusive evidence in favor of either the analytical model developed in this chapter or of the empirical assumptions used above. The level of statistical significance attributed to these results is undoubtedly exaggerated; the particular constructs used in the correlation analysis were neither the first used nor the only reasonable ones that could have been used. Hence, more degrees of freedom have in fact been used up than appears to be the case, and there is no formally correct way to adjust the results to account for this. In my judgment, the chances are better than even that the general pattern of the empirical results is substantive; that is, some such assumption as made above about movements in mean purchase probability among nonintenders is likely to improve purchase predictions based on buying intentions surveys. I doubt that the particular assumption made above is the most appropriate one, and I suspect that direct measurement of purchase probability among nonintenders would turn out to be a superior predictor than any proxy variable.

CHART 5

Change from Preceding Year in Twelve-Month Purchase Rates of New Automobiles Compared with Corresponding Change in Rate of Expected Purchases

x = Actual purchase rate
p' = Expected purchase rate of intenders
$(d + z)$ = Expected purchase rate of nonintenders

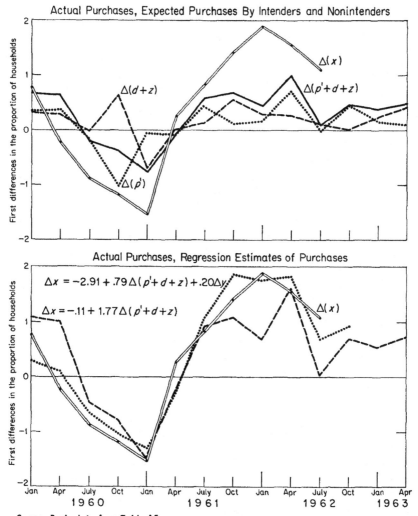

Source: Basic data from Table 15.

Summary

On the whole, the evidence tends to support the hypothesis that questions about intentions to buy elicit responses drawn from a continuous distribution of purchase probabilities. No convincing evidence is available on the shape or the stability of the distribution functions, nor is it known whether the mean of these functions can be accurately estimated from the proportion of the sample in the upper tail. It also seems clear that the typical intentions questions in current use tend to be relatively inefficient in that substantial numbers of households reporting that they "intend to buy" have lower purchase probabilities than some households not so reporting. Given these results, further experimentation with survey design seems to be called for, and the objective is self-evident. If a continuous distribution of purchase probabilities characterizes the universe, a survey should attempt to estimate the mean of this distribution. The simplest procedure is to estimate the distribution and compute the mean directly. In this way no assumptions need be made about the distribution function, its stability over time, or the relation between the mean and the proportion of households in the upper tail. It may turn out that only parts of the distribution are of interest for prediction purposes, but I see no way of deciding this question on a-priori grounds.

There are, of course, many possible procedures by which such information might be obtained, including the direct approach. I know of no convincing evidence that survey respondents would experience more difficulty in answering the question "What are the odds that you will buy A next year?" than in answering the kinds of questions currently used in intentions surveys, e.g., "Do you intend to buy A next year?" and "How certain are you of these plans?" It is even possible that the direct approach is the best, particularly since differences among households in the interpretation of a survey question may well be greater when literary terms are used than when numerical scales are explicit in the question. That is to say, on a-priori grounds it could be argued that the variance in cut-off probability (and, therefore, in purchase probability) among those reporting that they "definitely intend to buy within n months" is greater than the variance among those reporting that "the odds on buying within n months are better than two to one."[35] These are questions of judgment, however, and nothing in the above data suggests that one or another way of measuring subjective probability is superior. It may be that a more complicated procedure, involving combined responses to several questions,

[35] The illustration assumes that average probability is the same in both cases.

would be more accurate than simpler and more direct methods. This question is entirely open; but the conclusion seems inescapable that more precise and comprehensive scaling of the entire probability distribution is an essential requirement for increasing the accuracy of predictions based on survey data.

Granting that the probability model constitutes the most plausible interpretation of intentions data, a number of problems remain about how such data are to be used for predicting purchases of durable goods. First, is the cut-off probability corresponding to a given intentions question the same for all commodities and for all households in the population? If not, what are the characteristics to which the C_i are related? These questions are discussed in the next chapter. Second, how do unanticipated events (contingencies) influence the translation of initial probabilities into purchases? The third is similar to the second. Do concurrent attitudes have any effect on the initial probabilities associated with responses to questions about buying intentions or about explicit probabilities? These problems are discussed in Chapter 6. Finally, are the *ex ante* purchase probabilities associated with responses to a specific set of questions about buying intentions (or explicit probabilities) invariant over time? That is, are time series differences in average probability for the population accurately reflected in the changing proportion of responses to a fixed scale, or does the probability associated with a particular response vary systematically with particular kinds of circumstances, e.g., the level of unemployment, the state of business activity, etc.? In principle, one needs a series of observations $C_{i...j}$, relating to different time periods. My analysis implicitly assumes that a set of such observations will show only random variation due to sampling error. This problem is not discussed here; the necessary data cannot be readily obtained from any source, and cannot be obtained at all from the CU survey materials.

Appendix I: A Geometrical Model of the Subjective Probability Hypothesis

By amplifying the distribution function in Chart 1, I shall elaborate the subjective probability hypothesis and present some crude tests of its empirical content. The upper panel of Chart 6 shows the same distribution function as in Chart 1, i.e.,

$$1.0 \qquad\qquad n = f(Q),$$

and the cumulative distribution function obtained by summing from $C = 0$

CHART 6

Illustrative Distributions of Households
by Subjective Purchase Probability, by Expected Purchases,
and by Average and Marginal Purchase Probability

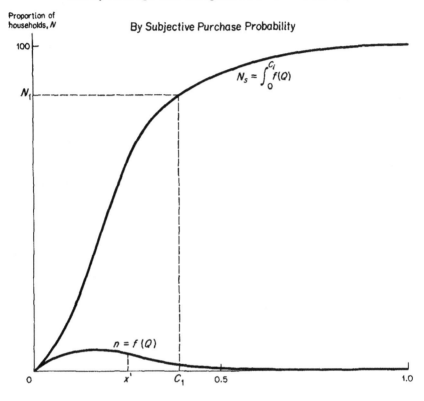

Proportion of households, N

By Subjective Purchase Probability

$$N_s = \int_0^{C_i} f(Q)$$

$n = f(Q)$

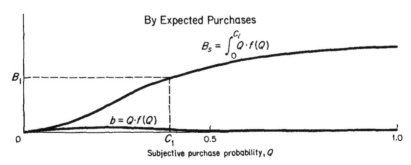

By Expected Purchases

$$B_s = \int_0^{C_i} Q \cdot f(Q)$$

$b = Q \cdot f(Q)$

Subjective purchase probability, Q

CHART 6 (concluded)

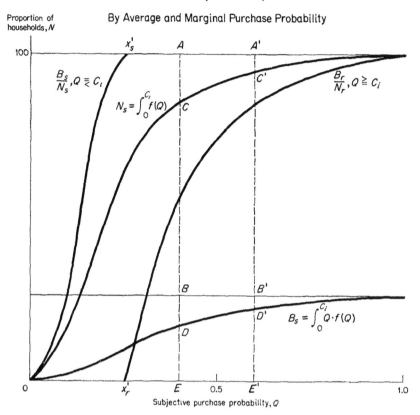

Proportion of households, N

By Average and Marginal Purchase Probability

Subjective purchase probability, Q

to $C = C_i$, that is,[36]

1.1
$$N_s = \int_0^{C_i} f(Q)dq.$$

The middle panel of Chart 6 shows an expected purchases (b) function obtained by multiplying the number of households at each probability level by the probability itself. If b households have purchase probabilities equal to 0.5, we expect these households, on the average, to make 0.5b purchases. The middle panel also contains a cumulative expected purchases function, obtained by summing from zero to C_i as above.

2.0
$$b = Q \cdot f(Q)$$

2.1
$$B_s = \int_0^{C_i} Q \cdot f(Q)dq$$

[36] I designate $\int_0^{C_i} f(Q)$, as N_s to indicate that it is the cumulative number of households with probabilities less than C_i, that is, the number that would not report intentions to buy if asked a question with a cut-off probability equal to C_i.

91

The two cumulative functions 1.1 and 2.1 have some useful properties. Equation 1.1 shows the number of households with probabilities equal to or less than C_i. Equation 2.1 shows the expected number of purchases by households with probabilities equal to or less than C_i. In the top panel of Chart 6, for example, N_1 households have subjective purchase probabilities equal to or less than C_1. These N_1 households, on the average, will make purchases equal to B_1, as indicated by the middle panel.

The ratio of these two cumulative functions—B_s/N_s—is thus the fraction of households with $Q \lesseqgtr C_i$ expected to purchase during the forecast period. When $C_i = 1.0$, this ratio is evidently equal to mean probability for the sample as a whole, i.e., to x'; when C_i approaches zero, this ratio will also approach zero. Two complementary cumulative functions, specifying the number of households and number of expected purchases for those with subjective probabilities equal to or *greater than* C_i, can also be constructed:

1.2 $$N_r = \int_{C_i}^{1} f(Q)dq$$

2.2 $$B_r = \int_{C_i}^{1} Q \cdot f(Q)dq$$

It follows that

1.3 $$N_r + N_s = \int_{0}^{1} f(Q)dq = N,$$

2.3 $$B_r + B_s = \int_{0}^{1} f(Q)dq = B,$$

and

3.0 $$B/N = x'$$

Further, B_r/N_r is the fraction of households with $Q \geq C_i$ expected to purchase during the forecast period. When C_i is zero this fraction is equal to the proportion of the entire sample that is expected to purchase, i.e., to x'. As C_i approaches 1.0, this fraction will also approach 1.0.

The bottom panel of Chart 6 reproduces the cumulative functions 1.1 and 2.1 from the upper panels and, in addition, shows the relation between N and both B_r/N_r and B_s/N_s. The last two are, of course, average purchase probability for those with $Q \geq C_i$ and $\lesseqgtr C_i$, respectively, since they relate numbers of expected purchases to numbers of people in the respective categories. These two ratios are plotted against the (horizontal) subjective probability scale. The ratio B_r/N_r varies from x' to 1.0 (and N varies from 0 to 100) as C_i varies from 0 to 1.0. The ratio B_s/N_s varies from 0 to x' as C_i varies from 0 to 1.0.

The construction of these ratios is illustrated in the bottom panel of Chart 6. When C_i is at E, N_s equals CE, and a proportion DE/CE is expected to purchase; when C_i increases to E', N_s increases to $C'E'$; and a smaller proportion, equal to $D'E'/C'E'$, is expected to purchase. When C_i approaches zero the ratio also approaches zero, and when C_i approaches unity the ratio approaches x'. The resulting values of B_s/N_s will trace out a curve from the lower left-hand corner of the diagram to x'_s at the top. Similarly for B_r/N_r: when C_i is at E, N_r equals AC; when C_i increases to E', N_r falls to $A'C'$. In the former case, a proportion equal to BD/AC is expected to purchase; and in the latter, a larger proportion, equal to $B'D'/A'C'$. When C_i approaches 1.0, N_r approaches zero, and B_r/N_r approaches unity. When C_i approaches zero, N_r approaches 100, and B_r/N_r approaches x'. The resulting values of B_r/N_r trace out a curve from x'_r at the bottom of the diagram to the upper right-hand corner.

I have noted above that B_r/N_r and B_s/N_s are essentially average purchase probability functions for households with $Q \geq C_i$ and $\leq C_i$, respectively. The cumulative frequency function—$N_s = \int_0^{C_i} f(Q)$—can also be interpreted as a probability function, marginal (in the sense used by economists in discussing cost or revenue functions) to both of the above average probability functions. The cumulative function 1.1 shows the number of households with probabilities equal to or less than some cut-off point, C_i. The marginal household in that function evidently has a probability of purchase, Q, equal to C_i. Consequently, the ratio of the slopes of the B and N functions at C_i must be the marginal probability of the C_ith household. Since the marginal probability is the same whether one is cumulating households from $C_i = 0$ to $C_i = 1.0$ or vice versa, the cumulative frequency distribution is marginal (in the above sense) to the average probability function with the origin in the lower left-hand corner $(B_s/N_s, Q \leq C_i)$, as well as to the average probability function with the origin in the upper left-hand corner $(B_r/N_r, Q \geq C_i)$.

Chart 7 is designed to make better use of the available data, and shows the lower panel of Chart 6 for alternative distributive functions. The axes have been rotated a quarter turn to the left, so that both marginal and average (subjective) probability are now on the vertical axes; the cumulative number (per cent) of households is on the horizontal. The horizontal axis represents the proportion of nonintenders when it is read as scaling 100 per cent to 0 per cent reading from left to right; it also represents the proportion of intenders when read as 100 per cent minus the proportion of nonintenders. The cumulative frequency function—

CHART 7

Illustrative Functional Relations Between
Alternative Intentions Questions and Purchase Rates
for Intenders and Nonintenders

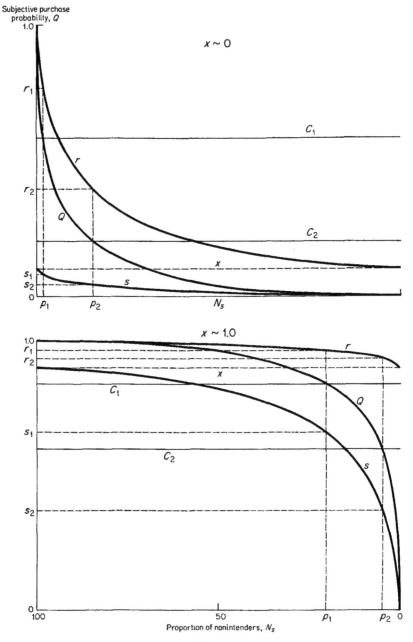

CHART 7 (concluded)

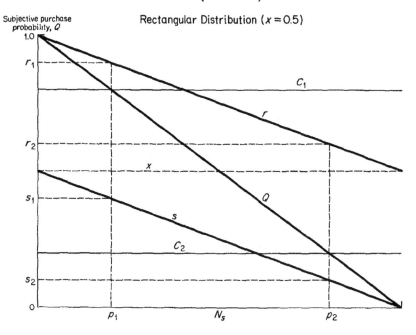

Rectangular Distribution ($x = 0.5$)

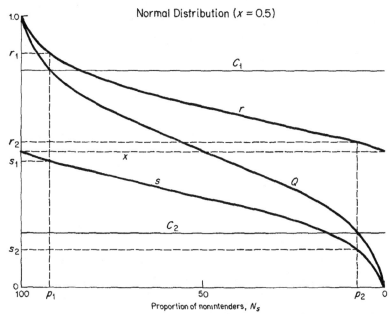

Normal Distribution ($x = 0.5$)

$N_s = \int_0^{C_i} f(Q)$—is the marginal probability curve, designated as Q. One average probability curve is the ratio B_r/N_r; the other is the ratio B_s/N_s. The first of these functions is designated r', the second s', in accordance with the nomenclature used above. A horizontal line has been drawn at x', the mean probability for the sample as a whole. The top panel of Chart 7 shows these functions for a probability distribution with a very small value of x'; second panel, the same functions for a distribution with a very large value of x'; the third panel, the same functions for a rectangular distribution with $x' = 0.5$; and the fourth panel, the same functions for a normal distribution with x' also equal to 0.5.

Given a survey of intentions to buy, the survey question having a cut-off probability of C_i, and a subsequent survey of purchases, we will observe some fraction (p_i) of the sample reporting intentions, a fraction $(1 - p_i)$ not reporting intentions, and fractions r_i and s_i of p_i and $1 - p_i$, respectively, actually purchasing. A fraction (x_i) of the sample as a whole will actually purchase. I assume that *ex ante* mean purchase probability for any group is equal to the *ex post* fraction of the group observed to purchase, although there is some regression bias in the relation between these two measures as discussed above. Thus, x_i is an estimate of x'_i; r_i, of r'_i; and s_i, of s'_i. Several combinations of points $(r,p)_i$ and $(s,1 - p)_i$ can be located from the empirical data, although there are not any directly observable measures of the corresponding cut-off probability, C_i. Two such combinations of points are illustrated in Chart 7, for cut-off points designated C_1 and C_2.

From Chart 7 the same generalizations can be elicited as in the text about the relation among r, s, p, and x. First, r exceeds s for any C_i; therefore, $r_i - s_i$ must always be positive. Second, both r_i and s_i are positively related to C_i, hence negatively related to p_i. These generalizations hold for the distribution functions in all four panels and are therefore independent of the value of x. Third, the relation between $r - s$ and p depends on x. When x is small (top panel), $r - s$ is positively related to C; hence, negatively related to p. When x is large (second panel), $r - s$ is negatively related to C; hence, positively related to p.[37] In the third

---

[37] The last two statements are clearly true in general for the functions shown in Chart 7: since $r - s$ is necessarily equal to x when p is 100 per cent—and $C = 0$—and to $1 - x$ when p is zero per cent—and $C = 1.0$—it follows that the correlation between $r - s$ and p will tend to be negative if $1 - x$ is larger than x, and to be positive if x is larger than $1 - x$. Thus, the correlation between $r - s$ and p must generally be negative for functions like that in the top panel, positive for functions like that in the second panel. It appears, however, that parts of the function may have the reverse relationship. For example, the correlation between $r - s$ and p for values of p close to 100 per cent

panel, where $x' = 0.5$, there is evidently a zero correlation between $r - s$ and p because the former is a constant (0.5) throughout the entire range of p. The last panel also has a distribution function with an x' of 0.5, but with the characteristics of a normal (Gaussian) function rather than of a rectangular function. In this panel there is zero linear correlation

CHART 8

Proportion of Sample Reporting Intentions to Buy Automobiles, and Proportion of Intenders and Nonintenders Purchasing Within a Six-Month Period

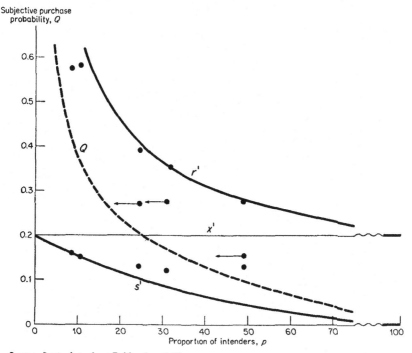

Source: Basic data from Tables 9 and 10.

between $r - s$ and p; however, there is a negative association between the two in the region where p is less than 0.5, a positive association where p is greater than 0.5. Finally, the variance in $r - s$, as a function of C or p,

might well be positive for functions like those in the top panel; and for functions like those in the second panel, the correlation might well be negative for values of p close to zero, i.e., where nonintenders are close to 100 per cent. If functions were drawn for values of x slightly under 0.5 (top panel) or slightly over 0.5 (second panel) it would be impossible to tell by visual inspection whether the correlation between $r - s$ and p was positive or negative or zero in either panel.

depends on the value of x. The closer x comes to 0.5, the smaller the variance of $(r - s)$; the closer x comes to either 0 or 1, the larger the variance. All these generalizations can be observed in the data, as already discussed in the text.

It is an interesting exercise to plot some of the observed $(r,p)_i$ and $(s, 1 - p)_i$ points to get a clearer view of the probability distributions for

CHART 9

Proportion of Sample Reporting Intentions to Buy
Washing Machines, and Proportion of Intenders and Nonintenders
Purchasing Within a Six-Month Period

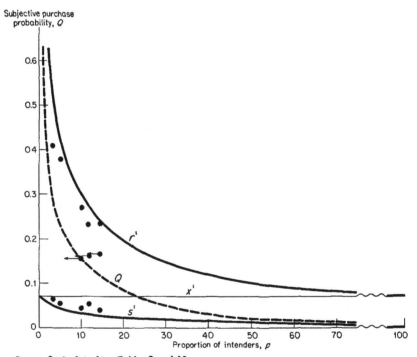

Source: Basic data from Tables 9 and 10.

different items. All observed functions have values of x that are below 0.5; consequently, functions like those in the top panel of Chart 7 are appropriate. The data for automobiles, for washing machines, and for clothes dryers are plotted in Charts 8, 9 and 10. These data are representative of the least skewed function (automobiles), the most skewed (clothes dryers), and the "typical" function (washing machines). Points on the r and s functions can be located precisely from the basic data in

Tables 9 and 10. Although some observations for the Q function are available, they all consist of averages for fairly large segments, that is, of mean probability between two unknown cut-off points. These are plotted at $(Q_{i...j}, p_j)$; that is, the mean probability for households with probabilities lower than i but higher than j is located at p_j. Such points are necessarily too far to the right, and an arrow indicates this fact.[38]

CHART 10

**Proportion of Sample Reporting Intentions to Buy
Clothes Dryers, and Proportion of Intenders and Nonintenders
Purchasing Within a Six-Month Period**

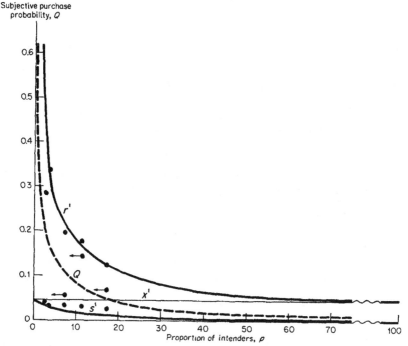

Source: Basic data from Tables 9 and 10.

The empirically observed points in these charts are plotted from data in Tables 9 and 10. Panel A in these tables contains points on the Q function; Panel B has points on the r' function; Panel C, points on the s' function. The r' and s' functions are drawn to correspond roughly to the observed points, account being taken of the regression bias noted above. Because of this bias the observed $(r,p)_i$ points will generally be below the

[38] It cannot be correct to plot these q points midway between p_i and p_j, since the Q function is not a straight line. The $i, \ldots, j$ points are so far apart that location at the midpoint is a poor estimate.

true $(r',p)_i$ point, since *ex ante* probability must be higher than the *ex post* purchase rate for groups of households in the upper tail of the distribution. Conversely, the observed $(s,1 - p)_i$ points will generally be above the true $(s',1 - p)_i$ points. In Charts 8, 9, and 10 the bias is clearly evident in the s' function; any reasonable estimate of this curve must lie below the observed s points, especially for relatively high values of p.

Appendix II: An Estimate of the Potential for Improvement in the Prediction of Purchases

One additional piece of empirical data can be brought to bear on the prediction problem. Granting the probability hypothesis, there are only two reasons that a survey of buying intentions will produce an erroneous forecast of the population purchase rate: first, the survey may not yield enough information for a reliable estimate of mean *ex ante* purchase probability, because the proportion reporting that they intend to buy is a less than perfect substitute for the mean; second, the *ex post* purchase rate may diverge from *ex ante* mean purchase probability because of unforeseen events. Evidently, only the first type of error can be reduced or eliminated by improvements in survey design.[39] But are errors of the first type large enough to merit a serious attempt to reduce or eliminate them?

The question cannot be answered with precision, but an estimate of the minimum size of type 1 errors can be obtained from the data. In Chapter 2 estimates are given of the proportion of the variance in actual purchases explained by responses to each of the intentions questions—that is, the cross-section r^2 (coefficient of determination) between X and P, where both X and P are dichotomous (1,0) variables. But $r^2_{X,P}$ is less than unity because of the effects of the two types of error just discussed.[40] And an

---

[39] Errors due to unforeseen events can be reduced only if both the functional relation between *ex ante* probability and unforeseen events, as well as the events themselves, can be specified. In that case perfectly accurate contingent forecasts would be possible.

[40] It may be objected that the cross-section correlation would be less than unity even if a perfectly accurate measure of *ex ante* purchase probability were available for each household and no unforeseen events took place during the period. The observed values of X are inherently dichotomous—either a household purchases the commodity or it does not—but *ex ante* probability is presumably a continuous function. Thus, of 100 households with probabilities of 0.1, on the average 10 will buy and 90 will not buy; and the cross-section correlation r^2_{XQ}, where Q is purchase probability, will be less than unity.

The objection, while valid, does not affect the analysis. The observed values of r^2_{XP}, where both X (purchases) and P (intentions to buy) are (1,0) variables, are unbiased estimates of r^2_{xp}, where x and p are the proportions of purchasers and intenders drawn from a number of randomly selected subsamples. But if purchase probability were an available datum, the correlation between values of mean purchase probability and the proportion of purchasers drawn from the same randomly selected subsamples would be unity, assuming that no unforeseen events occur and that the subsamples are very large.

estimate of the maximum size of type 2 errors can be obtained from the data; hence, also, an estimate of the minimum size of type 1 errors.

The argument is as follows: errors due to the influence of unforeseen events essentially constitute a regression bias. As noted above in the section "The Problem of Bias," this is one of the reasons that r_i is a downwardly biased estimate of r'_i; s_i, an upwardly biased estimate of s'_i. Although there is no way to estimate the true value of r'_i, there are several ways of estimating the maximum value of r'_i, given the commodity and the buying intentions question.

To begin with, it has previously been demonstrated that the following inequality must hold by definition:

$$1 \geqq r', s' \geqq 0;$$

that is, both r' and s' must be between zero and unity. Further, both r' and s' are also constrained by the definitional relation

$$x' = r'p + s'(1 - p)$$

Since r' cannot be greater than unity nor s' less than zero, it follows that

$$\text{mâx. } r' = \frac{x'}{p}, \text{ and}$$

$$\text{mîn. } s' = \frac{x' - p}{1 - p}$$

Thus when p is greater than x', r' will have a maximum value of less than unity and s' a minimum value of zero; where p is less than x', r' will have a maximum value of unity and s' a minimum value greater than zero.[41]

The above analysis thus provides two independently derived upper limits to the value of r'_i, and two independently derived lower limits to the value of s'_i.[42] These are

$$r'_i \gtreqless 1, \text{ and}$$

$$r'_i \gtreqless \frac{x'}{p}; \text{ in addition}$$

$$s'_i \geqq 0$$

$$s'_i \geqq x' - p/1 - p$$

[41] Both the above constraints are ineffective when x is approximately equal to p. In such cases the value of (mâx. r' − mîn. s') will be approximately unity, and the value of mâx. r^2x,p will also be close to unity.

[42] Estimates of mâx. r'_i and mîn. s'_i can also be obtained from Tchebycheff's Inequality, but the procedure is more complicated and the results are much the same. Given the true mean and standard deviation of any distribution, Tchebycheff's Inequality states that no more than $1/k^2$ cases will be beyond k standard deviations from the mean, regardless of the shape of the distribution. Turning this theorem around, the pro-

An estimate of the maximum correlation between X and P can evidently be obtained from the above maximum or minimum estimates, since

$$\text{mâx. } r^2{}_{X,P} = (\text{mâx. } r'_i - \text{mîn. } s'_i)^2 \frac{p(1 - p)}{x(1 - x)}$$

These estimates (of mâx. $r^2{}_{X,P}$) constitute the proportion of variance in purchases that could conceivably be explained by buying intentions if unforeseen events are given the maximum possible weight; the residual variance $(1 - \text{mâx. } r^2{}_{X,P})$ must therefore be an estimate of the minimum unexplained variation in purchases attributable to the use of a dichotomous $(1,0)$ buying-intentions variable, rather than a continuous distribution of *ex ante* probabilities, in making predictions. Table 18 summarizes these estimates for each of the thirteen commodities and for several of the buying-intentions questions; the observed proportion of the variance in X explained by P is also shown.

The data suggest that, although unforeseen events may have served to reduce the purchases-intentions correlation very considerably, any reasonable estimate of their importance still leaves a good deal of variation in purchases that cannot be explained by a dichotomous intentions variable. In very few cases does it appear that much more than two-thirds of the total variance in purchases could have been explained by intentions, making an extremely generous allowance for the part of total unexplained variance due to unforeseen events. I conclude that there is a considerable potential for improvement if a survey can be designed that will yield more information about the probability distribution. To what degree this potential can be realized is, of course, a question on which the available data shed no light at all.

---

portion of cases equal to $1/k^2$ can be no more than k standard deviations from the mean. Defining p as $1/k^2$, and assuming that the mean of the *ex ante* distribution, x', is equal to the observed purchase rate (x), it follows that p cases can be no more than the distance $x + \sigma'/\sqrt{p}$. But this is the same as saying that

$$\text{mâx. } C_i = x + \sigma'/\sqrt{p}$$

Given that $\sigma' = (r' - s')\sqrt{p(1 - p)}$ (see above, p. 53), and that $s' = \dfrac{x' - pr'}{1 - p}$

(see above, p. 52), and assuming that the distribution above C_i is rectangular, it turns out that

$$\text{mâx. } r'_i = \frac{1/2(1 + x' - x'\sqrt{1 - p})}{1 - 1/2\sqrt{1 - p}}.$$

Given mâx. r'_i, and mîn. s'_i, mâx. $r^2{}_{X,P}$ can be readily estimated. The distribution free assumption in the Tchebycheff theorem, however, typically provides estimates of mâx. r'_i that are much the same as those shown in Table 18.

TABLE 18

PROPORTION OF VARIANCE IN PURCHASES EXPLAINED BY
ALTERNATIVE BUYING INTENTIONS QUESTIONS

Commodity	Buying Intentions Questions[a]			
	A_1	C_1	D_1	$A_1 + A_2$
	OBSERVED PROPORTION (r^2_{XP})			
Automobiles	.080	.120	.079	.072
Furniture	.096	.118	.067	.063
Carpets & rugs	.077	.076	.027	.046
High-fidelity equipment	.043	.059	.060	.021
Range	.095	.130	.055	.079
Refrigerator	.098	.084	.089	.083
Washing machine	.055	.114	.068	.049
Television set	.010	.068	.040	.012
Air conditioner	.066	.072	.084	.082
Clothes dryer	.036	.063	.044	.050
Dishwasher	.103	.070	.078	.067
Food freezer	.053	.065	.047	.049
Garbage disposal	.044	.082	.044	.031
	ESTIMATED MAXIMUM PROPORTION (mâx. r^2_{XP})			
Automobiles	.373	.854	.753	.523
Furniture	.681	.580	.652	.487
Carpets & rugs	.740	.493	.504	.399
High-fidelity equipment	.642	.491	.500	.307
Range	.486	.735	.781	.598
Refrigerator	.432	.679	.892	.522
Washing machine	.421	.792	.685	.601
Television set	.459	.710	.606	.424
Air conditioner	.376	.725	.560	.427
Clothes dryer	.596	.551	.578	.374
Dishwasher	.725	.615	.610	.328
Food freezer	.584	.722	.506	.309
Garbage disposal	.647	.665	.553	.436

SOURCE: Data in upper panel derived from Chapter 2; data in lower panel estimated according to procedures described in the text.

[a] For a discussion of the intentions questions, see Chapter 2.

[b] The procedures for estimating mâx. r^2_{XP} are described in the text. An illustration is as follows: For question A_1—definite intentions to buy automobiles within twelve months—$x = 0.191$ and $p = 0.081$. Hence the appropriate estimate of mâx. r'_i is unity, since the alternative estimate—mâx. $r'_i = \dfrac{x}{p}$—yields a value of r'_i greater than unity. The appropriate estimate of mîn. s'_i is

Since

$$\text{mîn. } s_i = x' - p/1 - p = 0.110/0.919 = 0.120.$$

$$\text{mâx. } r^2_{XP} = (\text{mâx. } r'_i - \text{mîn. } s'_i)^2 \, p(1 - p)/x(1 - x),$$
$$\text{mâx. } r^2_{XP} = (1.0 - .120)^2 \, .081(.919)/.191(.809);$$
$$\text{mâx. } r^2_{XP} = .373.$$

CHAPTER 4

Buying Intentions and Purchase Probability: II

Introduction

THE analysis in Chapter 3 was concerned with the general relation between purchase probability and surveys of household buying intentions for particular durable commodities. In this chapter I examine some of the problems arising from the aggregation of purchase probabilities and their empirical counterpart, buying intentions.

I start with two problems that are closely related to the analysis in the previous chapter. First, are the cut-off probabilities associated with alternative measures of buying intentions—the C_i—the same for all commodities? If not, are the differences systematically related to identifiable characteristics of the commodity? Second, are the C_i the same for all groups in the population, or do they differ with identifiable household characteristics such as income, life-cycle status, ownership of the commodity in question, and so forth.

As noted above, there are no direct observations on the cut-off probabilities associated with variant intentions questions. However, C_i is closely related to the empirically observable magnitude r_i. Given the probability function $n = f(Q)$, it has been shown that C_i must be somewhat below r'_i, the mean of the distribution function above C_i. I assume that the observed magnitude r_i—the fraction of intenders purchasing—is a reasonably good proxy for r'_i, although r_i is subject to a downward bias. If the C_i differ among commodities or population groups, it seems reasonable to suppose that the r'_i and r_i will differ also, since C_i must be strongly correlated with both.

For the moment, assume that *ex ante* r'_i is equal to *ex post* r_i. It follows that r_i must be above C_i; the difference between the two will depend on the shape of the distribution function and on the characteristics of the ith intentions question. If the distribution function has a rapidly changing slope in the region of the cut-off points, as in the top panel of Chart 11, C_1 and C_2 will be quite close to the corresponding means, r'_1 ($= r_1$) and r'_2 ($= r_2$). On the other hand, if the distribution function has a flatter slope in the region of the cut-off points, as in the middle panel of Chart 11, both C_1 and C_2 will be further below their corresponding means. Generally speaking, the more skewed the distribution function, the steeper the slope in the region of relatively low cut-off points and the flatter the slope in the region of relatively high cut-off points. The amount of skewness in the distribution function is, in turn, related to mean probability for the entire function; the smaller the mean the more skewed the distribution

CHART 11

Illustrative Relation Between Slope of Distribution
Function and Cut-Off Probability

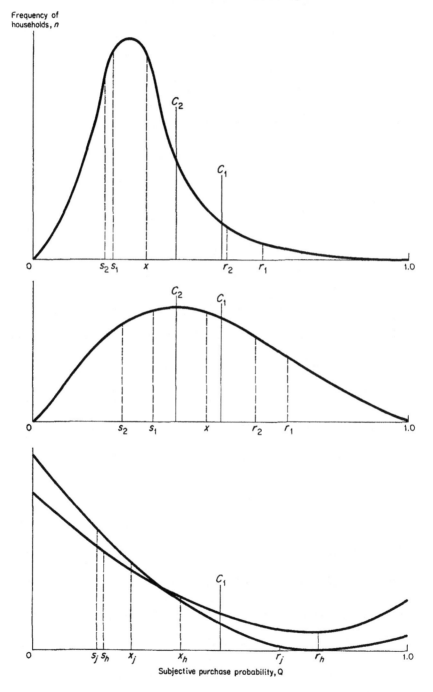

Frequency of
households, n

Subjective purchase probability, Q

function and the smaller the difference between r_i and C_i for relatively low values of the latter.

On the other hand, the distribution functions are not necessarily bell-shaped with greater or smaller amounts of skew. A U-shaped function is not at all improbable. The largest single number of households may have probabilities equal to zero: many households may simply have no interest at all in purchasing particular items, or they may have just acquired a new one. At the high-probability end of the distribution, households with probabilities approximately equal to unity may exceed those with probabilities of 0.7 or 0.8. Suppose the commodity in question were automobiles, for example. A fairly large number of households buy a new car every year as a matter of course; purchase probability for these households, if the forecast period covers the customary time of purchase, is bound to be unity or close to it. If the distribution functions happen to be U-shaped, the mean probability above any cut-off point located around the trough will probably be higher the higher the mean in the distribution as a whole. This situation is illustrated in the lower panel of Chart II, where r_j represents mean probability for low-income households, r_h the corresponding mean for high-income households.

Differences in Cut-off Probability Among Commodities and Households

The question of whether or not C differs among commodities or among households, given the specifications of the buying-intentions questions, can now be examined. Table 19 summarizes the observed values of r, and the corresponding fraction of households reporting intentions to buy, for two of the alternative questions—those asking about "definite" and about "definite, probable, and possible" purchases within a year. The last column shows the estimated mean probability for the sample as a whole, i.e., the observed purchase rate.

The data provide strong evidence that C_i is not the same for all items. For example, r for those definitely intending to buy a car within a year—r_d—is 0.566. The corresponding cut-off probability, C_d, must be lower than 0.566. The function must be highly skewed (even more so than the function at the top of Chart 11), since the mean is 0.191; hence, the C_d corresponding to an r_d of 0.566 is unlikely to be lower than 0.40 or 0.45. Taking account of the fact that r_d is a downwardly biased estimate of r'_d, the true C_d is probably somewhat higher than 0.40. Yet the *mean* probabilities for households definitely intending to buy a television set (0.197), a garbage disposal unit (0.275), or a high-fidelity set (0.304) are all well below 0.40. The corresponding values of C_d must be even lower, although perhaps not so much lower as in the case of automobiles because these distributions are more highly skewed and the cut-off probabilities are relatively low. But C_d cannot possibly be the same for automobiles and for garbage disposal units.

Assuming that these differences among commodities in r_i represent real differences in C_i, it appears from Table 19 that, given the intentions question, C is relatively high for commodities owned by most households (cars, ranges, refrigerators), and relatively low for commodities owned by few

TABLE 19

ESTIMATED PROBABILITY THAT INTENDERS WILL PURCHASE SPECIFIED COMMODITY, AND PER CENT OF INTENDERS IN SAMPLE

	Estimated Purchase Probability Among:			Per Cent of Sample Households with:	
Commodity	Definite Intenders	Definite, Probable, or Possible Intenders	Entire Sample	Definite Intentions	Definite, Probable, or Possible Intentions
Automobile	.566	.349	.191	8.1	31.0
Furniture	.493	.330	.187	13.5	31.9
Carpets and rugs	.376	.201	.076	5.7	17.1
Washing machine	.409	.233	.075	3.3	11.9
High-fidelity equipment	.304	.144	.065	4.3	17.0
Refrigerator	.508	.249	.056	2.5	10.6
Range	.478	.257	.052	2.5	8.4
Clothes dryer	.284	.177	.046	2.8	11.4
Television set	.197	.118	.053	2.5	11.6
Air conditioner	.463	.230	.054	2.1	11.8
Food freezer	.317	.148	.027	1.6	8.3
Dishwasher	.392	.172	.026	1.9	7.5
Garbage disposal unit	.275	.149	.023	1.5	5.1

SOURCE: Table 2, Chapter 2.

households (food freezers, garbage disposal units, dishwashers). Also, as noted above, differences in r_i (hence C_i) among commodities are positively correlated with differences in x; that is, commodities purchased by relatively few households tend to have low cut-off probabilities, and vice versa for commodities with relatively high purchase rates. Since mean probability (= purchase rate) and degree of skewness are necessarily associated, the degree of skewness in the probability function is also correlated with both r_i and C_i.[1]

[1] There is no way (from the data) of isolating the basic cause of this relationship. The rank correlation between purchase rate (x) and mean probability for intenders (r) is somewhat higher than that between the fraction owning and mean probability; both correlations are significant at the 0.05 level. I would guess that the basic rela-

I turn now to an examination of the variation in C among households with different characteristics, given the commodity and the buying-intentions question. Here the results are quite different. There is no evidence that C_i, given the commodity, varies among households with different levels of family income, life-cycle status, or educational level. Since C is not observable, r_6 and $1 - r_6$—the fractions purchasing and not purchasing among those intending to buy within six months—are used as the test statistics. For each of thirteen durables, I tested the relation between r_6 and, in turn, income (eight classes), life-cycle status (five classes), and educational level (five classes). Of thirty-nine such tests, contrasting the observed values of r_6 with those predicted by the hypothesis of no association, only one yielded a value of chi-square large enough to be statistically significant at the 5 per cent level.[2] I conclude that r_6 (hence also C_6) is invariant with respect to family income, life-cycle status, or education.[3]

---

tionship is between ownership and C_i. If a commodity is already being used by most households, the probability function is mainly determined by replacement considerations. If the commodity is not owned, the prospect of acquiring something "new" may well encourage a high degree of whimsey and wishful thinking in the estimate of purchase probability and in the response to questions about intentions to buy. It is also possible that buying-intentions questions are subject to this bias while questions about purchase probability might not be, although again I have no way of demonstrating the point.

[2] The test statistics are actually $r_6 p_6 N$ and $(1 - r_6)p_6 N$, that is, the number of households reporting buying intentions and purchasing (not purchasing) in the first, second, etc., age, income, or education group. The one case with a significant value of chi-square was actually very close to but below the critical value of chi-square for the 0.05 level.

[3] Examination of the r_6 patterns within these classifications does not provide any clear evidence that C_6 might actually be somewhat higher when family income is higher, or when educational level is higher, etc. For the majority of commodities the correlation between r and family income is positive though necessarily nonsignificant, given the chi-square results. However, the probability functions will generally be less skewed for high-income groups than for low-income groups, since the mean probability (= purchase rate) in the sample as a whole is positively correlated with income. Given the (relatively low) level of the C_6, the less skewed the distribution function the further apart are C_6 and r_6, and the further C_6 is likely to be below any given r_6. Hence, the correlation between C_6 and family income might be even weaker than the small positive correlation observed between r_6 and family income. The same is true of the relation between r_6 and the other two variables. The relation here, if any, consists of a slight tendency for r_6 to be higher for groups with relatively high purchase rates—households with more income, more education, or with younger heads. But even this weak relationship may be too strong as a measure of the correlation between these characteristics and C_6.

If the distribution functions are U-shaped, the same conclusion will hold. In this case functions with relatively large mean values are likely to have more rapidly rising slopes above the minimum point relative to functions with smaller mean values. Thus, the mean probability in any segment above the minimum point is likely to be greater when the overall mean is relatively high (see Chart 11).

Differences in Purchase Rates Among Households

The fact that r_i (hence C_i) does not vary among households with different characteristics implies that purchase rates for nonintenders, s_i, are likely to vary among the same classes of households provided that x differs. In connection with a quite different problem, I showed in Chapter 3 that differences in x are generally associated with differences in s if r is the same for both groups unless very special conditions prevail.[4] Hence, if the means of these probability distributions above the cut-off point happen to be about the same for groups that differ with respect to mean probability in the distribution as a whole (x), the means below the cut-off point (s_6) will generally be correlated with x. The point is illustrated in Chart 12, which is similar to Chart 3 in Chapter 3.

The expected empirical results show up quite clearly when s_6 is computed for the thirteen commodities within the same income, life-cycle, and educational classes. In testing for independence between the observed values of s_6 (for the same income, life-cycle, and educational classes) and the mean for all classes combined, seven of thirty-nine independent tests showed chi-square values that would be observed only once in 100 trials and fifteen of thirty-nine showed values that would be observed only once in 20 trials. The variation in s_6, given the commodity, is highly correlated with the variation in x, as is bound to be true.[5]

The observed differences in the purchase rates of nonintenders within different income, age, etc., classes can be rationalized in several ways. It may be that the probability distributions are symmetrical above the cut-off point but not below. Many households purchase automatically whenever a specified contingency arises (a breakdown, a major repair bill, acquisition of knowledge about a particular product, etc.). Such households will be nonintenders unless the contingency is regarded as probable.

[4] See Chapter 3, p. 76.

[5] The same pattern in the r and s data can be observed in buying-intentions surveys taken from carefully drawn probability samples. A large number of such surveys, and a few reinterviews, have been conducted by the Survey Research Center at the University of Michigan. Lawrence C. Klein and John B. Lansing, in "Decisions to Purchase Consumer Durable Goods," *Journal of Marketing*, October 1955, present data (Table II) on the purchase rates of intenders and nonintenders, classified by income. Both the chi-square test and regression analysis indicate that the relation between s and income class is significant, but not the relation between r and income class. See also Peter De Janosi, "Factors Influencing the Demand for New Automobiles," *Journal of Marketing*, April 1959, Table 2A, where the same relation among r, s, and income is also apparent.

Because of financial constraints, the reaction of low-income households to such contingencies is less likely to involve a purchase than the reaction of high-income households to the identical contingency. In effect, the joint probability that any given contingency will occur *and* that the reaction will consist of a decision to purchase is considerably larger among high-

CHART 12

Illustrative Probability Distributions for High- and Low-Income Households

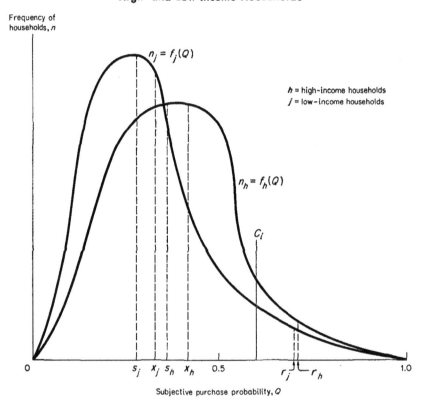

Subjective purchase probability, Q

than among low-income families, even though the probability of occurrence for any given contingency is the same for both. But in this case, mean purchase probability will be larger among high-income nonintenders than among low-income nonintenders, provided these factors enter into the households' *ex-ante* estimate of purchase probability; observed purchase rates will differ in any event. I see no logical reason why a similar difference would necessarily be observed among high- and low-income intenders.

Another possibility is that *exposure* to contingencies may be different among these groups. If so, the (*ex post*) fraction purchasing may be quite different, while (*ex ante*) mean probability is the same. High-income households will generally have larger stocks of durables than others, and unanticipated replacement may be more frequent. On the other hand, high-income households are likely to have newer as well as larger stocks and that factor would tend to work in the opposite direction.

I did not perform extensive tests to determine the degree to which this set of relations would be altered if some other intentions question, with a different cut-off probability, had been used. A comparison of responses to the "within six months" and "within twelve months" intentions questions seems to show that r_{12} is not as unrelated to family income or life-cycle status as the above tests showed r_6 to be. This finding is quite consistent with the hypothesis that C_t does not vary among households. C_{12} must be lower than C_6, and the slope of the distribution function is apt to change more rapidly between these two cut-off points the more skewed the function. Since the probability functions for high-income groups have higher mean values than those for low-income groups, they are less skewed. Therefore, different means are more likely to be observed in the segment above C_{12} than in the one above C_6. The point is illustrated in Chart 11, where the difference in r_2 between the top and middle panels is greater than the difference in r_1. Other factors may also be present. For example, high-income households might have higher cut-off probabilities than low-income ones for intentions questions characterized by a high degree of uncertainty, or they may systematically underestimate their purchase probability over relatively long time horizons.

Two conclusions follow from these results. First, aggregation of buying intentions across different commodities will not produce a homogeneous total for the expected dollar value of purchases, since expected values are lower for some items than others, given the specifications of the intentions question and the price of the item. This is not likely to be a serious difficulty in practice, because the items that make up the large majority of intended purchases are relatively homogeneous with respect to the probabilities associated with any given intentions questions. The items for which probabilities seem to be much lower are generally those purchased by relatively few households; hence, they are comparatively unimportant in the aggregate of either expected or actual dollar values of purchases. Secondly, the distribution of the population by variables like income, demographic status, or education evidently makes little or no difference to the purchase probabilities associated with responses to ques-

111

tions about buying intentions. In effect, there is no convincing evidence that responses to (dichotomous) buying intentions questions should be weighted according to whether income is high or low, etc., and this is a great convenience in making practical use of such data.

Cut-off Probabilities and Purchase Rates Related to Durable Goods Stock

Up to this point I have analyzed variations in C_i among different commodities and differently situated households, finding significant variation in C_i among commodities that is apparently related to characteristics of the commodity itself, but no significant variation in C_i for a given commodity among households with different family income, life-cycle status, and educational level. Examination of the relation between C_i and some other household characteristics tends to weaken this tentative conclusion of invariance among households, and also points up some specific problems in aggregating probabilities or buying intentions.

Data on the durable goods stock position of each household are available from the CU surveys. In addition, respondents were asked whether any items in their durables stock "needed to be replaced." Answers to this question seemed to combine a judgment concerning age or condition of the stock with attitudes toward obsolescence.

The data on stock position and subjective replacement need cover nine commodities. These items divide naturally into three groups: (1) automobiles; (2) ranges, refrigerators, washing machines, and television sets; (3) clothes dryers, dishwashers, food freezers, and air conditioners. Automobiles are treated separately because of their relatively high unit cost, their extremely high ownership ratio, and the possibility of extensive multiple ownership. The second class consists of items that are owned by the bulk of households in the sample; the third, of those owned by relatively few households.[6]

Because buying intentions and purchases were comparatively infrequent for some of these commodities, especially those in group 3, I combined intentions and purchases for commodities in both the second and the third groups. Thus the basic data consist of average purchase rates for groups of commodities among households classified with respect to stock position, subjective replacement need, and buying intentions. Three such classes were formed among both intenders and nonintenders; those who owned the commodity but did not report that it needed replacement (S), those

[6] The ownership ratios range from roughly 74 to 79 per cent of all households for category 2, from 16 to 34 per cent in category 3; about 92 per cent of these households own at least one automobile.

112

who owned and reported a need for replacement (R), and those who did not own the commodity at the time of interview (NS).[7] Table 20 summarizes the estimated mean probabilities (= observed purchase rates) for intenders and nonintenders among households classified by ownership and by replacement need. The sample used for the analysis was asked about intentions to buy within six months.

TABLE 20

ESTIMATED MEAN PURCHASE PROBABILITIES (OBSERVED PURCHASE RATES)
FOR THREE CLASSES OF COMMODITIES

Commodity Class	Sample Size (N)	Number of Intenders	Observed Purchase Rates for: Intenders (r_6)	Nonintenders (s_6)
1. S	2,583	138	.493	.142
R	759	225	.622	.242
NS	295	25	.640	.133
2. S	9,829	127	.331	.037
R	1,425	258	.264	.104
NS	3,294	205	.522	.056
3. S	3,290	53	.340	.048
R	136	19	.368	.068
NS	11,122	356	.272	.018

SOURCE: Basic data from Consumer Purchase Study, NBER.

NOTE: Commodity class 1 consists of automobiles; class 2: ranges, refrigerators, washing machines, and television sets; class 3: clothes dryers, dishwashers, food freezers, and air conditioners. S designates those who owned the items and did not indicate that they needed replacement; R, owners who stated that the specified items needed to be replaced; NS, nonowners. The number of nonintenders is the difference between the total number of observations (N) and the number of intenders. Sample size for each class is the number of households in the sample multiplied by the number of items in the class, i.e., N is four times as large in classes 2 and 3 as in class 1. The sample size distribution among households classified by S, R, and NS is essentially a distribution by commodity rather than by household; that is, the same household can be classified in S for ranges, R for refrigerators, and NS for television sets and washing machines.

The data examined in the first part of this chapter indicate that r_6, the estimated mean probability for intenders, does not vary systematically with family income, life-cycle status, or education. I inferred that the probability cut-off point, C_6, which is closely related to r_6, was also invariant with respect to these household characteristics. On the other hand, the data showed that s_6, the mean probability for nonintenders, was highly correlated with household characteristics such as income, being higher for those with relatively large incomes, etc. For the classifications summarized in Table 20, both r_6 and s_6 seem to vary with durable goods

[7] Obviously, the NS group could not have reported that replacement was necessary.

ownership and with the need for replacement; hence, C_6 cannot be the same for households with different S and R characteristics. The pattern of these relationships is quite interesting, and is puzzling in at least one respect.

AUTOMOBILES

For automobiles, mean probability among intenders (r_6) is significantly higher (0.05 level) for R households than for the S group; that is, households reporting that (one of) their automobile(s) needed to be replaced are more apt to buy than others. This is a sensible enough result except that both groups of households reported that they intended to buy, and there is no a priori reason why the condition of the automobile stock would not have been taken wholly into account when intentions were reported. It will be recalled that mean probability did not turn out to be significantly different for intenders in different income classes, but the replacement-need variable does not fit this pattern. Of course, C_6 for automobiles may really be the same for the S and R groups, with the difference in observed r_6 simply reflecting a different distribution of *probabilities for these two groups above the identical cut-off point.* This possibility cannot be tested with the data, although the difference in r_6 between these two groups is not so large that it can be disregarded.[8]

Mean purchase probability for automobiles is also closely related to stock and replacement needs among nonintenders, but this pattern is similar to that which had been observed previously for other household characteristics. The magnitude of s_6 is almost twice as large for R households as for either the S or NS ones. The sample sizes are all fairly larger here ($N > 250$), and the difference in s_6 between R and either of the other two classes is statistically significant at the 0.01 level. This difference probably reflects the influence of contingencies. Nonintenders indicating that an item needs to be replaced are essentially saying that they would purchase a new one if they could afford it because the old one is unsatisfactory. Thus, any favorable financial contingency is more apt to result in a purchase, and the unfavorable contingency of complete breakdown is also more probable.

HOUSEHOLD DURABLES

For the second and third commodity groups, most of the results are consistent with the proposition that r_6 is independent of the S and R character-

---

[8] The automobile purchase rate among *NS* intenders *is also higher than among* S intenders, and is about the same as for R. The difference in r_6 between S and NS intenders is not statistically significant, however, because the NS sample is so small.

istics, while s_6 is not. The r_6 values are not significantly different from each other for S and R households in either commodity group; the difference in s_6 is highly significant (0.01 level) for commodity group 2, not significant for 3.[9] In sum, contrasting the behavior of intenders and nonintenders among households that owned the item at the time of the survey, I find that intenders have essentially the same purchase rate, hence the same C, regardless of whether the item was thought to be in need of replacement. Nonintenders, on the other hand, are much more apt to purchase if they reported that the item needed to be replaced; this relation is especially strong in commodity group 2. All these results are wholly consistent with earlier findings about the behavior of intenders and nonintenders with different incomes, educational level, and life-cycle status.

However, the comparison of purchase rates for owners (S) and nonowners (NS) in commodity groups 2 and 3 shows some surprising results. Intenders who were nonowners had much *higher* mean probabilities than owners in commodity class 2; somewhat *lower* mean probabilities in commodity class 3. These differences are highly significant for class 2, not significant for 3. Differences in mean probabilities among nonintenders—s_6—follow a similar pattern, and these differences are highly significant in both commodity groups 2 and 3. To summarize: For commodity group 3, both intenders and nonintenders are *more* apt to purchase if they already own the item in question at the time of the survey; the differences are not significant for intenders, highly significant for nonintenders. For commodity group 2, in contrast, owners are significantly *less* likely to buy than nonowners among both intenders and nonintenders.

The upshot is that C_6 is probably not invariant among all classes of households. The difference in r_6 between owners and nonowners of ranges, refrigerators, etc., seems far too large to be due to either sampling error or differences in the shape of the distribution function above C_6. Hence, I conclude that C_6—and other C_i as well—must be substantially higher for nonowners than for owners of these commodities. Differences in r_6 among households are well within the limits of sampling variability for commodity class 3, partly because the sample sizes are relatively small. Finally, the data provide strong corroboratory evidence that purchase probability among nonintenders is significantly related to household characteristics associated with differences in purchase rates for the sample

[9] Very few householders who owned items in commodity group 3 reported that the items needed replacement, for the obvious reason that most of these commodities must have been acquired fairly recently. Hence, the sample size in the R group is quite small; and the difference between R and S, although in the expected direction, is not statistically significant at any reasonable level.

as a whole. Among nonintenders, those reporting that an item in their durables stock needs to be replaced are much more likely to buy than other households.[10]   Purchase probabilities for owners and nonowners are also significantly different for nonintenders, but the differences go in opposite directions for commodity classes 2 and 3.   The last observation is clearly in need of explanation.

DIFFERENCES BETWEEN MOVERS AND NONMOVERS

On a priori grounds, I would have thought that nonowners would be more apt to purchase than owners, other things equal, since the marginal returns from purchase of a newer model are normally less than the returns from a first purchase.   This proposition is well documented by studies that show a negative association (in time series) between the size of the durables stock and the purchase rate.[11]   Thus, the data for commodity group 2 seem sensible enough.   But what about commodity group 3, where the correlation between ownership and purchase probability is significantly *positive* among nonintenders, positive but nonsignificant among intenders?   One possible explanation is that owners of these commodities are more likely to buy than nonowners because they have higher incomes; another, that such households are more likely to move.   Once having owned a dishwasher or clothes dryer the family is unlikely to do without one, and a move to a new house is frequently accompanied by wholesale renovation of the stock of kitchen and laundry equipment—the equipment previously owned being sold as part of the old house.   Further, a prospective move of this kind may not be accompanied by "intentions" to buy new kitchen or laundry equipment.   The decision to leave the old durables and buy new ones may come up for consideration only when a satisfactory new house has been located and a prospective buyer found for the old house.   This interpretation is consistent with the data: only

[10] Another interesting piece of evidence that tends to corroborate these relationships, based on analysis of randomly selected population samples, is reported by Janet Fisher in "Consumer Durable Goods Expenditures, with Major Emphasis on the Role of Assets, Credit, and Intentions," *Journal of the American Statistical Association,* Sept. 1963, p. 653.   In a regression of durables purchases during 1957 on selected independent variables, she reports that nonintenders who purchased durables in the preceding year are significantly more likely to buy than other nonintenders   While intenders are significantly more likely to buy than nonintenders, it appears to make little difference to intenders' purchase rates whether they had or had not purchased durables in the preceding year.

[11] See, for example, Harold W. Watts and James Tobin, "Consumer Expenditures and the Capital Account," *Proceedings of the Conference on Consumption and Savings,* ed. Irwin Friend and Robert Jones, Philadelphia, University of Pennsylvania Press, 1960, Vol. II; and *The Demand for Durable Goods,* ed. Arnold C. Harberger, Chicago, University of Chicago Press, 1960.

about one out of five buying intentions in group 3 were reported by owners, but owners accounted for about half the purchases among nonintenders and almost half the total purchases.

The explanation via income differences seems to account for some of the observed positive correlation between s_6 and ownership, but not nearly enough. A test of the second explanation is provided by Table 21. Here

TABLE 21

ESTIMATED MEAN PURCHASE PROBABILITIES (OBSERVED PURCHASE RATES), BY HOME
OWNERSHIP STATUS, FOR THREE CLASSES OF COMMODITIES

			Observed Purchase Rates for:	
Commodity Class	Sample Size (N)	Number of Intenders	Intenders (r_6)	Nonintenders (s_6)
A. HOME OWNERS—NO PLANS TO MOVE, NO MOVE				
1. *S*	1,167	93	.462	.149
R	490	141	.660	.252
NS	168	11	.545	.127
2. *S*	7,145	65	.323	.028
R	976	169	.260	.099
NS	1,179	44	.432	.034
3. *S*	2,529	35	.314	.038
R	93	8	.250	.059
NS	6,678	176	.244	.018
B. NONOWNERS OF HOMES, AND HOME OWNERS WHO MOVED OR PLANNED TO MOVE				
1. *S*	916	45	.556	.129
R	269	84	.560	.222
NS	127	14	.714	.142
2. *S*	2,684	62	.339	.060
R	449	89	.270	.114
NS	2,115	161	.547	.069
3. *S*	761	18	.389	.083
R	43	11	.455	.094
NS	4,444	180	.300	.018

SOURCE: Basic data from Consumer Purchase Study, NBER.
NOTE: See Table 20 for definition of commodity classes and of *S*, *R*, *NS*, and *N*.

two classes of households are distinguished: first, those who owned their own homes at the survey date and neither reported intentions to buy a house nor purchased one; second, all other households, comprising those who did not own homes at the survey date, plus those who owned and either intended to buy or purchased another house. The same data as were shown in Table 20 are calculated separately for each of these groups of households in Table 21.

The r_6 column now seems to show significant differences among the *S*,

R, and *NS* groups in only two places. In panel A, those intending to buy automobiles have a significantly higher (0.01 level) mean probability if they also said that their automobile(s) needed replacement; in panel B, nonowners intending to buy ranges, etc., have a significantly higher (0.01 level) mean purchase probability. The results here are much the same as in Table 20. Some of the differences among nonintenders (s_0) are substantially altered, however. Among panel A households, the difference in mean purchase probability between owners and nonowners of class 3 commodities is apparently rather small; but it is highly significant because of the very large sample size. On the other hand, the difference among movers (panel B) is much sharper than before, and is of course highly significant (0.01 level). Taking account of income differences, it seems quite possible that, among nonintenders for class 3 commodities, the propensity of households that already own these items to buy them relatively more frequently than nonowners is entirely due to the greater likelihood that the former will move and will purchase replacements in the process.

Summary

On the whole, the pattern of variation in mean purchase rates among households that differ as to ownership and replacement needs for durable goods is reasonably consistent with the findings and analysis in the first part of this chapter. For the most part, mean probability for intenders, hence also the cut-off probability, is invariant among households that differ with respect to ownership and replacement need. On the other hand, mean probability for nonintenders is highly correlated with *R*; nonintenders reporting that a commodity needs to be replaced are much more likely to buy than other nonintenders. This relation is especially strong for household durables typically owned by most families—ranges, refrigerators, washing machines, television sets and automobiles. For automobiles, the relationship between replacement need and purchase probability is quite strong for intenders as well. Finally, there are no significant differences among nonintenders in purchase probabilities for owners and nonowners, with one exception: owners of class 3 commodities have significantly *higher* purchase probabilities than nonowners. This relationship is mainly—perhaps entirely—due to the behavior of households that changed residence during the forecast period.

These results suggest a rather formidable aggregation problem. Take the question: How are stocks of durables related to purchases, net of other factors? My results show that ownership of class 2 durables is likely to be associated with a smaller probability of purchasing, holding replacement needs and intentions to buy constant.   If replacement needs are not held constant, the relationship is likely to be reversed because only owners can be in need of replacement and replacement need is strongly correlated with purchase probability.   On the other hand, ownership of class 3 durables is associated with a substantially *larger* probability of purchasing, holding replacement need and intentions to buy constant.   Failure to account for replacement needs will make this relationship even stronger. Thus, the aggregate stock of durables may turn out to be completely unrelated to purchases, net of other factors, because the influence of ownership on purchase probability goes in diametrically opposite directions for the two important classes of consumer durables.[12]

Appendix: Predictions of Differences in Purchase Rates Among Households

The data developed in this chapter suggest another possible test of the proposition, discussed in Chapter 3, that mean *ex ante* purchase probability cannot be reliably estimated from the proportion of intenders—households with purchase probabilities above the cut-off probability associated with a given intentions question.   In principle the appropriate test involves the time series correlation between the observed purchase rate (x), which is an unbiased estimate of mean *ex ante* probability (x'), and the observed proportion of intenders (p).   Such correlations as have been estimated show that p explains a significant amount of the variation in x, but that substantial residual variation remains.[13]   The residual variation is presumably due either to the presence of intervening events or to the fact that p is an imperfect (linear) predictor of x'.

It has been shown above that the observed purchase rates within various income and life-cycle classes differed substantially from each other, that the observed purchase rates for nonintenders were strongly correlated with x, but that the observed purchase rates for intenders (r) generally had little or no relation to x.   As might be anticipated, these different

[12] If the stock were measured as aggregate value minus the amount in need of replacement, i.e., $S - R$, stock would show a significant negative relation to purchases because R has a significant positive relation.   This procedure is not unreasonable, since it amounts to assigning a value of zero to those items in the stock that the household says are in need of replacement.   Zero is too low a value, but if the choice is between zero and original cost the first is presumably a better estimate than the second.

[13] See Arthur Okun, "The Value of Anticipations Data in Forecasting National Product," *The Quality and Economic Significance of Anticipations Data*, Princeton for NBER, 1960 and Eva Mueller's "Comment," which follows the Okun article; and my *Consumer Expectations, Plans, and Purchases: A Progress Report*, Occasional Paper 70, New York, NBER, 1959.   An exploratory investigation of time series data is also contained in Chapter 3, above.

income or life-cycle classes exhibit substantial variability in p. If it is true that p is a perfect predictor of x', the cross-section correlation between p and x for groups of households classified according to income or life-cycle status ought to be unity except for the differential influence of intervening events among the groups, sampling variability aside.[14] Put another way, if p is a perfect linear predictor of x in time series, net of intervening events, it ought also to be a perfect cross-section predictor—again, net of intervening events. And if this is the case, no other variable can have a significant relation to x in a cross section *unless* it represents an unforeseen event with a differential impact on behavior in the several groups.

To test this proposition, I regressed x on p for each of ten commodities, using values generated by a classification according to income level and life-cycle status (four income, three life-cycle classes). Regressions of x on p net of income were also computed for each commodity, as were a few regressions net of both income and life-cycle status. Use of an income and life-cycle classification is essentially a way of generating some variance in x among groups of households. Neither variable represents an unforeseen event; in the terminology of Chapter 7, below, both are initial-data variables. It follows that no net relation should be observed between the purchase rate and either income or life-cycle class if the correlation between p and x' is perfect except for unforeseen events; on the other hand, some net relation might be observed if p and x' have a less than perfect linear relation.[15]

The data are summarized in Table 22. Although differences in the proportion of households that report buying intentions are a reasonably good linear predictor of differences in the purchase rate, the correlation is by no means perfect. More important, for about half of the commodities examined, both family-income class and life-cycle status make a significant contribution to the explanation of differences in the purchase rate, net of differences in the proportion of intenders. There is no evi-

---

[14] In one respect this test may be better than the conceptually correct time series test. Some kinds of intervening events are specific to individual households or groups of households; others are general, in that they influence all households. Both these kinds of intervening events may have some influence on the time series correlation, but only the former (specific to groups) will influence the cross-section correlation.

[15] The simple correlation between purchase rate and either income or life-cycle class is determined by the choice of class intervals. Evidently, a classification into those with incomes below $2,000 per year, between $2,000 and $25,000, and above $25,000 will yield a higher correlation between the purchase rate and income than a classification into groups with more evenly spaced class intervals. But the association between purchase rate and income net of the proportion of intenders will not be sensitive to such arbitrary choices, sampling variability aside.

TABLE 22

CROSS-SECTION CORRELATIONS OF PURCHASES WITH BUYING INTENTIONS,
LIFE-CYCLE STATUS, AND INCOME

	r^2_{12}	$R^2_{1.24}$	$r^2_{12.4}$	$r^2_{14.2}$
Automobile	.213	.646ª	.161	.550ª
Furniture	.656ª	.867ª	.640ª	.614ª
Washing machine	.219	.427	.287	.266
Refrigerator	.470ª	.516ª	.406ª	.086
Air conditioner	.161	.777ª	.044	.734ª
Dishwasher	.532ª	.543ª	.174	.024
Range	.590ª	.745ª	.586ª	.380ª
Clothes dryer	.756ª	.771ª	.758ª	.062
Garbage disposal unit	.357ª	.395	.366ª	.059
High-fidelity equipment	.067	.233	.006	.178
	$R^2_{1.234}$	$r^2_{12.34}$	$r^2_{13.24}$	$r^2_{14.23}$
Furniture	.894ª	.039	.199	.641ª
Refrigerator	.563	.370	.098	.004
Range	.865ª	.657ª	.472ª	.381
Clothes dryer	.870ª	.830ª	.431ª	.122

SOURCE: Basic data from Consumer Purchase Study, NBER.

NOTE: Subscript 1 denotes purchases; 2, buying intentions; 3, life-cycle status; and 4, family-income level.

ª Significantly different from zero at 0.05 level.

dence that a systematic nonlinearity in the (p,x') relation accounts for these results. These findings support the intuitively plausible proposition that the linear correlation between p and x, though significantly higher than zero, is likely to be considerably less than the (unobservable) correlation between x' and x. In short, knowledge of p is by no means a perfect substitute for knowledge of x'.[16]

[16] I do not think it can usefully be argued that these results simply show that the relevant relations may be nonlinear. From a practical point of view, one wants to use survey data to aid in predicting purchases. If there is in fact a unique but nonlinear relation between p and x', it would take some time and additional data to establish the functional form of the relation. Even then, one could never be sure that the true relation had been found unless it were fairly obvious from the data—which it is not. And on a priori grounds, it does not seem plausible to me that the relation is unique but simply nonlinear.

CHAPTER 5

Aggregate Intentions-Purchases Relationship

Introduction

THIS chapter deals with the relation between aggregate buying intentions and aggregate purchases. The main focus is on a comparison of intentions with other predictors of durable goods purchases, such as income, life-cycle status, etc. There is also a preliminary investigation of some possible interactions between buying intentions and other predictors of durable goods purchases.

The basic data are identical to those discussed in Chapters 2, 3, and 4, except that the individual-commodity buying intentions and purchases reported by each household have been combined into crudely weighted aggregates designed to measure intended and actual dollar magnitudes for each household. All commodities except automobiles are assigned equal weights of 1 ($=$ roughly \$300 worth of durables); these commodities are: room air conditioner, house air conditioner, carpets and rugs (over \$100 worth), clothes dryer, dishwasher, food freezer, furniture (over \$100 worth), garbage disposal unit, high-fidelity equipment, home heating system, movie camera, range, refrigerator, television set, and washing machine. Automobile weights are as follows:

	Assigned Weight
Automobile, used	2
Automobile, new	
Under \$2,500	4
\$2,500–\$3,500	5
Over \$3,500	6

Some of the unit weights are clearly inappropriate. First, prices paid for house air-conditioning systems, home heating systems, movie cameras, and garbage disposal units are rather different from prices typically paid for the other unit-weight items; for all other items the price ranges of popular models overlap to a considerable degree. Second, it is known that the probabilities associated with responses to an intentions question are not the same for all items, being higher for automobiles, say, than for dishwashers. I did not refine the weights to correct these two known biases, since (1) for the first three items mentioned above, an estimate of average price has little meaning because the range of possible prices is very large; (2) relatively few households either planned to buy or purchased any of the four items; (3) relatively few households purchased those items for which purchase probabilities, given the buying-intentions question, are quite different from the "typical" values. In effect, the gain in accuracy did not seem worth the cost of either adjustment.

The first step was to classify households by the level of aggregate buying intentions. The average level of purchases by households in each of the categories was then computed. The results (Table 23) are shown for several of the intentions questions. Correlations between aggregate buying intentions $(\hat{P})$ and aggregate purchases (P) are also shown; P is measured over the six months subsequent to the survey of intentions.

TABLE 23

BUYING INTENTIONS OF APRIL 1958 COMPARED WITH WEIGHTED AVERAGE PURCHASES, APRIL–OCTOBER 1958

Weighted Number of Buying Intentions, April 1958	Weighted Average Purchases of Households for Intentions Question[a]			
	A_1	B_1	C_1	D_1
0	1.30	1.26	1.01	1.14
1	1.82	1.52	1.14	1.30
2	2.06	1.86	1.74	1.62
3	2.83	2.31	1.98	1.80
4	3.11	2.84	2.35	2.04
5	3.46	3.51	2.79	2.57
6	3.76	3.70	3.16	2.55
7	4.04	3.57	3.26	3.32
8	4.36	3.71	3.18	3.54
9 or more	3.38	3.82	3.16	2.77
All households	1.65	1.62	1.63	1.65
REGRESSION STATISTICS $(P = a + b\hat{P})$[b]				
Square of correlation coefficient (r^2)	.093	.095	.124	.085
Intercept (a)	+1.337	+1.235	+.993	+1.730
Slope coefficient (b)	+.384	+.367	+.317	+.252
Standard error of b	±.020	±.019	±.014	±.014

SOURCE: Basic data from Consumer Purchase Study, NBER.

[a] The intentions questions are: A_1—definite plans within twelve months; B_1—plans within six months; C_1—plans within twelve months (if income is as expected); D_1—plans within twelve months. See Table 1 for a more complete description of the intentions questions.

[b] Data based on individual observations; P = purchases, $\hat{P}$ = buying intentions.

Aggregate Purchases and Buying Intentions

In examining Table 23, one is immediately impressed by the closeness of the buying intentions–purchases relationship, particularly when the data are grouped in order to reduce the random variation inherent in individual behavior. The average value of (aggregate) purchases rises steadily with the level of (aggregate) intentions for all four questions, although average purchases drop off somewhat at very high levels of intentions.[1] The correlation data also indicate a quite powerful relation between aggregate intentions and purchases, with intentions explaining from 9 to 12 per cent of the variance, depending on the group.[2]

Differences among the variant intentions groups in average purchases, keeping reported intentions constant, are generally consistent with the interpretation of intentions developed in Chapter 3. Average purchases corresponding to any given level of buying intentions are highest in group A_1, next highest in B_1, and lowest in D_1. From the analysis in Chapter 3 it is clear that average probability for intenders in groups A_1 and B_1 must be higher than for intenders in either C_1 or D_1.[3] The probability cut-off points implied by these four questions can be ranked by the fraction of households reporting intentions. On this scale, A_1 intenders would be expected to have a higher cut-off than those in B_1, and similarly for intenders in group C_1 compared to D_1. Thus, the model predicts that purchase probability for intenders in groups A_1, B_1, C_1, and D_1 would rank in that order, and the data on average purchases are consistent with such a prediction.

The regression coefficients are equally consistent with the probability model. These coefficients measure the average difference in purchases among households that differ by unity in the weighted aggregate of intended

---

[1] Most previous studies of buying intentions in relation to subsequent purchases have simply distinguished between households with and without intentions or purchases, or used ratios of intentions (purchases) to income (see James Tobin, "On the Predictive Value of Consumer Intentions and Attitudes," *Review of Economics and Statistics*, February 1959; Lawrence R. Klein and John B. Lansing, "Decisions to Purchase Consumer Durable Goods," *Journal of Marketing*, October 1955; Eva Mueller, "Effects of Consumer Attitudes on Purchases," *American Economic Review*, December 1957; and Peter De Janosi, "Factors Influencing the Demand for New Automobiles," *Journal of Marketing*, April 1959).

[2] This constitutes a very strong relationship as cross-section results go. By comparison, the results reported by Mueller show the following correlations in a cross-section study, using data from the Survey of Consumer Finances:

Regression Relation	*Squared Correlation Coefficient*
P on income	.032
P on age	.017
P on attitudes	.020
P on intentions	.036

Income explains less than 4 per cent of the variance for this sample, and buying intentions explain roughly the same amount.

[3] The cut-off probability for intenders must be higher in A_1 than in either C_1 or D_1. The intentions question for the former asked about "definite plans to buy within a year," while for groups C_1 and D_1 the questions asked about "plans within a year." The cut-off probability must also be higher for B_1 than for either C_1 or D_1 because the former question asked about "plans within six months."

purchases. According to the model, a given difference in intended purchases should be associated with a larger difference in actual purchases for households in group A_1 than for those in groups B_1, C_1, or D_1, because the purchase probability associated with a reported "intention to buy" is larger in A_1 than elsewhere. More generally, the model predicts that the regression coefficients of intentions will rank in the order A_1, B_1, C_1, D_1; and this prediction corresponds to the observed ranking.

One of the most interesting results in Table 23 is the sizable difference between C_1 and D_1 both in the $(P, \hat{P})$ correlation and in the level of average purchases associated with any given level of intentions. Both groups were asked what seemed to be an identical question about buying intentions, i.e., "Do you plan to buy within the next twelve months or so?" But the intentions question for C_1 contained two additional and specifically contingent parts as well, which asked about intentions if income were to be higher or lower than expected (see Chapter 2). It is quite clear that the purchase probability associated with buying intentions reported on the noncontingent part of variant C—C_1—were affected by the existence of the two contingent parts. The fraction of intenders is lower in C_1 than D_1 for almost every item, and the purchase rates for intenders are higher in C_1.[4] And from Table 23, it is clear that both correlation and regression coefficients are noticeably higher for C_1 than for D_1, and that a given level of intentions is generally associated with larger average purchases in C_1 than in D_1. The above aggregate results accord with my findings in Chapters 2 and 3 for individual-commodity data.

It is also interesting that the correlation between six-month purchases and the intentions question with a six-month time horizon (variant B_1) is not very different from the correlations for A_1 and D_1, both of which asked about intentions over a twelve-month period. The inference seems to be that the time horizon attached to a question about intentions should not be taken as an indicator of the probable date of purchase. A question with a relatively short time horizon seems to serve somewhat the same function as one with a longer horizon but with restrictive specifications about the degree of certainty; that is, asking about "plans within six months" seems to elicit much the same general pattern of intentions and purchases as asking about "definite plans within twelve months." These aggregate data again confirm the results in Chapters 2 and 3, where roughly the same purchase probability was found to be associated with responses to these two questions.

[4] See Chapter 2 above, and my *Consumer Expectations, Plans, and Purchases: A Progress Report*, Occasional Paper 70, New York, NBER, 1959, Chap. 3, Table 9.

Aggregate Purchases and Contingent Buying Intentions

So far, I have discussed the relation between aggregate buying intentions and purchases for alternative intentions variables, obtained from survey questions asked of different samples of households. Supplementary measures of intentions, with lower probability cut-off points, are also available for several of these samples. I now turn to the problem of combining intentions variables such as those in the several parts of A and C in order to achieve the best possible explanation of purchases.

I designate responses to the relatively high-probability part of a multiple intentions question as "standard" intentions, $\hat{P}$. Thus, "definite" buying intentions are standard for the A group; "intentions within twelve months," for the C group. Responses to the relatively low-probability part of the question are designated "contingent" intentions, $\hat{P}_c$. Thus "probable or possible" purchases are contingent for the A group; "intentions if income is higher than expected," for the C group. Groups A, B, and C have both a standard and a contingent intentions variable; group D has only a standard intentions variable (see Chapter 2).

The analysis of individual commodity data in Chapter 3 suggests the undesirability of relating the sum $\hat{P} + \hat{P}_c$ for each household to the sum of purchases (P). This procedure is tantamount to assigning equal weights to both kinds of intentions, and it is known that the purchase probabilities associated with standard intentions are substantially higher than those associated with contingent intentions.[5] If the purchase probabilities are different, the regression coefficients are presumably different also.

The simplest procedure is to estimate coefficients from an equation of the form

1.0 $$P = b_0 + b_1\hat{P} + b_2\hat{P}_c + u,$$

allowing the data to choose the weights assigned to $\hat{P}$ and $\hat{P}_c$. By so doing it is assumed that both variables are linearly related to purchases and that contingent intentions have the same influence on purchases for every level of standard intentions. Evidence against a linear relationship is not strong, but the assumption of independence between the $(P,\hat{P}_c)$ relation and the level of $\hat{P}$ seems questionable. I have already shown that variables like income and life cycle apparently have a stronger influence on the

---

[5] This relation holds within any of the groups for which both $\hat{P}$ and $\hat{P}_c$ were obtained, although it does not of course follow that $\hat{P}$ for one group necessarily has a higher cut-off or mean probability than $\hat{P}_c$ for a different group. In fact, the $\hat{P}$ variables in groups A, B, and C all seem to have higher cut-off probabilities than any of the $\hat{P}_c$ variables, but this is due to the particular questions asked.

purchases of nonintenders than of intenders. The probable reasons have been discussed (see Chapters 3 and 4). The logic of the argument suggests that the influence of contingent intentions may well be stronger when standard intentions are zero or relatively small than when they are relatively large. If so, coefficients for the buying intentions variables should be estimated from equations like these:

2.0
$$P = b_0 + b_1\hat{P} + b_2\hat{P}_c + b_3\hat{P}\hat{P}_c + u,$$

or

3.0
$$P = b_0 + b_1\hat{P} + b_2\hat{P}_c + b_3Z\hat{P}_c + u,$$

where $Z = 1$ when $\hat{P} = 0$
$\quad\quad Z = 0$ when $\hat{P} > 0$

Both these equations permit the relation between contingent intentions and purchases to vary with the level of standard intentions. In equation 2.0 the slope coefficient of $\hat{P}_c$ is $b_2 + \hat{P}b_3$; since b_3 is expected to be negative, the entire expression is at a maximum when $\hat{P}$ is zero. As $\hat{P}$ increases the expression becomes steadily smaller, presumably becoming negative at some point. In equation 3.0, the regression coefficient of $\hat{P}_c$ is $b_2 + Zb_3$; hence there are two different slopes for the $(\hat{P}_c,P)$ relation, depending on whether the value of Z is unity or zero. Since b_3 is expected to be positive, the coefficient of $\hat{P}_c$ will be larger when $\hat{P}$ is zero than when it is not.

One rather straightforward empirical test of the general notion that contingent intentions are more closely associated with purchases when standard intentions are zero involves the computation of separate regressions for households with zero and nonzero values of $\hat{P}$. Using the A group, the following results are obtained:

For the entire sample,

1.1
$$P = 1.081 + .390\hat{P} + .117\hat{P}_c, \; R^2 = .110$$
$$\quad\quad\quad\quad (.020) \quad (.014)$$

For households with $\hat{P} > 0$,

1.2
$$P = 1.327 + .351\hat{P} + .072\hat{P}_c, \; R^2 = .090$$
$$\quad\quad\quad\quad (.010) \quad (.009)$$

For households with $\hat{P} = 0$,

1.3
$$P = 1.012 + .138\hat{P}_c, \; R^2 = .031$$
$$\quad\quad\quad\quad (.016)$$

The coefficient of $\hat{P}_c$ differs in the predicted direction, being about

127

twice as large when $\hat{P} = 0$ than when $\hat{P} > 0$. Contingent intentions explain about 3 per cent of the variance in purchases when standard intentions are zero, compared to an incremental explained variance of around 2 per cent for households with nonzero standard intentions.

TABLE 24

<small>Selected Relations Among Durable Goods Buying Intentions and Purchases</small>

		Net Regression Coefficients		
		DOLLAR SCALES		
Group A	$\hat{P}$	$\hat{P}_c$	$\hat{P}\hat{P}_c$	r^2 or R^2
$P = f(\hat{P})$	+.394[a]			.089
$P = f(\hat{P},\hat{P}_c)$	+.397[a]	+.095[a]		.101
$P = f(\hat{P},\hat{P}_c,\hat{P}\hat{P}_c)$	+.566[a]	+.155[a]	−.095[a]	.117
Group C				
$P = f(\hat{P})$	+.378[a]			.148
$P = f(\hat{P},\hat{P}_c)$	+.387[a]	+.081[a]		.152
$P = f(\hat{P},\hat{P}_c,\hat{P}\hat{P}_c)$	+.446[a]	+.128[a]	−.031[a]	.156
		DICHOTOMOUS SCALES		
Group A	$\hat{P}$	$\hat{P}_c$	$Z\hat{P}_c$[b]	r^2 or R^2
$P = f(\hat{P})$	+.243[a]			.057
$P = f(\hat{P},\hat{P}_c)$	+.233[a]	+.170[a]		.082
$P = f(\hat{P},\hat{P}_c,Z\hat{P}_c)$	+.401[a]	+.017	+.229[a]	.092
Group C				
$P = f(\hat{P})$	+.218[a]			.046
$P = f(\hat{P},\hat{P}_c)$	+.218[a]	+.055		.048
$P = f(\hat{P},\hat{P}_c,Z\hat{P}_c)$	+.230[a]	+.050	+.016	.048

Source: Basic data from Consumer Purchase Study, NBER.

Note: The data cover only husband-wife households with the head between twenty-five and thirty-four years old. P represents durable goods purchases. In Group A, $\hat{P}$ represents definite intentions to buy within a year; $\hat{P}_c$, probable or possible intentions to buy within a year; and $N = 852$. In Group C, $\hat{P}$ represents intentions to buy within a year if income is as expected; $\hat{P}_c$, intentions to buy within a year if income is 10 to 15 per cent higher than expected; and $N = 815$. For further explanation, see accompanying text.

[a] Significantly different from zero at 0.05 level, using t test.

[b] $Z = 1$ when $\hat{P} = 0$; otherwise, $Z = 0$.

The results obtained from equations 2.0 and 3.0 are shown above. To make the test somewhat more rigorous I have stratified the sample by life-cycle status; the regressions in Table 24 are based on observations that include only husband-wife households with the head between twenty-five and thirty-four years old. Four sets of coefficients are shown. The top panel contains regression coefficients obtained by fitting equation 2.0 to the data for groups A and C; all variables (P, $\hat{P}$, and $\hat{P}_c$) are the usual weighted aggregates designed to represent dollar scales. The lower panel shows regression coefficients obtained by fitting equation 3.0 to the data for the same groups. For these regressions the variables are scaled dichotomously; that is, P, $\hat{P}$, and $\hat{P}_c$ take on values of either zero or one depending on whether or not the household reported any standard or contingent intentions or purchased any durable good.[6] The coefficients are computed in a stepwise manner; variables are added one at a time and the regression recomputed. We can thus observe the effect on the coefficient of $\hat{P}$ of adding $\hat{P}_c$, or the effect on the coefficient of $\hat{P}_c$ of introducing interaction.

The empirical results conform rather well to theoretical expectations. Interpreting the regression coefficients in the upper panel as the probability of purchasing one unit of durables if one unit of intentions is reported, it appears that $\hat{P}$ is associated with roughly four times the probability of purchasing as $\hat{P}_c$. The coefficients of both $\hat{P}$ and $\hat{P}_c$ are highly significant net of each other, and the cross-product interaction $\hat{P}\hat{P}_c$ adds significantly to an explanation of the variance in purchases and has the predicted negative sign in both groups. Thus, the purchase probabilities associated with $\hat{P}_c$ depend on the value of $\hat{P}$, and vice versa. When $\hat{P}$ is zero the purchase probabilities associated with $\hat{P}_c$ are 0.155 and 0.128 for the A and C intentions questions, respectively. In group A, when the value of $\hat{P}$ is equal to approximately two units, the probability associated with $\hat{P}_c$ falls to zero; the coefficient of $\hat{P}_c$ for the C group falls to zero when $\hat{P}$ is about four units. The coefficients of $\hat{P}$ behave similarly, being highest when $\hat{P}_c$ is zero and gradually diminishing as $\hat{P}_c$ rises.

The regression coefficients of $\hat{P}$ and $\hat{P}_c$ in the lower panel, where the scaling is dichotomous, measure the probability of purchasing one or more durables when the respondent reports one or more intentions. In the A group the respective probabilities for $\hat{P}$ and $\hat{P}_c$ are both highly significant and not much different in size. For the C group, however, $\hat{P}_c$ appears to be almost unrelated to purchases, while $\hat{P}$ is highly significant and about the same size as in the A group. This is not surprising. Both $\hat{P}$ and $\hat{P}_c$ have relatively high cut-off probabilities (for individual commodities) in the A group. As a consequence, substantial numbers of households reported neither standard nor contingent buying intentions for any of the items, and their $\hat{P}$ and $\hat{P}_c$ are therefore zero when dichotomous scaling is used. These households are much less apt to purchase than the others. On the other hand the probability cut-off (for individual items) is very low for the $\hat{P}_c$ variant in group C, while the cut-off for the $\hat{P}$ variant in this

---

[6] Since regressions for group B show much the same results as those for group C, they are not shown. A measure of $\hat{P}_c$ cannot be obtained for variant D, since it contains only a high-probability intentions variable.

group is not very different from the cut-off point for the $\hat{P}_c$ variant in group A (see Chapter 3). Practically all group C households reported contingent intentions to buy at least one item, and $\hat{P}_c$ has a value of one for these households when dichotomous scaling is used. As a consequence, the dichotomous $\hat{P}_c$ variable in group C has almost no variance. Further, the behavior of households reporting some contingent buying intentions ($\hat{P}_c$) differs little from that of those reporting none, and is apt to reflect variations in the interpretation of the question rather than real differences in *ex ante* purchase probability.

The interaction term in the lower panel ($Z\hat{P}_c$, where $Z = 1$ when $\hat{P} = 0$, $Z = 0$, when $\hat{P} > 0$) is significant only for the A group, although it has the expected sign in group C as well. Before $Z\hat{P}_c$ is added to the regression in the A group, $\hat{P}_c$ appears to have as strong an association with P as does $\hat{P}$. When $Z\hat{P}_c$ is added the influence of $\hat{P}_c$ disappears almost entirely, indicating that contingent intentions are associated with purchases, net of standard intentions, only for those households that do not report standard intentions, i.e., with $\hat{P} = 0$. The inclusion of $Z\hat{P}_c$ also causes a substantial increase in the coefficient of $\hat{P}$, suggesting that the net effect of $\hat{P}$ on P will be underestimated unless account can be taken of the differential influence of $\hat{P}_c$ on P.

On the whole, the results provide support at the aggregate level for several of the propositions advanced earlier. The regression coefficients for both standard ($\hat{P}$) and contingent ($\hat{P}_c$) intentions to buy all behave in accord with the probability model. The coefficients of the $\hat{P}$ and $\hat{P}_c$ variables are higher in group A than in group C, and the coefficient of $\hat{P}$ is substantially higher than that of $\hat{P}_c$ within both groups. There is convincing evidence that the probability scale represented by the $\hat{P}$ variable is noticeably improved by the refinement embodied in $\hat{P}_c$, since $\hat{P}_c$ makes a highly significant contribution to the explanation of purchases provided by standard intentions to buy. Further, there is strong evidence that the usefulness of this refinement varies with the value of $\hat{P}$; $\hat{P}_c$ is of maximum usefulness when $\hat{P}$ is zero, becoming less important as $\hat{P}$ increases. The common-sense interpretation of these results is as follows: We can tell quite a bit about differences in the dollar amount of actual purchases among households from data on the dollar amount of prospective purchases. Ability to predict differences in purchases is enhanced if the dollar amount of contingent prospective purchases is also known, but it is enhanced much more for households that reported "none" for the standard intentions category. The basic reason appears to be variation among households in the probabilities implicitly attached to survey questions about buying intentions. Such variation will mean that households reporting "none" when asked about their intentions to buy, that is, households classed as nonintenders, comprise two quite different groups of people. On the one hand, there are those with the "average" interpretation of the intentions question and a relatively low probability of purchase. On the other hand, there are those who have a relatively high probability of purchase but assign an even higher cut-off probability to the intentions question. As a consequence, there is a relatively large variance in actual (but unobserved) purchase probabilities for those reporting zero standard intentions, and these probabilities are apparently correlated with responses to questions about more contingent or less certain future purchases.

Intentions as a Proxy for Other Variables

It is clear enough from these data that aggregate buying intentions are very strongly associated with aggregate purchases. It does not necessarily follow, however, that intentions help to explain differences in purchase behavior among households after allowing for the influence of common factors. Variables such as family income, stage of the life-cycle, expectations and attitudes, etc., are related to both durable goods purchases and to durable goods buying intentions. The aggregate relationship observed above may therefore be a consequence of the fact that young-married, optimistic, or high-income consumers buy relatively many durable goods and report relatively many buying intentions. If so, the appropriate predictor of purchases is not buying intentions but some combination of family income, stage of the life cycle, degree of optimism, etc.

Similarly, it is possible that the aggregate intentions-purchases correlation is dominated by the close association between automobile-buying intentions and automobile purchases, or by the close association between house-buying intentions and housing purchases. Automobile intentions and purchases comprise roughly half the weighted aggregate value of durable goods intentions and purchases. And while the above measures of aggregate intentions and purchases do not include houses, intentions and purchases for household durables like refrigerators, dishwashers, furniture, etc., are known to be closely related to house-buying intentions and housing purchases. Thus it is necessary to find out whether the strong aggregate correlations observed above represent real phenomena or simply reflect factors that exert a common influence on both purchases and buying intentions.

TABLE 25

WEIGHTED AVERAGE NUMBER OF BUYING INTENTIONS AND PURCHASES WITHIN
INCOME AND LIFE-CYCLE CLASSES

	HUSBAND-WIFE HOUSEHOLDS WITH HEAD							
	Under 35		*35–44*		*45–64*		*Over 65*	
	Buying Inten-tions	Pur-chases	Buying Inten-tions	Pur-chases	Buying Inten-tions	Pur-chases	Buying Inten-tions	Pur-chases
INCOME CLASS								
			SAMPLE B					
Under $5,000	0.95	1.52	0.67[a]	1.16[a]	0.86[a]	1.16[a]		
$5,000–$9,999	1.03	1.59	0.90	1.42	0.80	1.33	0.51[a]	0.86[a]
$10,000 or more	1.39	2.16	1.34	2.02	1.33	1.98		
			SAMPLE C					
Under $5,000	1.80	1.57	1.47[a]	1.00[a]	1.24[a]	1.26[a]		
$5,000–$9,999	1.89	1.60	1.81	1.38	1.48	1.34	1.52[a]	1.21[a]
$10,000 or more	2.74	2.26	2.56	2.02	2.51	1.96		

SOURCE: Basic data from Consumer Purchase Study, NBER.
[a] Less than 100 households in cell.

INCOME AND LIFE-CYCLE STATUS

In Table 25 I present mean (aggregate) purchases and buying intentions for two of the variant groups within several income (Y) and life-cycle (L) classes. Since the data show that intentions and purchases are similarly related to both variables, the high $P,\hat{P}$ correlations observed may be due wholly or mainly to the common influence of Y and/or L.

The most conclusive test would involve fitting the data to the following equation:

$$4.0 \qquad P = b_0 + b_1\hat{P} + b_2Y + b_3L + b_4(Y,L) + u$$

where P = aggregate purchases of durables
$\hat{P}$ = aggregate intentions to buy durables
Y = family income
L = family life-cycle status
Y,L = interactions between Y and L

If the coefficient of $\hat{P}$ were to become statistically nonsignificant when Y and L were held constant, it would be concluded that the observed simple correlation between P and $\hat{P}$ was due wholly to the common influence of Y and L. This test cannot be used, because the data for family income or life-cycle status are available only in class intervals; that is, it is known only whether family income is between, say, $5,000 and $7,500 per year, or whether the household head is between twenty-five and thirty years of age. Given this limitation, the best available test consists of a comparison of the proportion of total within-class variance in purchases that is explained by buying intentions with the proportion that might conceivably be explained by a combination of family income and life-cycle status. The first proportion can be computed directly; the second can be approximated if we can estimate (1) the true slope of the within-class regressions between P and both Y and L and (2) the true within-class variance of P, Y, and L. I designate b_{yp} and b_{ap} as the slopes of the regressions between (Y,P) and (L,P) respectively; M_{yy}, M_{aa}, and M_{pp} as the variances of income, life cycle, and purchases, respectively; and M_{yp}, M_{ap}, etc., as the respective covariances. The within-class correlations between purchases and income (r_{yp}) and between purchases and life-cycle status (r_{ap}) can be written

$$r_{yp} = \sqrt{\frac{M^2_{yp}}{M_{yy}M_{pp}}}$$

$$r_{ap} = \sqrt{\frac{M^2_{ap}}{M_{aa}M_{pp}}}$$

Since $M_{yp} = M_{yy}b_{yp}$, and $M_{ap} = M_{aa}b_{ap}$, it follows that

$$r_{yp} = \sqrt{\frac{M_{yy}b^2_{yp}}{M_{pp}}}$$

and

$$r_{ap} = \sqrt{\frac{M_{aa}b^2_{ap}}{M_{pp}}}$$

Thus it is necessary to estimate M_{pp}, M_{yy}, M_{aa}, b_{yp}, and b_{ap}. The required variances cannot be computed directly from the data (except for M_{pp}), since only class intervals are available; but they can readily be estimated if it can be assumed that the within-class distribution of Y and L is rectangular.[7] From the proportions of households in the various income and life-cycle classes, I judge that the distribution of both Y and L is approximately rectangular for the group of husband-wife households with the head between thirty-five and forty-five years of age and with family income between $5,000 and $10,000 per year. The slopes of the Y,P and L,P regressions within this class can be fairly well approximated from data on average purchases by households in this and the two adjacent classifications.[8]

Let us err on the side of caution and accept relatively high estimates for the within-class slopes; for b_{yp} let us accept 0.0001 as the true slope; and

[7] A rectangular distribution simply implies that observations are spaced equally between the beginning and end points of the class; hence the mean is the class midpoint, and the variance depends on the width of the class interval.

[8] Table 25 shows that the average purchases of households in the three income classes

for b_{ap}, 0.020. Using values for M_{pp} calculated directly from the data and estimating M_{yy} and M_{aa} on the basis of an assumed rectangular distribution within the specified group, I calculate that family income cannot explain more than 0.6 per cent of the within-class variance in purchases; a similar computation indicates that life-cycle status (age, in this case) cannot explain more than 0.1 per cent of the within-class variance in purchases. These estimates of maximum explained variance in P attributable to Y and L are almost precisely the same for samples B and C, since the computed variance in purchases (the only possible source of difference, given the procedure) is almost identical (3.46 compared to 3.49). On the other hand, buying intentions explain almost 14 per cent of the variance in purchases for the relevant B sample, over 18 per cent for the relevant C sample. Hence, I conclude that the strong correlations observed between buying intentions and purchases cannot be due to the joint influence of Y or L on both, since the maximum proportion of the variance in purchases explained by the combined influence of Y and L cannot begin to account for the proportion of variance explained by intentions to buy. This conclusion would not be altered if similar computations were performed on groups of households in other income or life-cycle classes, or if all income and life-cycle classes had been combined so that the variance of Y and L took on its maximum value (see below, Chapter 7).[9]

INTENTIONS TO BUY HOUSES OR AUTOMOBILES

One further explanation of the close relation observed between aggregate buying intentions and aggregate purchases requires examination. It is

---

indicated are as follows:

	Class 1: Under $5,000	Class 2: $5,000– $9,999	Class 3: $10,000 and Over
Sample B	1.16	1.42	2.02
Sample C	1.00	1.38	2.02

If the mean incomes for households within these three classes are, respectively, $3,750, $7,500, and $15,000, the slope of the income-purchases regression between income classes 1 and 2 in sample B would be 1.42 − 1.16 ÷ $7,500 − $3,750, or 0.26 ÷ 3,750, or roughly 0.00006; the regression slope would be 1.38 − 1.00 ÷ $7,500 − $3,750, or roughly 0.00010 for sample C. A similar computation indicates that the income-purchases regression would have a slope of roughly 0.00008 between income classes 2 and 3 in both samples. If the regression slope *within* income class 2 is the same as these between-class slopes, I would estimate the within-class slope as roughly 0.00008. A comparable procedure would yield estimates of the within-class slope for the age-purchases regression.

[9] The extent of the difference in variance explained by Y,L and buying intentions would not generally be as great, because the proportion of variance explained by

possible that the aggregate $P, \hat{P}$ relation is dominated either by the relation between intentions to buy and actual purchases of automobiles, or between intentions to buy and actual purchases of housing. Automobiles are a significant part of the aggregates for both intentions and purchases, amounting to roughly half of each. It would not be surprising if survey questions about intentions (or purchase probability) were much more accurate predictors of spending behavior for relatively high-unit-cost commodities than for others. If so, the intentions-purchases relationship would be appreciably less close for durables other than automobiles, since the observed aggregate relationship would be dominated by the auto-mobile component.[10] Similarly, it may be that the relationship between aggregate intentions to buy and aggregate purchases of household durables comes about wholly or in part because people planning to buy (and buying) houses report relatively many intentions and make relatively many purchases. If so, the appropriate predictor is not durable goods buying intentions but house buying intentions.

These possibilities are easily tested by stratification. The sample was split by three alternative criteria: (1) a household either reports intentions to buy an automobile or does not; (2) a household either reports intentions to buy some household durable or does not; (3) a household either reports intentions to buy a house or does not. Aggregate intentions and purchases ($\hat{P}, P$) were divided into intentions and purchases with respect to all household durables ($\hat{P}_h, P_h$) and to automobiles ($\hat{P}_a, P_a$). The following correlations were then computed for the indicated classification:

Intend to buy a car:

5.1 $$P_h = b_0 + b_1 \hat{P}_h$$
5.2 $$P_a = b_0 + b_1 \hat{P}_a$$
5.3 $$P = b_0 + b_1 \hat{P}$$

---

intentions is typically lower in other groups than in the two examined above. Using the classifications of Table 25, there are ten income-life-cycle groups in both the B and C samples. The distribution of these twenty groups, by proportion of variance in purchases explained by intentions to buy, is as follows:

Proportion of M_{pp} explained by $\hat{P}$ (per cent)	0–4.9	5–9.9	10–14.9	15 and over	Total
Number of groups in each class	4	6	7	3	20

Further, as noted above, the variance attributable to Y and/or L would be somewhat higher if the analysis had been carried out on all income and life-cycle classes combined.

[10] There is some evidence that buying intentions do not improve time series predictions of household durables, although they do improve predictions for automobiles (see Arthur Okun, "The Value of Anticipations Data in Forecasting National Product," *The Quality and Economic Significance of Anticipations Data*, Princeton for NBER, 1960).

Do not intend to buy a car:

5.4
$$P_h = b_0 + b_1 \hat{P}_h$$

5.5
$$P_a = b_0 + b_1 \hat{P}_a$$

5.6
$$P = b_0 + b_1 \hat{P}$$

Continuing, there are six similar correlations, 6.1–6.6, for those intending (not intending) to buy some household durable; six more, 7.1–7.6, for those intending (not intending) to buy a house; and three, 8.1–8.3, for the entire sample.

TABLE 26

RELATIONSHIPS BETWEEN BUYING INTENTIONS AND PURCHASES OF HOUSEHOLD DURABLES AND OF AUTOMOBILES

Subgroup	Sample Size	Square of Correlation Coefficient Relating Intentions to Buy and Purchases of		
		Household Durables[a]	Automobiles[b]	Total Durables[c]
Intend to buy auto	382	.094	.082	.064
Do not intend to buy auto	3,216	.122	[d]	.040
Intend to buy some household durable	1,391	.101	.102	.087
Do not intend to buy any household durable	2,207	[d]	.105	.079
Intend to buy house	260	.128	.120	.108
Do not intend to buy house	3,338	.088	.101	.085
Entire sample	3,598	.118	.102	.094

SOURCE: Basic data from Consumer Purchase Study, NBER.
NOTE: The respondents are those in group B, intentions question B_1 (see Chapter 2). All regression coefficients are more than three times their standard errors.
[a] The regression equation is: $P_h = a + b\hat{P}_h$.
[b] The regression equation is: $P_a = a + b\hat{P}_a$.
[c] The regression equation is: $P = a + b\hat{P}$.
[d] Correlation coefficient necessarily zero because the independent variable (intentions to buy) is zero for all households.

If the durables of very large unit cost (autos and housing) have a dominant influence on the aggregate $P,\hat{P}$ relationship, equations 5.1 and 5.4 ought to have significantly lower correlations than 6.2 and 6.5; 7.4 ought to have a significantly lower correlation than either 7.1, 7.2, or 7.5; and 8.1, a significantly lower correlation than 8.2. In sum:

$$r_{5.1}, r_{5.4} < r_{6.2}, r_{6.5}$$
$$r_{7.4} < r_{7.1}, r_{7.2}, r_{7.5}$$
$$r_{8.1} < r_{8.2}$$

Table 26 tabulates the relevant correlation and regression coefficients.

These data give scant indication that the aggregate $P,\hat{P}$ correlation is attributable to the indirect influence of either automobile or housing intentions and purchases. The correlation between P_h and $\hat{P}_h$ is just as strong as that between P_a and $\hat{P}_a$, and it makes no appreciable difference to either correlation whether the household intended to purchase only household durables, only an automobile, or both. The $P,\hat{P}$ correlations seem somewhat stronger for *both* household durables and autos if the household also reported plans to buy a house, but the differences are well within the limits of sampling variability. In terms of the set of tests specified above, the predicted differences show up in direction more than half the time, but they are not very large and none are statistically significant. I conclude that there is no evidence to suggest that the observed relation between aggregate buying intentions and aggregate purchases is due either to the direct or indirect dominance of the aggregates by durables of relatively large unit cost.

Some Analytical Considerations

These results confirm the explanatory power of the buying-intentions variable in an incontrovertible manner. Why should buying intentions be so much more strongly associated with purchases than are variables such as income and life-cycle stage? To get at the answer to this question, consider the nature of the buying intentions variable compared to other variables that are associated with household behavior; also, consider the nature of the cross-section data used to discover, verify, or quantify these relationships.

The factors customarily used to explain household behavior are essentially designed to explain average or aggregate behavior. For example, no one would expect that *all* households with annual incomes between $4,000 and $5,000 will buy fewer durable goods than *all* households with annual incomes between $10,000 and $15,000. Similarly, not every household in the "low average purchase" category of variables such as life cycle, assets, debts, age and condition of the stock of durables, expected income, etc., is expected to buy less than every household in the "high average purchase" category. Yet for reasons having to do with utility maximization, average purchases for a sample of households are expected to be strongly related to variables like these.

One of the reasons for expecting systematic patterns in average behavior but considerable variation among individuals is that most of the variables relevant to individual behavior are not ordinarily measured. One household will buy because, given its structure of wants, an income increase permits it to carry a greater debt-repayment burden, and it has recourse to temporary financial help if the payment becomes burdensome.

Another, with an identical want structure, may not buy if income were to rise because it deems the increase too uncertain and regards the use of temporary financial assistance in the event of trouble as undesirable. A third with the same want structure and an income increase will not buy because it hopes to receive the item from a close friend or relative when the latter redecorates—and so on, ad infinitum.

The number of possible combinations of factors and interactions among factors that add up to a given probability of purchasing X during the next Y months is obviously very great. Probably one could, in principle, measure and analyze all or most of these factors, but surely everyone would agree that such a goal is not now in sight and may never be reached or even approximated. Further, explanation of all these idiosyncratic combinations is not necessary for accurate predictions of aggregate behavior. But a survey of intentions to buy goes a long way toward isolating precisely those combinations of specific circumstances that result in the vast variety of causal relationships underlying individual purchase decisions. For this reason buying intentions are an extremely powerful tool for the analysis of differences in purchases among households.

Buying intentions are, indeed, a rather unusual variable in the empirical analysis of purchases. The object of such analysis is to quantify the influence of variables that are significantly associated with purchases, so that movements in these variables may be used to predict changes in purchases. Income, income prospects, age, stock of durables, etc., can be said to reflect either present or prospective ability to pay for durable goods or the structure of preferences for them. But buying intentions surely measure (directly) neither ability nor need, now or in the future. Rather, they reflect each household's judgment about the probability of purchase in the near future, given the weight attached by the household to ability to pay now and in the future along with need now and in the future. Thus, buying intentions obviously encompass factors that have already entered the household's own calculating apparatus.

It thus seems plausible that intentions to buy would contribute substantially to an explanation of purchases in the analysis of cross-section data. What is not so clear, perhaps, is why anything *else* contributes, given the above interpretation.[11] The explanation lies partly in the

---

[11] It is obvious, of course, that variables reflecting unforeseen alterations in household circumstances should contribute substantially to the explanation of purchases. (See Okun, "Forecasting National Product"; and Juster, *Consumer Expectations;* Juster, "Prediction and Consumer Buying Intentions," *American Economic Review*, May 1960; Juster, "The Predictive Value of Consumers Union Spending-Intentions Data," *The Quality and Economic Significance of Anticipations Data.*

variation in subjective probability among households that report that they intend or do not intend to purchase during some specified period, as discussed earlier. It seems self-evident that the cut-off probability attached to such a statement varies from respondent to respondent, although practically nothing is known empirically about this problem. Moreover, some households must give impressionistic responses that are essentially unrelated to reality. Others may attach no operational meaning to words like "plan" or "intend" and simply report no intentions regardless of circumstances. It follows that variables like income, assets, age, etc., will show some relationship to purchases for the sample as a whole, net of buying intentions, because subjective purchase probability is not measured with enough precision by the intentions question.

Let us suppose that the above analysis is correct, and that intentions to buy show a strong empirical relation to subsequent purchases (in cross sections) because they isolate sets of favorable or unfavorable circumstances that are essentially idiosyncratic to individual households. It follows that intentions may not be as useful, in a relative sense, for predicting changes over time as in predicting differences among households at the same point in time.[12] Further, buying intentions may be useful for time series predictions largely because they not only measure the influence of factors specific to individual households, but also reflect the impact of factors or combinations of factors that affect many households in the same way at the same time. Wholly idiosyncratic circumstances are randomly distributed among the population at every point in time; the buying intentions that reflect these circumstances would thus be invariant over time. Therefore, some proportion—perhaps a substantial one—of the cross-section variance explained by intentions to buy probably reflects the influence of factors that are uninteresting if one is concerned with time series predictions.

---

[12] Buying intentions may still be the most important single variable for analyzing time series changes. But its advantages over alternative variables would not be so great as it seems to be in the cross-section data.

CHAPTER 6

The Influence of Attitudes and Expectations on Purchases

Introduction

A MAJOR part of the existing research using consumer survey data has been concerned with relating attitudes and expectations to purchase behavior, both in time series and in cross sections. It is here that one finds the sharpest difference of opinion among researchers, both as to the interpretation of empirical results and the related question of usefulness in prediction.[1]

PREVAILING HYPOTHESES

One view is that consumer attitudes (thought of as generalized feelings of well-being reflecting relative optimism or pessimism) are fundamental determinants of spending and saving behavior and that both expectations (judgments about the course of events external to the household) and intentions (judgments about events internal to the household) are basically attitudes carrying a time dimension. Under this interpretation an appropriate measure of consumer sentiment blends all three kinds of variables in the same way as the characterization of a voter as prospectively Democratic or Republican combines his opinions on philosophical questions, his actual voting record in the past, his economic self-interest as reflected by income status, etc.

[1] On the one side are the works of Katona and Mueller: George Katona and Eva Mueller, *Consumer Attitudes and Demand, 1950–1952*, Ann Arbor, Michigan University Survey Research Center, n.d., pp. 51–61; Katona and Mueller, *Consumer Expectations, 1953–1956*, Ann Arbor, Michigan University Survey Research Center, n.d.; Katona, "Business Expectations in the Framework of Psychological Economics," *Expectations, Uncertainty, and Business Behavior*, ed. M. J. Bowman, Ann Arbor, Michigan University Survey Research Center, 1958; Mueller, "Effects of Consumer Attitudes on Purchases," *American Economic Review*, December 1957; Mueller, "Consumer Attitudes—Their Influence and Forecasting Value," *The Quality and Economic Significance of Anticipations Data*, Princeton for NBER, 1960; and, most recently, Katona, *The Powerful Consumer*, New York, McGraw-Hill, 1960. Compare the foregoing with James Tobin, "On the Predictive Value of Consumer Intentions and Attitudes," in *Review of Economics and Statistics*, February 1959; Arthur Okun, "The Value of Anticipations Data in Forecasting National Product," in *Anticipations Data; Reports of Federal Reserve Consultant Committees on Economic Statistics*, Joint Committee on the Economic Report, 84th Cong., 1st sess., 1955; F. Thomas Juster, *Consumer Expectations, Plans, and Purchases: A Progress Report*, Occasional Paper 70, New York, NBER, 1959; Juster, "Prediction and Consumer Buying Intentions," *American Economic Review*, May 1960; and Juster, "The Predictive Value of Consumers Union Spending-Intentions Data," in *Anticipations Data*. See also Peter De Janosi, "Factors Influencing the Demand for New Automobiles," *Journal of Marketing*, April 1959; Lawrence R. Klein and John B. Lansing, "Decision to Purchase Consumer Durable Goods," *Journal of Marketing*, October 1955; and Lansing and Stephen B. Withey, "Consumer Anticipations: Their Use in Forecasting Consumer Behavior," *Short-Term Economic Forecasting*, Princeton for NBER, 1955.

Thus any factor reflecting greater (lesser) optimism will tend to increase (decrease) an individual's optimism index. Holding other attitudes constant, households that report buying intentions or expect increased incomes, *ceteris paribus*, will have higher index scores and should purchase more than if they reported no buying intentions or expected decreased incomes. Similarly, households with the same expectations and intentions but feeling "better off than last year" will have higher scores than those feeling "worse off," and will make more purchases. In a previous publication I have labeled this viewpoint the "additivity" hypothesis, on the grounds that its proponents argue that any attitude, expectation, or intention reflecting optimism will, *ceteris paribus*, result in a more favorable disposition towards durable goods purchases, hence be associated with a greater amount of purchases.[2]

An alternative viewpoint is that attitudes, expectations, and intentions should be taken at face value. That is to say, expectations reflect the household's judgment about the future course of events external to the household; intentions, on the other hand, reflect tentative plans to undertake specified actions in the light of these judgments. Attitudes influence both expectations and the relation between expectations and intentions. In this view, purchases (actions) are directly related to (or predicted by) intentions, modified by the incidence of unforeseen developments. I have previously labeled this viewpoint the "contingent-action" hypothesis.

Both of these views relate to the interpretation of responses to survey questions about attitudes, expectations, or intentions. Proponents of both views would agree that these responses are more than a simple extrapolation of the respondent's experience. For if buying intentions or expectations could themselves be predicted from the underlying "real" factors—data on stocks of goods, income, income change, occupation, etc.—measurement of consumer anticipations would be unnecessary. Indeed, many economists regard anticipatory variables as essentially epiphenomena, in that they contain no useful information over and above that provided by knowledge of the household's real situation—its level and rate of change in income, demographic composition, and so forth. However, these economists would probably agree that the availability and timeliness of anticipatory data may well make them of considerable

---

[2] See *Consumer Expectations* and "Prediction and Consumer Buying Intentions." The terminology is not intended to convey the impression that any or all possible measures of sentiment carry equal weight or that none interact with others; it is designed to indicate that all measures of consumer sentiment that reflect optimism increase index scores and, hence, are associated with higher rates of purchase, while all measures that reflect pessimism have the reverse effect.

value in forecasting, even though they may be of no help in understanding or explaining behavior.

The test of these alternative viewpoints is clearly their ability to predict empirically observable phenomena. Appropriate tests are neither simple to construct nor straightforward in interpretation. Take the relation between expected change in income, actual change in income, intentions to buy durables, and actual purchases of durables. The additivity hypothesis predicts that expected change in income will be positively associated with purchases, holding buying intentions and actual income change constant, since the larger the expected income increase the more optimistic the household; hence, the greater the amount of purchases. On the other hand, the contingent-action hypothesis predicts a negative association between expected change in income and purchases, holding intentions and actual income change constant; the larger the expected income increase the less agreeably surprised the household and, hence, the smaller the amount of purchases relative to buying intentions. The third possibility is that no association exists between expected income change and purchases, holding actual income change and past income changes constant, because expected change is nothing more than some kind of weighted average of past changes.

EXISTING EVIDENCE

These hypotheses can be tested with data from the CU surveys. The relevant test indicates no statistically significant association between $\Delta \hat{Y}$ (expected change in income) and P (purchases of durable goods), holding $\hat{P}$ (buying intentions) and ΔY (actual change in income) constant. This conclusion may be correct; but it is quite possible that the observed relation is not significant because the actual relation is more complicated. For example, it is doubtful whether a single-valued estimate of expected change in income is an adequate measure of income expectations. If the structure of such expectations is best described by a probability distribution of the possible outcomes, both the mean and the dispersion of the distribution are surely relevant. A single-valued response is presumably to be interpreted as an estimate of the mean; but we obviously cannot be sure of this. Further, no good measure of dispersion is available.[3] As a consequence, the difference between actual change in income and my

---

[3] The basic data contain an estimate of the range of income changes regarded as "at all likely" by the respondent, but this estimate is not available for the time period on which I have concentrated in this monograph.

single-valued measure of expected change may not be an accurate and unbiased measure of income surprise; and if it is not, the data cannot discriminate among the alternative hypotheses.

Previous investigations into the relation between durable goods purchases and anticipatory variables have generally provided support for the proposition that at least some anticipatory variables are associated with purchases. In particular, buying intentions have always shown a strong statistical relation to purchases in reinterview studies. On the other hand, a relatively weak or nil association has generally been found between attitudes or expectations and purchases.[4] Tobin's results showed no significant net association between purchases and a number of variables representing attitudes and expectations; buying intentions were significantly related to purchases—actually, to the ratio of durables' purchases to income. A study of the attitude index constructed by Katona and Mueller showed a positive relation between attitudes and purchases net of intentions, income, and age for the second half of 1954, but no significant relation in the first half of 1955.[5] In an earlier multivariate study, using dichotomous variables for purchases and intentions to buy, Klein and Lansing could find no important behavioral association between the attitude-expectation variables and purchases; buying intentions, as is customarily the case, were significantly related to purchases. In another earlier study, Lansing and Withey found significant associations between various attitudes or expectations and purchases, but the empirical tests generally involved little netting out of the effects of other variables. Lansing and Withey also found that the difference between expected and actual income change (income surprise) was significantly related to purchases of automobiles, net of intentions to buy.

---

[4] The findings discussed here relate entirely to studies of behavioral differences among a cross section of households. Studies of time series relationships between purchases of durables and expectational variables have been based on relatively few observations; more important for my purposes, the time series studies have not generally attempted to test anticipatory variables net of a sophisticated (objective) model, largely because of the limited number of observations.

The available time series results are relatively more favorable to the hypothesis that attitudes and expectations, as distinct from intentions to buy, are related to purchase behavior. Both intentions ($\hat{P}$) and an index of attitudes (A) show significant relations to purchases in some of these studies. Depending on the time period and the particular choice of variables, it has been found that $\hat{P}$ is more important than A or vice versa (see Okun; and Mueller, "Consumer Attitudes—Their Influence and Forecasting Value").

[5] Mueller, "Effects of Consumer Attitudes on Purchases." In this study both purchases and intentions are modified yes-no constructs rather than dollar amounts, which may tend to weaken all the relationships somewhat.

In my judgment, existing studies of cross-section data have failed to provide convincing evidence in support of any of the hypotheses described above. On the whole, I read the evidence as suggesting that both attitudes and expectations are essentially unrelated to purchase behavior, while buying intentions are strongly related. It is also possible, however, that these studies have failed to uncover relationships that really exist. Research on these problems has been handicapped to some degree by the relatively small sample sizes available. It is true that six or seven hundred cases are ample for multivariate analysis involving a large number of explanatory factors. But this sample size becomes less satisfactory if some of the variables are important for the young but not for the old, or for households with buying intentions but not for nonintenders, or if combinations of extreme expectations or attitudes are much more important than moderate ones, etc.

On a priori grounds, there is some reason to suppose that the influence of anticipatory variables on purchase behavior is not the same for all subgroups in the population, that the effect of expectations and attitudes is not independent of buying intentions or other attitudes and expectations, and so on. My object in the next two chapters is to explore some of these possibilities at greater length. In the balance of this chapter I analyze the interrelationships among a number of measures bearing on attitudes or expectations, aggregate buying intentions, and aggregate purchases of durable goods. In the next chapter I summarize the results of an extensive multivariate regression analysis.

Purchases and Expectations

My first concern is with the relation between purchases and a cluster of variables that may be construed as either attitudes or expectations. The relation between purchases and an index of attitudes has been examined in a number of publications by Katona and Mueller.[6] The component parts of their attitude index have included variables such as expected and past change in financial well being, expectations about general business conditions, opinions about market conditions for durables (good-bad time to buy durables), expectations about price changes plus an evaluation of whether these changes are "to the good" or "to the bad," and buying intentions for durable goods. The index in their cross-section tests is

---

[6] For example, see *Consumer Attitudes and Demand*, pp. 51–61; and *Consumer Expectations*, p. 10.

essentially a scale of unweighted scores obtained from a trichotomous distribution of respondents by each of the component variables.[7] That is to say, respondents are assigned scores of 2, 1, or 0, depending on whether they expect to be "better off," "the same," or "worse off" in the future. If six such questions are included in the attitude index, scores may range from 12, corresponding to the maximum degree of optimism, to zero, the maximum degree of pessimism.

Two kinds of problems are involved in the construction of such indexes. First, at face value, some of the components are statements of expectations, i.e., they represent judgments about future events that may or may not happen. The relation between optimistic expectations and purchases may or may not involve a positive association, since, as pointed out above, the net correlation between the two may depend on the difference between expectations and outcomes. If so, optimistic expectations cannot be assigned a score until the corresponding outcome is known, although on the average the appropriate score for a household with optimistic expectations would be lower than that for a household with pessimistic expectations if buying intentions are held constant. On the other hand, statements that seem to represent judgments about future events may really be nothing more than a general indicator of optimism, in which case the Katona-Mueller procedure is the appropriate one.[8]

The second is the problem of weighting, both within and between the variables that constitute the index. A trichotomous (2,1,0) scale for better-same-worse or up-no change-down supposes that the difference between better-worse is just twice as large as that between better-same or worse-same, and that households reporting "better" are distributed at the upper end of the true optimism scale in the same way as those reporting "same" are distributed in the middle part of the scale and those reporting "worse" at the lower end of the scale. Similar assumptions must hold for comparisons across the variables that are index components.

For the most part the CU data do not lend themselves to a thorough examination of this range of problems, since the surveys were not designed for exhaustive tests of this nature. However, enough information is available to explore the question of whether the relation between attitudes (or expectations) and subsequent purchases is suitably described by a trichotomous classification of the sort just discussed.

---

[7] The rationale for the procedure is described in Katona and Mueller, *Consumer Expectations*.

[8] In practice this difficulty only arises when both buying intentions and expectations are components of the index, since the possible negative association between expectations and purchases would be observed only when intentions are held constant.

To examine the question of appropriate weighting I use responses to three variables that relate to household attitudes.[9] These questions concern (1) actual change in family income over the past year; (2) expected change in family income during the next year; (3) expected change in general business conditions during the next year. All three questions were accompanied by a five-point scale: large increase (improvement), small increase (improvement), no change, and small or large decreases (deterioration). In addition, respondents could check categories labeled "don't know," "too uncertain to guess," or "other," depending on the particular question.

Alternative methods of scoring these responses were utilized. In the first, 1 = increase (large or small) 2 = no change, and 3 = decrease (large or small); households with any other responses were excluded from the sample. Hence, the index scores range from a maximum of 9 (the most pessimistic group) to a minimum of 3 (the most optimistic group). For husband-wife households with heads between twenty-five and thirty-four years of age, the weighted average number of durable goods purchased by each index score group is shown in Table 27.

This index, composed of three trichotomous classifications within each of three variables, has a highly significant relation to purchases. A one-way analysis of variance on the cell means yields an F ratio of 3.49, significantly different from unity at the 0.01 level. The pattern of the cell averages is consistent—except for the group with an attitude score of 7—with the proposition that favorable or optimistic attitudes are associated with relatively high purchases; pessimistic attitudes, with relatively low purchases. While it is true that those with optimistic attitudes tend to have relatively higher incomes than those with pessimistic attitudes, adjusting for the influence of family income weakens but does not alter the above relationship; differences in purchases among attitude classes are still significant at the 0.01 level, holding family income constant. The

---

[9] For present purposes I bypass two problems of considerable importance. First, are these questions really about attitudes, or about expectations, or about simple fact? Secondly, are these the appropriate questions to use in order to construct the best possible index of attitudes? Both are obviously significant questions. I put them aside now because the question of appropriate weighting is important regardless of whether the index really measures fact, diffuse attitudes, or expectations, and regardless of whether the best index should include more or different components. These particular questions happen to be available, and I do not claim that they constitute an optimal combination of variables that relate to (or measure) household optimism or pessimism.

TABLE 27

COMPARISON OF THREE-POINT ATTITUDE INDEX SCORES AND MEAN DURABLE
GOODS PURCHASES

Number of Households (N)	Score on Attitude Index (A)	Weighted Average Number of Purchases (P̄)
942	3	1.951
1,191	4	1.827
1,421	5	1.718
830	6	1.582
509	7	1.636
138	8	1.536
71	9	1.507
5,102	Total	1.748

SOURCE: Basic data from Consumer Purchase Study, NBER.
NOTE: $F = 3.49$, significant at 0.01 level.

regression of the cell averages ($\bar{P}$) against the index scores (A), weighting the averages by the number of cases in each cell, yields

1.0
$$\bar{P} = 2.175 - 0.087A + u, \; r^2 = 0.0036$$
$$(0.020)$$

(with the variance of P taken as the actual variance for all 5,102 cases). There is no indication of nonlinearity in the pattern of residuals.

INDICATIONS OF NONLINEARITY

Next I revised the scoring system to include the five-point scale for each of the three variables, counting large increase as 1, small increase as 2, no change as 3, small decrease as 4, and large decrease as 5. By this count, scores will range from 3 (extreme optimism) to 15 (extreme pessimism). The distribution of households by attitude scores (A'), and mean purchases for each group, are shown in Table 28. Regressing purchases on these index scores,

2.0
$$\bar{P} = 2.439 - 0.086A' + u, \; r^2 = 0.0056$$
$$(0.016)$$

Some of the results here are not very different from those obtained for the simpler classification; for example, the F ratio for the cell means and the regression coefficient relating attitudes to purchases are about the same. A' explains more of the variance in P than does A, but this is largely because the A' scale itself has substantially greater variance than the A scale. However, the pattern of residuals in equation 2.0 clearly

147

TABLE 28

COMPARISON OF FIVE-POINT ATTITUDE INDEX SCORES AND MEAN DURABLE
GOODS PURCHASES

Number of Households (N)	Score on Attitude Index (A')	Weighted Average Number of Purchases (P̄)
2	3	4.000
48	4	2.542
253	5	2.217
924	6	1.887
1,130	7	1.762
1,162	8	1.669
764	9	1.569
489	10	1.744
192	11	1.526
88	12	1.511
22	13	1.545
17	14	1.118
6	15	0.667
5,102	Total	1.748

SOURCE: Basic data from Consumer Purchase Study, NBER.
NOTE: $F = 3.95$, significant at 0.01 level.

shows that a linear regression is inappropriate. An F test for non-linearity indicates that the relation between A' and $\bar{P}$ is significantly non-linear (0.05 level) even though all of the departures from linearity occur at the extremes, where the observations receive very little weight because the cell sizes are so small.

Partitioning of the sample by index score groups show the nonlinearity quite clearly. Linear regressions were calculated for the top four groups, the bottom four, and the five in the middle. The results are shown below (standard errors are in parentheses):

A' Index Scores	N	Mean Purchases	Regression Coefficient of $\bar{P}$ on A'	r^2
3, 4, 5, 6	1,232	1.993	−.386 (.107)	.010
7, 8, 9, 10, 11	3,737	1.679	−.038 (.030)	.0004
12, 13, 14, 15	133	1.429	−.209 (.166)	.012
All	5,102	1.748	−.089 (.016)	.006

There is fairly conclusive evidence that only rather extreme expected or experienced changes are associated with subsequent differences in purchases of durables. Differences in the degree of optimism among a group that includes only fairly optimistic households are associated with large and statistically significant differences in purchases; that is, extreme optimists purchase substantially and significantly more than moderate optimists. The same is true of the association between differences in the degree of pessimism among pessimists and differences in purchases, although these differences are not statistically significant partly because the sample contains relatively few pessimistic households. On the other hand, equally wide (index score) differences in the degree of optimism or pessimism among those who are moderately one or the other (or completely neutral) are not associated with significant differences in purchases despite the very large sample of households in this category; for the moderate group, differences in purchases per scale unit are only about one-tenth as large as for either of the other two groups. Thus, all of the observed significant relationship between index scores and purchases is apparently due to the behavior of households at the extremes of the index score range.

SOME NONLINEAR FUNCTIONS

Further experiments involved fitting some nonlinear functions to these data. Nonlinear scores were introduced by assigning values of 1, 4, 5, 6, and 9 in place of the 1, 2, 3, 4, 5 weighting underlying the Table 28 classification. The resulting scores range from 3 to 27. I then estimated the three regressions shown below:

3.0 $$\bar{P} = b_0 + b_1 T + u,$$

where T is the rescaled A' index.

4.0 $$\bar{P} = b_0 + b_1 T' + u,$$

where $T' = \left(\dfrac{1}{T} - \dfrac{1}{30 - T} \right).$

5.0 $$\bar{P} = b_0 + b_1 T + b_2 T^2 + b_3 T^3 + u.$$

Since equation 3.0 is simply a linear version of the nonlinear scale (1,4,5,6,9) described above, it is a moderately nonlinear regression. Differences in behavior among those expecting or experiencing large changes, small changes, no change, etc., are presumed to be adequately reflected by the ratios of 1:4:5:6:9; that is, those anticipating large increases are expected to show three times as much of a difference in purchases, relative to those anticipating small increases, as those antici-pating small increases relative to those anticipating no change or no change relative to small decreases. Regressions 4.0 and 5.0 reflect the general relationship shown above—that the larger and more consistent are anticipated changes the greater will be the difference in purchases. Equation 4.0 imposes symmetry, in that the shape of the curve from 0 to 15 (the scale midpoint) must be a reversed (mirror) image of the shape in the 15-to-30 range; equation 4.0 also imposes a slope of infinity at scale values of 0 or 30. Equation 5.0 does not contain any of these constraints; it could show that optimism and purchases are positively related in several segments of the scale and negatively related or unrelated elsewhere. The computed regressions, weighted by cell frequencies, are plotted in the top panel of Chart 13 and summarized below.

3.1 $\bar{P} = 2.608 - 0.0632\,T + u, r^2 = 0.0067$
$\phantom{3.1\ \ \bar{P} = }(0.011)$

4.1 $\bar{P} = 1.670 + 5.6467\,T' + u, r^2 = 0.0075$
$\phantom{4.1\ \ \bar{P} = }(0.910)$

5.1 $\bar{P} = 5.630 - 0.689\,T + 0.040\,T^2 - 0.0008\,T^3 + u, R^2 = 0.0093$
$\phantom{5.1\ \ \bar{P} = }(0.191)\quad\ \ (0.013)\quad\ \ (0.0003)$

Unweighted regressions based entirely on the cell means, shown below, are plotted in the lower panel of Chart 13.

3.2 $\bar{P} = 3.25 - 0.095\,T + u, r^2 = 0.746$
$\phantom{3.2\ \ \bar{P} = }(0.012)$

4.2 $\bar{P} = 1.818 + 5.845\,T' + u, r^2 = 0.840$
$\phantom{4.2\ \ \bar{P} = }(0.557)$

5.2 $\bar{P} = 5.517 - 0.668 + 0.039\,T^2 - 0.0008\,T^3 + u, R^2 - 0.850$
$\phantom{5.2\ \ \bar{P} = }(0.330)\ \ (0.024)\quad\ \ (0.0005)$

Chart 13 shows the computed regressions; the observed points are shown as heavy dots. The top panel (with the weighted regressions) shows the linear 3.1 equation and equation 4.1 plotted against the lower scale for attitude scores. The linear regression and equation 5.1 are plotted against the upper scale for attitude scores, and several of the observed points are redrawn as hollow dots. The two nonlinear functions are so close together in the middle range that it would be hard to tell them apart if both were shown on the same scale.

These results are quite interesting in several respects. First, both equations 4.1 and 5.1 constitute a significant improvement over equation 3.1; allowing for the loss of additional degrees of freedom, the F ratio for the additional explained variance is significant (0.05 level) for both weighted and unweighted versions of 4.0 and 5.0. Secondly, the differences between the weighted and unweighted regressions are rather striking.

CHART 13

Regressions of Purchases
on Attitude Index Scores

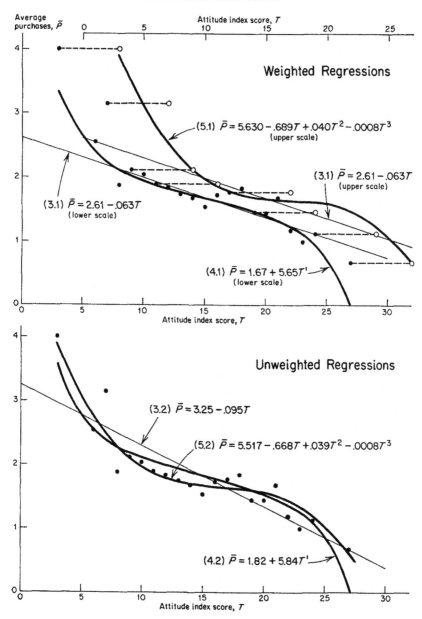

Average purchases, $\bar{P}$

Attitude index score, T

Weighted Regressions

(5.1) $\bar{P} = 5.630 - .689T + .040T^2 - .0008T^3$
(upper scale)

(3.1) $\bar{P} = 2.61 - .063T$
(upper scale)

(3.1) $\bar{P} = 2.61 - .063T$
(lower scale)

(4.1) $\bar{P} = 1.67 + 5.65T'$
(lower scale)

Attitude index score, T

Unweighted Regressions

(3.2) $\bar{P} = 3.25 - .095T$

(5.2) $\bar{P} = 5.517 - .668T + .039T^2 - .0008T^3$

(4.2) $\bar{P} = 1.82 + 5.84T'$

Attitude index score, T

Regression 3.2 (unweighted) has a much larger (absolute) slope than 3.1 (weighted) because the extreme observations, which are well above the regression line at the optimism end of the scale and well below at the pessimism end, are given equal weight instead of a weight proportional to cell size. But the apparent fit of the 4.0 and 5.0 regressions is practically the same in both weighted and unweighted versions. Since the weights are arbitrary in the sense that they reflect the particular sample being surveyed, the unweighted regressions may be more meaningful as a measure of behavior for households with different characteristics provided that sampling errors in the cell means can be neglected. The fact that these regressions show the same results either weighted or unweighted indicates to me that they probably constitute a substantially accurate description of the true relationship between these variables.

Finally, equation 5.0 turns out to have a slope of close to zero in the middle range of attitude scores in both weighted and unweighted versions. As noted before, this regression is not constrained at all. But it is almost symmetrical about the scale midpoint, with a slope that indicates very little difference in purchases over the range of attitude scores from about 12 to 20—out of a total range of scores from 3 to 27. Both nonlinear functions have flatter slopes than the linear function in the middle of the scale, indicating that differences in moderate attitudes are not as useful in discriminating between households with relatively high or low purchase rates as are differences in extreme attitudes.

The above results suggest that differences in purchase behavior are dominated by the behavior of households expecting or experiencing large changes. Further tests of this hypothesis can be constructed. I divided the sample into the same number of groups as in the A index (Table 27), but defined the groups on the assumption that expecting or experiencing large changes is the dominant cause of differences in purchases. Thus I lumped together all households that did not report any large actual or expected change on all three questions, and defined this group as having neutral attitudes. The remaining households were divided into three groups of optimists and three of pessimists,[10] depending on the relative balance of optimistic and pessimistic replies on the three questions; the cell averages resulting from this classification (A'') are shown in Table 29. The same tests were then run on this as on the Table 27 classification.

The classification in Table 29 is clearly superior to that in Table 27; the F ratio is about twice as high, and the A'' index scores explain about

[10] A small residual group that had a pattern of optimism-pessimism-no change was also included in the neutral group.

twice as much of the variance in P. The A'' classification is somewhat arbitrary; one can always improve (*ex post*) on a classification by rearranging households. Nonetheless, it is interesting to note the behavior of the "neutral" classification in Table 29. It comprises about three-quarters of all households in the sample, ranging all the way from those reporting

TABLE 29

COMPARISON OF NONLINEAR ATTITUDE INDEX SCORES AND MEAN DURABLE
GOODS PURCHASES

Number of Households (N)	Score on Attitude Index (A'')[a]	Weighted Average Number of Purchases $(\bar{P})$
84	3	2.880
572	4	2.002
231	5	1.922
3,980	6	1.697
74	7	1.635
134	8	1.395
27	9	1.000
5,102	Total	1.748

SOURCE: Basic data from Consumer Purchase Study, NBER.
NOTE: The regression equation is

$$\bar{P} = 2.912 - 0.202A'' + u,$$
$$(0.033)$$
$$r^2 = 0.0074,$$
$$F = 7.7,$$

significant at 0.01 level.

[a] Scores 3 (9) are extreme optimism (pessimism), comprising at least two very optimistic (pessimistic) responses and a third of optimism (pessimism) or no change.

Scores 4 (8) are moderate optimism (pessimism), comprising one very optimistic (pessimistic) and one moderately optimistic (pessimistic) response; the third response must be neutral or optimistic (pessimistic). A few cases comprising two very optimistic (pessimistic) responses and a third of some degree of pessimism (optimism) were also included here.

Scores 5 (7) are slight optimism (pessimism), consisting of one very optimistic (pessimistic) response, one moderately optimistic (pessimistic) response, and a third of some degree of pessimism (optimism).

Score 6 is the neutral category, consisting of all households with no extremely optimistic or pessimistic response on any of the three questions. A few (173) cases that do not fit anywhere else are also included in this category.

actual or expected small increases to those reporting actual or expected decreases on all three questions. It cannot be shown that households in this group are significantly heterogeneous with respect to purchase behavior. This (neutral) A'' subgroup can itself be readily divided into seven subgroups, using the classification basis of Table 27. Analysis of variance on the cell means yields an F ratio that is not significantly different from unity despite a sample size of close to four thousand cases.

CONCLUSIONS

On the whole, the evidence strongly suggests that extreme combinations of attitudes or expectations are significantly related to purchase behavior, while moderate ones are apparently either unrelated or quite weakly related. These relationships hold for a sample of relatively young families with the head of household between twenty-five and thirty-four years of age. It should be noted, however, that the same pattern was not found among older families with heads between forty-five and sixty-four. Here the data show that the relation between purchases and attitudes is relatively weak in general, although it is statistically significant for a linear classification like that in Table 28. Further, there is no evidence at all that a nonlinear classification such as A'' is an improvement. On the other hand, there is no indication that the neutral group in the A'' classification for these older families, comprising close to three thousand cases, is significantly heterogeneous, even though the range of (linear) attitude scores covers fully half the range of the entire classification. In sum, I would regard the evidence on the importance of extreme and the unimportance of moderate attitudes and expectations as strongly suggestive though not wholly conclusive.

Purchases, Buying Intentions, and "Surprises"

I turn now to the relation among expectations, outcomes, intentions, and purchases to find out whether surprises or whether expectations themselves seem to be associated with purchases net of intentions to buy. The relevant classifications can readily be constructed, since data are available on both expected and actual income change on a five-point scale ranging from large increase to large decrease. Thus, income surprise can be defined as actual change minus expected change ($\Delta Y - \Delta \hat{Y}$), where both ΔY and $\Delta \hat{Y}$ range from 5 (large increase) to 1 (large decrease).

According to the contingent-action hypothesis, discussed earlier in this chapter, $\Delta Y - \Delta \hat{Y}$ should be positively correlated with purchases, holding buying intentions constant; groups of households with relatively large (algebraic) values of $\Delta Y - \Delta \hat{Y}$ should buy more, relative to intentions, than those with relatively small values of the surprise variable. As pointed out earlier, this measure of income surprise may be seriously deficient, because it depends wholly on a single-valued estimate of $\Delta \hat{Y}$ and does not take any account of dispersion. According to the additivity hypothesis, also discussed earlier, optimistic expectations should be associated with relatively heavy purchases net of buying intentions.

Since increases in income would also tend to be associated with relatively heavy purchases, the additivity hypothesis can be interpreted as saying that $\Delta Y + \Delta \hat{Y}$ should be positively correlated with P net of intentions because both components have a positive association.[11]

SOME PREVIOUS EVIDENCE RE-EXAMINED

Extensive tests of the relation between purchases (P), buying intentions $(\hat{P})$, and expected and actual change in income ($\Delta \hat{Y}$ and ΔY, respectively) failed to uncover any systematic net relation between P and the income expectation variable. Some of my investigations in earlier stages of this project[12] had indicated that, using grouped data, an equation of the form

$$6.0 \qquad\qquad P/\hat{P} = b_0 + b_1 \Delta Y + b_2 \Delta \hat{Y} + u$$

yielded negative coefficients for $\Delta \hat{Y}$ and positive ones for ΔY that were statistically significant. Thus, favorable income surprises appeared to be associated with high purchases relative to intentions, as predicted by the contingent-action hypothesis, while expectations themselves were associated with low purchases relative to intentions, contradicting the additivity hypothesis. The same paper also reported that an equation of the form

$$6.1 \qquad\qquad P = b_0 + b_1 \hat{P} + b_2 \Delta Y + b_3 \Delta \hat{Y} + u$$

yielded nonsignificant coefficients for both expected and actual change in income. The negative results of equation 6.1 were attributed to the differential impact of expected income change on purchases by intenders and nonintenders. The argument essentially is that expectations about income change may be acting as a probability-scaling device for those reporting zero buying intentions, while for those reporting nonzero intentions probability-scaling is dominated by the income-surprise role of income expectations. Hence, the net relation between purchases and expectations is positive for nonintenders, negative for intenders, and may not show up at all if both groups are averaged.

This explanation for the negative results of equation 6.1 may well be correct. However, the results of equation 6.0 clearly do not support the contingent-action hypothesis, since they are largely, if not entirely, due to a *spurious correlation between expected change in income and the*

---

[11] Blending both hypotheses, one could argue that all three variables—ΔY, $\Delta \hat{Y}$, and $\Delta Y - \Delta \hat{Y}$—ought to have a positive association with purchases net of buying intentions. In this case the relation between $\Delta \hat{Y}$ and P becomes impossible to predict, since it depends on whether the optimism or the surprise effect of $\Delta \hat{Y}$ predominates.

[12] See "Prediction and Consumer Buying Intentions," pp. 604–617.

ratio of purchases to intentions.[13]   The spurious element in the correlation disappears if purchases and intentions are introduced as separate variables.[14]   Hence, the empirical tests that use group averages do not show any relation at all between the income change variables and purchases, net of buying intentions.

SOME EXPERIMENTAL RESULTS

The apparent lack of association between purchases and either expectations or surprises net of buying intentions is also shown by the results of an

[13] I am indebted to George Katona for calling my attention to the spurious relation between income surprise and the *ratio* of aggregate purchases to aggregate intentions.

[14] The explanation is as follows: We are interested only in whether households with pessimistic (optimistic) income expectations, holding income change constant, tend to buy more (less) relative to intentions than those with optimistic (pessimistic) expectations.   If this turns out to be the case, it follows that agreeable or favorable surprises are positively correlated with purchases, given intentions.   Let us take a group of households with varying expectations about income change, all of whom experienced no change in income.   Some fraction of each income expectation class will report buying intentions for each of the commodities on the list, and another fraction will report that they have purchased; the dependent variable in equation 6.0 is the ratio of these two fractions, summed across commodities.   That is,

$$P = \Sigma x, \text{ and}$$
$$\hat{P} = \Sigma p; \text{ hence}$$
$$P/\hat{P} = \Sigma x/\Sigma p.$$

But it has been shown above that, using the notation of Chapters 2 and 3, $x = pr + (1 - p)s$; hence

$$P/\hat{P} = \frac{\Sigma[pr + (1 - p)s]}{\Sigma p} = \frac{\Sigma pr}{\Sigma p} + \frac{\Sigma s(1 - p)}{\Sigma p}$$

Suppose, for the sake of argument, that income surprise is completely unrelated to behavior, i.e., that the contingent-action hypothesis has no empirical content.   It follows that r (the fraction of intenders who buy) and s (the fraction of nonintenders who buy) will be the same for each of the income-surprise classifications; for if income surprise has no relation to behavior, it clearly will not influence either r or s.   But from the formulation above it is apparent that even if both r and s are invariant with respect to income surprise, $P/\hat{P}$ will be related to surprise provided that p (the fraction of the group reporting intentions) happens to be related.   It is known (empirically) that p is correlated with income expectations; the more optimistic are expectations, the greater the fraction of households that report intentions.   But holding actual change in income constant, expectations must be inversely correlated with income surprise; hence, a group of households with unfavorable income surprises (i.e., optimistic expectations) will have a higher value of p than a group with favorable surprises (i.e., pessimistic expectations).   The higher the value of p, holding r and s constant, the lower the ratio of P to $\hat{P}$.   As a consequence, households with unfavorable income surprises will show relatively low ratios of P to $\hat{P}$ because of differences in p, even though r and s may be identical for all groups.

This spurious element is powerful enough to force a statistically significant negative correlation between ΔY and $P/\hat{P}$.   Suppose, for example, that $r = 0.5$ and $s = 0.2$, and that both r and s are the same for all commodities and also for optimists and pessimists.   Suppose further that p is 0.3 for optimists, 0.2 for pessimists.   Then $P/\hat{P}$ for optimists is $0.5 + [0.2(0.7/0.3)] = 0.97$; for pessimists, $P/\hat{P}$ equals

$$0.5 + [0.2(0.8/0.2)] = 1.30.$$

extensive multiple correlation analysis, using individual households as the unit of observation. The sample was stratified into relatively homogeneous life-cycle groups, since it seemed likely that these variables might have differential effects on behavior for young-old, married-unmarried, etc. The following regressions were computed for different life-cycle groups and for several of the intentions questions.

7.0 $\quad P = b_0 + b_1\hat{P} + b_2\Delta Y + b_3\Delta\hat{Y} + \cdots + u$

8.0 $\quad P = b_0 + b_1\hat{P} + b_2(\Delta Y - \Delta\hat{Y}) + \cdots + u$

7.1 $\quad P = b_0 + b_1\hat{P} + b_2\Delta Y + b_3\Delta\hat{Y} + b_4Z\Delta\hat{Y} + \cdots + u$

8.1 $\quad P + b_0 + b_1\hat{P} + b_2(\Delta Y - \Delta\hat{Y}) + b_3Z(\Delta Y - \Delta\hat{Y}) + \cdots + u$

In 7.1 and 8.1, $Z = 1$ when $\hat{P} = 0$; otherwise $Z = 0$.

On the whole, the results were discouraging. Significant positive coefficients for income surprise or significant negative coefficients for income expectations appeared on occasion; but so did significant coefficients with the opposite sign; and the bulk of the $\Delta\hat{Y}$ and $\Delta Y - \Delta\hat{Y}$ coefficients were nonsignificant despite sample sizes of typically over seven hundred cases. If any systematic pattern was present in these coefficients, it was not readily apparent.

The lack of positive results could be due to several factors. First, either expectations, or surprises, or both may in fact be unrelated to behavior. Secondly, a relation between expectations and purchases may actually exist but cannot be observed unless a good measure of the dispersion of expectations can be included in the analysis; as pointed out before, my data do not have such a measure. Finally, it is possible that the relation among expectations, outcomes, purchases, and buying intentions depends on the level of purchase probability associated with intentions.

As regards the second point, correspondence between analytical concepts and the survey variables used to represent them is not necessarily close. For example, we speak of testing to determine whether or not subjectively held expectations about income are related to purchase behavior. But we are not really testing income expectations per se; rather, the test variable consists of responses to a particular question bearing on income prospects. If the empirical results indicate that subjective income expectations are unrelated to purchases, it may mean only that the particular question is an unsatisfactory representation of expectations. Income expectations (properly measured) undoubtedly have a bearing on decisions to buy durable goods, although subjective statements concerning income prospects may not be useful.

In a way, empirical analysis of survey data is an attempt to find particular questions that are capable of being used as proxies for analytically relevant variables. In some cases it is known from theory that a factor is related to behavior in a particular way, and it is required to find out if the relationship is strong or weak, or whether it has the same influence in all groups. If survey responses that purport to represent this factor are tested and no relationship is found, the presumption is that the particular question is poorly suited. In other cases it may not be known whether the measuring rod is faulty or whether there simply is no important behavioral relationship present.

As regards the third point, let us now take a closer look at the relation between purchases, intentions to buy, and deviations between expected and actual income changes (surprises). It was argued above that those with favorable or agreeable surprises ought to purchase more, relative to intentions, than those with no surprises; by the same token, those with unfavorable or disagreeable surprises ought to purchase less, relative to intentions, than those with no surprises. The empirical evidence did not support the existence of such a relation, either because the relation in fact does not exist or because the measure of surprise is deficient.

But it can also be plausibly argued that these relations depend on the specification of a "buying intention," in particular, on the purchase probability associated with a statement of intention to buy. Suppose that two kinds of intentions are reported by households—those with a very high purchase probability and those with a probability that is relatively low but significantly higher than zero. Let us designate high-probability buying intentions as "standard" ($\hat{P}$), low-probability intentions as "contingent" ($\hat{P}_c$).[15] It could be argued that favorable surprises will have comparatively little influence on the *ex post* probability of purchase by households with standard ($\hat{P}$) intentions because *ex ante* purchase probability is already very high;[16] unfavorable surprises, on the other hand, might have a relatively strong effect on *ex post* purchase probability for these households. High *ex ante* purchase probability must have been predicated on a set of expectations, at least one of which (income expecta-

[15] The designation is the same as that used in Chapter 5 for a similar purpose.

[16] By *ex ante* purchase probability I have in mind the respondent's subjective purchase probability as of the survey date; by *ex post* purchase probability, his subjective probability as of the survey date if he had known with certainty the actual course of external events during the forecast period. Thus, *ex ante* and *ex post* purchase probability are the same for a respondent with perfectly certain expectations about external events all of which occur. *Ex ante* probability is greater than *ex post* probability for a respondent who experiences unfavorable (and unforeseen) changes; and the reverse is true for a respondent who experiences favorable (and unforeseen) changes during the forecast period.

tions) has resulted in disappointment for the group experiencing unfavorable or disagreeable surprises. As a consequence, some households in this group may be unable or unwilling to purchase in accordance with their *ex ante* probabilities.

A similar dichotomy may be present with respect to the relation among purchases, contingent intentions ($\hat{P}_c$), and surprises. Favorable surprises would be expected to have an especially strong influence on the purchases of households with contingent intentions, since the intentions themselves may have been contingent (*ex ante*) precisely because income had not been expected to change in as favorable a way as it actually did. On the other hand, the groups with no surprises or with unfavorable ones might be expected to show the normally weak relation between P and $\hat{P}_c$; since the relation is weak to begin with, those with unfavorable surprises may act in much the same way as those with no surprises.

In sum, the association between purchases and standard intentions may be significantly weaker for the unfavorably surprised than for others, and may be somewhat stronger for the favorably surprised than for the no-surprise group. The relation between purchases and contingent intentions may be especially strong for the favorably surprised, perhaps somewhat weaker for the unfavorably surprised than for the no-surprise group.

It must be remembered that these analytical concepts are very imperfectly represented by the data. In particular, lacking a measure of the dispersion of expectations, the surprise variable is suspect. As noted before, mean expected change, which is to be compared with reported change, is hardly an adequate description of expectations. Further, a clean distinction between standard and contingent plans, as these terms are used above, is lacking.

As a first step, I separated out households with agreeable or disagreeable income surprises and estimated regression coefficients for purchases on standard and contingent intentions. The results were more consistent than those found in previous tests, but the differences were rather small and hardly ever significant. Next, I adopted a more rigorous definition of surprise, requiring that households report unexpectedly favorable or unfavorable developments with respect to both income and general business conditions. The rationale is simply that one can be more confident that a given household actually received a pleasant surprise if it received more income than its (mean) expectation and also thought that business conditions had developed more favorably than anticipated at the survey date. Similarly, I felt more confident that a given household had been unpleasantly surprised if it received less income than expected and also thought that business conditions had developed less favorably than anticipated.

This redefinition of income surprise, and the hypotheses discussed above, were tested on two of the variant groups—the A sample, where $\hat{P}$ represents definite intentions to buy within a year and $\hat{P}_c$, probable-possible intentions to buy within a year; and the C sample, where $\hat{P}$ represents intentions to buy within a year, and $\hat{P}_c$ intentions to buy within a year if income were to be 10 to 15 per cent higher than expected. At first glance it looks as if the intentions questions asked of the C sample are ideally suited for this test because one of the intentions questions is specifically contingent on unexpectedly favorable income developments. However, the analysis suggests that the dichotomy between purchases and the effect of surprises for those with standard or contingent intentions should be most evident when $\hat{P}$ includes only those intentions with very high purchase probabilities and $\hat{P}_c$ includes only intentions with probabilities significantly higher than zero and lower than $\hat{P}$. As I have shown in Chapter 3, the purchase probabilities associated with $\hat{P}$ and $\hat{P}_c$ for the A group come much closer to this analytical definition than do the probabilities associated with $\hat{P}$ and $\hat{P}_c$ for the C group.

Table 30 summarizes correlations for husband-wife households with the head between twenty-five and thirty-four years of age. The top panel shows simple correlation and regression coefficients for the A and C samples and for the two samples combined. The middle panel has coefficients for a multiple regression in which $\hat{P}$ and $\hat{P}_c$ are assumed to be linearly related to P. Results of a multiple regression that allows for interaction between $\hat{P}$ and $\hat{P}_c$ (along the lines discussed in Chapter 5) are summarized in the bottom panel.

The data in Table 30 are rather encouraging, considering the hodge-podge of coefficients in the regression analysis described earlier. The linear multiple regressions are apt to be the most reliable, since the interaction term in the bottom panel tends to make the regression coefficients quite sensitive to sampling variations; because of the way in which surprise is defined, both the favorably surprised group (F) and the unfavorably surprised group (U) are quite small. The A sample shows results that are almost wholly in accord with the proposition that $\hat{P}$ is less closely associated with P for those with unfavorable surprises than for either of the other two groups, and that $\hat{P}_c$ is more closely associated with P for those with favorable surprises than for either of the other groups. The net regression coefficient of $\hat{P}$ in the two lower panels is substantially lower for the U group than for either of the other two groups; the differences are significant (0.05 level) for the linear multiple regression but not for the regression with interaction. The $\hat{P}$ coefficient is also higher for F than N in both panels, though the differences are relatively small and not statistically significant. The $\hat{P}_c$ coefficients behave equally well, being highest for the F group and lowest for the U group in both panels. All of the

TABLE 30

<small>Effect of Income Surprise on Relation Between Purchases and Intentions</small>

	A Sample Subgroups			*C Sample Subgroups*			*A + C Sample Subgroups*		
	F (84)	N (718)	U (50)	F (68)	N (682)	U (64)	F (152)	N (1400)	U (114)
				SIMPLE CORRELATIONS					
b_{12}	+.539ᵃ	+.396ᵃ	+.077	+.289ᵇ	+.384ᵃ	+.353ᵃ	+.358ᵃ	+.368ᵃ	+.254ᵃ
r^2_{12}	.130	.092	.003	.085	.146	.164	.084	.118	.071
b_{13}	+.228ᵇ	+.083ᵃ	−.010	+.066	+.043	+.089	+.127	+.066ᵃ	+.051
r^2_{13}	.048	.010	.000	.009	.002	.013	.021	.005	.004
				MULTIPLE CORRELATIONS					
$b_{12.3}$	+.564ᵃ	+.402ᵃ	+.093	+.308ᵇ	+.394ᵃ	+.349ᵃ	+.373ᵃ	+.374ᵃ	+.251ᵃ
$b_{13.2}$	+.255ᵇ	+.094ᵃ	−.031	+.095	+.082ᵇ	+.074	+.147ᵇ	+.086ᵃ	+.019
$R^2_{1.23}$	.190	.104	.005	.104	.153	.173	.112	.127	.072
				MULTIPLE CORRELATIONS WITH INTERACTION					
$b_{12.34}$	+.634ᵃ	+.561ᵃ	+.341	+.273ᵇ	+.460ᵃ	+.384ᵃ	+.414ᵃ	+.469ᵃ	+.308ᵃ
$b_{13.24}$	+.282ᵇ	+.150ᵃ	+.055	+.072	+.135ᵃ	+.105	+.169ᵇ	+.139ᵃ	+.061
$b_{14.23}$	−.046	−.092ᵃ	−.093	+.019	−.034	−.020	−.025	−.052ᵃ	−.030
$R^2_{1.234}$	.192	.120	.014	.105	.157	.174	.114	.134	.074

Source: Basic data from Consumer Purchase Study, NBER.

Note: The data cover husband-wife households with head of house between twenty-five and thirty-four years old. F represents the group of households experiencing favorable income surprise; N, no surprise; U, unfavorable surprise (see accompanying text for definition of income surprise). The sample size for each group is given in parentheses beside the symbol. A and C refer to buying intentions questions (see text). The variables are as follows:

$$X_1 = P = \text{purchases}$$
$$X_2 = \hat{P} = \text{standard intentions}$$
$$X_3 = \hat{P}_c = \text{contingent intentions}$$
$$X_4 = \hat{P}\hat{P}_c = \text{interaction of standard and contingent intentions}$$

ᵃ Significantly different from zero at 0.01 level, using t test.
ᵇ Significantly different from zero at 0.05 level, using t test.

differences in the middle panel are statistically significant; the $\hat{P}_c$ coefficient for the U group is significantly smaller than that for the other two groups in the lowest panel.

On the other hand, none of these generalizations holds for the C group. Here there are no significant differences among the $\hat{P}$ or $\hat{P}_c$ coefficients in any of the three groups, perhaps because the $\hat{P}$ variant in the C group is clearly not limited to high-probability buying intentions. In fact, the $\hat{P}$

variable for group C is not very different from the algebraic sum of $\hat{P}$ and $\hat{P}_c$ in group A, judging from data in Chapter 2.

When the two groups are combined, the pattern shown by the A group is somewhat diluted but still clearly apparent. The reliability of the combined results is greater because the sample sizes for the F and U groups are about twice as large as before; but the reliability is presumably reduced by the difference in the meaning of standard and contingent intentions in the two groups. In the bottom panel the U group has a lower $\hat{P}$ coefficient than either F or N, and the $\hat{P}$ coefficient is not significantly different for F and N. The F group has the highest $\hat{P}_c$ coefficient; the U group, the lowest.

An interesting sidelight on these results is the behavior of the interaction variable. Interaction between standard and contingent intentions appears to be stronger for households in the N group than for households in either of the groups experiencing surprises. This fact makes little difference for comparisons involving the U group, but it widens the difference between the $\hat{P}_c$ coefficients for the F and N groups whenever $\hat{P}$ takes on values greater than zero. The tabulation below illustrates the behavior of the $\hat{P}_c$ coefficients for the F and N groups, taking account of the interaction between this variable and $\hat{P}$. Data are shown for the A group and for the combined A and C groups.

	A Sample		A + C Samples	
Estimated value of $b_3\hat{P}_c + b_4\hat{P}\hat{P}_c$	F	N	F	N
When $\hat{P} = 0$	+.282	+.150	+.169	+.139
When $\hat{P} = 1$	+.236	+.058	+.144	+.087
When $\hat{P} = 2$	+.190	−.034	+.119	+.035

As can be seen, the estimated net influence of contingent intentions on purchases for the N group moves rapidly to zero as standard intentions increase, but continues to be strongly positive for the F group. It thus seems to be the case that the differential influence of $\hat{P}_c$ on P, as a function of the level of $\hat{P}$, is less important in the F group. Since this group starts out with a higher $\hat{P}_c$ coefficient when $\hat{P}$ is zero, it appears that $\hat{P}_c$ is always more important in the F than in the N group, but the differential is wider when $\hat{P}$ has relatively large values.

The last test relating to this problem involves estimating coefficients for a multiple regression designed as a more general test of the proposition that $\hat{P}$ (for the U group) and $\hat{P}_c$ (for the F group) have special significance relative to the N group. The regression has the form

9.0 $$P = b_0 + b_1\hat{P} + b_2\hat{P}_c + b_3Z\hat{P} + b_4Z_1\hat{P}_c + u$$

where P = purchases of durables

$\hat{P}$ = standard intentions to buy durables

$\hat{P}_c$ = contingent intentions to buy durables

$Z\hat{P}$ = standard intentions to buy durables

Z = 1 for U households and 0 for all other households

$Z_1\hat{P}_c$ = contingent intentions to buy durables

Z_1 = 1 for F households and 0 for all other households

TABLE 31

DIFFERENTIAL IMPORTANCE OF INCOME SURPRISE ON THE RELATION BETWEEN
INTENTIONS AND PURCHASES

$\hat{P}$	$\hat{P}_c$	$Z\hat{P}$	$Z_1\hat{P}_c$	r^2 or R^2	F Ratio for Added Variable(s)
		Net Regression Coefficients			
			A SAMPLE		
+.394	a	a	a	.0887	75.4[b]
a	+.088	a	a	.0103	8.8[b]
+.397	+.095	a	a	.1007	11.2[b]
+.405	a	−.245	a	.0908	2.0
a	+.080	a	+.137	.0139	3.1
+.407	+.089	−.186	+.116	.1056	2.3
		A AND C SAMPLES COMBINED			
+.312	a	a	a	.0970	161.4[b]
a	.070	a	a	.0062	10.3[b]
+.364	+.085	a	a	.1210	44.3[b]
+.367	a	−.121	a	.1128	29.1[b]
a	+.068	a	+.024	.0063	0.2
+.373	+.085	−.111	+.071	.1231	2.0

SOURCE: Basic data from Consumer Purchase Study, NBER.

NOTE: For the A sample, $N = 852$; for the A and C samples combined, $N = 1,666$. See accompanying text for explanation of table.

[a] Variable excluded from regression.

[b] Significantly different from unity at 0.01 level.

If the standard intentions of unfavorably surprised households are less closely associated with purchases than is the case for other households, b_3 should be less than zero. Similarly, if the contingent intentions of favorably surprised households are more closely associated with purchases than is the case for other households, b_4 should be greater than zero. Both b_1 and b_2 should be greater than zero, since both standard and contingent buying intentions are expected to be positively associated with purchases even if any special influences of $\hat{P}$ for the U group and $\hat{P}_c$ for the F group are held constant. The data are summarized in Table 31, with regressions shown for different clusters of variables.

The signs of all regression coefficients are in accord with the propositions advanced above, although the Z and Z_1 terms generally do not make a statistically significant contribution to explained variance. The most appropriate test of the two interaction variables consists of comparing the results for the last equation in each panel with those for the third. The difference between these two equations is that both interaction variables have been added to a regression including $\hat{P}$ and $\hat{P}_c$; in neither panel does the combined influence of the additional variables add significantly to the explanation of purchases. On the other hand, $Z\hat{P}$ makes a significant contribution to the explanation of P in the lower panel (compare the first and fourth equations), and some of the other variables involving Z or Z_1 are significant at the 0.10 level, though not at 0.05.[17]

Tests similar to those summarized in Table 31 were run on different subgroups with results that were not as consistent. In other subsamples one of the interactions generally had the expected sign while the other behaved erratically. For example, in the subsample composed of husband-wife households with the head between thirty-five and forty-four years old, the U group had a smaller coefficient for standard intentions than either the F or N group, as predicted. But this same group also had a larger coefficient for contingent intentions than either the F or N group, which makes no particular sense. The contingent-plan coefficient for F was in turn higher than that for N, in accordance with expectations. None of the differences in regression coefficients were large enough to be statistically significant.

Summary

The results of this investigation into the relation among durable goods purchases, buying intentions, expectations, and/or surprises can best be categorized as suggestive of possible relationships but inconclusive as to whether expectations and/or surprises are actually related to purchases net of buying intentions. A nonlinear relation between expectations and purchases seems quite probable, because extremely optimistic (pessimistic) expectations are associated with relatively high (low) purchases, while moderate optimism (pessimism) appears to be unrelated to purchases. Whether this relation continues to exist net of buying intentions has not been examined above, but evidence to be presented later suggests that

---

[17] These interaction terms do not show significance partly because each is relevant for only a small proportion of the total cases and, hence, each makes a relatively small contribution to total explained variance for all cases taken together. This seems to be the reason why the $Z\hat{P}$ term in the top panel increases explained variance by a trifling amount (compare the first and fourth equations) despite its very large absolute size. The $Z\hat{P}$ term is relevant in only 50 (of 852) cases. Although these cases fit considerably better when $Z\hat{P}$ is included along with $\hat{P}$, the remaining cases are affected only very slightly. The net improvement is not statistically significant.

some net relation between a nonlinear index of expectations and purchases may well be present. Still, even the best fit obtained (between purchases and a cubic equation involving expectations) was able to explain less than 1 per cent of the variance in purchases. This performance stands in sharp contrast to the 10 to 20 per cent of the variance in purchases typically explained by intentions to buy.

Similarly, I was unable to find any simple relation between surprises and purchases net of buying intentions. Experiments with a more stringent definition of favorable and unfavorable surprise suggested the possibility that favorable surprises, in interaction with contingent buying intentions, may be positively related to purchases; unfavorable surprises in interaction with standard buying intentions may be negatively related to purchases. The evidence in support of these propositions is a long way from being convincing. While the data generally yield regression coefficients with the appropriate signs, many of the coefficients are not significantly different from zero; the contribution to explained variance is generally very small; and in some cases, the data yield coefficients with inappropriate signs. Still, the results are sufficiently promising to suggest that these relations are worth further investigation and are potentially valuable in explaining consumer behavior.

Finally, the results in this chapter suggest that only rather large deviations from average experience are of much value in explaining the relation of expectations and/or surprises to purchase behavior. In effect, these results seem to indicate that households with very optimistic expectations or very favorable surprises are likely to buy considerably more durable goods, other things being equal; those with very pessimistic expectations or very unfavorable surprises, considerably fewer. These extreme cases are of little quantitative importance to the sort of data I have been using. The vast bulk of households in a cross section do not fall into either of these categories, and the evidence suggests that the necessarily modest differences in expectations or surprises among households in the middle group are not related to differences in behavior. But it does not follow that these variables play an equally minor role in the explanation of differences in purchase behavior over time. Although only a small (absolute) number of households experience either extreme expectations or surprises during any one period, the time series variance in the number of such households is likely to be considerable. This fact, coupled with the possibility of a quantitatively important association between extreme expectations or surprises and purchases, may mean that an important part of the time series variation in purchases is associated with changes in the proportion or number of households in these extreme categories.

CHAPTER 7

Multivariate Analysis of Aggregate Purchases and Buying Intentions[1]

Introduction

IN THE preceding chapters a selected set of relations between consumer purchases of durable goods and consumer anticipations has been examined. The focus has been mainly on analysis of intentions to buy durable goods: in Chapters 2, 3, and 4 an interpretation of buying intentions as representing judgments about subjective purchase probability was developed and tested; in Chapter 5, the possibility was investigated that the strong statistical association between aggregate intentions and purchases was due to the common influence of other factors; and in Chapter 6, the relations among intentions, expectations, surprises, and purchases were explored.

The data available in the Consumers Union surveys permit a test of the simultaneous influence of a number of factors on household decisions to purchase durable goods. It has been argued earlier that buying intentions reflect judgments about *ex ante* purchase probability for a given forecast period. A wholly accurate measure of purchase probability would in principle be perfectly correlated with subsequent purchases except for the influence of events that were either not foreseen or imperfectly foreseen by the respondent. I designate such unforeseen events as intervening variables. On the other hand, the set of factors underlying the household's (wholly accurate) estimate of purchase probability would have no net relation to purchases, their influence being accounted for in purchase probability. I designate such factors as initial-data variables.

Consider a multivariate model in which household purchases during period t are a function of (1) *ex ante* purchase probability measured at the beginning of t; (2) nonanticipatory, or objective, variables, such as household income, stocks of durable goods, etc., measured at the beginning of t; (3) anticipatory variables, such as expectations about income measured at the beginning of t; and (4) intervening variables, reflecting partly or wholly unforeseen events that occur during period t. This model would show that only *ex ante* probability and intervening events—variables in the first and fourth categories—have a net association with purchases.

---

[1] The basic line of analysis pursued in this Chapter—that an interesting test of the probability hypothesis would contrast the influence of buying intentions on the partial correlation of purchases with initial-data variables, on the one hand, and with intervening variables on the other—grew out of a suggestion by Jacob Mincer. The dearth of intervening variables that could be measured led to construction of the classification variables for house-buying intentions and housing purchases.

The initial-data variables in the second and third categories would be completely unrelated to purchases net of purchase probability. And intervening variables would be more strongly associated with purchases, holding initial-data variables constant, than otherwise. For example, a given change in income would have more influence on purchases if expected change in income were held constant, since the intervening variable "unexpected change in income" is more accurately measured by the difference between actual and expected change than by actual change alone.

The relation of both purchases and purchase probability to the expectations, attitudes, and financial situation of the household is relevant for the analysis of consumer behavior quite aside from the question of whether the latter variables are useful for prediction. The probability variable is, after all, simply a convenient short cut for measuring the influence of the underlying factors associated with purchases; the short cut may or may not be the most accurate way to make predictions about the future, but it tells us nothing per se about the basic reasons for differences in behavior. However, an analysis of factors associated with purchase probability ought to yield insights into the fundamental determinants of behavior. And it may turn out that the probability short cut has inherent limitations that make it desirable to build a predictive model incorporating the major determinants of purchase probability but not the probability variable itself.[2]

Given a precise measure of purchase probability, the above analysis suggests that initial-data variables will be associated with both purchases and purchase probability but that the association with probability will be stronger. In the absence of intervening events, initial-data variables would show the same association with both purchases and probability because the two would be identical. If intervening events have any importance, actual purchases will differ from purchase probability, and the initial-data variables will be less strongly associated with the (*ex post*) variable purchases than with the (*ex ante*) variable purchase probability.

[2] The above analysis fits the general framework developed by Franco Modigliani and outlined in the introduction to "*The Quality and Economic Significance of Anticipations Data*, Princeton for NBER, 1960. Modigliani speaks of an expectation function, a planning function, and a realization function. The planning function relates purchase probability (buying intentions or plans) to the initial-data variables. It answers the question "why do households have certain probabilities or plans?" The realization function relates purchases to initial probability and intervening variables. It answers the question "why do households purchase what they do, given their plans and the difference between expected and actual events?" The initial-data variables, in principle, are redundant in a realization function because such variables are presumably embodied in purchase probability.

On the other hand, intervening variables will be associated with purchases while having no direct relation to purchase probability.

Data Limitations

From preceding chapters it is quite clear that the data do not contain a precise measure of *ex ante* purchase probability. The household's reported intentions to buy durables—basically a classification into dichotomous (or trichotomous) probability groups—constitute a proxy variable. Not only is the intentions variable discontinuous while probability itself is not, but it is known that many of the intender-nonintender classifications are inefficient in the sense that some intenders appear to have lower purchase probabilities than some nonintenders.[3] As a consequence, use of buying intentions as a proxy for purchase probability will mean that a number of these relations may either not be observable at all, or will be weaker than predicted. For example, initial-data variables might not be wholly redundant to probability as measured by intentions, although these variables ought to be more strongly associated with intentions than with purchases. Similarly, intervening variables may not be more strongly associated with purchases when initial-data variables are held constant, nor may intervening variables be independent of buying intentions. It would be supposed, however, that intervening variables ought to be more strongly associated with purchases than with intentions.

Description of Variables

Fifteen independent variables are used in the multivariate regression analysis. Seven are classified as initial-data variables, five as intervening variables,[4] and three are the buying-intentions variables used to represent purchase probability. Two dependent variables are examined—durable goods purchases and intentions to buy durable goods, aggregated for each household. The designation and description of these variables follows.

INDEPENDENT VARIABLES

Objective Initial-Data Variables

$X_1 = Y$ Normal family income before taxes, scaled:

under $3,000 = 2.0	$7,500 − $9,999 = 8.8
$3,000–$3,999 = 3.5	$10,000–$14,999 = 12.5
$4,000–$4,999 = 4.5	$15,000–$24,999 = 20.0
$5,000–$7,499 = 6.2	$25,000 and over = 40.0

[3] See above, Chapters 2 and 3.
[4] With one exception, all the intervening variables represent events that are only partly unforeseen (see below).

Normal income is essentially the income bracket reported for a period that includes the forecast period (April 1958–October 1958), with some adjustment in particular cases.

The data indicate the bracket into which actual family income fell for 1957 (from the April 1958 questionnaire) and the bracket for actual 1958 income (from the October 1958 reinterview survey). It is also known whether these income figures were regarded as being "unusually high" or "unusually low." In cases where the income bracket was the same in both surveys and was not regarded as unusually high or low in either case, I assigned the bracket midpoint as the normal income level. In cases where the bracket differed and one year was unusual while the other was not, I assigned the income for the normal year as the normal income. In cases where the bracket was the same and both years were unusually high (low) I took the midpoint of the next lower (higher) bracket as normal income provided that the family expected a decrease (increase) in income for 1959. In cases where the bracket differed but both years were regarded as normal I used 1958 income. Finally, in cases where the reported pattern of income, unusually high or low income, and income expectations did not make any sense, the household was excluded from the sample.

$X_2 = \Delta L_{-1}$ Change in liquid assets during the twelve months ending April 1958, scaled:

increase	$= +1$
no change	$= 0$
decrease	$= -1$

$X_3 = \Delta Y_{-1}$ Change in family income over the twelve months ending April 1958, scaled:

increased substantially (20% or more)	$= 6$
increased somewhat (5 to 20%)	$= 4$
no change	$= 3$
decreased somewhat (5 to 20%)	$= 2$
decreased substantially (20% or more)	$= 0$

$X_4 = S'$ Durables stock adjustment. Respondents were asked in April 1958 whether any of a list of nine items in their durable goods inventory "need to be replaced." It is assumed that the weighted sum of such responses (autos $= 4$, other durables $= 1$ each) represents a difference between the household's actual and desired stock of durable goods.

The procedure is tantamount to assuming that a durable that "needs replacing" has a value equal to zero, one that does not need replacing a value equal to original cost. The S' variable is obviously a crude measure of desired change in current inventory, but is the best measure available from the CU survey.

Anticipatory Initial-Data Variables

$X_5 = \hat{E}$ Index of the household's April 1958 expectations with regard to changes in their own income, Y, and changes in general business conditions, B. The data in Chapter 6 suggest that only extreme expected changes are related to behavior, hence $\hat{E}$ is scaled:

expect substantial increase (improvement) in both Y and B or substantial increase in one and moderate in the other	$= 2$
expect substantial decrease (deterioration) in both Y and B or substantial decrease in one and moderate in the other	$= 0$
all other combinations	$= 1$

$X_6 = 0$ The household's April 1958 opinion about current buying conditions for durable goods, scaled:

good time (for respondent) to buy durables	$= 2$
pro-con, other, don't know	$= 1$
bad time (for respondent) to buy durables	$= 0$

$X_7 = \hat{E}_5$ The household's April 1958 expectations about financial prospects for a five-year forward period, scaled:

expect substantial improvement	$= 2$
expect moderate improvement	$= 1$
all other responses	$= 0$

This variable was originally reported on a nine-point scale—expect substantial, moderate, or slight improvement (deterioration), expect no change, too uncertain to say, and other. Preliminary tests indicated that the truncated scale shown above was more closely associated with behavior, possibly due to the erratic behavior of the very small cell size groups that were combined into the "all other" category. (About two-thirds of the sample fall into the 2 and 1 scales shown above.) In addition some *ex post* (October 1958) data were used to assign scales, although the basic scale is *ex ante* (April 1958). Households that expected "substantial improvement" in April 1958 but only "slight improvement" or worse in October 1958 were assigned scales of 0 rather than 2, while those expecting "moderate improvement" in April 1958 and "no change" or worse in October 1958 were assigned scales of 0 rather than 1. These shifts must be due either to the respondent's misunderstanding of the question in the April survey or to a drastic downward revision in the respondent's long-term financial expectations. In my judgment, the number of cases with a legitimate downward revision of this magnitude would be trivial, hence it was assumed that all such cases represented misinterpretation of the original question.

Intervening Variables

$X_8 = \Delta Y$ Change in family income during the forecast period, scaled:

substantial increase (20% or more)	= 6
moderate increase (5 to 20%)	= 4
no change	= 3
moderate decrease (5 to 20%)	= 2
substantial decrease (20% or more)	= 0

$X_9 = \Delta Y_t$ Transitory income during the forecast period, scaled:

positive transitory	= +1
no transitory	= 0
negative transitory	= −1

This variable was constructed from several pieces of information. Households classified as having a positive (negative) transitory income component are those reporting that their incomes were "higher (lower) due to unusual circumstances" (see the description of normal income, X_1, above). Some exceptions were made, based on a comparison of responses to the transitory income question with responses to questions dealing with 1957 and 1958 income, April 1958 income expectations, and October 1958 income expectations. For example, households reporting that their April–October income was "unusually" high, that 1958 income was higher than in the previous year, and (in October 1958) that they expected their incomes to rise even more during the coming year, were reclassified as having a zero transitory income component, since these households apparently could not distinguish between "unusually higher" and "higher." Similarly, households reporting that their incomes were unusually low but expecting further declines were reclassified as not having transitory income components during the forecast period.[5]   Households reporting wholly inconsistent information were eliminated completely from the sample, as noted above in the description of normal income.

$X_{10} = H_{01}$ Unanticipated purchase of a house during the forecast period, scaled:

> households not reporting intentions to buy a house
> in April 1958 but purchasing between April
> and October 1958 $= 1$
> all other households $= 0$

$X_{11} = H_{10}$ Unfulfilled April 1958 intentions to buy a house, scaled:

> households reporting intentions to buy a house in
> April 1958 but not purchasing between April
> and October 1958 $= 1$
> all other households $= 0$

$X_{12} = H_{11}$ Anticipated purchase of a house during the forecast period, scaled:

> households reporting April 1958 intentions to buy
> a house and purchasing between April and
> October $= 1$
> all other households $= 0$

The three housing variables constitute different combinations of April 1958 house-buying intentions and purchases between April and October 1958.   The April 1958 survey asked whether respondents "intended to buy a house during the next twelve months."   The October 1958 survey asked whether respondents had purchased a house during the April-October period.   Four possible combinations exist:

Intended to buy and purchased, designated H_{11}
Intended to buy and did not purchase, designated H_{10}
Did not intend to buy and purchased, designated H_{01}
Neither intended to buy or purchased, designated H_{00}.

---

[5] A later questionnaire sent to this same group (not analyzed in the current monograph) indicated clearly that many households reporting such transitory income changes were really talking about normal raises or about reductions in current income due to retirement.   Hence, this kind of misinterpretation was known to be fairly common before it was decided to undertake the reclassification described above.

The H_{00} combination is omitted from the list of independent variables to avoid overdetermining the system.

The first three combinations represent situations that, to some degree, reflect the impact of intervening events—even the H_{11} classification. The mean *ex ante* probability of purchasing a house for those responding "yes" to the question about house buying plans (the H_{10} and H_{11} groups) is obviously less than unity; and *ex ante* probability is likely to have been higher for buyers (H_{11}) than for nonbuyers (H_{10}). *Ex post*, none of the households in H_{10} purchased; hence, unfavorable intervening events must have occurred in some of these households. *Ex post*, all of the households in H_{11} purchased; hence, favorable intervening events must have occurred here, on the average. In a similar vein, those in H_{00} and H_{01} must have had a relatively low (but higher than zero) mean *ex ante* probability of purchasing a house, and it is likely that purchase probability was higher in H_{01}. *Ex post*, everyone in the H_{01} group purchased; hence, favorable intervening events must have been common. In the H_{00} group, on the other hand, unfavorable intervening events must have occurred on balance, since no housing purchases were made in that group. Further, because mean *ex ante* probability must have been higher for house buyers that reported intentions, favorable intervening events must have been more important in H_{01} than in H_{11}. Similarly, because *ex ante* probability must have been higher in H_{10} than in H_{00}, unfavorable intervening events must have been more important in the former than in the latter group.

Buying Intentions Variables

$X_{13} = \hat{P}$ April 1958 "standard" intentions to buy durable goods, aggregated for each household and scaled from 0 to 9. (See Chapter 6, "Introduction," for description of the aggregation.)

$X_{14} = \hat{P}_c$ April 1958 "contingent" intentions to buy durable goods, aggregated for each household and scaled from 0 to 6. (See Chapter 6, "Introduction," for description of the aggregation.)

$X_{15} = Z\hat{P}_c$ April 1958 contingent intentions to buy durable goods, aggregated for each household and scaled the same as $\hat{P}_c$ if $\hat{P} = 0$, scaled zero if $\hat{P} > 0$.

That is, X_{15} is the same as X_{14} multiplied by the factor Z, where

$Z = 1$ when $\hat{P} = 0$

$Z = 0$ when $\hat{P} > 0$

DEPENDENT VARIABLES

$Y_1 = P$ Purchases of durable goods between April and October 1958, aggregated for each household and scaled from 0 to 9. (See Chapter 6 for description of the aggregation.)

$Y_2 = \hat{P}$ April 1958 standard intentions to buy durable goods; this variable is identical to the independent variable X_{13}.

Other variables in addition to those listed above are utilized in another set of multivariate regressions discussed in Appendix A, where the focus is on the net relation between durable goods purchases and a large number of anticipatory and objective initial-data variables. Included in this analysis are a number of interactions designed to test the proposition that initial-data variables help to scale purchase probability for nonintenders while being essentially redundant for intenders.

Sample Stratification

Separate regressions were estimated for a number of subgroups. As noted earlier, the Consumers Union sample was originally split into five randomly selected subgroups, each of which received a different set of questions about intentions to buy. Four of the five groups contain both a standard and a contingent intentions variable, but one of these variant questions was systematically misinterpreted and has never been fully processed.[6] Regressions are estimated for three of the original subgroups, with the buying intentions variables obtained from responses to the following questions.

Subgroup A: Standard intentions to buy $(\hat{P})$—"definitely intend to buy within twelve months"

Contingent intentions $(\hat{P}_c)$—"probably or possibly may buy within twelve months"

Subgroup B: Standard intentions $(\hat{P})$—"intend to buy within 6 months"

Contingent Intentions $(\hat{P}_c)$—"intend to buy later"

Subgroup C: Standard intentions $(\hat{P})$—"intend to buy within twelve months"

Contingent intentions $(\hat{P}_c)$—"will buy within 12 months if income is 10–15 per cent higher than expected"

In addition, the sample is stratified by demographic status, designated by

---

[6] See Chapter 2, above, and Juster, *Consumer Expectations, Plans, and Purchases: A Progress Report*, Occasional Paper 70, New York, NBER, 1959.

subscript as follows: 1, husband-wife households, head between 25 and 34; 2, husband-wife households, head between 35 and 44; 3, husband-wife households, head between 45 and 64; 4, husband-wife households, head 65 and over; and 5, all other households.

Only the first three demographic groups are analyzed below, largely because the remaining groups contain relatively few households; hence, a total of nine subgroups are included in the analysis (A_1, A_2, A_3, B_1, B_2, B_3, C_1, C_2, and C_3). The demographic stratification is used in preference to the construction of independent variables for age and marital status because it seemed desirable to test the proposition that the influence of many factors, especially anticipatory ones, is not the same for households with relatively young and relatively old heads. For example, it has been argued by many that wealth (discounted future income plus net worth from property) is a more important determinant of consumption behavior than is current income.[7] If so anticipatory variables, which are likely to be more highly correlated with wealth than with current income, ought to be of greater significance in the purchase decisions of younger than of older households, and vice versa for variables that reflect the current financial situation.

Before proceeding to discuss the hypotheses under test, a brief digression on degrees of freedom is in order. The regressions presented below and in Appendix A were not the first regressions computed during this investigation; as a consequence, some degrees of freedom have been used up. Some of the variables represent the survivors from a more comprehensive list originally tested on one subgroup. Since nine subgroups are available, the results for the other subgroups represent legitimate tests rather than a recomputation omitting variables known to be nonsignificant. In other cases a particular variable was tested with one scale, the scale redesigned on the basis of the results, and the regression recomputed. The redesigned variable is bound to show the appropriate result in the test subgroup, but constitutes an hypothesis to be tested in other subgroups.

On the whole, it is fair to say that the empirical results presented in the text of this chapter are less suspect, because of preliminary investigation, than are the regressions shown in Appendix A. At a fairly late stage in the project the focus of the regression analysis was altered to concentrate

---

[7] This view, or variations of it, underlies much of the recent theoretical and empirical research on consumer behavior. See, for example, Milton Friedman, *A Theory of the Consumption Function*, Princeton for NBER, 1957; and Franco Modigliani and R. E. Brumberg, "Utility Analysis and the Consumption Function" reprinted in K. K. Kurihara (ed.), *Post-Keynesian Economics*, New Brunswick, N.J., Rutgers University Press, 1954.

on the differential impact of buying intentions on the association between purchases and initial-data variables, on the one hand, and purchases and intervening variables, on the other. Also, it was decided to compute regressions with both purchases and standard buying intentions as dependent variables, using a common set of independent variables. The procedure involved selecting (on the basis of the results in Appendix A) the initial-data variables most consistently related to purchases, then adding a number of intervening variables—notably, the dummies for house-purchases and house-buying intentions. As a consequence, the results in this chapter represent tests of hypotheses in the strict sense except that the initial-data variables have been selected partly on the basis of a preliminary investigation.

Hypotheses Under Test

The hypotheses being tested mainly constitute implications of the basic thesis of the monograph—that buying intentions are a reflection of the household's subjective purchase probability, and that the distribution of these purchase probabilities is a continuous function. As already noted, initial-data variables are expected to be more closely related to buying intentions than to purchases, intervening variables are expected to be more closely related to purchases than to intentions, and the introduction of intentions into a regression of purchases on variables in both categories should reduce the net influence of initial-data variables more than that of intervening variables.

It has been noted above that intentions are a relatively crude proxy for purchase probability.[8] The consequences of this fact are worth examining more carefully. For illustration, take the relation between family income and purchases. If purchase probability is not standardized, income and purchases will be positively related, since families with relatively high incomes tend to buy more, other things equal, than families with relatively low incomes. But if purchase probability is held constant, there is no a-priori reason why income should have any net influence on purchases; high-income families will tend to have higher purchase probabilities than low-income ones; and the full effect of income differences ought to be included in probability *differences because families* know their incomes at the time they report probabilities. Income might continue to show a net influence on purchases if favorable intervening events were more common in relatively high-income families, but even here income and pur-

---

[8] See "Data Limitations," above.

chases would show no net association provided variables reflecting these intervening events were also included in the analysis.

However, suppose that a precise measure of purchase probability is not available. Buying intentions serve as a proxy for probability in that intenders have higher mean probabilities than nonintenders. But further suppose that, in the lexicon of Chapter 3, relatively high-income households tend to have systematically higher cut-off probabilities than relatively low-income ones, given the intentions question, or that they have higher mean probabilities in the segment of the distribution either above or below the probability cut-off. In that case intenders and/or nonintenders would have higher mean purchase probabilities if their incomes were high than if they were low; this fact would be reflected in the regression coefficient of income, holding buying intentions constant. Income will be associated with purchases, net of buying intentions, because income is serving as a proxy for purchase probability even after account is taken of the intentions variable. In effect, any variable that tends to be correlated with purchase probability, *given* buying intentions, will tend to show (empirically) a net association with purchases for that reason.

The hypotheses underlying the housing variables can now be discussed more precisely. As noted earlier, three dummy variables related to housing are employed in the analysis; these are designated H_{01} (unanticipated housing purchases), H_{10} (unfulfilled house-buying intentions), and H_{11} (anticipated housing purchases). The regression coefficient of each of these variables measures the difference in average purchases between households in each of the respective housing categories and those in the fourth (neither intended to buy nor purchased a house). Ignoring purchase probability or its proxy, buying intentions, it is clear that those purchasing a house are likely to buy relatively many durable goods whether or not they reported house-buying intentions. As the data will show, those anticipating the housing purchase tend to buy more durables than other house buyers, possibly because a lengthier period of preparation facilitates a more rapid acquisition of the durables with which to furnish and equip the house.[9] It is not evident, a priori, whether those reporting house-buying intentions but not purchasing will tend to buy more durable goods than those doing neither, although it appears from the results that they typically do.

When buying intentions are introduced into the analysis, it is expected that the regression coefficient of H_{01} will be positive; that of H_{10}, negative.

---

[9] This difference in purchases might well disappear if a longer forecast period had been employed in the analysis, say twelve months instead of six months.

On the average, those in H_{01} must have experienced intervening events favorable to purchases; those in H_{10}, unfavorable intervening events; and the coefficients of H_{01} and H_{10} will reflect these influences. By the same token, it appears that households in the H_{11} group should buy more durables net of intentions than those neither intending to buy nor buying a house, since they must, on average, have experienced favorable intervening events. Hence, the regression coefficient of H_{11} should also be positive. But this group should buy fewer durables relative to intentions than those in H_{01}, since they must have experienced favorable intervening events to a lesser degree. Consequently, the regression coefficient of H_{11}, net of buying intentions, should be smaller than that of H_{01}.[10]

Finally, the buying-intentions variable constitutes a measure of mean *ex ante* purchase probability for durable goods: more precisely, the regression coefficient of buying intentions is an estimate of the mean difference in *ex ante* purchase probability between intenders and nonintenders; in the terminology of Chapter 3, the regression coefficient of intentions is an estimate of $r' - s'$. The model predicts that this regression coefficient will be relatively large when the cut-off probability associated with the intentions question is relatively high, given the skew in the underlying probability distributions. (See Chapter 3, especially the analysis of the data in Tables 9 and 10.)

Description of Basic Data Tables

The basic correlation and regression data are shown in Tables 42–44, at the end of this chapter; these tables relate to the respective subgroups designated above as $A_1, \ldots, C_3$. Independent variables are listed in the stub in order of their introduction: objective initial-data variables

---

[10] This conclusion follows from the facts that households in H_{11} had a higher *ex ante* probability of house purchase than those in H_{01} and that *ex post*, both groups purchased. It should be noted, however, that the analysis holds only on the assumption that the mean *ex ante* probability associated with *durable goods* buying intentions is the same in all housing groups. As will be discussed, the assumption probably does not hold.

To anticipate the argument, mean *ex ante* purchase probability (for durables) among intenders and nonintenders is not likely to be the same for households in the different housing categories. Those intending to buy and buying a house presumably had a higher mean *ex ante* probability of purchasing the *house* than those either intending to buy and not purchasing or those not reporting intentions but purchasing. To the extent that the durable goods buying intentions of H_{11} households are contingent on the purchase of a house, it seems reasonable to assume that the mean *ex ante* probability associated with the durable goods buying intentions of H_{11} households is also likely to be higher than for others. That is to say, intenders in this group are likely to have higher mean *ex ante* probabilities, given their buying intentions, than those in either H_{10} or H_{01}. Statistically, this fact would be reflected in a positive regression coefficient for the H_{11} dummy variable, other things equal.

$(Y,\Delta L_{-1},\Delta Y_{-1},S')$ first, then anticipatory initial-data variables $(\hat{E},O,\hat{E}_5)$, then intervening variables $(\Delta Y,\Delta Y_t,H_{01},H_{10},H_{11})$, and finally, buying-intentions variables $(\hat{P},\hat{P}_c,Z\hat{P}_c)$. Columns 1 through 3 show net regression coefficients with standard buying intentions $(\hat{P})$ as the dependent variable; in column 1 coefficients are shown for the four objective initial-data variables; in column 2, for the three anticipatory and the four objective variables; and in column 3, for the five intervening variables plus the objective and anticipatory initial-data variables. These three regressions are designated as $X_1, \ldots ,X_4, X_1, \ldots ,X_7$, and $X_1, \ldots ,X_{12}$, respectively, corresponding to the variables included in each. The significance levels for regression coefficients are indicated by asterisks—$** = 0.01$ level; $* = 0.05$ level.[11] The constant term and the multiple correlation coefficient are shown at the bottom of the table.

In addition to the net regression coefficients, F ratios are shown both for groups of variables and for some individual variables; all these F ratios are net of all variables included in the respective regression equations. In the first column of Table 42, for example, the joint F ratio for objective initial-data variables is 9.0, based on the variance explained by these four variables. In the second column, the joint F ratio for anticipatory initial-data variables is 15.9, based on the (incremental) variance explained by these three variables. A new joint F ratio (7.7) for the objective variables net of the anticipatory ones is also shown in the second column; but this measure is an approximation.[12]

Columns 4–7 show regression coefficients and F ratios for equations having durable goods purchases as the dependent variable. Columns 4, 5, and 6 are comparable to columns 1, 2, and 3, respectively, in that a common set of independent variables is used. Column 7 has net regression coefficients for all fifteen independent variables; thus, columns 6 and 7 differ only in that the latter includes the three buying intentions variables while the former excludes them. The F ratios in columns

[11] Because some degrees of freedom have been used up in preliminary regressions, somewhat conservative t tests were used. The 0.05 level thus means a t ratio of at least 2; the 0.01 level, a t ratio of at least 3.

[12] The computer program did not yield the incremental variance explained by, $X_1, \ldots ,X_4$ net of $X_5, \ldots ,X_7$. Joint F ratios that could not be computed directly from the incremental explained variance were estimated from t ratios; in the second column of Table 42, for example, the joint F ratio of 7.7 for objective variables is the mean of the squared t ratios for the four variables. This procedure gives a biased estimate of the true F ratio for a group of variables to the extent that intercorrelation exists among the variables in the group; if the within-group intercorrelations are all zero, the mean F ratio, as estimated from the t ratios, is identical to the joint F ratio. Since the relevant intercorrelations are actually quite small, all joint F ratios shown in these tables are close approximations to the true numbers.

4 through 7 are again exact estimates for incremental groups of variables, approximations for groups of variables previously included in the regression. The last two columns show F ratios for each of the fifteen independent variables against both intentions (column 8) and purchases (column 9); these ratios were computed from zero-order correlation coefficients.[18]

Empirical Results

SUMMARY

On the whole the data provide rather impressive support for the basic hypotheses. In all nine subgroups, the partial correlations of both groups of initial-data variables (objective and anticipatory) are stronger with buying intentions than with purchases, measuring the partial correlation by the joint F ratio. The contrast is strongest for the subgroups $(C_1, C_2, \text{ and } C_3)$ with an intentions question that, since it maximizes the correlation between intentions and purchases, is the closest available proxy for purchase probability. Also, about two-thirds of the regression coefficients for the seven initial-data variables are larger when buying intentions rather than purchases are the dependent variable. For the intervening variables, twenty-two of the twenty-seven partial correlations (ΔY and ΔY_t jointly, H_{10} and H_{01} separately, within each of nine subgroups) are stronger with purchases than with intentions, as predicted. The data for H_{11} are less consistent: the partial correlations are about the same with intentions as with purchases, and the regression coefficients are also about the same. Special circumstances are relevant here, and this problem is discussed below. (All these statements are based on comparisons of columns 3 and 6 in Tables 42–44, that is, on regressions that do not include buying intentions as an independent variable but regress both purchases and intentions on a common set of initial-data and intervening variables.)

The data also clearly evidence the predicted differential influence of buying intentions on the relation between initial-data or intervening variables and purchases. Given nine subgroups, the total numbers of observations on (seven) initial-data and (four) intervening variables are sixty-three and thirty-six, respectively, again excluding the H_{11} variable.

---

[18] The means of the F ratios in columns 8 and 9 for any group of variables are the joint F ratios that would have been observed if there were in fact zero intercorrelation not only among variables within a group but among all independent variables shown. A comparison of such mean F ratios—for example, as computed from column 8 with the joint F ratio in column 1 for the objective group of variables, or as computed from column 9 with the joint F ratio in column 4—indicates that intercorrelation within this group of variables is in fact close to zero.

Table 32 summarizes the total number of cases in which variables in these respective categories have the predicted algebraic sign and a significance level of 0.05 or the predicted sign and a significance level of 0.01, before and after buying intentions are held constant. Summary data are shown

TABLE 32

SUMMARY OF RESULTS FROM MULTIVARIATE REGRESSION ANALYSIS: NUMBERS OF STATISTICALLY SIGNIFICANT REGRESSION COEFFICIENTS AND MEAN OF F RATIOS

| | NUMBER OF NET REGRESSION COEFFICIENTS THAT HAVE PREDICTED SIGN AND HAVE t RATIO | | | | | |
| | Greater than 2 | | Greater than 3 | | Mean of F Ratios | |
SUBGROUP	Before Intentions	After Intentions	Before Intentions	After Intentions	Before Intentions	After Intentions
OBJECTIVE INITIAL-DATA [a]						
A_1, B_1, C_1	6	3	6	2	9.4	4.4
A_2, B_2, C_2	6	6	6	3	11.6	4.7
A_3, B_3, C_3	6	4	4	2	7.8	4.1
Total or mean	18	13	16	7	9.6	4.4
ANTICIPATORY INITIAL-DATA [b]						
A_1, B_1, C_1	4	3	3	1	8.0	4.4
A_2, B_2, C_2	3	3	3	1	7.2	3.7
A_3, B_3, C_3	4	2	1	0	4.1	2.1
Total or mean	11	8	7	2	6.4	3.4
COMBINED OBJECTIVE AND ANTICIPATORY INITIAL-DATA						
Total or mean	29	21	23	9	8.2	4.0
INTERVENING [c]						
A_1, B_1, C_1	4	5	3	4	8.3	7.7
A_2, B_2, C_2	5	5	2	2	5.0	5.5
A_3, B_3, C_3	2	3	1	1	3.2	3.1
Total or mean	11	13	6	7	5.5	5.4

SOURCE: Tables 42–44.

[a] Variables included are normal family income (Y), change in liquid assets (ΔL_{-1}) and in family income (ΔY_{-1}) prior to the survey, and stock adjustment (S').

[b] Variables included are expectations index ($\hat{E}$), opinion about buying conditions (O), and long-range financial prospects ($\hat{E}_5$).

[c] Variables included are income change during the forecast periods (ΔY), transitory income (ΔY_t), unexpected housing purchase (H_{01}), and unfulfilled plan to buy house (H_{10}).

for the three life-cycle groups. The mean of the joint F ratios is also shown, both before and after the inclusion of buying intentions.

A number of points stand out clearly. First, the F ratios for both categories of initial-data variables decline sharply when buying intentions are included in the regression, while the F ratios for intervening variables are hardly affected at all. In fact, the joint F ratios for both categories of initial-data variables decline in every one of the nine subgroups when buying intentions are added to the regression. In only about 10 per cent of the 63 cases does the partial correlation between purchases and any initial-data variable show an increase when intentions are held constant. In contrast, both correlation and regression coefficients for intervening variables increase in about half the cases when buying intentions are held constant.

Secondly, the number of initial-data variables with a statistically significant relation to purchases differs sharply depending on whether or not intentions are held constant; this is not the case for intervening variables. The contrast is most evident from a comparison of the third and fourth columns in Table 32. Before intentions are included in the regression, initial-data variables are significantly related to purchases at the 0.01 level in twenty-three cases (sixteen objective and seven anticipatory); intervening variables have this strong an association with purchases in six cases. After the inclusion of buying intentions, only nine of the original twenty-three cases involving initial-data variables still show significance at the 0.01 level, while seven intervening variables—a net increase—now show an 0.01-level association with purchases.[14]

Finally, there is some indication that the relative importance of objective and anticipatory initial-data variables differs among life-cycle groups. The anticipatory variables are clearly more important for households with relatively young heads, judging both from the joint F ratios and from the number of cases that show a statistically significant relation to purchases at the 0.01 level. However, it does not appear from these data that objective variables are more important for households with older heads; rather, there seems to be no pattern at all in this regard. But data to be presented later suggests that objective variables may in fact be more important for households with older heads.

A more detailed summary of results from the multivariate analysis is given by Table 33, which shows the algebraic sign and significance level for each variable in all nine subgroups, based on regressions from columns 3 and 7 of Tables 42–44.

Looking first at the regression with buying intentions dependent, it

---

[14] Although the intervening variables that show a significant association with purchases at the 0.01 level are all housing dummy variables (H_{01} and H_{10}), the other intervening variables show the same pattern. For example, there are four cases in which income change or transitory income are significantly related to purchases (0.05 level) before inclusion of buying intentions; all four of these cases are still significant at the 0.05 level after inclusion of intentions, and the regression coefficients are practically unchanged.

TABLE 33

SUMMARY OF RESULTS FROM MULTIVARIATE REGRESSION ANALYSIS: ALGEBRAIC SIGNS OF ALL NET REGRESSION COEFFICIENTS AND t RATIOS

Independent Variables				Subgroup Designation						Number of Net Regression Coefficients		
	A_1	A_2	A_3	B_1	B_2	B_3	C_1	C_2	C_3	+	* or **	**
REGRESSIONS WITH BUYING INTENTIONS DEPENDENT												
Initial-data												
Objective												
Y	+	**	+	**	**	**	**	*	**	9	7	6
ΔL_{-1}	+	0	+	+	*	*	+	+	+	8	2	0
ΔY_{-1}	+	+	0	+	0	+	**	+	*	7	2	1
S'	**	**	**	**	**	**	**	**	**	9	9	9
Anticipatory												
$\hat{E}$	+	0	+	0	+	*	+	*	0	6	2	0
O	**	**	**	**	**	**	**	**	**	9	9	9
$\hat{E}_6$	*	+	**	+	+	+	*	0	+	8	3	1
Intervening												
Income change												
ΔY	0	+	+	0	0	+	0	*	+	5	1	0
ΔY_t	0	+	0	+	+	+	+	+	0	6	0	0
Housing												
H_{01}	*	*	+	+	+	+	*	+	+	9	3	0
H_{10}	+	**	0	**	**	**	**	**	**	8	7	7
H_{11}	**	+	**	**	**	**	**	**	+	9	7	7
REGRESSIONS WITH PURCHASES DEPENDENT												
Initial-data												
Objective												
Y	**	*	**	**	**	**	+	**	*	9	8	6
ΔL_{-1}	0	+	+	+	0	+	+	+	0	6	0	0
ΔY_{-1}	0	0	+	+	0	+	0	0	+	4	0	0
S'	+	*	+	*	**	*	+	*	+	9	5	1
Anticipatory												
$\hat{E}$	0	0	0	+	+	0	+	+	+	5	0	0
O	**	+	*	+	**	+	*	*	*	9	6	2
$\hat{E}_6$	0	0	+	+	0	+	*	*	+	6	2	0
Intervening												
Income change												
ΔY	*	*	+	0	+	+	0	+	+	7	2	0
ΔY_t	+	*	+	+	0	*	+	+	+	8	2	0
Housing[a]												
H_{01}	**	+	+	**	**	**	**	**	+	9	6	6
H_{10}	0	0	+	0	*(0)	0	**(0)	0	*(0)	1	3	1
H_{11}	**	**	*	**	**	**	*	**	+	9	8	6
Buying intentions[b]												
$\hat{P}$	**	**	**	**	**	**	**	**	**	9	9	9
$\hat{P}_c, Z\hat{P}_c$	**	**	+	*	+	0	*	+	+	8	4	2

+ = positive net regression coefficient, t ratio <2
0 = negative net regression coefficient, t ratio <2
* = positive net regression coefficient, t ratio >2
*(0) = negative net regression coefficient, t ratio >2
** = positive net regression coefficient, t ratio >3
**(0) = negative net regression coefficient, t ratio >3

SOURCE: Tables 42–44. Independent variables are defined above, in "Description of Variables."

[a] The predicted regression coefficient of H_{10}, net of buying intentions, is negative.

[b] Algebraic sign for $\hat{P}_c$, $Z\hat{P}_c$ is taken from the regression that includes $\hat{P}_c$ only and not $Z\hat{P}_c$; significance level is that for $\hat{P}_c$ before adding $Z\hat{P}_c$ or that for $Z\hat{P}_c$, whichever is higher.

appears that five of the twelve independent variables are significantly related to intentions in almost every subgroup, usually at the 0.01 level. These include normal family income, desired stock adjustment, opinion about buying conditions, unfulfilled plans to buy a house, and anticipated purchases of housing. Four others (income and liquid-asset change prior to the survey, the expectations index, and long-range financial prospects) generally have the predicted algebraic sign and are significant in at least two of the nine groups; these variables, especially the first two, are generally significant at the 0.01 level in a zero-order regression but are redundant to other variables—notably, to opinion about buying conditions. Of the remaining three variables, the hypotheses tested do not predict the sign of one (unexpected housing purchases), although the signs are all positive; the other two (intervening income changes) are predicted not to have any net association with buying intentions. On the whole, therefore, the results accord quite well with the hypotheses.

Turning to the regressions with durable goods purchases dependent, the strongest and most consistent variables are normal family income, unanticipated housing purchases, anticipated housing purchases, and standard buying intentions. Two others—desired stock adjustment and opinion about buying conditions—always have the predicted sign and are generally significant at the 0.05 level, though not at the 0.01 level. The two intervening income-change variables, as well as contingent buying intention, long-range financial prospects, and unfulfilled house-buying intentions, usually have the predicted sign (positive for the first four, negative for H_{10}), and are significant in at least two of the subgroups. Finally, three variables seem to be essentially unrelated to purchases—change in income and change in liquid assets prior to the survey date and the expectations index.

In terms of the classification via initial-data, intervening, and buying-intentions variables, standard buying intentions are clearly the strongest variable of the fifteen; this variable accounts for close to half the total explained variance. The intervening housing variables are consistently significant, and the intervening income-change variables are consistent with respect to algebraic sign though they are generally not statistically significant. Some of the initial-data variables continue to exert a strong influence on purchases net of buying intentions, although in every case their influence is sharply reduced when intentions are included in the regression.

It should be noted that the subgroups differ markedly in the degree to which the respective intentions questions constitute an adequate proxy for purchase probability. The regression analysis confirms the earlier finding (Chapter 2) that the intentions questions in the C subgroups are the best of those available in the CU data; both the simple and partial correlation between intentions and purchases is consistently stronger in the C groups. As a consequence, initial-data variables ought to be less strongly associated with purchases net of intentions in the C subgroups than elsewhere, while the influence of intervening variables ought to be about the same. It appears from Table 33 (and from the basic data tables) that this is in fact the case: for example, the net relation between the income or stock adjustment variables and purchases is clearly less strong in C_1, C_2, and C_3 than elsewhere, while the intervening housing variables H_{10} and H_{01} are at least as strong net of buying intentions in the C groups as in other groups.

Finally, Table 33 provides an additional test of the proposition that initial-data variables will be more strongly related to buying intentions than to purchases, and that the converse ought to be true with respect to intervening variables. A glance at the summary statistics on the right-hand side of Table 33 confirms that this is the typical pattern. For every variable in the initial-data category the same or more subgroups have the predicted sign in the intentions regression than in the purchases regression, and the same or more subgroups have both the predicted sign and any given level of statistical significance (with one exception—family income, 0.05 significance level). For every variable in the intervening category, the converse is true.[15]

The data in Table 33 indicate that a number of variables have a negligible net influence on both intentions and purchases. One last general summary—Table 34—is therefore presented; regression coefficients and F ratios before and after buying intentions are held constant are shown for those initial-data and intervening variables that are significantly related to purchases (0.05 level) in at least two of the nine groups, net of all independent variables. Data from only the A and C subgroups are presented, since the results are about the same in the B groups as in A. The independent variables comprise two objective initial-data variables

---

[15] There appear to be two exceptions to this statement: H_{10} shows a preponderance of plus signs and coefficients significant at the 0.01 level in the intentions regression; this is as predicted, since those with (unfulfilled) house-buying intentions ought to have relatively more durable goods buying intentions than other households. In the purchases regression, H_{10} generally has negative coefficients, a few of which are significant; but this is again as predicted, since households in this category (planned to buy a house but did not purchase) are expected to buy relatively fewer durables, holding buying intentions constant, than others, because they must have experienced unfavorable intervening events. The other apparent exception is H_{11}, which is analyzed below.

TABLE 34
SUMMARY OF RESULTS FROM MULTIVARIATE REGRESSION ANALYSIS: EFFECT OF ADDING
DURABLE GOODS BUYING INTENTIONS TO REGRESSIONS OF PURCHASES ON SELECTED VARIABLES
(mean F ratios are shown in brackets)

Independent Variables	Net Regression Coefficients					
	Before	After	Before	After	Before	After
	A_1		A_2		A_3	
Initial-data Objective						
Y	[13 4] 0.048**	[7.7] 0.039**	[21.1] 0.035**	[6.3] 0.021*	[11.0] 0.035**	[6.2] 0.033**
S'	0.106**	0.020	0.168**	0.078*	0.114*	0.042
Anticipatory						
O	[16.3] 0.383**	[10.1] 0.291**	[6 2] 0.247**	[1.8] 0.131	[6.5] 0.281*	[3.2] 0.214*
$\hat{E}_s$	0.043	−0.010	0.030	−0.022	0.262*	0.166
Intervening Income Change						
ΔY	[3.7] 0.126*	[4 3] 0.125*	[5.8] 0.152*	[5.8] 0 148*	[0 6] 0.100	[0.4] 0 077
ΔY_t	0.252	0.289	0.494*	0.488*	−0.005	0.051
Housing						
H_{01}	[16.9] 1.196**	[14.8] 1.055**	[3 1] 0.664*	[2.5] 0.488	[2.2] 0.679	[2.2] 0.657
H_{10}	−0.094	−0 234	−0.013	−0.312	0 541	0.540
Housing						
H_{11}	[39 7] 1.519**	[19.4] 1.053**	[14.4] 1.253**	[10 2] 1.027**	[14.4] 2.038**	[6 8] 1.388*
	C_1		C_2		C_3	
Initial-data Objective						
Y	[15.5] 0.038**	[2.5] 0.022	[24.1] 0.041**	[9.3] 0.032**	[12.1] 0.030*	[2.6] 0.020*
S'	0 151**	0.043	0.186**	0.072*	0.158**	0.045
Anticipatory						
O	[16.2] 0.308**	[8.4] 0.192*	[11.9] 0.334**	[5.6] 0.190*	[7.3] 0.324**	[3.2] 0.212*
$\hat{E}_s$	0 273**	0.208*	0.172	0.176*	0.134	0.086
Intervening Income Change						
ΔY	[2.3] −0.082	[1.6] −0.066	[1.5] 0.108	[0.8] 0.060	[0.3] 0.032	[0.4] 0.013
ΔY_t	0.262	0.208	0.201	0.184	0.163	0.198
Housing						
H_{01}	[18.8] 1.387**	[19.9] 1.100**	[10.2] 1.274**	[12.8] 1.320**	[1.2] 0.448	[2.8] 0.396
H_{10}	−0.397	−0.893**	−0.060	−0.402	−0.456	−0.859*
Housing						
H_{11}	[24.0] 1.384**	[7.8] 0.785*	[24 0] 1.940**	[11.6] 1.328**	[0.8] 0.616	[0.6] 0.514

* = t ratio >2.
** = t ratio >3.
SOURCE: Tables 42–44; regression coefficients are from columns 6 and 7. The independent variables are defined above, in "Description of Variables."

(normal family income, Y, and desired stock adjustment, S'); two anticipatory initial-data variables (opinion about buying conditions, O, and long-range financial prospects, $\hat{E}_5$); two intervening income-change variables (change in income during the forecast period, ΔY, and transitory income, ΔY_t); two intervening housing variables (H_{01}, unanticipated housing purchase, and H_{10}, unfulfilled plans to buy a house); and the one variable that has a pronounced element of both intervening and initial-data considerations (H_{11}, anticipated purchase of a house). Mean F ratios for the four pairs of variables and the F ratio for H_{11} are shown in brackets.

The differential impact of buying intentions on the relation between purchases and initial-data or intervening variables is strikingly evidenced in Table 34. In subgroup A_2, for example, the objective initial-data variables Y and S' have a mean F ratio of 21.1 before intentions are held constant; the anticipatory initial-data variables O and $\hat{E}_5$, a mean F ratio of 6.2. After intentions are held constant, these F ratios fall to 6.3 and 1.8, respectively. But the intervening variables ΔY and ΔY_t have the same mean F ratio (5.8) both before and after. In the subgroup C_1 the same objective and anticipatory initial-data variables have mean F ratios of, respectively, 15.5 and 16.2 before, 2.5 and 8.4 after; the intervening income-change variables, in contrast show a small decline—from 2.3 to 1.6.[16]

[16] The difference between the A and C subgroups in the relative influence of buying intentions on the relation between purchases and initial-data variables should again be noted. This difference must be due to the buying intentions questions asked of households in these groups, sampling variation aside. The before-intentions and after-intentions mean F ratios for the specified initial-data variables are:

		Y, S'		$O, \hat{E}_5$	
		Before	After	Before	After
A_1		13.4	7.7	16.3	10.1
A_2		21.1	6.3	6.2	1.8
A_3		11.0	6.2	6.5	3.2
	Mean of A Subgroups	15 2	6.7	9.7	5.0
C_1		15.5	2.5	16.2	8.4
C_2		24.1	9.3	11.9	5.6
C_3		12.1	2.6	7.3	3.2
	Mean of C Subgroups	17.2	4.8	11.8	5.7

On the basis of these data the initial-data variables apparently are somewhat more strongly related to purchases in the C subgroups than in A, *prior* to the introduction of intentions. This is presumably a sampling phenomenon, since these variables are identical in each subgroup and the subgroups themselves were selected at random. Net of buying intentions, however, the Y and S' variables have *less* influence in the C

The two housing variables that are mainly intervening are not influenced much by the inclusion of buying intentions. In three of the six groups the mean F ratio for H_{01} and H_{10} increases when buying intentions are held constant, and in the other three groups the change is either nil or a negligible decline. For H_{11}, which is partly an intervening and partly an initial-data variable, the F ratio declines in all six groups, although in no case does the addition of buying intentions reduce a statistically significant H_{11} coefficient to a nonsignificant one. Nonetheless, the H_{11} coefficients all drop considerably and the F ratios are roughly halved, comparing the situation before and after buying intentions are included in the regression on purchases.

Further, it is clear from both Table 34 and the basic data tables that the regression coefficient of H_{11} (anticipated housing purchases) is generally *larger* than that of H_{01} (unanticipated housing purchases) net of intentions to buy durables. Ordinarily, H_{11} has a much larger regression coefficient than H_{01} before durable goods intentions are included in the regression, a slightly larger one after intentions are held constant; that is, holding intentions constant reduces the H_{11} coefficient much more than that of H_{01}, but not enough more to reverse the direction of difference. Since favorable intervening events must have been more frequent or more important in H_{01} than in H_{11} (see above), this result is inconsistent with predictions of the probability model. Because the problem is complicated, I have deferred further examination of it until the remaining results have been discussed.

DIFFERENCES BETWEEN LIFE-CYCLE CLASSES

It has already been noted that anticipatory initial-data variables are more closely related to purchases in households with younger heads, while objective initial-data variables seemed to have no life-cycle pattern at all vis-à-vis purchases. Table 35 facilitates a more careful examination of this proposition; F ratios from the regression of purchases on anticipatory and objective initial-data variables are shown for each of the nine sub-groups, as is the F ratio for durable goods buying intentions. Two sets of these ratios are included: one is the mean of the F ratios calculated from the simple correlation between each independent variable and purchases;

groups; the O and $\hat{E}_5$ variables just slightly more. A comparison of paired observations in the respective subgroups (A_1 versus C_1, etc.) suggests that the C intentions question exerts a stronger influence on the initial-data variables in almost every case. The reason presumably is that the intentions question in the C groups is a better proxy for purchase probability than the question in A; hence, the initial-data variables are more redundant to buying intentions in the C groups.

the other is the mean of the F ratios estimated from the partial correlations in the complete (fifteen-variable) regression.

The hypothesized life-cycle pattern for both anticipatory initial-data variables and buying intentions is clearly in evidence: households with relatively young heads tend to have the highest F ratios based on either the simple or partial correlation with purchases; those with relatively older heads, the lowest F ratios. But there seems to be no discernible life-cycle pattern to the F ratios for objective initial-data variables. However, these observations are based on the relation between initial-data

TABLE 35

MEAN F RATIOS FOR RELATION BETWEEN GROUPS OF INDEPENDENT VARIABLES
AND DURABLE GOODS PURCHASES, BY LIFE-CYCLE CLASS

| | INITIAL-DATA VARIABLES | | | | Buying Intentions[a] | |
| | Objective | | Anticipatory | | | |
SUBGROUP	Simple	Net	Simple	Net	Simple	Net
A_1	10.2	4.1	20.2	6.8	133.3	80.7
B_1	16.8	7.9	6.7	0.8	128.1	71.7
C_1	9.8	1.2	16.0	5.7	154.8	87.0
Mean	12.3	4 4	14.3	4 4	138.7	79.8
A_2	12.9	3.3	6.1	1.6	91.4	61.0
B_2	13 0	6.1	9.9	5.6	115.2	56.2
C_2	12.4	4 8	13.8	4.0	140.2	73.3
Mean	12.8	4.7	9.9	3.7	115.6	63.5
A_3	9.0	3.6	9.8	2.6	48.2	24.2
B_3	11.6	7.2	4.2	1.1	63.5	24.7
C_3	6 6	1.6	9.4	2.6	67.5	38.8
Mean	9.1	4.1	7.8	2.1	59.7	29.2

SOURCE: Tables 42–44.

[a] Standard buying intentions ($\hat{P}$) only; contingent buying intentions ($\hat{P}_c$) and the interaction variable $Z\hat{P}_c$ have a small net effect except in the A groups, although they generally have the predicted signs in other groups as well.

variables and actual purchases. Intervening events may have an important influence on this relation, particularly in view of the relatively short forecast period in the analysis. It can be argued, therefore, that the relation between initial-data variables and *buying intentions* provides a more accurate picture of the relative importance of objective and anticipatory variables in the decision-making process, since intervening events should have little or no influence on this relation.

FACTORS DETERMINING PURCHASE PROBABILITY

The data contain, not one measure of buying intentions, but several; the relation between initial-data variables and buying intentions depends on which intentions question is used. For example, buying intentions in the A subgroups constitute responses to a question with a relatively high probability cut-off point and a relatively small proportion of yes responses. The intentions question asked of the C subgroups has a much lower cut-off probability than that asked of A, and the C subgroups show a correspondingly much higher proportion of yes responses. Thus, an analysis of the relation between buying intentions and initial-data variables yields different results in the A, B, and C samples because of differences in the intentions variables themselves. An indication of the extent of these differences is provided by Table 36, which shows the proportion of total variance in buying intentions explained by a common set of independent variables in each of the nine subgroups.

TABLE 36

PROPORTION OF VARIANCE IN BUYING INTENTIONS EXPLAINED BY SEVEN INITIAL-DATA VARIABLES

| | Life-Cycle Class | | |
Group	1	2	3
A	.073	.109	.099
B	.100	.110	.148
C	.170	.201	.238

SOURCE: Tables 42–44.

The intentions variable in the C samples is evidently much more closely associated with initial-data factors than that in the A or B samples, and the same is true for the intentions variable in the B sample relative to that in A. The reason is simple enough. The C buying-intentions variable elicited many more yes responses for each of the commodities included in the aggregate, as noted above. A minority of households in the C samples (about 35 per cent) reported no buying intentions at all; the remaining households reported numbers of intentions ranging from one to nine. Thus "aggregate intentions" is a number greater than zero for most C households, and those reporting no intentions at all presumably constitute a relatively homogeneous subsample with relatively low *ex ante* purchase probabilities.

On the other hand, the A intentions variable elicited relatively few yes responses, although many A respondents, other than the small number reporting that they "definitely" would buy, replied that they "probably or possibly" would purchase. A majority of sample A households (about 65 per cent) reported no definite buying intentions; the remainder, numbers of definite intentions varying from one to nine. But the 65 per cent of the A sample who are nonintenders constitute a relatively heterogeneous group, in that their *ex ante* purchase probabilities have a substantial variance. Although aggregate buying intentions—and *ex ante* probability—among those reporting at least one buying intention is as closely (probably more closely) associated with initial-data factors among A households as among those in C, the variance in *ex ante* probability among those reporting no buying intentions is bound to be much greater in the A groups. Since the intentions variable is evidently unable to explain any of the variance in *ex ante* probability among nonintenders, it will necessarily be unrelated to initial-data factors associated with differences in *ex ante* purchase probability for the nonintenders.[17] In sum, the data suggest that the relation between the observed variable "aggregate buying intentions" and the unobserved variable "aggregate *ex ante* purchase probability" is much stronger in the C samples than in A; although the association between aggregate *ex ante* probability and initial-data factors must be the same in both groups, the association between these factors and aggregate buying intentions would be stronger in C than in A if aggregate C intentions were more strongly correlated with aggregate *ex ante* probability; and this appears to be the case.

These considerations suggest that the relation between initial-data variables and purchase probability is most closely approximated by the relation between initial-data variables and buying intentions for the C samples; the next-best intentions variable for this purpose is that in the B samples.[18] Hence, Table 37 summarizes the net regression coefficients and joint F ratios from the regression of aggregate buying intentions on initial-data variables in the B and C samples.

The data indicate that the initial-data variables most closely associated with buying intentions (and, hence, purchase probability) are desired stock adjustment (S'), and opinion about buying conditions for durables (O). Both variables are significant at the 0.01 level net of all seven

---

[17] The argument is basically empirical, not a priori. There is no logical reason why the association between aggregate intentions and initial-data variables might not be stronger the higher the cut-off probability of the intentions question.

[18] Both standard and contingent buying intentions are proxies for purchase probability, and the A sample appears to have the best contingent-intentions variable among the three groups. But the regressions were run only on the standard buying-intentions variable in each sample, not on contingent intentions. I would guess that the relation between A contingent intentions and initial-data variables is probably as close as that between A standard intentions and these variables; this statement would not be true for the other samples. Further, it is fairly evident that a combination of standard and contingent A intentions—perhaps even so crude a combination as the sum of the two—would yield results that are not very different from those for the C standard-intentions variable.

independent variables, and they account for roughly three-fourths of the total explained variance. Before the anticipatory variables are included in the regression, family income (Y) is also significantly related to intentions at the 0.01 level in all subgroups, and liquid-asset change prior to the intentions survey (ΔL_{-1}) is significant at the 0.05 level in all groups. But the anticipatory variables—mainly O—reduce the influence of both these variables considerably. Income is still significant at the 0.05 level

TABLE 37

NET REGRESSION COEFFICIENT AND JOINT F RATIOS FOR INITIAL-DATA VARIABLES RELATED TO STANDARD BUYING INTENTIONS

Subgroup	Objective Variables					Anticipatory Variables			
	Y	ΔL_{-1}	ΔY_{-1}	S'	Joint F Ratio	$\hat{E}$	O	$\hat{E}_s$	Joint F Ratio
OBJECTIVE VARIABLES ONLY									
B₁	035ᵃ	.178ᵇ	.053	.199ᵃ	20.0				
B₂	.028ᵃ	.284ᵃ	− 075	.208ᵃ	22.3				
B₃	.035ᵃ	.275ᵇ	.095	.282ᵃ	24.6				
C₁	.063ᵃ	232ᵇ	.221ᵃ	.316ᵃ	34.0				
C₂	.038ᵃ	.241ᵇ	.095	.375ᵃ	34.2				
C₃	.050ᵃ	.288ᵇ	.264ᵃ	.444ᵃ	38.0				
OBJECTIVE AND ANTICIPATORY VARIABLES									
B₁	.028ᵇ	.126	.047	.205ᵃ	17.6	−.193	.326ᵃ	.076	11.0
B₂	.023ᵇ	.215ᵇ	− .103	.212ᵃ	19.0	.167	.311ᵃ	.041	9.3
B₃	.031ᵃ	.239ᵇ	.039	.288ᵃ	24.5	.702ᵇ	.291ᵃ	.005	8.8
C₁	.047ᵃ	.141	167ᵃ	.322ᵃ	29.3	.656	.501ᵃ	.220ᵇ	20.8
C₂	.028ᵇ	.113	.078	.369ᵃ	31.7	.852ᵇ	.551ᵃ	.012	20.9
C₃	.036ᵃ	.149	.184ᵇ	.439ᵃ	35.0	− .257	.479ᵃ	.234	11.0

SOURCE: Tables 42–44, columns 1 and 2.
ᵃ = Significantly different from zero at 0.01 level.
ᵇ = Significantly different from zero at 0.05 level.

in all groups; at the 0.01 level, it is significant in only three of the six. In addition, all the income regression coefficients decline markedly. The effect of the anticipatory variables on liquid-asset change is even stronger; only two of the six groups show a significant (0.05 level) relation between (ΔL_{-1}) and buying intentions after the anticipatory variables are included in the regression; and all the coefficients show a noticeable drop. In contrast, the coefficient of S' is completely unaffected when anticipatory variables are included in the regression.

The data in Table 37 exhibit consistent and fairly strong differences among life-cycle classes in the relative influence of objective and anticipatory variables on buying intentions. In both the B and C samples the joint F ratio for objective variables is larger the older the head of household. All four objective variables contribute to this pattern, although differences in the partial correlation of S' with $\hat{P}$ are mainly responsible. The anticipatory variables follow the opposite pattern with respect to differences among life-cycle classes; the younger the household head, the more closely are these variables related to buying intentions. This result is almost entirely due to differences in the partial correlation of O with $\hat{P}$; the other two anticipatory variables behave erratically, although in the C samples both $\hat{E}$ and $\hat{E}_5$ appear to be somewhat more strongly related to intentions for households with relatively young heads.

The observed differences among life-cycle classes are consistent with the hypothesis that expenditures on durables are more closely associated with wealth (defined to include the discounted value of future income) than with current income. The correlation between wealth and current income is bound to be relatively weak in households with younger heads because the variance of discounted future earnings, current income held constant, is greater the younger the household head. Hence anticipatory variables, which are correlated more closely with wealth than with current income, will have a relatively stronger net influence on purchase probability in younger households. Conversely, objective variables, which reflect differences among households in their current financial situation, will have a relatively stronger net influence on the decisions of older households because they constitute a better proxy for wealth in such a group.

A DIGRESSION ON TASTE VARIABLES

One of the most interesting results in Table 37 is the powerful influence of the stock adjustment variable, S', on buying intentions.[19] Investigation of the relation between durables stock and purchases (discussed in Appendix A) indicated a weak positive association between the two, instead of the negative relation anticipated a priori. The positive stock-purchases correlation is probably due to the correlation between stock of durables and household tastes, i.e., to what have been called personality correlations. S', however, contains a strong subjective element; a household may have a large and relatively new stock of durables and yet report that many items need replacement precisely because its members have

---

[19] S' represents the (weighted) number of durables in the household's inventory that were regarded as "in need of replacement." The statement that a particular item needed replacement was interpreted as indicating a difference between the household's actual and desired stock of durables.

a taste for durables, while another household with a smaller and older stock may report that no items are in need of replacement for the converse reason. To some extent, therefore, S' tends to standardize for differences in tastes. The data can thus be interpreted as suggesting that the influence of durables stock on purchases, taste for durables held constant, is really quite powerful; the observed correlation between S' and both purchases and buying intentions is positive and quite strong; and S', while it may standardize tastes, is clearly a very crude measure of the difference between actual and desired stock.

A DIGRESSION ON IDIOSYNCRATIC VARIABLES

The same line of analysis may explain why the opinion variable (O) obtained from responses to the question "Is the present a good or bad time for you to buy durables?" is so strongly related to both purchases and buying intentions in the CU data. Both the form of the question and the intercorrelation between O and other initial-data variables indicate that respondents are essentially saying: "Taking everything into account (our current and prospective income, asset and debt position, etc.), this is a [good, bad, pro-con] time for us to be spending money on durables." Thus, O reflects the household's own judgment about the joint influence of objectively observable factors like income, income change, assets, and debts on its current financial position. Since different households necessarily assign different weights to these factors, the O variable combines them in whatever way is most appropriate for each household. Because it is partly an idiosyncratic variable, it can be argued that O ought to explain more of the variance in purchases or intentions to buy than any simple combination of the underlying factors, and would probably explain more variance than any conceivable combination of these factors.[20]

[20] Several points of interest in connection with this variable should be noted. First, O is not necessarily the same as the apparently identical variable obtained by the Survey Research Center and reported in the annual *Survey of Consumer Finances* or in their own Interim Surveys. The SRC uses a projective question: "Is this a [good, bad, pro-con] time for *people like yourselves* to buy durables?" The responses to this question may thus differ from responses to the similar but personally oriented question asked on the CU surveys. Moreover, the SRC has interpreted responses to the projective question as reflecting judgments about market conditions rather than about the current state of the household's finances. That is to say, the SRC argues that responses to the projective question relate to the household's expectations about current and prospective prices, and this view is supported by responses to a follow-up question, "Why do you say so [that this is a good, etc., time for people like yourselves to buy]?" For further discussion, see Appendix A.

Secondly, the Federal Reserve Board's Consultant Committee on Economic Statistics found that the SRC opinion question was the only attitude variable strongly related to

BUYING INTENTIONS VARIABLES

One of the most important empirical tests in this chapter concerns the structure of the regression coefficients for durable goods buying intentions. The basic thesis of the monograph is that a classification of households into intenders and nonintenders essentially constitutes a classification into groups with relatively high and relatively low mean *ex ante* purchase probability, drawn from a universe characterized by a continuous distribution of *ex ante* purchase probabilities. The mean probability for both intenders and nonintenders depends on the cut-off probability that respondents assign to the question about buying intentions. As pointed out earlier in this chapter, the constant term in a simple linear regression of purchases on intentions is an estimate of mean probability among nonintenders, while the regression coefficient of intentions is an estimate of the difference in mean probability between intenders and nonintenders.[21]

The data in Tables 42–44 contain six different buying intentions variables; the A, B, and C subsamples contain both a standard and a contingent intentions variable, each of which is constructed from responses to questions with different (implicit) cut-off probabilities. A priori, it is clear that the standard intentions variable in each of these (A,B,C) samples has a higher cut-off probability than the contingent intentions variable in the same sample, and that the standard intentions variable in A has a higher probability cut-off than that in C (see Chapters 2 and 3). On the basis of evidence that is partly a priori and partly empirical (the proportion of households responding yes to the alternative questions), the ordering of the cut-off probabilities for the remaining intentions questions can be fixed with a fair degree of confidence.

Given the variation in cut-off probability for the six intentions ques-

---

time series changes in expenditures on durables (see *Reports of Federal Reserve Consultant Committees on Economic Statistics*, Joint Committee on the Economic Report, 84th Cong., 1st sess., 1955). Thus these cross-section results are consistent with an analysis of time series changes based on responses (to a roughly similar question) from a random sample of the population.

[21] The fact that the empirical data relate aggregate intentions for each household to aggregate household purchases makes little difference in principle. The linear regression coefficient of aggregate purchases on intentions is still an estimate of the difference in mean probability between intenders and nonintenders, except that it constitutes a weighted average of intender-nonintender probability differences for all commodities included in the aggregate. The constant term, however, becomes the probability that a nonintender will purchase *any of* the commodities in the aggregate. Dividing the constant by the number of commodities aggregated will produce an estimate of the weighted mean probability that nonintenders will purchase the "average" commodity.

tions, it is anticipated that there will be relatively little difference in mean probability among nonintenders, relatively much among intenders (again, see Chapter 3). As a consequence, differences in mean probability between intenders and nonintenders should be positively (though not linearly) correlated with the cut-off probability. Since the regression coefficients of the respective buying-intentions variables are estimates of the respective differences in mean probability between intenders and nonintenders, the test involves a comparison of the respective cut-off probabilities for the six intentions variables—which can be ordered on partly a priori and partly empirical grounds—with the corresponding coefficients estimated in the multivariate regressions.

Table 38 contains two sets of coefficients for the relevant intentions variables. The upper panel contains data from the regressions analyzed in this chapter, while the lower panel contains data from the regressions discussed in Appendix A.[22] The observed regression coefficients follow the predicted pattern closely in all life-cycle classes; the conformity is almost perfect in the youngest age groups, more erratic in the oldest. All coefficients but one are positive, and the size of the differences among coefficients seem generally reasonable. These generalizations apply to the coefficients in either panel, although some of the mean probabilities implied by the Panel B coefficients seem rather large. For example, the mean *ex ante* probability associated with definite buying intentions for households in the 25–34 age group appears to be somewhere around 0.7 or 0.8, judging from the data in the lower panel. The estimated mean difference in observed purchase rates between intenders and nonintenders is calculated as 0.52, and nonintenders must have had purchase rates in excess of zero—say, roughly 0.07; hence, the mean purchase rate for intenders is estimated as roughly 0.6. By implication, mean *ex ante*

---

[22] The upper and lower panels differ in three important respects. First, the number of cases included in each of the regressions is smaller in the lower panel; the Appendix A regressions excluded all households either intending to buy or purchasing a house. Second, the complete set of independent variables—for the regression equation from which the respective intentions coefficients are taken—is not the same in the upper and lower panels; compare $X_1, \ldots, X_{12}$ listed in the first part of this chapter with $X_{1a}, \ldots, X_{13a}$ listed in Appendix A. Third, interaction between standard and contingent intentions assumes a different form: in the upper panel the interaction variable is $Z\hat{P}_c$, where $Z = 1$ when $\hat{P}$ is zero, $Z = 0$ otherwise; in the lower panel the interaction variable is the cross-product, $\hat{P}\hat{P}_c$.

The most important difference is the third. The cross-product interaction generally tends to increase the coefficients for both standard and contingent intentions to a greater degree than the other $(Z\hat{P}_c)$; hence, most of the coefficients in the lower panel are higher than their counterparts in the upper panel. While the ordering is about the same, the differences among intentions variables are somewhat more pronounced in the lower panel.

probability among intenders should have been considerably higher than 0.6 because of regression bias, and I would doubt that this is the case.

The data in Table 38 also indicate that the regression coefficient of buying intentions is a function of life-cycle status, being systematically larger for groups of households with relatively young heads. It is not

TABLE 38
NET REGRESSION COEFFICIENTS FOR ALTERNATIVE MEASURES OF DURABLE GOODS BUYING INTENTIONS

Predicted Order of Cut-off Probability	Observed Coefficients, Life-Cycle Class:		
	1	2	3
REGRESSIONS FROM TABLES 42–44			
1. $\hat{P}$ in A sample	.375*	.292*	.267*
2. $\hat{P}$ in B sample	.359*	.291*	.220*
3. $\hat{P}$ in C sample	.287*	.316*	.253*
4. $\hat{P}_c$ in A sample[a]	.126*	.139*	.052
5. $\hat{P}_c$ in C sample[a]	.082	.067	.036
6. $\hat{P}_c$ in B sample[a]	.049	.021	−.026
REGRESSIONS FROM APPENDIX A			
1. $\hat{P}$ in A sample[b]	.520*	.452*	.179*
2. $\hat{P}$ in B sample[b]	.334*	.416*	.274*
3. $\hat{P}$ in C sample[b]	.406*	.336*	.297*
4. $\hat{P}_c$ in A sample[c]	.147*	.159*	.087*
5. $\hat{P}_c$ in C sample[c]	.136*	.004	.066
6. $\hat{P}_c$ in B sample[c]	.055	.062	−.004

SOURCE: Data in upper panel taken from Tables 42–44, column 7, i.e., from equation that regresses durables goods purchases on all fifteen independent variables. Data in lower panel taken from Appendix A, Tables A-1 through A-9, column 3, i.e., from regressions that do not include the interaction variables—ZS', ZY, $\hat{E}\hat{P}$, ZO, and $Z_1\hat{P}_c$.
* = Significantly different from zero at 0.01 level.
[a] Figure shown is the coefficient of contingent buying intentions when standard intentions are zero. The $Z\hat{P}_c$ interaction behaves erratically and also causes erratic movements in $\hat{P}_c$; hence, the combined influence of both variables is a better measure than either taken alone.
[b] Figure shown is the coefficient of standard intentions when contingent intentions are zero.
[c] Figure shown is the coefficient of contingent intentions when standard intentions are zero.

clear why this is so. The simple correlations between intentions and purchases, as well as the corresponding regression coefficients, tend to be slightly smaller in the older age groups, although the differences are not so pronounced as those shown above and are well within the limits of sampling variability. On the other hand, the association between buying intentions and initial-data variables is typically stronger among households in the older age groups; hence, the partial correlation and regression coefficients for buying intentions are weaker, relative to the zero-order relationships, in the older age groups. By implication, intervening events (not necessarily those observable in the data) must have been relatively more important as an explanation of differences in purchases among older households. It does not necessarily follow that intervening events were more common—indeed, they may have been less so. But unexpected developments—especially adverse ones—may well result in a greater divergence between intentions and purchases among older than among younger households. For example, younger households faced with unexpected financial adversity may be more willing to make use of both accumulated savings and credit than older households faced with a similar situation; if so, the relation between *savings intentions* and *actual savings* would be closer in older households, that between *spending intentions* and *actual spending* closer in younger ones, other things being equal.

A Re-examination of the Housing Variables

The last section of this chapter is concerned with a re-examination of the three variables representing house purchases or house-buying intentions—H_{10}, H_{01}, and H_{11}. As already discussed, the regression coefficients of these (classification) variables, net of durable goods buying intentions, are presumed to measure the relative importance of intervening events. The events themselves are not directly observable but are inferred from the fact that housing purchases in the respective groups were observed to be more (or less) frequent than indicated by the *ex ante* mean probability of housing purchases. Thus, households who purchased houses but did not report house-buying intentions (H_{01}) are presumed to have experienced favorable intervening events to a greater degree, on the average, than those who purchased houses and had also reported house-buying intentions (H_{11}); similarly, households reporting intentions to buy houses but not purchasing (H_{10}) are presumed to have experienced unfavorable intervening events to a greater degree on average than those neither intending to buy nor purchasing houses (H_{00}). The net regression coefficients of H_{01}, H_{10}, and H_{11} measure the respective differences in average purchases, other things being equal, between households in these three groups and those in H_{00}. Consequently, in an equation of the general form

$$P = b_0 + b_1\hat{P} + b_2 H_{01} + b_3 H_{10} + b_4 H_{11} + \cdots + u,$$

where the variables are defined as above, the regression coefficients should be ordered

$$H_{01} > H_{11} > 0 > H_{10}.$$

Instead, the data examined above indicate that, in most subgroups, the net regression coefficients of these variables are ordered

$$H_{11} > H_{01} > 0 > H_{10}.$$

It will be recalled that the regression coefficient of $\hat{P}$, durable goods buying intentions, is an estimate of the difference in mean purchase probability between (durable goods) intenders and nonintenders. Suppose, however, that $\hat{P}$ has not one value but multiple values, depending on the particular circumstances of groups of households. The evidence in Chapters 3 and 4 suggests that the coefficient of $\hat{P}$ probably varies little (if at all) with household characteristics such as income, age, etc. However, the housing variables are so constituted that differences among H_{01}, H_{10}, H_{11}, and H_{00} in mean *ex ante* purchase probability for intenders are not only possible, but likely.

To begin with, durable goods buying intentions are consistently higher in the H_{11} groups than in H_{10} (both reported house-buying intentions, but only those in H_{11} purchased); on a priori grounds, the *ex ante* mean probability of a housing purchase must have been higher in H_{11} than in H_{10}.[23] In the same vein, intentions to buy durables were consistently higher in H_{01} than in H_{00} (neither group "intended" to buy a house, but those in H_{01} bought); a priori, the *ex ante* mean probability of a housing purchase is likely to have been higher in H_{01} than in H_{00}. It is a reasonable supposition that, in these groups, the mean probability associated with buying intentions for durable goods is related to the mean probability of a housing purchase, given the strong complementarity between purchases of housing and purchases of durables. On this line of reasoning the mean probability associated with intentions to buy durables ought to be substantially higher in H_{11} than in H_{10}, somewhat higher in H_{01} than in H_{00}. Moreover, given the nature of these classifications, the mean *ex ante* probability associated with the durables buying intentions of H_{11} households is likely to have been higher than in either H_{01} or H_{00}, while among H_{10} households the *ex ante* mean is likely to have been lower than in either of these groups. That is to say, it can plausibly be argued that mean durable goods purchase probability among intenders ranks in the order

$$H_{11} > H_{01} > H_{00} > H_{10}.$$

There seems to be no a priori reason to suppose that mean *ex ante* purchase

[23] The question on house-buying intentions asked about "the next twelve months." Households that reported intentions to buy houses and purchased within the six-month forecast period surely had higher *ex ante* probabilities of purchasing houses, on the average, than those who reported intentions but did not buy.

probability among nonintenders would necessarily follow the same pattern; even if it did, it is likely that differences among nonintenders would be much less pronounced than among intenders.[24]

If purchase probability varies in this way, the probability model no longer predicts that the coefficient of H_{01} will necessarily exceed that of H_{11} in the regressions summarized in Tables 42–44. If the mean *ex ante* purchase probability associated with durable goods buying intentions varies among the housing groups, the regression coefficients of the housing classification variables will reflect this fact as well as the fact of differences in intervening events. Thus, the coefficient of H_{11} might exceed that of H_{01} even though intervening events were more important in the latter group provided that mean *ex ante* purchase probability were higher among H_{11} than among H_{01} intenders by enough to offset the difference.

This possibility can be explored empirically. For the moment, two assumptions must be made: first, that among households in each of the respective housing categories, the incidence of intervening events is independent of the level (number) of reported buying intentions; second, that in each of the respective groups the *ex ante* probability associated with intentions is independent of the level of intentions. Designating favorable intervening events as F, unfavorable ones as U, and durable goods purchases (buying intentions) for households in the respective housing categories H_{01}, H_{10}, H_{11}, and H_{00} as $P_{01}(\hat{P}_{01})$, . . . ,$P_{00}(\hat{P}_{00})$, we can write

$$\text{within } H_{01}, P_{01} = c_{01} + a_{01}\hat{P}_{01} + b_{01}(F_{01} + U_{01}) + e_{01},$$
$$\text{within } H_{10}, P_{10} = c_{10} + a_{10}\hat{P}_{10} + b_{10}(F_{10} + U_{10}) + e_{10},$$
$$\text{within } H_{11}, P_{11} = c_{11} + a_{11}\hat{P}_{11} + b_{11}(F_{11} + U_{11}) + e_{11},$$
$$\text{within } H_{00}, P_{00} = c_{00} + a_{00}\hat{P}_{00} + b_{00}(F_{00} + U_{00}) + e_{00}$$

It is clear that favorable intervening events must have outweighed unfavorable ones in subgroups that purchased houses (H_{01} and H_{11}), and that this must have been true to a greater extent in H_{01} than in H_{11}. Unfavorable intervening events must have outweighed favorable ones in H_{10}; and the same should be true in H_{00}, although to a lesser extent. It follows that:

$$(\bar{F}_{01} + \bar{U}_{01}) > (\bar{F}_{11} + \bar{U}_{11}) > 0 > (\bar{F}_{00} + \bar{U}_{00}) > (\bar{F}_{10} + \bar{U}_{10})$$

The *ex ante* purchase probability associated with the durable goods buying intentions of households in these four groups is expected to vary as

[24] *Ex post*, of course, nonintenders who purchase houses will buy considerably more than other nonintenders; but this is in large part attributable to the influence of intervening events, not to differences in the mean *ex ante* probability associated with durable goods buying intentions.

hypothesized above. The probability associated with intentions to buy any given product is presumably highest among those in H_{11}, lowest among those in H_{10}. And the analysis suggests that the probability associated with intentions to buy durable goods might well be higher in H_{01} than in H_{00}. On this basis, it should be observed that:

$$a_{11} > a_{01}, a_{00} > a_{10} > 0,$$

and it may be that

$$a_{01} > a_{00}$$

Finally, it can be argued that the constant term should be positive, with little if any variation among the groups. Buying intentions, the only available measure of durable goods purchase probability, is basically a dichotomous variable. In an equation of the form

$$P_0 = c_0 + a_0\hat{P}_0 + b_0(F_0 + U_0) + e_0,$$

the a_0 coefficient measures the average difference in the purchase rates of intenders and nonintenders, while the constant is an estimate of the mean purchase rate of nonintenders, other things equal. Since nonintenders have a mean purchase rate greater than zero, c_0 will exceed zero.[25] It follows that

$$c_{01} \sim c_{10} \sim c_{11} \sim c_{00} > 0.$$

The empirical data do not, of course, contain variables that represent favorable or unfavorable intervening events per se, but can be fitted only to equations of the form

$$P = c' + a\hat{P} + e',$$

where $c' = c + b(\bar{F} + \bar{U})$
$e' = e + \text{Var.} (F + U).$

Thus the constant term in a simple linear regression of purchases on buying intentions is an estimate of the combined influence of intervening events and the mean purchase rate of nonintenders. Since the latter is not expected to show much variation among the groups, other things equal, differences in the constant can be attributed primarily to the differential importance of intervening events.

In sum, the analysis suggests that, designating the constant term in a simple linear regression of purchases on buying intentions as k, the slope

[25] Data in Chapter 6, Table 23, indicate that mean purchases among nonintenders are typically greater than 1.0 durables.

coefficient as p, and the respective housing groups $H_{01}, \ldots, H_{00}$ by subscripts,[26]

$$k_{01} > k_{11} > k_{00} > k_{10},$$

and

$$p_{11} > p_{01}, p_{00} > p_{10} > 0;$$

perhaps,

$$p_{01} > p_{00}.$$

Differences in the influence of intervening events on purchases in these four groups ought to show up as differences in the constant term, while differences in the mean *ex ante* probability associated with durable goods buying intentions ought to show up as differences in the slope of the regression coefficient for buying intentions.

Differences among these groups in the correlation between purchases and buying intentions should also be observable. A priori, groups in which the variance of intervening events is relatively large ought to show a relatively weak $P, \hat{P}$ correlation, since the error variance will include the within-group variance of $F + U$. The variance of $F + U$ probably *tends to be greater for groups in which intervening events are more important*—H_{01} and H_{10}. On that count the intentions-purchases correlation ought to be stronger in H_{00} than in the other three groups, and it can be argued that the $P, \hat{P}$ correlation should be stronger in H_{11} than in H_{01} or H_{10}.[27]

---

[26] It cannot be determined a priori whether all of the k coefficients will be greater than zero. k_{01}, k_{11}, and k_{00} clearly ought to exceed zero; the balance of intervening events is either favorable or very slightly unfavorable, while the mean purchase rate of nonintenders is considerably above zero and should outweigh the (slight) negative influence of intervening events in the H_{00} group. In H_{10}, however, it is not clear that the negative influence of unfavorable intervening events will *exceed the mean purchase rate of nonintenders.*

[27] The reasoning is as follows. The mean *ex ante* probability of a house purchase among those reporting intentions to buy a house can be roughly estimated as about 0.55; approximately 35 to 40 per cent of all intenders purchased a house, and the regression bias is likely to be fairly strong. The mean *ex ante* probability of a house purchase among those not intending to buy a house is likely to be around 0.05, perhaps less. Mean probability among intenders is the weighted average of the means in H_{10} and H_{11}; since the former group did not purchase and the latter group purchased, mean *ex ante* probability is presumed to be higher in H_{11}. It might be reasonable to assume that the mean *ex ante* probability of a housing purchase was roughly 0.80 in H_{11} and 0.50 in H_{10}. Similarly, the mean probability of 0.05 for nonintenders is the weighted average of the means for H_{01} and H_{00}. A reasonable set of figures here might be 0.30 for H_{01} and 0.04 for H_{00}.

Now the variance of $F + U$ in any of these groups depends largely on the mean *ex ante* probability of a housing purchase. I would judge that an appropriate measure of the variance involves the assumption that an *ex ante* mean of 0.50 in a group where all purchased houses is tantamount to saying that half of the group experienced favora-

The empirical results are summarized in Table 39. Because of the small sample sizes of the groups of households that purchased or intended to buy houses, a regression combining the A, B, and C groups in each life-cycle class is shown in addition to separate regressions for each of the groups.

TABLE 39

BUYING INTENTIONS-PURCHASES CORRELATION WITHIN GROUPS CLASSIFIED BY LIFE-CYCLE AND HOUSING STATUS

	Life-Cycle Group 1				Life-Cycle Group 2				Life-Cycle Group 3			
	H_{01}	H_{10}	H_{11}	H_{00}	H_{01}	H_{10}	H_{11}	H_{00}	H_{01}	H_{10}	H_{11}	H_{00}
A subsamples												
k	2.29	1.27	2.37	0.88	2.40	1.21	2.20	1.29	1.78	2.26	1.17	1.43
p	0.44[a]	0.11	0.37[a]	0.49[a]	−0.16	0.26[a]	0.55[b]	0.41[a]	0.61[b]	0.18	0.88[a]	0.23[a]
r^2	0.12	0.02	0.14	0.13	0.02	0.15	0.12	0.10	0.15	0.01	0.68	0.04
N	85	83	61	852	50	54	32	863	20	31	14	559
B subsamples												
k	1.98	1.62	2.08	1.19	2.18	1.07	2.06	1.17	3.09	1.64	1.80	1.19
p	0.31	0.20[b]	0.44[a]	0.41[a]	0.35	0.11	0.53[a]	0.38[a]	0.11	−0.13	0.57[a]	0.32[a]
r^2	0.05	0.06	0.14	0.10	0.08	0.02	0.32	0.09	0.01	0.03	0.33	0.07
N	60	70	46	866	47	59	32	836	30	20	14	678
C subsamples												
k	2.00	1.23	1.48	0.97	0.82	1.30	0.69	0.82	0.61	0.84	1.46	1.08
p	0.40[a]	0.05	0.45[a]	0.37[a]	1.04[a]	0.09	0.67[a]	0.34[a]	0.73[a]	0.08	0.45[a]	0.29[a]
r^2	0.14	0.00	0.28	0.14	0.41	0.00	0.43	0.14	0.32	0.00	0.62	0.10
N	65	94	47	814	44	65	22	691	19	26	8	570
A, B, C, samples combined												
k	2.13	1.36	1.95	1.14	2.11	1.16	1.92	1.13	2.21	1.81	1.34	1.24
p	0.39[a]	0.09[b]	0.42[a]	0.37[a]	0.29[a]	0.15[a]	0.52[a]	0.34[a]	0.30[b]	−0.07	0.71[a]	0.27[a]
r^2	0.12	0.02	0.19	0.11	0.06	0.04	0.26	0.09	0.06	0.01	0.54	0.06
N	210	247	154	2,533	141	178	86	2,390	69	77	36	1,807

SOURCE: Basic data from Consumer Purchase Study, NBER. See accompanying text for description of procedures.

[a] = Significantly different from zero at 0.01 level, using t test.
[b] = Significantly different from zero at 0.05 level, using t test.

The pattern of the results, though erratic because of small sample sizes, is reasonably consistent with the propositions that mean *ex ante* purchase probability and the influence of intervening events differ along the lines discussed above. The groups that purchased houses (H_{01} and H_{11})

ble intervening events and the other half experienced nothing unforeseen. If "intervening events" are scaled $+1, -1, 0$, corresponding to favorable, unfavorable, or none, the respective means and variances would be:

Housing Group	Mean Value of $F + U$	Variance of $F + U$
H_{01}	$+.70$	.21
H_{10}	$-.50$	.25
H_{11}	$+.20$	.16
H_{00}	$-.04$	.04

generally have larger constants than the nonpurchase groups (H_{10} and H_{00}). But while H_{11} is apt to have a smaller constant than H_{01}, as predicted, there are numerous cases in which the reverse is true; and it is generally not the case that H_{10} has a smaller constant than H_{00}, as the analysis predicts. Further, there are cases in which H_{10} has the largest constant in any of the four groups. The ordering of the slope coefficients is uniformly in accord with predictions, although the size of many of these differences seems unduly large. The regression coefficient of intentions is larger for H_{11} than for H_{00} in eight of the nine subgroups; H_{10} has a smaller slope than H_{00} in all nine subgroups. There is no apparent difference in slope between H_{01} and H_{00}—in five groups, the slope in H_{01} is lower; and in the other four groups it is higher. There are, however, a few cases in which H_{01} has an extremely large slope.

Given these results, it is probable that some of the assumptions do not hold. For example, the slopes in the H_{10} groups are generally very small, and some are negative. It does not seem plausible that these coefficients are estimates of the difference in mean *ex ante* purchase probability between H_{10} intenders and nonintenders. By the same token, some of the slope coefficients in H_{01} and H_{11} seem unreasonably large. If the slope coefficients are seriously biased, it necessarily follows that the constants will be biased in the opposite direction. Thus, an adequate explanation for the observed facts—that H_{10} generally has a larger constant than consistent with the analysis, or that H_{01} and H_{11} frequently have smaller constants than predicted—may simply be that the estimated slope coefficients in these groups are systematically biased.

The analysis underlying Table 39 depends heavily on two critical assumptions: (1) within each of the housing groups the level of durable goods buying intentions is uncorrelated with intervening events; and (2) within each group the *ex ante* probability associated with durable goods buying intentions is also uncorrelated with the level of buying intentions. If favorable intervening events were positively correlated with the level of buying intentions, the regression coefficient of intentions (p) would then be too large as a measure of the mean difference in *ex ante* probability between intenders and nonintenders; the constant term (k) would be too small as a measure of the influence attributable to intervening events. The reverse would be true if U and $\hat{P}$ were positively correlated. Similarly, if the *ex ante* probability associated with intentions were higher for households that reported a relatively large number of buying intentions, the regression coefficient of $\hat{P}$ would be too large in that particular group, the constant term too small.

A comparison of mean purchases and buying intentions in the H_{01} and H_{11} groups, where the mean *ex ante* probability of a housing purchase is likely to be quite different (both purchased houses, but only those in H_{11} reported house-buying intentions), suggests that the higher the *ex ante* probability of buying a house, the larger are both intentions to buy and purchases of durable goods, given that a house is purchased. But if this is true for a comparison between households in H_{01} and H_{11}, it should apply equally well within these groups. If so, households in H_{01} or H_{11} with the highest (lowest) *ex ante* probability of purchasing a house would have reported the most (fewest) durable goods buying intentions and made the most (fewest) purchases, relative to other households in the same groups. To the extent that this is the case, the regression coefficient of buying intentions on purchases will be too large as a measure of the difference between intenders and nonintenders in mean purchase probability, the constant term too small as a measure of the importance of intervening events.

Similarly, mean durable goods buying intentions are generally much smaller in H_{10} than in H_{11} (both groups reported intentions to buy a house, but only those in H_{11} purchased), again indicating that the *ex ante* probability of buying a house is correlated with the number of buying intentions for durable goods. If this is also true within each of these groups, those with the largest number of durable goods buying intentions would have had relatively high *ex ante* probabilities of purchasing the house. Since none of the households in H_{10} purchased, those with relatively large numbers of durable goods buying intentions must therefore have experienced unfavorable intervening events to a greater degree than others in the same group. The consequence here is a *downward* bias in the regression coefficient of durable goods buying intentions in the H_{10} group, an *upward* bias in the constant term.

These considerations also bear on the within-group correlations between intentions and purchases. The data show that the correlation between purchases and intentions is generally weaker in H_{01} and H_{10} than in H_{11}, and generally stronger in H_{00} than in H_{10}, as predicted. That is,

$$r_{11} > r_{01}, r_{10}$$
$$r_{00} > r_{10},$$

where the subscripts denote the housing groups and r is the simple correlation between purchases and durable goods buying intentions. However, it is also true that r_{11} is always greater than r_{00}, and that r_{01} is frequently greater than r_{00} and almost always greater than r_{10}. Both r_{11} and r_{01} thus tend to be higher than anticipated and r_{10} tends to be lower than anticipated, observations consistent with the presence of within-group intercorrelations between the *ex ante* probability associated with buying intentions and the level of intentions.

One experiment that shows rather interesting results is to substitute a set of partially a priori regression coefficients for those shown in Table 39 and then to recompute the constant. The data provide empirical evidence that

$$p_{11} > p_{01}, \; p_{00} > p_{10},$$

but the quantative differences seem unduly large. Suppose it is assumed that p_{00} is an unbiased estimate of p^*_{00}—the "true" regression coefficient in H_{00}. Since the sample size in H_{00} is extremely large and the importance of intervening events is presumably less than in any of the other groups, any bias ought not to be serious. The data indicate that p_{10} is smaller than p_{00}, but the differences seem too large on a priori grounds. So p^*_{10} is arbitrarily set equal to $p^*_{00} - 0.05$. There is no empirical evidence that p_{01} differs from p_{00}; hence, p^*_{01} is set equal to p^*_{00}. Finally, the empirical evidence indicates that p_{11} is greater than p_{00}, but again the difference seems too large in many of the groups. In addition, it appears that the difference between p_{11} and p_{00} varies with life-cycle status; a careful scrutiny of Table 39 suggests that $p_{11} - p_{00}$ is quite small in the youngest age group, quite large in the oldest age group, and of moderate size in the central age group. Accordingly, it is assumed that in A_1, B_1, and C_1: $p^*_{11} = p^*_{00} + 0.05$; in A_2, B_2, and C_2: $p^*_{11} = p^*_{00} + 0.15$; and in A_3, B_3, and C_3: $p^*_{11} = p^*_{00} + 0.25$.[28] Given these assumptions a new set of constants—k^*—can be estimated.[29] These are shown in Table 40, with the original k values included for comparison.

[28] It is not quite accurate to designate all of the p^* estimates as "assumptions." The p coefficients are of course empirically obtained. Since p^*_{00} is assumed equal to p_{00}, it is basically an empirical estimate. Similarly, p^*_{01} is assumed equal to p^*_{00}, but p_{01} shows no systematic tendency to differ from p_{00}. The estimate of p^*_{10} is essentially arbitrary, since the data suggest only that p^*_{10} is lower than p^*_{00}. Finally, the p^*_{11} estimates are reasonably close to the (observed) average p_{11} for the A, B, and C samples in the respective life-cycle classes, as can be seen from the following tabulation.

Life-cycle Class	Computed Mean p_{11}	Mean Estimate of p^*_{11}
1	.42	.47
2	.58	.53
3	.63	.57

[29] In the A_3 group shown in Table 39, the estimate of p_{00} seemed unduly low. The estimates of k^* are based on the assumption that all the p_{00} regression coefficients are unbiased except for this one, which was raised from 0.23 to 0.35. This adjustment has some effect on the differentials in p^* but serves mainly to reduce all the k^* values in the A_3 group.

The k^* estimates are almost wholly consistent with the hypotheses advanced earlier, except in the A sample. The rank ordering of the k^* estimates is perfectly consistent with the predicted ordering for all three life-cycle classes in the combined (A + B + C) sample, for the mean of the k^* estimates in the separate samples, and for the C sample.

TABLE 40

ESTIMATED AND COMPUTED VALUES OF THE CONSTANT TERM IN A LINEAR REGRESSION OF PURCHASES ON BUYING INTENTIONS WITHIN SPECIFIED LIFE-CYCLE AND HOUSING STATUS GROUPS

	Estimated k^*					Computed k				
	A	B	C	A + B + C	Mean of A, B, C	A	B	C	A + B + C	Mean of A, B, C
Life-cycle group 1										
H_{01}	2.23	1.85	2.06	2.16	2.04	2.29	1.98	2.00	2.13	2.09
H_{10}	0.94	1.30	0.31	0.85	0.85	1.27	1.62	1.23	1.36	1.37
H_{11}	2.01	2.03	1.59	1.95	1.87	2.37	2.08	1.48	1.95	1.97
H_{00}	0.88	1.19	0.97	1.14	1.01	0.88	1.19	0.97	1.14	1.01
Life-cycle group 2										
H_{01}	1.68	2.15	2.15	2.03	1.99	2.40	2.18	0.82	2.11	1.80
H_{10}	1.03	0.60	0.64	0.80	0.75	1.21	1.07	1.30	1.16	1.19
H_{11}	2.19	2.06	1.39	2.00	1.88	2.20	2.06	0.69	1.92	1.65
H_{00}	1.29	1.17	0.82	1.13	1.09	1.29	1.17	0.82	1.13	1 09
Life-cycle group 3										
H_{01}	2.00	2.74	1.45	2.24	2.06	1.78	3.09	0.61	2.21	1.82
H_{10}	2.17	0.62	0.31	1.21	1.03	2.26	1.64	0.84	1.81	1.58
H_{11}	2.05	1.79	1.27	1.95	1.70	1.17	1.80	1.46	1.34	1.48
H_{00}	1.35	1.19	1.08	1.24	1.20	1.43	1.19	1.08	1.24	1.23
Rank[a] r^2	0.16	0.75	1.00	1.00	1.00	0.16	0.64	0.00	0.44	0.44

SOURCE: Computed values of k from Table 39; see accompanying text for discussion of the k^* estimate.

[a] Predicted versus observed rank.

These results suggest a basis for recomputation of the net regression coefficients for H_{01}, H_{10}, and H_{11} in the multivariate analysis. If the mean probability associated with buying intentions is such that

$$p^*_{11} > p^*_{01}, \quad p^*_{00} > p^*_{10}$$

and if the numerical relations are those estimated above, the equation used to estimate the coefficients of H_{01}, H_{10} and H_{11} was not properly specified. Instead of one buying intentions variable there ought to have been several, reflecting the fact that the mean probability associated with durable goods buying intentions differs among the housing groups. A rough estimate of the coefficients that would have been observed for H_{01}, H_{10}, and H_{11} if separate intentions variables had been included in the analysis can be obtained from the p^* values.

The coefficients of the housing variables in Tables 42–44 are estimates of the difference in mean purchases of durables between households in H_{00} and those in the other three groups, other things equal. The coefficient of buying intentions is an estimate of the difference between intenders and nonintenders in mean purchase probability. The above analysis suggests that mean probability among intenders is a function of whether the household is in H_{01}, H_{10}, H_{11}, or H_{00}; that mean probability among nonintenders is about the same for households in all four groups; and that the difference among these four groups in the mean probability associated with buying intentions is adequately measured by the p^* estimates. Granting these propositions, the appropriate coefficients for H_{01}, H_{10}, and H_{11} can be approximated by the following procedure.

1. Start with the coefficients of the housing dummy variables in the regression that does not include buying intentions (column 6 in Tables 42–44). These coefficients are estimates of mean differences in purchases of durables between H_{00} and the other groups, other things equal but ignoring intentions to buy durables.

2. Assume that p^*_{00}—the true regression coefficient of buying intentions in H_{00}—is equal to the net regression coefficient of buying intentions for the sample as a whole, as estimated in column 7 of Tables 42–44. The "true" coefficients of buying intentions in H_{01}, H_{10}, or H_{11} are then estimated from the assumed differences between p^*_{00} and p^*_{01}, p^*_{10}, or p^*_{11}.

3. Multiply the p^* coefficients in step 2 by the mean difference between H_{00} and the other three groups in the level of buying intentions. This calculation indicates the degree to which purchases in H_{01}, H_{10}, or H_{11} are expected to be higher or lower than purchases in H_{00} because of differences among these groups either in the level of buying intentions or in the mean probability associated with intentions.

4. Adjust the housing coefficients estimated in step 1 by adding (subtracting) the differences calculated in step 3. The resulting figure is an estimate of what H_{01}, H_{10}, and H_{11} would have been if the "true" coefficient of buying intentions for each group, rather than one coefficient reflecting a weighted average for all groups, had been used in the regressions. The calculation rests on the assumption that interrelations among purchases, buying intentions, housing status, and all other variables included in Tables 42–44 regressions

would not be affected if separate intentions variables, reflecting the mean probability associated with buying intentions in each of the groups, had been used in place of the single intentions variable actually employed. Since all these interrelations appear to be quite weak, this assumption is unlikely to cause serious difficulty.

Table 41 summarizes alternative estimates of the regression coefficients for H_{01}, H_{10}, and H_{11}. The first estimate is taken from step 1 above; it consists of the mean differences in durable goods purchases between H_{00} and the other groups, as estimated by the multiple regression before account is taken of buying intentions but after standardizing for the influence of seven initial-data and two intervening variables. The second estimate is also taken directly from the multiple regressions; it measures differences among housing groups in mean purchases net of buying intentions, initial-data, and intervening variables on the implicit

TABLE 41

ALTERNATIVE ESTIMATES OF REGRESSION COEFFICIENTS FOR HOUSING CLASSIFICATION VARIABLES

Estimate Number	H_{01}	H_{10}	H_{11}	H_{01}	H_{10}	H_{11}	H_{01}	H_{10}	H_{11}
	A_1 SUBGROUP			A_2 SUBGROUP			A_3 SUBGROUP		
1.	1.20	−0.09	1.52	0.66	−0.13	1.25	0.68	0.54	2.04
2.	1.05	−0.23	1.05	0.49	−0.31	1.03	0.66	0.54	1.39
3.	0.99	−0.19	1.00	0.51	−0.44	1.08	0.64	0.53	1.38
4.	0.99	−0.18	0.93	0.51	−0.39	1.00	0.64	0.53	0.77
5.	1.35	0.06	1.13	0.39	−0.26	0.90	0.65	0.83	0.70
	B_1 SUBGROUP			B_2 SUBGROUP			B_3 SUBGROUP		
1.	0.77	0.30	1.53	1.14	−0.33	2.08	1.69	−0.27	2.26
2.	0.71	−0.03	1.06	1.05	−0.63	1.48	1.54	−0.53	1.78
3.	0.68	−0.10	0.95	1.04	−0.68	1.41	1.53	−0.61	1.59
4.	0.68	−0.04	0.87	1.04	−0.62	1.07	1.53	−0.54	0.82
5.	0.66	0.11	0.84	0.98	−0.57	0.89	1.55	−0.57	0.60
	C_1 SUBGROUP			C_2 SUBGROUP			C_3 SUBGROUP		
1.	1.39	−0.40	1.38	1.27	−0.06	1.94	0.45	−0.46	0.62
2.	1.10	−0.89	0.78	1.32	−0.40	1.33	0.40	−0.86	0.51
3.	1.09	−0.88	0.83	1.21	−0.58	1.26	0.43	−0.83	0.56
4.	1.09	−0.80	0.74	1.21	−0.49	0.94	0.43	−0.76	0.49
5.	1.09	−0.66	0.62	1.33	−0.18	0.57	0.37	−0.77	0.19
	$A_1 + B_1 + C_1$ SUBGROUP			$A_2 + B_2 + C_2$ SUBGROUP			$A_3 + B_3 + C_3$ SUBGROUP		
5.[a]	1.02	−0.29	0.81	0.90	−0.33	0.87	1.00	−0.03	0.71

SOURCE: See accompanying text for explanation of estimates.

[a] Multiple regression not computed; hence, estimates 1 through 4 could not be calculated.

assumption used in the first part of this chapter—that the mean probability associated with intentions does *not* vary systematically among the housing groups. The third estimate is similar in derivation to that described in step 4 above, but the coefficients of H_{01}, H_{10}, and H_{11} are based on the same assumption as in estimate 2—that the mean purchase probability associated with buying intentions is the same in all housing groups and is equal to the net coefficient of intentions in the basic multiple regressions. The fourth estimate is the one described in step 4; it measures differences in purchases net of buying intentions on the assumption that the probability associated with intentions is such that

in life-cycle class 1: $p^*_{11} - 0.05 = p^*_{01} = p^*_{00} = p^*_{10} + 0.05;$
in life-cycle class 2: $p^*_{11} - 0.15 = p^*_{01} = p^*_{00} = p^*_{10} + 0.05;$
in life-cycle class 3: $p^*_{11} - 0.25 = p^*_{01} = p^*_{00} = p^*_{10} + 0.05;$

and that in all three cases $p^*_{00} = X_{13}$, the net coefficient of intentions in Tables 42–44. The last estimate is derived from k^*; the mean differences in purchases between H_{00} and H_{01}, H_{10} or H_{11} are calculated as the respective differences between k^*_{00} and k^*_{01}, k^*_{10}, or k^*_{11}.

A comparison of the second and third estimates indicates the extent to which the rough-cut procedure described above is able to reproduce the results of a formal regression. The third and fourth estimates differ only with respect to assumptions about the mean purchase probability associated with buying intentions for durable goods; both estimates are derived from the first estimate in exactly the same way. A comparison of the third with the fourth estimate is therefore a fair measure of the change in the H_{01}, H_{10}, and H_{11} regression coefficients that would take place if the assumptions about differential mean probability among the housing groups were correct.

Averaging the data for all nine subgroups, the results indicate that those in H_{11} purchase 0.60 more durables than those in H_{01} when the influence of buying intentions is ignored, standardizing for the effect of initial-data and intervening variables (estimate 1). Taking account of intentions but assuming that the mean *ex ante* probability associated with intentions is the same for all housing groups, those in H_{11} still purchase more than those in H_{01}; but the average difference is considerably smaller—0.23 durables instead of 0.60 (estimate 2). A conceptually comparable figure based on a rough approximation (estimate 3) yields an average difference of 0.22. If it is assumed that mean *ex ante* probability varies according to the p^* values, the differential is reversed on average, although the mean difference is small—0.05 durables (estimate 4). Finally, the k^* estimate

(5) indicates that those in H_{01} purchase more net of intentions than those in H_{11}, the average differential for all nine groups being 0.21 durables. These results support the proposition that the H_{01} coefficient would in fact be greater than H_{11} if the *ex ante* probability differences associated with intentions were held constant, or if a good measure of purchase probability itself, rather than intentions to buy, were available.

In sum, the model predicts that the coefficient of H_{01} must exceed that for H_{11}, holding purchase probability constant, because favorable intervening events must have been more common in H_{01}. The regression data in Tables 42–44 indicate that the reverse is true, a finding that I would regard as strong contradictory evidence vis-à-vis the probability model. But the simple regressions of purchases on intentions within the housing groups clearly suggest that mean *ex ante* probability is likely to be different for intenders in these groups, and reasonable assumptions about the size of the differences are sufficient to reverse the original result.

Summary

The results in this chapter lend additional support to the hypothesis that consumer responses to questions about intentions to buy durable goods are basically a reflection of purchase probability. To a considerable degree, information about income, assets, durables stock, expectations, and attitudes is not needed to explain differences among households in reported durable goods purchases; it may be that these variables are not completely redundant to intentions because the latter constitutes a less than adequate proxy for purchase probability. On the other hand, variables that reflect wholly or partly unforseen events are strongly associated with durable goods purchases net of all other explanatory factors, as predicted. The summary tabulation below shows the mean of the F ratios (i.e., the means of the squared t ratios for each variable in the respective groups, taken from column 7 in Tables 42–44) for the groups of independent variables discussed at the beginning of the chapter—objective initial-data variables, of which the model contains four, anticipatory initial-data variables (three), intervening variables (five), and buying intentions variables (three).

Class of Variables	Number of Variables	Subsample								
		A_1	A_2	A_3	B_1	B_2	B_3	C_1	C_2	C_3
Initial-Data										
Objective	4	4.1	3.3	3.6	7.9	6.1	7.2	1.2	4.8	1.6
Anticipatory	3	6.8	1.6	2.6	0.8	5.6	1.1	5.7	4.0	2.6
Intervening	5	11.5	5.3	2.4	5.2	8.4	7.3	10.1	7.8	1.4
Buying Intentions	3	46.0	45.0	13.4	36.0	28.0	13.0	45.3	36.7	19.5

In all nine groups, intentions to buy durable goods have by far the strongest net relation to durable goods purchases; in six of the nine groups, intervening variables are more strongly related to purchases, on average, than either category of initial-data variables.[30] More importantly, the net influence of initial-data variables is reduced in all eighteen cases (nine subgroups, both objective and anticipatory categories) when buying intentions are held constant; in contrast, the net influence of intervening variables is increased in nine of eighteen comparable cases (nine subgroups, both income-change and housing categories). Finally, in the only instance where the empirical results generally stand in apparent contradiction to the model—the regression coefficient of anticipated housing purchases generally exceeds that of unanticipated housing purchases—it can be shown that the contradiction is only apparent: A simplifying assumption that holds in most cases clearly does not hold for the housing variables, and relaxation of the assumption makes enough difference to reverse the original results.

[30] It is true that the intervening income-change variables (ΔY and ΔY_t) are less strongly related to purchases than some of the initial-data variables, net of intentions to buy. However, the intervening income-change variables happen to be less strongly related to purchases throughout, and the model predicts that the net influence of initial-data variables will be *reduced* to a greater degree than that of intervening variables when intentions are held constant, not that the net influence of initial-data variables will be less. A glance at Tables 42–44 indicates clearly that intentions have less influence on the intervening income-change variables than on the initial-data variables, and that the former are generally less closely related to purchases than the latter.

TABLE 42

SUMMARY OF CORRELATION DATA FOR TWELVE-MONTH DEFINITE AND PROBABLE-POSSIBLE INTENDERS CLASSIFIED BY LIFE-CYCLE STATUS

INDEPENDENT VARIABLES	REGRESSION COEFFICIENTS FOR CORRELATION BETWEEN							F RATIOS FOR ZERO-ORDER CORRELATION WITH P	
	Buying Intentions ($\hat{P}$) and			Durable Goods Purchases (P) and				$\hat{P}$	P
	$x_1 \ldots x_4$	$x_1 \ldots x_7$	$x_1 \ldots x_{12}$	$x_1 \ldots x_4$	$x_1 \ldots x_7$	$x_1 \ldots x_{12}$	$x_1 \ldots x_{16}$		
	(1)	(2)	(3)	(4)	(5)	(6)	(7)	(8)	(9)
A_1—HUSBAND-WIFE HOUSEHOLDS, HEAD BETWEEN 25 AND 34 YEARS OLD									
Initial-Data									
Objective	(9.0)	(7.7)	(8.8)	(10.2)	(7.4)	(6.8)	(4.1)		
Y	.019	.010	.007	.064**	.052**	.048**	.039*	4.3	28.8
ΔL_{-1}	.088	.024	.004	.093	.004	.000	−.000	3.2	3.2
ΔY_{-1}	.065	.024	.037	.025	−.010	−.024	−.039	4.3	1.1
S'	.135**	.140**	.147**	.100*	.108*	.106**	.020	24.3	7.6
Anticipatory		(15.9)	(12.7)		(14.8)	(10.9)	(6.8)		
E		.361	.260		.286	−.019	−.100	6.5	4.3
O		.305**	.283**		.436**	.383**	.291**	35.7	53.2
$\hat{E}_s$		.186**	.157*		.086	.043	−.010	15.3	3.2
Intervening									
Income Changes			(0.9)			(3.7)	(4.3)		
ΔY			−.034			.126*	.125*	0.0	13.1
ΔY_i			−.106			.252	.289	0.0	4.3
Housing									
Unanticipated P			(5.2)			(33.6)	(28.1)		
H_{01}			.422*			1.196**	1.055**	6.5	34.5
Unfulfilled $\hat{P}$			(1.9)			(0.2)	(1.4)		
H_{10}			.242			−.094	−.234	0.0	2.2
Anticipated P			(40.0)			(39.7)	(19.4)		
H_{11}			1.275**			1.519**	1.053**	42.6	38.0
Buying Intentions[a]							(46.0)		
$\hat{P}$							.375**		133.3
$\hat{P}_c$							.081		16.4
$Z\hat{P}_c$							.132		
Constant	.478**	−.132	.015	.946**	.428	.264	.045		
R^2	.032	.073	.113	.036	.075	.139	.210		

(continued)

213

TABLE 42 (continued)

	REGRESSION COEFFICIENTS FOR CORRELATION BETWEEN							F RATIOS FOR ZERO-ORDER CORRELATION WITH	
	Buying Intentions ($\hat{P}$) and			Durable Goods Purchases (P) and					
INDEPENDENT VARIABLES	$x_1 \ldots x_4$	$x_1 \ldots x_7$	$x_1 \ldots x_{12}$	$x_1 \ldots x_4$	$x_1 \ldots x_7$	$x_1 \ldots x_{12}$	$x_1 \ldots x_{15}$	$\hat{P}$	P
	(1)	(2)	(3)	(4)	(5)	(6)	(7)	(8)	(9)
A_2—HUSBAND-WIFE HOUSEHOLDS, HEAD BETWEEN 35 AND 44 YEARS OLD									
Initial-Data									
Objective									
Y	(16.8) .044**	(14.7) .036**	(15.6) .034**	(12.0) .039**	(10.2) .034**	(10.7) .035**	(3.3) .021*	33.0	20.3
ΔL_{-1}	.003	−.092	−.109	.132	.080	.058	.055	0.1	6.0
ΔY_{-1}	.081	.011	.006	.073	.038	−.011	−.030	4.0	3.0
S'	.153**	(16.4) .164**	(15.3) .167**	.156**	(4.2) .162**	(4.5) .168**	(1.6) .078*	29.8	22.4
Anticipatory									
$\hat{E}$		−.038	−.101		−.250	−.355	−.372	0.0	0.0
O		.398**	.382**		.247**	.247**	.131	53.6	18.3
$\hat{E}_s$		.120	.110		.039	.030	−.022	5.0	0.1
Intervening									
Income Changes									
ΔY			(0.0) .017			(5.8) .152*	.148*	0.0	6.0
ΔY_s			.001			.494*	.488*	0.0	8.0
Housing									
Unanticipated P									
H_{01}			(4.8) .548*			(6.2) .664*	(3.6) .488	3.0	4.0
Unfulfilled $\hat{P}$									
H_{10}			(20.4) .966**			(0.0) −.013	(1.4) −.312	22.4	0.0
Anticipated P									
H_{11}			(1.7) .451			(14.4) 1.253**	(10.2) 1.027**	3.0	15.0
Buying Intentions[a]									
$\hat{P}$				.958**	1.056**	.608	(45.0) .292**	91.4	35.1
$\hat{P}_c$							.148**		
$Z\hat{P}_c$							−.009		
Constant	.127	−.096	−.141				.527		
R^2	.064	.109	.132	.046	.058	.089	.158		

(continued)

214

TABLE 42 (concluded)

A_3—HUSBAND-WIFE HOUSEHOLDS, HEAD BETWEEN 45 AND 64 YEARS OLD

Initial-Data								F	F
Objective	(9.1)	(9.8)	(11.1)	(8.2)	(4.9)	(5.9)	(3.6)		
Y	.012	.005	.004	.043**	.035**	.035**	.033**	3.2	22.5
ΔL_{-1}	.100	.042	.046	.106	.046	.065	.047	0.6	2.5
ΔY_{-1}	−.052	−.109	−.086	.160	.102	.100	.126	0.0	5.6
S	.196**	.204**	.215**	.100*	.107*	.114*	.042	32.0	5.6
Anticipatory									
$\hat{E}$		(10.0) .227	(7.6) .135		(5.8) −.113	(4.7) −.300	(2.6) −.351	3.2	0.0
O		.269**	.250**		.309**	.281*	.214*	14.6	19.9
$\hat{E}_5$		.379**	.336**		.325*	.262*	.166	13.8	9.5
Intervening									
Income Changes									
ΔY			(1.5) .066			(0.6) .100	(0.4) .077	1.2	1.9
ΔY_t			−.233			−.005	.051	2.5	0.0
Housing									
Unanticipated P									
H_{01}			(0.0) .073			(2.2) .679	(2.2) .657	0.0	1.9
Unfulfilled $\hat{P}$									
H_{10}			(0.4) −.246			(2.2) .541	(2.2) .540	0.0	3.8
Anticipated P									
H_{11}			(33.2) 2.326**			(14.4) 2.038**	(6.8) 1.388*	34.0	18.5
Buying Intentions[a]									
$\hat{P}$							(13.4) .267**		48.2
$\hat{P}_e$							.054		
$Z\hat{P}_e$							−.002		3.8
Constant	.348*	−.123	−.265	.982**	.826	.859	.898		
R^2	.055	.099	.151	.050	.076	.111	.148		

SOURCE: Basic data from Consumer Purchase Study, NBER.
NOTE: Figures in parentheses in first seven columns are either F ratios or joint F ratios.

* = t ratio > 2.
** = t ratio > 3.
[a] $\hat{P}$ signifies definite intentions to buy within a year; $\hat{P}_e$, probable-possible intentions to buy within a year.

TABLE 43

SUMMARY OF CORRELATION DATA FOR SIX-MONTH AND "LATER" INTENDERS CLASSIFIED BY LIFE-CYCLE STATUS

| INDEPENDENT VARIABLES | REGRESSION COEFFICIENTS FOR CORRELATION BETWEEN | | | | | | | F RATIOS FOR ZERO-ORDER CORRELATION WITH | |
| | Buying Intentions ($\hat{P}$) and | | | Durable Goods Purchases (P) and | | | | | |
	$x_1 \ldots x_4$ (1)	$x_1 \ldots x_7$ (2)	$x_1 \ldots x_{12}$ (3)	$x_1 \ldots x_4$ (4)	$x_1 \ldots x_7$ (5)	$x_1 \ldots x_{12}$ (6)	$x_1 \ldots x_{15}$ (7)	$\hat{P}$ (8)	P (9)
B₁—HUSBAND-WIFE HOUSEHOLDS, HEAD BETWEEN 25 AND 34 YEARS OLD									
Initial-Data									
Objective									
Y	(20.0) .035**	(17.6) .028*	(16.9) .033**	(15.6) .064**	(13.0) .059**	(13.5) .066**	(7.9) .056**	13.7	30.0
ΔL_{-1}	.178*	.126	.102	.138	.101	.077	.047	10.5	7.4
ΔY_{-1}	.053	.047	.020	.104*	.100*	.077	.073	4.2	8.4
S'	.199**	.205**	.197**	.147**	.151**	.144**	.079*	53.6	21.2
Anticipatory									
$\hat{E}$		(11.0) -.193	(8.3) -.247		(3.8) .098	(2.1) -.018	(0.8) .056	0.0	2.1
O		.326**	.257**		.225**	.160*	.085	34.4	16.9
$\hat{E}_s$		.076	.091		.033	.036	.006	2.1	1.0
Intervening									
Income Changes									
ΔY			(1.4) -.058			(2.3) -.058	-.036	0.0	0.0
ΔY_t			.220			.307	.234	3.1	4.2
Housing									
Unanticipated P									
H_{01}			(0.4) .205			(10.2) .773**	(9.0) .710**	0.0	6.3
Unfulfilled $\hat{P}$									
H_{10}			(24.3) .936**			(1.7) .300	(0.0) -.032	25.6	2.1
Anticipated P									
H_{11}			(34.5) 1.443**			(30.2) 1.530**	(14.4) 1.062**	38.8	31.1
Buying Intentions[a]									
$\hat{P}$							(36.0) .359**		128.1
$\hat{P}_c$							-.019		1.0
$Z\hat{P}_c$							.068*		
Constant	.476**	.457	.588*	.882**	.664*	.842*	.550		
R^2	.071	.100	.152	.057	.067	.104	.165		

(continued)

216

TABLE 43 (continued)

B₂—HUSBAND-WIFE HOUSEHOLDS, HEAD BETWEEN 35 AND 44 YEARS OLD

Initial-Data									
Objective	(22.3)	(19.0)	(22.1)	(13.0)	(12.1)	(11.9)	(6.1)		
Y	.028**	.023*	.025**	.038**	.032**	.033**	.026**	16.8	18.8
ΔL_{-1}	.284**	.215*	.194*	.112	.032	.048	−.004	14.8	2.0
ΔY_{-1}	−.075	−.103	−.068	−.098	−.138*	−.119	−.103	0.0	2.0
S'	.208**	.212**	.210**	.170**	.177**	.172**	.109**	57.6	29.0
Anticipatory		(9.3)	(8.3)		(9.2)	(8.3)	(5.6)		
$\hat{E}$		.167	−.050		.655*	.463	.480	0.0	3.9
O		.311**	.284**		.332**	.333**	.256**	33.2	25.9
$\hat{E}_s$		.041	.004		.038	−.013	−.019	0.0	0.0
Intervening									
Income Changes			(0.0)			(0.0)	(0.3)		
ΔY			−.036			.049	.055	0.0	0.0
ΔY_t			.026			−.023	−.018	0.0	0.0
Housing									
Unanticipated P			(2.0)			(16.8)	(15.2)		
H_{01}			.409			1.136**	1.046**	0.0	12.8
Unfulfilled $\hat{P}$			(27.2)			(1.7)	(6.8)		
H_{10}			1.119**			−.331	.634*	22.9	2.0
Anticipated P			(57.9)			(38.4)	(19.4)		
H_{11}			2.234**			2.079**	1.475**	54.4	40.5
Buying Intentions[a]							(28.0)		
$\hat{P}$							.291**		115.2
$\hat{P}_c$							.003		0.0
$Z\hat{P}_c$							.018		
Constant	.412**	.068*	.259	.972**	.148	.141	−.032		
R^2	.085	.110	.185	.050	.076	.130	.179		

(continued)

TABLE 43 (concluded)

| | REGRESSION COEFFICIENTS FOR CORRELATION BETWEEN | | | | | | | F RATIOS FOR ZERO-ORDER CORRELATION WITH | |
| | Buying Intentions ($\hat{P}$) and | | | Durable Goods Purchases (P) and | | | | | |
INDEPENDENT VARIABLES	$x_1 \ldots x_4$ (1)	$x_1 \ldots x_7$ (2)	$x_1 \ldots x_{12}$ (3)	$x_1 \ldots x_4$ (4)	$x_1 \ldots x_7$ (5)	$x_1 \ldots x_{12}$ (6)	$x_1 \ldots x_{15}$ (7)	$\hat{P}$ (8)	P (9)
			B_3—HUSBAND-WIFE HOUSEHOLDS, HEAD BETWEEN 45 AND 64 YEARS OLD						
Initial-Data									
Objective									
Y	(24.6) .035**	(24.5) .031**	(24 4) .031**	(12.4) .052**	(11.6) .049**	(11.2) .050**	(7.2) .044**	16.6	30.8
ΔL_{-1}	.275*	.239*	.202*	.100	.065	.046	.006	10.5	2.2
ΔY_{-1}	.095	.039	.004	.143	.123	.052	.053	2.2	3.7
S'	.282**	.288**	.269**	.150**	.153**	.142**	.093**	59.1	9.7
Anticipatory									
$\hat{E}$		(8.8) .702*	(7.5) .601*		(2.6) -.048	(2.3) -.076	(1.1) -.218	6.7	0.0
O		.291**	.287**		-.235*	.219*	.142	23.7	12.0
$\hat{E}_s$		.005	.001		.024	.000	.004	0.7	0.7
Intervening									
Income Changes									
ΔY			(1.1) .067			(3.8) .054	(3.2) .052	0.7	1.3
ΔY_t			.216			.562*	.524*	0.7	4.5
Housing									
Unanticipated $\hat{P}$									
H_{01}			(3.0) .582			(22.1) 1.687**	(17.6) 1.535**	3.7	21.3
Unfulfilled $\hat{P}$									
H_{10}			(14.8) 1.448**			(0.4) -.274	(1.4) -.532	13.6	0.7
Anticipated P									
H_{11}			(33.1) 2.585**			(18.5) 2.257**	(10.9) 1.776**	40.6	21.3
Buying Intentions[a]									
$\hat{P}$							(13.0) .220**	63.5	2.2
$\hat{P}_c$							-.056		
$Z\hat{P}_c$							-.030		
Constant	.205	-.666*	-.836*	.740**	.622	.523	.702		
R^2	.117	.148	.207	.063	.073	.130	.162		

SOURCE: Basic data from Consumer Purchase Study, NBER.

NOTE: Figures in parentheses in first seven columns are either F ratios or joint F ratios.

* = t ratio > 2.

** = t ratio > 3.

[a] $\hat{P}$ signifies intentions to buy within six months; $\hat{P}_c$, intentions to buy later.

TABLE 44

SUMMARY OF CORRELATION DATA FOR TWELVE-MONTH AND INCOME-CONTINGENT INTENDERS CLASSIFIED BY LIFE-CYCLE STATUS

| | REGRESSION COEFFICIENTS FOR CORRELATION BETWEEN | | | | | | | F RATIOS FOR ZERO-ORDER CORRELATION WITH | |
| | Buying Intentions ($\hat{P}$) and | | | Durable Goods Purchases (P) and | | | | | |
INDEPENDENT VARIABLES	$x_1 \ldots x_4$ (1)	$x_1 \ldots x_7$ (2)	$x_1 \ldots x_{12}$ (3)	$x_1 \ldots x_4$ (4)	$x_1 \ldots x_7$ (5)	$x_1 \ldots x_{12}$ (6)	$x_1 \ldots x_{15}$ (7)	$\hat{P}$ (8)	P (9)
c_1—HUSBAND-WIFE HOUSEHOLDS, HEAD BETWEEN 25 AND 34 YEARS OLD									
Initial-Data									
Objective									
Y	(34.0)	(29.3)	(36.0)	(9.7)	(7.2)	(8.0)	(1.2)		
	.063**	.047**	.053**	.046	.034*	.038**	.022	21.8	13.4
ΔL_{-1}	.232*	.141	.072	.138	.076	.034	.010	13.4	5.1
ΔY_{-1}	.221**	.167**	.162**	.083	.043	.039	-.006	20.8	4.1
S'	.316**	.322**	.321**	.144**	.148**	.151**	.043	73.1	16.6
Anticipatory									
$\hat{E}$		(20.8)	(16.6)		(11.7)	(11.0)	(5.7)		
		.656	.299		.318	.283	.199	6.1	3.1
O		.501**	.449**		.343**	.308*	.192*	64.6	32.6
$\hat{E}_5$		.220*	.199*		.228*	.273**	.208*	13.4	12.3
Intervening									
Income Changes									
ΔY			(0.9)			(2.3)	(1.6)		
			-.063			-.082	-.066	0.0	0.0
ΔY_t			.231			.262	.208	1.0	1.0
Housing									
Unanticipated P									
H_{01}			(6.7)			(33.6)	(22.1)		
			.790*			1.387**	1.100**	8.2	36.9
Unfulfilled $\hat{P}$			(49.4)			(4.0)	(17.6)		
H_{10}			1.474**			-.397	-.893**	44.6	4.1
Anticipated P			(34.0)			(24.0)	(7.8)		
H_{11}			1.863**			1.384**	.785*	28.2	22.9
Buying Intentions[a]									
$\hat{P}$							(45.3)		
							.287**	154.8	
$\hat{P}_c$							.048		20.8
$Z\hat{P}_c$							.034		
Constant	.872**	-.153	.174	1.056**	.424	.638	.423		
R^2	.118	.170	.241	.037	.069	.130	.203		

(continued)

219

TABLE 44 (continued)

INDEPENDENT VARIABLES	Buying Intentions ($\hat{P}$) and			Durable Goods Purchases (P) and				F RATIOS FOR ZERO-ORDER CORRELATION WITH	
	$x_1 \ldots x_4$ (1)	$x_1 \ldots x_7$ (2)	$x_1 \ldots x_{12}$ (3)	$x_1 \ldots x_4$ (4)	$x_1 \ldots x_7$ (5)	$x_1 \ldots x_{12}$ (6)	$x_1 \ldots x_{15}$ (7)	$\hat{P}$ (8)	P (9)
C_2—HUSBAND-WIFE HOUSEHOLDS, HEAD BETWEEN 35 AND 44 YEARS OLD									
Initial-Data									
Objective									
Y	(34.2) .038**	(31.7) .028*	(34.8) .028*	(13.4) .051**	(12.0) .043**	(12.2) .041**	(4.8) .032**	10.8	21.9
ΔL_{-1}	.241*	.113	.127	.075	−.014	.040	.006	9.1	1.6
ΔY_{-1}	.095	.078	.062	−.008	−.032	−.056	−.070	3.3	0.0
S'	.375**	.369**	.372**	.189**	.186**	.186**	−.072*	105.5	26.2
Anticipatory									
$\hat{E}$		(20.9) .852*	(16.7) .696*		(10.2) .467	(8.7) .472	(4.0) .289	10.8	4.1
O		.551**	.492**		.358**	.334**	.190*	61.7	30.6
$\hat{E}_s$		.012	−.045		.175	.172	.176*	1.6	6.6
Intervening									
Income Changes									
ΔY			(2.5) .163*			(1.5) .108	(0.8) .060	4.9	4.1
ΔY_t			.062			.201	.184	0.0	0.8
Housing									
Unanticipated P									
H_{01}			(0.0) .012			(20.2) 1.274**	(23.0) 1.320**	0.0	21.0
Unfulfilled $\hat{P}$									
H_{10}			(27.0) 1.245**			(0.1) −.060	(2.6) −.402	34.2	0.0
Anticipated P									
H_{11}			(27.5) 2.131**			(24.0) 1.940**	(11.6) 1.328**	20.2	19.3
Buying Intentions[a]									
$\hat{P}$							(36.7) .316**		140.2
$\hat{P}_c$							−.011		6.6
$Z\hat{P}_c$							.078		
Constant	.834**	−.253	−.710	.648**	−.053	−.536	−.446		
R^2	.141	.201	.257	.061	.095	.145	.219		

(continued)

TABLE 44 (concluded)

C_3—HUSBAND-WIFE HOUSEHOLDS, HEAD BETWEEN 45 AND 64 YEARS OLD

								F	F
Initial-Data									
Objective									
Y	(38.0) .050**	(35.0) .036**	(35.3) .038**	(7.6) .037**	(6.6) .029*	(6.4) .030*	(1.6) .020*	14.0	11.4
ΔL_{-1}	.288*	.149	.130	−.012	−.118	−.101	−.132	7.5	0.0
ΔY_{-1}	.264**	.184*	.181**	.150	.089	.070	.026	10.7	3.1
S'	.444**	.439**	.441**	.158**	.160**	.158**	.045	96.9	12.0
Anticipatory									
$\dot{E}$	(11.0) −.257	(10.9) −.335			(6.0) .449	(5.3) .394	(2.6) .461	0.0	1.9
O	.479**	.486**			.328**	.324**	.212*	42.4	21.8
$\dot{E}_s$	.234	.187			.141	.134	.086	8.2	4.4
Intervening									
Income Changes									
ΔY			(0.7) .085			(0.3) .032	(0.4) .013	2.5	1.2
ΔY_t			−.147			.163	.198	0.0	1.9
Housing									
Unanticipated P, H_{01}			(0.0) .089			(1.0) .448	(0.8) .396	12.7	1.2
Unfulfilled $\hat{P}$, H_{10}			(15.9) 1.482**			(1.4) .456	(4.8) −.859*	0.0	1.9
Anticipated P, H_{11}			(0.5) .311			(0.8) .616	(0.6) .514	0.0	1.2
Buying Intentions[a]									
$\hat{P}$				.899**			(19.5) .253**	67.5	
$\hat{P}_e$							.011	0.0	
$Z\hat{P}_e$							.025		
Constant	.582**	.529	.262		.259	.134	.043		
R^2	.196	.238	.259	.047	.075	.082	.137		

SOURCE: Basic data from Consumer Purchase Study, NBER.

NOTE: Figures in parentheses in first seven columns are either F ratios or joint F ratios.

* = t ratio > 2.
** = t ratio > 3.

[a] $\hat{P}$ signifies intentions to buy within twelve months; $\hat{P}_e$, intentions to buy within twelve months if income is higher than expected.

APPENDIXES

APPENDIX A

Results from the Preliminary Regression Analysis

Introduction

As NOTED, an intensive investigation of the relation of durables purchases to initial-data variables and buying intentions preceded the empirical analysis in Chapter 7; this investigation focused on a somewhat different set of problems than those discussed in the text.

First, it seemed clearly desirable to construct a model that would explain purchases as a function of purely objective (nonanticipatory) variables, such as income, asset level, amount of debt, durable goods stock, number of children, and so forth. In order to evaluate the usefulness of consumer anticipations it is essential to demonstrate that they are not redundant to readily available objective factors; hence, the latter have first priority, so to speak. Secondly, it seemed desirable to investigate alternative ways of introducing anticipatory variables into the model. For example, test regressions were designed to find out how expected and actual income change influence purchase behavior. These can be treated as separate variables or combined into an "income surprise" construct (actual change minus expected change). The difficulty is that a variable purporting to measure income surprise may be related to purchases simply because actual change in income is so related. This would clearly be the case if expectations were a random variable, since surprise would then be actual change minus a random error. Thus it is necessary to know whether expected and actual changes are separately related to purchases in order to know whether surprise is simply a proxy for actual change or is a meaningful variable in its own right. The test regressions were also used to experiment with the scaling assigned to qualitative variables.

Finally, it is clear from the analysis in the text that extensive testing for interactions may well be fruitful. In some cases separate regressions were computed for intenders and nonintenders to see if the coefficients were uniform. In other cases the entire sample was used and interaction variables introduced. These interactions usually had the form ZX, where X is any initial-data variable, $Z = 1$ when standard intentions are zero, $Z = 0$ otherwise. If the equation to be tested is

$$P = b_0 + b_1X + b_2ZX,$$

the estimated regression coefficient of X is $b_1 + b_2Z$. When $Z = 0$, the estimated regression coefficient of X is thus b_1; when $Z = 1$, it is $b_1 + b_2$. Other interactions were introduced in the form of cross-product terms, that is,

$$P = b_0 + b_1 X + b_2 Y + b_3 XY.$$

Here the coefficient of X is $b_1 + b_3 Y$; that of Y, $b_2 + b_3 X$.

Testing for interaction tends to limit the usefulness of significance tests involving standard errors. There is bound to be a relatively large covariance between any variable and an interaction term involving the same variable, for example, between X and ZX. Thus, the standard error of X will rise substantially when ZX or XY is introduced into a regression along with X. In some cases it turned out that neither X nor ZX was statistically significant, although X was significant before adding ZX, and ZX had a larger coefficient than X.

In addition to the difference in focus, the regressions in this appendix are estimated from samples that eliminated all households which either purchased houses during the forecast period or reported intentions to buy houses at the beginning of the forecast period; these are the groups designated in Chapter 7 as H_{01}, H_{10}, and H_{11}. Most of the households in these three groups purchased very large numbers of durables and reported large numbers of buying intentions, and it seemed preferable to test the potentially explanatory variables without allowing their possible inter-relations with house purchases or house-buying intentions to influence the results. In addition, a number of other households were excluded from the sample in both the Appendix A and Chapter 7 regressions, as indicated in the discussion of basic data sources contained in Appendix C.

Regressions were estimated for the same set of (nine) subgroups analyzed above. To repeat the notation, subgroups are designated by a letter and a subscript. The letter refers to the particular set of questions asked about intentions to buy; the subscript, to life-cycle stage. The designations for the nine groups are as follows:

Group A (definitely or probably—possibly plan to buy within twelve months)
    A_1—married, head between 25 and 34 years old
    A_2—married, head between 35 and 44
    A_3—married, head between 45 and 64
Group B (plan to buy within six months or later)
    B_1—married, head between 25 and 34
    B_2—married, head between 35 and 44
    B_3—married, head between 45 and 64

Group C (plan to buy within twelve months if income is higher, lower, as expected)

C₁—married, head between 25 and 34
C₂—married, head between 35 and 44
C₃—married, head between 45 and 64

Test regressions were run in several of these subgroups. Some variables were tested once or twice and then excluded; others were tested, then rescaled and tested again or tested in interaction. The results presented below are influenced by these tests; in effect, part of the data have been used to refine hypotheses.

Description and Analysis of Variables

The variables that seemed to have some promise as predictors of purchases are shown below, listed in the order of introduction into the regression. Many of these are identical to variables analyzed in Chapter 7; hence, the numerical designation in Chapter 7 is shown (X_1, X_2, etc.), as well as the designation in this appendix (X_{1a}, X_{2a}, etc.).

Independent Variables			*Scale*	*Designation in Chapter 7*
Objective variables:				
X_{1a}	Y	Normal family income, before tax (bracket mid-points)	$000	X_1
X_{2a}	ΔL_{-1}	Change in liquid assets prior to forecast period	+1 = increase 0 = no change −1 = decrease	X_2
X_{3a}	ΔY_{-1}	Change in income prior to forecast period	+3 = large increase +1 = small increase 0 = no change −1 = small decrease −3 = large decrease	X_3
X_{4a}	ΔY_t	Transitory income during the forecast period	+1 = positive transitory 0 = no transitory −1 = negative transitory	X_9
X_{5a}	T	Education level of household head	1 = college graduate 0 = otherwise	
X_{6a}	H	Housing status	1 = own home 0 = otherwise	
X_{7a}	S'	Desired stock adjustment	12 = maximum 0 = minimum	X_4
Anticipatory variables:				
	$\Delta \hat{Y}$	Expected change in income	5 = large increase 4 = small increase 3 = no change 2 = small decrease 1 = large decrease	
	$\Delta \hat{B}$	Expected change in general business conditions	Same as $\Delta \hat{Y}$	

		Independent Variables	Scale	Designation in Chapter 7
X_{8a}	$\hat{E}$	Index of expectations, combining $\Delta\hat{Y}$ and $\Delta\hat{B}$	$2 = \Delta\hat{Y} \times \Delta\hat{B} \geq 20$ $1 =$ otherwise $0 = \Delta\hat{Y} \times \Delta\hat{B} \leq 2$	X_5
	Y_s	Unexpected income developments	$(\Delta Y - \Delta\hat{Y}) + 5$ Maximum value $= 9$ Minimum value $= 1$	
	B_s	Unexpected developments in general business conditions	$(\Delta B - \Delta\hat{B}) + 5$ Maximum value $= 9$ Minimum value $= 1$	
X_{9a}	$E - \hat{E}$	Index of surprises combining Y_s and B_s	$2 = Y_s B_s \geq 36$ $1 =$ otherwise $0 = Y_s B_s \leq 16$	
X_{10a}	O	Opinion about current buying conditions	$2 =$ good time to buy $1 =$ pro-con, other $0 =$ bad time to buy	X_6
X_{11a}	$\hat{E}_b$	Long-range financial expectations	$2 =$ very optimistic $1 =$ moderately optimistic $0 =$ otherwise	X_7
X_{12a}	$O\hat{E}_b$			
X_{13a}	$\hat{C}$	Expected change in prices	$1 =$ expect decrease $0 =$ otherwise	

Buying intentions variables:

X_{14a}	$\hat{P}$	"Standard" intentions to buy durables	Weighted sum of items listed $6 =$ maximum $0 =$ minimum	X_{13}
X_{15a}	$\hat{P}_c$	"Contingent" intentions to buy durables	Weighted sum of items listed $6 =$ maximum $0 =$ minimum	X_{14}
X_{16a}	$\hat{P}\hat{P}_c$			

Interactions:

($Z = 1$ when $\hat{P} = 0$, $Z = 0$ when $P > 0$; $Z_1 = 1$ when $E - \hat{E} = 2$, $Z_1 = 0$ when $E - \hat{E} < 2$)

X_{17a}	ZS'
X_{18a}	ZY
X_{19a}	$\hat{E}\hat{P}$
X_{20a}	ZO
X_{21a}	$Z_1\hat{P}_c$

These variables fall roughly into four categories, which are noted in the list: objective variables, anticipatory variables, intentions to buy, and interactions. A few variables test interaction between variables in the same category, and these are analyzed with the category. All variables except Y_t, $E - \hat{E}$, and $Z_1\hat{P}_c$ are either initial-data variables (in the terminology of Chapter 7), buying-intentions variables, or interactions involving initial-data variables.

OBJECTIVE VARIABLES

The objective model, comprising the first seven variables, provides a bench mark against which to measure the performance of anticipatory variables. All seven are expected to have positive regression coefficients.

Income and income change prior to the forecast period need no explanation. Liquid-asset change is intended to reflect the influence of two factors. Windfalls prior to the forecast period ought to result in increased liquid-asset holdings, as should saving for the purpose of acquiring durables. Also, the inverse relation between purchases in t_{-1} and purchases in t may be reflected in liquid-asset accumulation or diminution. The transitory income variable departs from a pure forecast model, since the information was not obtained until the end of the period. This variable constitutes a partial test of the permanent income hypothesis, since it measures the influence of a (subjective) transitory income component on durable goods purchases, net of both past income change and "normal" income change during the forecast period.[1]

The education variable is intended to measure the influence of long-run income expectations, since young households with more education, given current income, should have relatively favorable future earnings prospects. Thus, a higher level of education should be associated with less current saving among young households, and perhaps with a greater willingness to incur indebtedness and acquire durables. The home ownership variable is intended to reflect the possibility that owners have more needs for durables, both because of their living pattern and because they must ordinarily purchase most household equipment, whereas many renters have these items supplied by the landlord.

The stock adjustment variable consists of responses to a question about whether or not items in the household's stock of durable goods "need to be replaced." These responses presumably reflect unsatisfactory functioning of the durables stock in a mechanical sense, due to age or hard use, as well as dissatisfaction due to the availability of newer and technically more advanced models.[2] The variable is treated as a measure of the difference between actual and desired stock of durables, as discussed in Chapter 7.

Other objective variables were tested in preliminary regressions and discarded. These include assets, nonmortgage debt, number of children, house purchases prior to the forecast period, and stock of durable goods.

[1] The permanent income hypothesis predicts a higher propensity to save (counting additions to the stock of durables as saving) out of the transitory component of income than out of the permanent component. Our data test whether households with positive or negative transitory income buy more or less durables, holding income and income change constant. Thus a finding of no net association does not contradict the permanent income hypothesis, since the transitory component might have its full effect on saving in the form of financial assets.

[2] Similar questions have been included in past surveys by the Survey Research Center (Michigan University) and in surveys conducted by the Census Bureau. I am not aware of any published analysis of results.

The probable reason for the failure of some of these variables to show a significant relation to purchases is that they are balance sheet or "stock" variables that reflect the tastes and preferences of the household. Purchases are a "flow" variable, and constitute the most important way of adjusting any difference between actual and preferred asset structure. Hence, it seems likely that what James Tobin has called personality correlations have a strong influence on the observed relation between current purchases and debts, assets, or stock of durables. Some households with relatively small debts, large assets, and small stocks of durables are in that position precisely because of their preference structure; they have and will continue to purchase relatively few durables. The reverse is true for some households with large debts, small asset holdings, and large stocks of durables—they have a taste for durables, and have and will continue to purchase relatively many.

Consequently, one could argue that the *lack* of a significant relation in cross sections between purchases and assets, debts, and durable goods stocks could mean that the latter variables actually do exert an influence on purchases in the expected direction. If they did not, personality correlations would produce a negative statistical association between purchases and asset holdings and positive ones between purchases and debt or durable goods stock. In fact, small positive regression coefficients appear for both debt and stock of durables, while households with assets over $10,000 make somewhat fewer purchases than others. But none of these relations is statistically significant.

An attempt was made to test the influence of durable goods stocks in groups stratified by a measure of personality. It is reasonable to assume that those with a taste for durable goods ought to own at least one durable in addition to a car or the basic household items—range, refrigerator, washing machine, and television set. Separate regressions were run on groups with only the basic items (or less) and those with more than the basic amount. The latter group showed a positive association between durables stock and purchases, net of all the important explanatory variables; those with the basic items only showed a negative association between stock and purchases. Neither coefficient was significant at the 5 per cent level.[3] These results suggest that the behavioral relationship would probably show through if personality differences could really be eliminated. The positive coefficient for S in the second equation may be due to the heterogeneity of the group characterized by a stronger than mini-

[3] The net regression coefficients are as follows, using the notation above and designating the stock of durables as S. Equation (1) includes the entire sample, (2) includes

mum preference for durables (i.e., to personality correlations *within* the group), and to the fact that ownership of some commodities (dishwashers, etc.) seems to be associated with a higher probability of purchase than nonownership because of its intercorrelation with the probability of a housing purchase (see Chapter 4, Tables 20 and 21). The third group is almost certainly more homogeneous with respect to taste than the second, and is less likely to purchase housing; and a negative association does turn up there.

ANTICIPATORY VARIABLES

The next six variables represent either attitudes, expectations, or surprises. The expectations index $(\hat{E})$ represents a combination of short-term expectations about income and general business conditions. The surprise index $(E - \hat{E})$ represents a similar combination of unexpected developments with respect to income and general business conditions. It was argued above (Chapter 6) that only extreme expected or actual changes exert an influence on purchase behavior. An index of expectations was therefore constructed that distinguished only between very optimistic, very pessimistic, and in-between views. A surprise index, reflecting the same emphasis on the extremes, was also constructed. It is hypothesized that both expectations and surprises have an influence on purchases. The relationship under test amounts to the following, where E is an index of actual change and $\hat{E}$ is an index of expected change, both scaled to emphasize the extremes.

$$1.0 \qquad P = b_0 + b_1\hat{E} + b_2(E - \hat{E}) + \cdots + u$$

It is anticipated that b_1 and b_2 will both be positive. Thus, expected change enters the regression in two ways. Expectations themselves are associated with purchases; and surprises, holding expectations constant,

---

households with more than "basic" S, and (3) those with basic S or less (asterisk denotes coefficient significant at 5 per cent level, using t test).

NET REGRESSION COEFFICIENTS FOR INDEPENDENT VARIABLES

	Y	ΔL_{-1}	ΔY_{-1}	ΔY_t	S	S'	$\hat{P}$	R^2
(1)	+.0087*	+.178	+.090	+.769*	+.029	+.113*	+.287*	.199
(2)	+.0068*	+.165	+.076	+.847*	+.215	+.059	+.301*	.166
(3)	+.0084*	+.258	+.098	+.574*	−.060	+.182*	+.301*	.200

Equation 1 is not wholly comparable with the other two because it also included some other variables not shown, one of which accounted for about 2 per cent of the total explained variance.

are also associated with purchases. Note that this relation is equivalent to:

$$1.1 \qquad P = b_0 + b_3 E + b_4 \hat{E} + \cdots + u$$

If 1.0 is the true relationship, and if $b_1 \sim b_2$, testing 1.1 would show $b_3 > 0$ and $b_4 \sim 0$, even though expectations actually do have an impact on purchases. Testing equation 1.0 in a stepwise regression would show that for

$$P = a + b_1 \hat{E} + \cdots + u,$$

$b_1 \sim 0$; and that for

$$P = a + b_1 \hat{E} + b_2 (E - \hat{E}) + \cdots + u.$$

$b_1 > 0, b_2 > 0$.

The next three variables can be construed either as attitudes or as judgments about the short- and long-term financial outlook for the household. Opinion about buying conditions (O) is obtained from responses to a question about whether "the present is a [good, bad, other] time for you to buy, *taking into account the financial situation in your household.*" A question asked respondents in the Survey of Consumer Finances is essentially the same as this one but uses a projective technique, i.e., "Is this a (good, bad) time for people *like yourselves* to buy household items?" The projective question has generally been interpreted as reflecting an evaluation of market conditions.[4] The opinion variable is included in the attitude index, along with expected price developments, in the group of variables headed "Attitudes Towards Market Conditions." Katona and Mueller present evidence that what people mean when they say "it's a good time to buy" is that prices are low or not rising, discounts are available, etc.; when people say "it's a bad time to buy" they mean that prices are too high or will fall later, discounts are not available, etc. There are also substantial numbers of people who refer to present or prospective financial circumstances as the reason why it's a good (bad) time to buy, i.e., "people can't afford to buy now" or "times are good now," etc.; this is especially true for those with favorable opinions about buying conditions.[5]

The Katona-Mueller interpretation of this variable may well be correct when a projective technique is used to obtain responses. However, the

[4] See George Katona and Eva Mueller, *Consumer Attitudes and Demand, 1950–1952*, Ann Arbor, Michigan University Survey Research Center, n.d.; and Katona and Mueller, *Consumer Expectations, 1953–1956*, Ann Arbor, Michigan University Survey Research Center, n.d.

[5] Katona and Mueller, *Consumer Attitudes and Demand*, pp. 17–19, and *Consumer Expectations*, p. 34.

opinion variable from the CU data does not appear to reflect market conditions in this sense. Rather, the matrix of correlation coefficients indicates that O is most closely associated with factors such as recent changes in liquid assets and income, income expectations, and expectations about general business conditions. There is some relation between price expectations and opinion about buying conditions, but this relation is much weaker than the others. The O variable thus seems to constitute a kind of subjective weighting of the factors that influence short-term financial outlook, much as the buying intentions variable reflects a subjective weighting of factors associated with purchase probability.

The next variable—long-range financial prospects $(\hat{E}_5)$—represents another subjective judgment by the household. This variable was originally obtained on a nine-point scale, including three gradients of optimism and pessimism, no change, other, and an uncertain category. Preliminary tests indicated that the association between purchases and the original scale was quite weak, although generally in the appropriate direction. A truncated scale, differentiating only among very optimistic, moderately optimistic, and all other households, was more strongly associated with purchases and is used below.[6]

The last of the three financial prospect variables consists of the interaction between O and $\hat{E}_5$; a cross-product interaction term is used. It seemed to me that optimism or pessimism regarding short-range prospects might as well be doubly reinforced by similar judgments about longer-range prospects. If so, those with favorable short-range prospects would tend to make relatively heavier purchases if their long-range prospects were also very favorable than if they were not, and vice versa.

The remaining variable in this category consists of expectations about price movements $(\hat{C})$. During the period covered by this study the common expectation (in this sample, at any rate) was that prices would either rise or remain the same; only about 10 per cent expected a price decline. The price variable was included in the preliminary regressions in a variety of ways; the only consistent evidence suggested that those anticipating a decline in prices might have purchased relatively more durables than the others. I would interpret this as evidence of bargain-hunting—those who expected price declines had been holding off purchases in the hope of lower prices; when the 1957–58 recession came to an

[6] As noted in Chapter 7, the criteria actually consisted of extreme or moderate optimism on the April 1958 survey and either no change or a one-category shift in optimism on the succeeding one. It did not seem plausible that a meaningful judgment about long-range prospects could change radically during a six-month interval; hence, those households with a substantial shift were put into the "all other" category.

end (at about the time of the survey) these households decided to go ahead, either because they actually found lower prices, higher discounts, etc., or because they ceased to expect that prices would go any lower. This interpretation is suggested by two supporting pieces of evidence: first, the expectation of price declines is associated with relatively many buying intentions; second, this association is stronger in the older age groups, where one anticipates bargain-hunting in a sample of Consumers Union subscribers. Thus, the $\hat{C}$ variable distinguishes only between those expecting price declines and all others.

BUYING INTENTIONS VARIABLES

The three variables included here have been discussed extensively in the text. They are "standard" intentions to buy durables ($\hat{P}$), "contingent" intentions to buy durables ($\hat{P}_c$), and the cross-product interaction term $\hat{P}\hat{P}_c$. $\hat{P}$ represents responses to the relatively high-probability part of a multiple intentions question; $\hat{P}_c$, responses to the relatively low-probability part of such a question. Also, these variables mean different things in the A, B, and C samples. For example, $\hat{P}$ is associated with a considerably higher mean purchase probability in the A and B samples than in the C sample, while $\hat{P}_c$ is associated with a mugh higher mean purchase probability in the A sample than in either B or C.[7] The interaction variable $\hat{P}\hat{P}_c$ is designed to permit the influence of $\hat{P}_c$ to vary with the level of $\hat{P}$. It is anticipated that the coefficient of the interaction variable will be negative and, hence, that the influence of $\hat{P}_c$ on P will be stronger when $\hat{P}$ is zero than when $\hat{P}$ is positive.[8] That is, it is anticipated that contingent intentions will be more closely associated with purchases when standard intentions are zero, less closely associated with purchases when standard intentions are positive.

INTERACTION VARIABLES

With two exceptions, these are designed to test the hypothesis that the effect of specified variables on purchases is different for (standard) intenders and nonintenders. Three variables were selected from the first two

---

[7] See Chapters 2 and 3.

[8] In a regression of the form

$$P = b_0 + b_1\hat{P} + b_2\hat{P}_c + b_3\hat{P}\hat{P}_c,$$

it is expected that b_1 and b_2 will be >0, $b_3 < 0$. If so, there is some level of $\hat{P}$ at which the net effect of $\hat{P}_c$ is zero; at higher levels of $\hat{P}$ the computed net effect of $\hat{P}_c$ would be negative, a logically untenable outcome. However, the size of b_2 and b_3 is rather completely determined by what happens between $0 \leq \hat{P} \geq 2$, and in this zone the net effect of $\hat{P}_c$ is generally positive.

categories that seemed, on preliminary analysis, to be strongly related to purchase behavior—normal income (Y), opinion about buying conditions (O) and stock adjustment (S'). Interaction variables of the form

$$P = b_o + b_1\hat{P} + b_2[X] + b_3Z[X],$$

where $Z = 1$ when $\hat{P} = 0$,
$\quad\quad Z = 0$ when $\hat{P} > 0$

are introduced for the Y, O, and S' variables.

The last two interaction terms test for the existence of special relations between buying intentions and particular anticipatory variables. Data analyzed in connection with Chapter 6 suggest that buying intentions might be more closely associated with purchases for households with very favorable expectations about both income prospects and business conditions. Therefore, I introduce the three-way interaction $\Delta\hat{Y} \times \Delta\hat{B} \times \hat{P}$, anticipating that the coefficient will be positive; the variable actually used is $\hat{E} \times \hat{P}$, since $\hat{E}$ is essentially a nonlinear version of $\Delta\hat{Y} \times \Delta\hat{B}$. The last variable tests for interaction between contingent intentions to buy $(\hat{P}_c)$ and favorable surprises. The analysis in Chapter 6 suggests that the association between purchases and contingent intentions might be stronger for households experiencing unexpectedly favorable events than for others.[9] Therefore, the interaction variable $Z_1\hat{P}_c$ is introduced, where $Z_1 = 1$ when $E - \hat{E} = 2$, $Z_1 = 0$ when $E - \hat{E} < 2$.[10]

Some systematic differences are predicted among groups asked different buying-intentions questions, and among groups asked the same intentions questions but whose life-cycle status differed. It should be observed that the net influence of both objective and anticipatory initial-data variables is relatively stronger when standard intentions are so defined that the probability cut-off point is relatively high. When this is the case interactions involving differences between intenders and nonintenders should have a stronger effect. In addition, it is anticipated that the regression coefficients of $\hat{P}$ and $\hat{P}_c$ will be consistent with predictions of the probability model as discussed in Chapter 7. Among life-cycle groups, expectational variables are expected to have more (and objective variables less) influence among younger households, simply because the future has a wider range of possible outcomes (and the past has less relevance) for the younger groups. In more technical terms, there should be greater variance in

---

[9] See Chapter 6. I have also discussed this in "Some Interrelationships Among Expectational Variables and Durable Goods Purchases," unpublished paper read at December 1960 meeting of the Econometric Society.

[10] $E - \hat{E} = 2$ for households that experience unexpectedly favorable developments with respect to both their own income and general business conditions.

wealth (including the discounted value of future earnings) among younger households, and wealth should be correlated with responses to expectational questions.

Basic Data

The regression data for the nine samples are presented in Tables A-1 through A-9; the subgroup designations are those discussed above in "Description and Analysis of Variables." Each table is identical in general format. The stub lists the variables in order of their introduction. The first four columns summarize net regression coefficients for objective variables, then for objective and anticipatory variables, and so on. Regression coefficients that are significantly different from zero at the

TABLE A-1

CORRELATION DATA RELATING AGGREGATE PURCHASES OF CONSUMER DURABLES TO OBJECTIVE, ANTICIPATORY, AND BUYING INTENTIONS VARIABLES, GROUP A_1[a]

Independent Variables	Regression Coefficients for Independent Variables				Simple Correlations with	
	$X_1 \ldots X_7$[b]	$X_1 \ldots X_{13}$	$X_1 \ldots X_{16}$	$X_1 \ldots X_{21}$	P	$\hat{P}$
Objective						
Y	.046*	.033*	.021	041*	0.11	0.10
ΔL_{-1}	.137	.029	.012	005	0.07	0.08
ΔY_{-1}	.000	−.025	−.043	− 039	0.03	0.07
ΔY_t	.354*	.282	.309*	.274	0.07	−0.04
T	−.146	−.117	−.137	−.147	0.00	0.00
H	−.084	−.077	−.021	−.022	−0.00	−0.04
S'	.089*	.089*	.002	−.073	0 08	0.19
Anticipatory						
$\hat{E}$		.517	.580	.577	0.06	0.00
$E − \hat{E}$		.332	.265	087	0.01	0.00
O		.424*	.326*	.144	0.24	0.16
$\hat{E}_b$		.114	.002	− 003	0.07	0.17
$O\hat{E}_b$		.049	.059	.082	0.20	0.19
$\hat{C}$		.117	.010	.034	−0.01	0.05
Buying Intentions						
$\hat{P}$			.520*	521*	0.30	1.00
$\hat{P}_c$			.147*	132*	0.10	−0.03
$\hat{P}\hat{P}_c$			−.095*	− 089*	0.15	0.66
Interactions						
ZS'				.118	−0.01	−0.25
ZY				−.035*	−0.14	−0.55
$\hat{E}\hat{P}$				.001	0.28	0.91
ZO				.281*	0.08	−0.28
$Z_1\hat{P}_c$				.153	0.08	−0.01
Multiple R	.179	.290	.406	.420		
Multiple R^2	.032	.084	.165	.176		

For notes, see end of Table A-9.

TABLE A-2

CORRELATION DATA RELATING AGGREGATE PURCHASES OF CONSUMER DURABLES TO
OBJECTIVE, ANTICIPATORY, AND BUYING INTENTIONS VARIABLES, GROUP A_2[a]

Independent Variables	Regression Coefficients for Independent Variables				Simple Correlations with	
	$X_1 \ldots X_7$[b]	$X_1 \ldots X_{13}$	$X_1 \ldots X_{16}$	$X_1 \ldots X_{21}$	P	$\hat{P}$
Objective						
Y	.036*	.030*	.014	.011	0.11	0.17
ΔL_{-1}	.126	.071	.076	.075	0.07	0.03
ΔY_{-1}	.026	.003	$-.024$	$-.024$	0.06	0.07
ΔY_t	.625*	.621*	.592*	.577*	0.11	0.01
T	$-.047$	$-.051$	.031	.035	0.02	-0.00
H	.025	-001	$-.075$	$-.075$	0.02	0.08
S'	.166*	.166*	.069*	.068	0.17	0.21
Anticipatory						
$\hat{E}$		$-.252$	$-.111$	$-.054$	-0.02	-0.02
$E - \hat{E}$		.254	.348	.264	0.05	0.01
O		.196*	.083	.040	0.12	0.25
$\hat{E}_5$		$-.016$	$-.043$	$-.039$	0.01	0.10
$O\hat{E}_5$		.062	$-.006$	.003	0.10	0.25
$\hat{C}$		.215	.131	.126	0.05	0.06
Buying Intentions						
$\hat{P}$			.452*	.525*	0.31	1.00
$\hat{P}_c$			.159*	.153*	0.16	-0.03
$\hat{P}\hat{P}_c$			$-.041$	$-.040$	0.23	0.66
Interactions						
ZS'				.004	0.00	-0.26
ZY				.000	-0.14	-0.56
$\hat{E}\hat{P}$				$-.004$	0.27	0.92
ZO				.064	-0.04	-0.31
$Z_1\hat{P}_c$				.050	0.09	0.03
Multiple R	.239	.267	.392	.393		
Multiple R^2	.057	.071	.153	.154		

For notes, see end of Table A-9.

5 per cent level are noted by an asterisk. The last two columns show zero-order correlations of all independent variables with both purchases and standard buying intentions.

The empirical results are summarized briefly below. Each category of variables is then analyzed in turn, and regression coefficients are presented net and gross of the different categories to the extent that this can be done. The sequence of variables was designed to permit measurement of the influence of anticipations net of objective variables, and of the influence of intentions net of both anticipations and objective variables. The influence of anticipatory variables (as a group) net of intentions, or of objective variables (as a group) net of either of the other two groups,

TABLE A-3

CORRELATION DATA RELATING AGGREGATE PURCHASES OF CONSUMER DURABLES TO OBJECTIVE, ANTICIPATORY, AND BUYING INTENTIONS VARIABLES, GROUP A_3[a]

Independent Variables	Regression Coefficients for Independent Variables				Simple Correlations with	
	$X_1 \ldots X_7$[b]	$X_1 \ldots X_{13}$	$X_1 \ldots X_{16}$	$X_1 \ldots X_{21}$	P	$\hat{P}$
Objective						
Y	.047*	.042*	.039*	.041*	0.22	0.05
ΔL_{-1}	.131	.117	.098	.102	0.07	0.03
ΔY_{-1}	.141	.075	.082	.088	0.11	0.02
ΔY_t	.062	.045	.096	.119	0.02	−0.07
T	.081	.114	.157	.152	0.08	−0.07
H	−.494*	−.505*	−.496*	−.466*	−0.08	−0.04
S'	.100*	.100*	.033	−.022	0.10	0.25
Anticipatory						
$\hat{E}$		−.274	−.341	−.239	−0.02	0.04
$E - \hat{E}$		.255	.233	.308	0.01	−0.01
O		.075	.027	.097	0.15	0.16
$\hat{E}_s$		.041	−.012	.004	0.12	0.11
$O\hat{E}_s$		.317*	.311*	.315*	0.19	0.16
$\hat{C}$		−.166	−.148	−.177	−0.05	−0.05
Buying Intentions						
$\hat{P}$			.179*	.367*	0.19	1.00
$\hat{P}_c$			.087*	.090*	0.10	−0.11
$\hat{P}\hat{P}_c$			.014	.022	0.16	0.56
Interactions						
ZS'				.079	0.00	−0.23
ZY				−.004	0.03	−0.48
$\hat{E}\hat{P}$				−.019	0.14	0.91
ZO				−.097	0.02	−0.32
$Z_1\hat{P}_c$				−.058	0.03	−0.01
Multiple R	.274	.321	.361	.370		
Multiple R^2	.075	.103	.130	.137		

For notes, see end of Table A-9.

cannot be measured because of the computer program used.[11] However, the relation between regression coefficients and standard errors will convey an accurate impression of the net influence of individual variables unless interactions are involved.

[11] The program obtained total explained variance for the sum of all variables every time a new variable was added. Thus, incremental explained variance is calculated only in one direction, so to speak. $R^2_{1.234}$ can be compared with $R^2_{1.23}$, and $r^2_{14.23}$ can be estimated by a simple calculation. But $r^2_{12.34}$ or $r^2_{13.24}$ would be more difficult to compute. This is not a problem if one is interested in incremental explained variance for individual variables. However, incremental explained variance for *groups* of variables that *precede* others cannot be obtained; the computation is feasible only for groups that follow others in the sequence of introduction into the stepwise regression. For example, given the computer program, one cannot obtain the incremental variance explained by $X_1, \ldots, X_6$ in an equation including $X_1, \ldots, X_{13}$; all that is known is the total variance explained by $X_1, \ldots, X_n$ or $X_1, \ldots, X_{n-a}$, not the total explained by $X_b, \ldots, X_n$.

TABLE A-4

CORRELATION DATA RELATING AGGREGATE PURCHASES OF CONSUMER DURABLES TO OBJECTIVE, ANTICIPATORY, AND BUYING INTENTIONS VARIABLES, GROUP B_1[a]

Independent Variables	Regression Coefficients for Independent Variables				Simple Correlations with	
	$X_1 \ldots X_7$[b]	$X_1 \ldots X_{13}$	$X_1 \ldots X_{16}$	$X_1 \ldots X_{21}$	P	$\hat{P}$
Objective						
Y	.056*	.054*	.050*	.047*	.16	0.10
ΔL_{-1}	.124	.102	.046	.041	.09	0.12
ΔY_{-1}	.127*	.116*	.110*	.112*	.12	0.07
ΔY_t	.123	.094	.089	.053	.03	0.03
T	.012	.034	−.039	−.043	.04	0.05
H	.009	−.102	−.102	−.092	.02	0.05
S'	.206*	.206*	.135*	.106*	.22	0.28
Anticipatory						
$\hat{E}$		−.013	−.013	−.012	.03	0.05
$E - \hat{E}$		−.010	−.008	−.007	−.03	−0.04
O		.248*	.187	.049	.10	0.12
$\hat{E}_5$		.090	.073	.074	.03	0.04
$O\hat{E}_5$		−.121	−.114	−.112	.05	0.12
$\hat{C}$		−.085	−.131	−.131	−.03	0.01
Buying Intentions						
$\hat{P}$			.334*	.419*	.29	1.00
$\hat{P}_c$			.055	.059	.08	−0.01
$\hat{P}\hat{P}_c$			−.015	−.016	.23	0.76
Interactions						
ZS'				.057	.05	−0.26
ZY				.005	−.08	−0.57
$\hat{E}\hat{P}$				−.000	.27	0.91
ZO				.308*	.02	−0.25
$Z_1\hat{P}_c$				−.017	−.01	−0.02
Multiple R	.296	.309	.376	.387		
Multiple R^2	.087	.095	.142	.150		

For notes, see end of Table A-9.

TABLE A-5

CORRELATION DATA RELATING AGGREGATE PURCHASES OF CONSUMER DURABLES TO
OBJECTIVE, ANTICIPATORY, AND BUYING INTENTIONS VARIABLES, GROUP B_2[a]

Independent Variables	Regression Coefficients for Independent Variables				Simple Correlations with	
	$X_1 \ldots X_7$[b]	$X_1 \ldots X_{13}$	$X_1 \ldots X_{16}$	$X_1 \ldots X_{21}$	P	$\hat{P}$
Objective						
Y	.040*	.035*	.028*	.030*	.16	0.14
ΔL_{-1}	.072	−.021	−.057	−.053	.04	0.11
ΔY_{-1}	−.064	−.096	−.090	−.094	−.03	0.01
ΔY_t	.055	.019	.038	.019	−.01	−0.00
T	.042	.047	.063	.060	.05	0.01
H	−.157	.203	−.083	−.066	−.02	−0.09
S'	.199*	.199*	.131*	.140*	.21	0.27
Anticipatory						
$\hat{E}$		.491	.392	.357	.06	0.07
$E - \hat{E}$		−.326	−.292	−.317	−.05	−0.04
O		.304*	.225*	.077	.14	0.18
$\hat{E}_s$		.069	.040	.022	.01	0.03
$O\hat{E}_s$		−.076	−.070	−.056	.06	0.11
$\hat{C}$		.087	.047	.066	−.00	0.01
Buying Intentions						
$\hat{P}$			.416*	.370*	.30	1.00
$\hat{P}_c$			.062*	.065*	.04	−0.05
$\hat{P}\hat{P}_c$			−.046*	−.049*	.19	0.71
Interactions						
ZS'				−.015	.00	−0.28
ZY				−.005	−.09	−0.52
$\hat{E}\hat{P}$				.009	.28	0.90
ZO				.259	.00	−0.32
$Z_1\hat{P}_c$				.010	−.02	−0.04
Multiple R	.268	.303	.380	.386		
Multiple R^2	.072	.092	.144	.149		

For notes, see end of Table A-9.

TABLE A-6
CORRELATION DATA RELATING AGGREGATE PURCHASES OF CONSUMER DURABLES TO
OBJECTIVE, ANTICIPATORY, AND BUYING INTENTIONS VARIABLES, GROUP B_3[a]

Independent Variables	Regression Coefficients for Independent Variables				Simple Correlations with	
	$X_1 \ldots X_7$[b]	$X_1 \ldots X_{13}$	$X_1 \ldots X_{16}$	$X_1 \ldots X_{21}$	P	$\hat{P}$
Objective						
Y	.051*	.050*	.044*	.047*	.21	0.15
ΔL_{-1}	.063	.041	−.006	−.007	.05	0.13
ΔY_{-1}	.071	.079	.077	.072	.06	0.06
ΔY_t	.408	.465*	.455*	.478*	.07	0.02
T	.016	−.039	−.032	−.019	.07	0.05
H	−.196	−.316	−.237	−.214	−.02	−0.03
S'	.179*	.179*	.127*	.144*	.14	0.24
Anticipatory						
$\hat{E}$		.311	.171	.066	.01	0.07
$E − \hat{E}$		.690*	.653*	.856*	.08	0.02
O		.249*	.182	.317*	.14	0.18
$\hat{E}_5$		−.052	−.046	−.053	.01	0.07
$O\hat{E}_5$		.019	−.018	−.070	.06	0.15
$\hat{C}$		.100	−.006	−.039	.03	0.12
Buying Intentions						
$\hat{P}$			.274*	.042	.27	1.00
$\hat{P}_c$			− 004	007	−.05	−0.17
$\hat{P}\hat{P}_c$			−.036	−.045	09	0.52
Interactions						
ZS'				−.042	−.02	−0.23
ZY				−.001	−.04	−0.50
$\hat{E}\hat{P}$				.017	.26	0.89
ZO				− 235	− 07	−0.35
$Z_1\hat{P}_c$				− 076	−.02	−0.08
Multiple R	.286	.321	.372	.387		
Multiple R^2	.082	.103	.139	.150		

For notes, see end of Table A-9.

TABLE A-7
Correlation Data Relating Aggregate Purchases of Consumer Durables to Objective, Anticipatory, and Buying Intentions Variables, Group C_1[a]

Independent Variables	Regression Coefficients for Independent Variables				Simple Correlations with	
	$X_1 \ldots X_7$[b]	$X_1 \ldots X_{13}$	$X_1 \ldots X_{16}$	$X_1 \ldots X_{21}$	P	$\hat{P}$
Objective						
Y	.047*	.038*	.017	.011	.13	0.18
ΔL_{-1}	.074	.016	−.016	−.020	.05	0.08
ΔY_{-1}	−.002	−.042	−.076	−.075	.03	0.12
ΔY_t	.297	.428*	.353*	.350*	.05	0.04
T	.039	−.040	−.046	−.042	.04	0.07
H	−.022	−.117	−.040	−.027	.02	−0.01
S'	.150*	.150*	.024	.043	.12	0.26
Anticipatory						
$\hat{E}$		.066	.165	.084	.02	−0.00
$E - \hat{E}$		−.197	−.021	.021	−.02	−0.06
O		.226*	.114	.095	.20	0.20
$\hat{E}_b$		.126	.063	.052	.11	0.08
$O\hat{E}_b$		.196*	.204*	.196*	.22	0.16
$\hat{C}$		.443*	.376	.420*	.05	0.01
Buying Intentions						
$\hat{P}$			.406*	.410*	.38	1.00
$\hat{P}_c$			.136*	.146*	.05	−0.10
$\hat{P}\hat{P}_c$			− 034	−.037*	.24	0.58
Interactions						
ZS'				−.081	−.11	−0.28
ZY				.035	−.16	−0.58
$\hat{E}\hat{P}$				.004	.36	0.89
ZO				.091	−.01	−0.29
$Z_1\hat{P}_c$				− 010	−.02	−0.07
Multiple R	.207	.309	.443	.449		
Multiple R^2	.043	.096	.196	.202		

For notes, see end of Table A-9.

TABLE A-8

CORRELATION DATA RELATING AGGREGATE PURCHASES OF CONSUMER DURABLES TO
OBJECTIVE, ANTICIPATORY, AND BUYING INTENTIONS VARIABLES, GROUP C_2[a]

Independent Variables	Regression Coefficients for Independent Variables				Simple Correlations with	
	$X_1 \ldots X_7$[b]	$X_1 \ldots X_{13}$	$X_1 \ldots X_{16}$	$X_1 \ldots X_{21}$	P	$\hat{P}$
Objective						
Y	.042*	.039*	.032*	.034*	.15	0.08
ΔL_{-1}	.087	.013	−.004	−.019	.05	0.08
ΔY_{-1}	.036	.006	−.031	−.022	.03	0.07
ΔY_t	.063	.117	.075	.070	.01	0.03
T	−.123	−.100	−.058	−.070	−.00	−0.03
H	.029	.027	.046	.050	.03	0.01
S'	.155*	.155*	.036	.018	.15	0.36
Anticipatory						
$\hat{E}$		.720*	.461	.280	.09	0.09
$E - \hat{E}$		−.005	−.034	.186	−.03	−0.03
O		.151	.032	.087	.14	0.22
$\hat{E}_5$		.054	.081	.048	.08	0.02
$O\hat{E}_5$		.124	.092	.084	.15	0.15
$\hat{C}$		.050	.016	.070	−.02	−0.02
Buying Intentions						
$\hat{P}$			.336*	.199*	.38	1.00
$\hat{P}_c$			.004	.006	−.03	−0.06
$\hat{P}\hat{P}_c$			−.006	−.002	.20	0.55
Interactions						
ZS'				.086	−.07	−0.26
ZY				.001	−.16	−0.51
$\hat{E}\hat{P}$				.010	.39	0.90
ZO				−.222	−.13	−0.31
$Z_1\hat{P}_c$				−.136	−.09	−0.08
Multiple R	.228	.279	.417	.430		
Multiple R^2	.052	.078	.174	.185		

For notes, see end of Table A-9.

TABLE A-9

Correlation Data Relating Aggregate Purchases of Consumer Durables to Objective, Anticipatory, and Buying Intentions Variables, Group C_3[a]

Independent Variables	Regression Coefficients for Independent Variables				Simple Correlations with	
	$X_1 \ldots X_7$[b]	$X_1 \ldots X_{13}$	$X_1 \ldots X_{16}$	$X_1 \ldots X_{21}$	P	$\hat{P}$
Objective						
Y	040*	.035*	.028*	.028*	.13	0.12
ΔL_{-1}	003	−.102	− 136	−.134	03	0 11
ΔY_{-1}	.140	096	042	033	.07	0.13
ΔY_t	.390	.243	.325	.382	.05	−0.01
T	− .329*	− .338*	− .330*	− 345*	− .02	0.03
H	.308	.236	.225	.264	.05	0.04
S'	148*	.148*	.020	.032	.13	0.39
Anticipatory						
$\hat{E}$		668	.736*	1 016*	07	−0.05
$E - \hat{E}$		.306	.140	.052	01	0.09
O		.322*	.180	.140	19	0 26
$\hat{E}_5$		.045	− .038	− .008	.08	0 09
$O\hat{E}_5$		.092	123	.157	.13	0.13
$\hat{C}$		.093	.004	− .062	−.01	0 05
Buying Intentions						
$\hat{P}$			.297*	.485*	.32	1 00
$\hat{P}_c$			.066	.069	− 01	−0.12
$\hat{P}\hat{P}_c$			− 023	−.020	.13	0 45
Interactions						
ZS'				− .048	− .09	−0.25
ZY				− .005	− .15	−0.52
$\hat{E}\hat{P}$				− 020*	.25	0 86
ZO				.168	− .04	−0.36
$Z_1\hat{P}_c$				−.051	.01	0.02
Multiple R	.235	296	.381	.399		
Multiple R^2	.055	087	.145	.159		

NOTES TO TABLES A-1 THROUGH A-9

Source: Basic data from Consumer Purchase Study, NBER.

* = coefficient > 1.96 times standard error.

[a]

Sample Designation	Buying Intentions Question
A	Which of the following products do you *definitely* plan to buy within the next twelve months?
B	Which of the following products do you plan to buy within the next six months?
C	Which of the following products do you plan to buy within the next twelve months (if income is as expected)?

Subscript Designation	Age-Marital Status
1	Married; head of household, 25–34 years old.
2	Married; head of household, 35–44 years old.
3	Married; head of household, 45–64 years old.

[b] In computing the regression coefficients, S' was added after the objective and anticipatory variables. The coefficient of S', holding only the objective variables constant, was thus not computed. Tables 42–44 show that the anticipatory variables exert little influence on the S' coefficient; therefore, I assume that the S' coefficient net of objective variables ($X_1, \ldots ,X_7$) equals the observed S' coefficient net of objective and anticipatory variables ($X_1, \ldots , X_{13}$). The incremental variance explained by S' net of both objective and anticipatory variables is added to the variance explained by the first six objective variables to get the variance explained by $X_1, \ldots , X_7$.

Empirical Results

SUMMARY

A summary of results from the multivariate regression analysis is provided by Tables A-10, A-11, and A-12. Table A-10 contains the means and variances for all variables, except for the interactions, in each of the nine

TABLE A-10
SUMMARY OF RESULTS FROM MULTIVARIATE REGRESSION ANALYSIS:
MEAN AND VARIANCE OF ALL VARIABLES
(variance shown in parentheses)

	Subgroup:								
	A_1	B_1	C_1	A_2	B_2	C_2	A_3	B_3	C_3
Independent variables									
Objective									
Y	8,705	8,447	8,794	10,963	11,170	11,045	12,244	12,057	12,104
	(2,237)	(2,256)	(2,299)	(3,677)	(4,836)	(3,884)	(6,631)	(6,506)	(6,057)
ΔL_{-1}	0.30	0.30	0.30	0.35	0.31	0.35	0.35	0.31	0.33
	(0.52)	(0.51)	(0.53)	(0.48)	(0.50)	(0.44)	(0.47)	(0.47)	(0.45)
ΔY_{-1}	0.63	0.48	0.56	0.37	0.36	0.37	0.23	0.13	0.19
	(1.52)	(1.66)	(1.56)	(1.00)	(0.81)	(0.92)	(0.84)	(0.90)	(0.84)
ΔY_t	+0.02	−0.002	+0.004	−0.007	+0.007	−0.02	−0.02	−0.02	−0.002
	(0.15)	(0.16)	(0.12)	(0.11)	(0.12)	(0.10)	(0.15)	(0.12)	(0.14)
T	0.74	0.71	0.72	0.61	0.60	0.56	0.43	0.42	0.44
	(0.19)	(0.21)	(0.20)	(0.24)	(0.24)	(0.25)	(0.24)	(0.24)	(0.25)
H	0.57	0.56	0.59	0.79	0.81	0.81	0.88	0.85	0 83
	(0.24)	(0.25)	(0.24)	(0.16)	(0.15)	(0.15)	(0.10)	(0.13)	(0.14)
S'	1.17	1.24	1.26	1.31	1.43	1.41	1.23	1.18	1.33
	(3.25)	(3.36)	(3.22)	(3.40)	(3.67)	(3.48)	(3.24)	(3.23)	(3.48)
Anticipatory									
$\hat{E}$	0.98	0.97	0.98	0.98	0.97	0.97	0.96	0.95	0.95
	(0.03)	(0.04)	(0.02)	(0.04)	(0.03)	(0.04)	(0.05)	(0.05)	(0.05)
$E - \hat{E}$	1.07	1.06	1.05	1.05	1.06	1.06	1.08	1.07	1.07
	(0.06)	(0.06)	(0.05)	(0.05)	(0.07)	(0.06)	(0.08)	(0.06)	(0.06)
O	0.67	0.53	0.68	0.78	0.76	0.74	0.81	0.85	0.93
	(0.71)	(0.68)	(0.74)	(0.77)	(0.78)	(0.77)	(0.75)	(0.78)	(0.80)
$\hat{E}_5$	0.83	0.88	0.91	0.59	0.60	0.58	0.37	0.33	0.34
	(0.60)	(0.62)	(0.60)	(0.47)	(0.47)	(0.52)	(0.33)	(0.31)	(0.31)
$\hat{C}$	0.12	0.11	0.10	0.12	0.14	0.15	0.17	0.17	0.16
	(0.11)	(0.10)	(0.09)	(0.11)	(0.12)	(0.12)	(0.14)	(0.14)	(0.14)
Buying Intentions									
P	0.73	0.92	1.72	0.74	0.92	1.73	0.70	0.94	1.86
	(1.78)	(1.91)	(3.23)	(1.95)	(2.09)	(3.46)	(2.24)	(2.51)	(4.14)
$\hat{P}_c$	2.09	3.34	2.23	2.10	3.03	2.04	1.78	2.49	1.83
	(4.12)	(5.22)	(3.91)	(4.08)	(5.17)	(4.12)	(4.27)	(5.66)	(4.20)
Dependent variable									
P	1.48	1.58	1.59	1.59	1.52	1.37	1.58	1.49	1.58
	(3.10)	(3.07)	(3.19)	(3.39)	(3.29)	(3.05)	(3.36)	(3.58)	(3.69)
Sample Size	852	866	814	863	836	691	559	678	570

SOURCE: Basic data from Consumer Purchase Study, NBER.

subgroups. Table A-11 shows the net regression coefficients for the most consistently significant of the twenty-one variables. Table A-12 shows the proportion of variance in purchases explained by each of the four groups of variables.

The influence of life-cycle status is apparent in these data, as is the influence of differences in the buying-intentions variable associated with the variant questions. Table A-10 indicates that there are consistent differences among the means for life-cycle groups with respect to income (Y), income change (ΔY_{-1}), education (T), home ownership (H), opinion about current buying conditions (O), long-range financial prospects $(\hat{E}_5)$, and price expectations $(\hat{C})$. Younger households have a lower income level, a more rapid rate of increase in income, more education, are less likely to own homes, have less favorable opinions about current buying conditions for durables, have more optimistic long-range financial prospects, and are more likely to expect rising prices.[12] The only marked difference in the variances is that older households show much greater variability in current family income than do younger households. Interestingly enough, young and old appear to report about the same number of standard buying intentions and purchases, although relative to income the young would report a great deal more of both. In addition, younger households generally report many more contingent buying intentions than others.

Net regression coefficients for the nine variables most consistently related to purchases are summarized in Table A-11. In the objective category, normal income, transitory income, and stock adjustment have the predicted signs in all subgroups; Y, ΔY_t, and S' are statistically significant (5 per cent level) in six, four and four of the nine subgroups, respectively. The data suggest, however, that S' is almost completely redundant to buying intentions when the latter is defined in the optimal way. Three of the four significant S' coefficients are found in the B subsamples, which contain the least efficient combination of $\hat{P}$ and $\hat{P}_c$. In the C subsamples, which were asked what seems to be the best (most efficient) of the intentions questions, none of the S' coefficients come close to being significant.

[12] One interesting result is the behavior of O. The group means show very clearly that O—opinion about current buying conditions—tends to be *more* favorable among older than younger households, on the average. This fact is consistent with the proposition that O is primarily a judgment about the household's current financial position rather than a judgment about the prevalence of "bargains" in the market; older households are typically in a stronger current financial position than younger ones because they have relatively higher incomes, larger asset holdings, lower debts, etc. I interpret this as one additional piece of evidence that the opinion variable in the CU data is not as closely related to market conditions as to personal financial situation.

TABLE A-11
Summary of Results from Multivariate Regression Analysis: Selected Net Regression Coefficients

				Independent Variables					
Subgroup	Y	ΔY_t	S'	$\hat{E}$	[O	ZO]ᵃ	$\hat{P}$	$\hat{P}_c$	$\hat{P}\hat{P}_c$
A₁	+.0021	+.309*	+.002	+.580	[+.224	+.286]*	+.520*	+.147*	−.095*
A₂	+.0014	+.592*	+.069*	−.111	[+.037	+.069]	+.452*	+.159*	−.041
A₃	+.0039*	+.096	+.033	−.341	[+.406	−.088]*	+.179*	+.087*	+.014
B₁	+.0050*	+.089	+.135*	−.013	[−.063	+.308]*	+.334*	+.055	−.015
B₂	+.0028*	+.038	+.131*	+.392	[+.022	+.258]*	+.416*	+.062*	−.046*
B₃	+.0044*	+.455*	+.127*	+.171	[+.246	−.233]*	+.274*	−.004	−.036
C₁	+.0017	+.353*	+.024	+.165	[+.290	+.091]*	+.406*	+.136*	−.034
C₂	+.0032*	+.075	+.036	+.461	[+.173	−.231]	+.336*	+.004	−.006
C₃	+.0028*	+.325	+.020	+.736*	[+.297	+.162]	+.297*	+.066	−.023

Source: Tables A-1 through A-9, third column except as noted in a. All coefficients are net of each other and of eight other variables not shown, including ΔL_{-1}, ΔY_{-1}, H, T, $E - \hat{E}$, $\hat{E}_5$, $O\hat{E}_5$, and $\hat{C}$.

ᵃ Coefficient of O includes effect of interaction variable $O\hat{E}_5$; the coefficient shown is the value of $O + O\hat{E}_5$ when $\hat{E}_5 = 1$. Of the six statistically significant coefficients, two are due to a significant interaction between O and E_5 rather than to a significant net coefficient for O; in both these cases O was significant before introduction of the interaction term. The significance level shown is for *either* O or ZO, whichever has the stronger relation to purchases.

Both ZO and O are net of the twenty variables included in the next-to-last regression. The interaction term ZO was the next to last variable added in the sequence; hence, the coefficients of these two variables, net of only those variables listed in the note, cannot be obtained.

* = Significantly different from zero at 0.05 level, using t test.

I conclude that S' adds little if anything to the explanation of purchases net of buying intentions, except where the intentions questions are relatively inefficient.

In the anticipatory category, the expectations index, $\hat{E}$, has the predicted sign in seven of the nine groups but is significant in only one; still, this variable has (absolutely) large positive coefficients in six groups and may well be quantitatively important for those (relatively few) cases where it takes on values different from the neutral classification. Opinion about buying conditions (O) has the right sign in all subgroups but one, and here the explanation is plainly the presence of interaction between intenders and nonintenders as represented by the ZO variable. O is statistically significant in three subgroups, although in two of these the significant variable is not O itself but an interaction between O and $\hat{E}_5$. If $O\hat{E}_5$ were eliminated from the regression, O would become significant in the three groups as shown. Further, the ZO interaction is significant in three additional groups; consequently, either O or an interaction involving it shows a significant positive relation to purchases in six of the nine groups. The ZO interaction has the predicted sign in six groups, behaves perversely in two (although not significantly so), and has little influence in the remaining group. It is also observable that ZO, which represents an interaction between intenders and nonintenders, is significant only when intenders are defined so as to include only households with relatively high purchase probabilities, i.e., those in the A and B groups; none of the ZO coefficients is significant in the C group. These results accord with predictions of the model.

The remaining variables that are consistently related to purchases are all measures of buying intentions—"standard" intentions $(\hat{P})$, contingent intentions $(\hat{P}_c)$, and the interaction of the two. $\hat{P}$ is clearly the strongest variable in the entire regression, being statistically significant in every subgroup, generally at the 0.01 level. Contingent buying intentions $(\hat{P}_c)$ is not quite so strongly related to purchases as is $\hat{P}$, but it has the predicted sign in all but one group and is significantly related to purchases in five of the nine groups. The influence of $\hat{P}_c$ differs considerably among the groups, varying according to the way in which contingent intentions are defined; this variable is much stronger in the A groups, for instance. Finally, the interaction $\hat{P}\hat{P}_c$ has the predicted (negative) association with purchases in all but one group and is statistically significant in two of the nine groups.

It is evident from Table A-12 (and also from Table A-11) that the relative importance of objective and anticipatory variables depends on life-cycle status. Sometimes this shows up in the regression coefficients (note the pattern of the $\hat{P}$ and $\hat{P}_c$ coefficients in Table A-11); more often it shows up as a difference in explained variance.

The data indicate that objective variables tend to explain relatively more of the variance in purchases for older households, while anticipatory variables are relatively more important for younger households. In Table A-12 the objective variables consistently explain more variance in the 45–64 age groups than in the other two groups; the anticipatory variables generally explain more variance in the 25–34 age groups than elsewhere, and the buying-intentions variables explain more variance in the two younger groups than in the 45–64 group.[13]

The wealth position of relatively young households is presumably highly variable in relation to current income and financial position. Younger households also show a great deal of variation in their expectations about

[13] The B_1 subsample constitutes an exception to the first two generalizations; this sample shows a relatively high proportion of variance explained by objective variables and a relatively low proportion explained by anticipatory ones, compared to the other groups.

financial resources and commitments. These expectations are importantly related to wealth; and if wealth is an important determinant of current purchases of durables, anticipatory variables will explain a relatively large fraction of the variance in purchases. In contrast, variables reflecting financial position, being less closely associated with wealth for younger households, will explain a relatively small fraction of the variance in purchases.[14] On the other hand, the wealth position of older households is presumably less variable relative to current income, since the

TABLE A-12

SUMMARY OF RESULTS FROM MULTIVARIATE REGRESSION ANALYSIS:
PROPORTION OF VARIANCE IN PURCHASES EXPLAINED
BY SPECIFIED GROUPS OF VARIABLES

| | R^2 FOR GROUPS OF VARIABLES | | | | | | | |
| | Objective | | Anticipatory | | Intentions to Buy | | Interactions | |
SUBGROUP	$R^2_{1.\alpha}$	$R^2_{1\alpha}$	$R^2_{1.\alpha\beta}$	$R^2_{1\beta.\alpha}$	$R^2_{1.\alpha\beta\gamma}$	$R^2_{1\gamma.\alpha\beta}$	$R^2_{1.\alpha\beta\gamma\delta}$	$R^2_{1\delta.\alpha\beta\gamma}$
A_1	.032	.032	.084	.054	.165	.088	.176	.013
A_2	.057	.057	.071	.015	.153	.088	.154	.001
A_3	.075	.075	.103	.030	.130	.030	.137	.008
B_1	.087	.087	.095	.009	.142	.052	.150	009
B_2	.072	.072	.092	.022	.144	.057	.149	.006
B_3	.082	.082	.103	.023	.139	.040	.150	012
C_1	.043	.043	.096	.055	.196	.111	.202	008
C_2	.052	.052	.078	.027	.174	.104	.185	.012
C_3	.055	.055	.087	.034	.145	.065	.159	.015

SOURCE: Derived from Tables A-1 through A-9. The subscripts designate the following variables (see above for definitions):
1—Purchases
α—Objective variables (X_1 . . . X_7)
β—Anticipatory variables (X_8 . . . X_{13})
γ—Buying intentions variables (X_{14} . . . X_{16})
δ—Interactions (X_{17} . . . X_{21})

present circumstances of these people must give a fairly accurate picture of prospective circumstances.[15] Hence, forward-looking variables are relatively less important, and the current financial situation more important, for the explanation of current purchases among older households.

---

[14] For purposes of the above discussion I define wealth as the capitalized value of permanent income. The most important component of wealth thus defined is the capitalized value of prospective earnings, rather than the current market value of real tangible assets.

[15] Some kinds of uncertainties are important for older households, especially those bearing on prospective expenses, but their current financial situation is bound to provide a relatively more accurate picture of their future situation than would be true of younger households.

The same reasoning may also explain the differential association between intentions to buy and purchases, since this variable, while not measuring anticipations directly, is bound to reflect them. Thus, greater variance in buying intentions relative to current income is anticipated among a group of younger households; and differences in wealth among these households should be correlated with both intentions to buy and purchases.

Other factors in addition to wealth may also be relevant for an explanation of differences among age groups in the explanatory power of the intentions variable. One quite different possibility is that the durable goods purchases of older households are more likely to constitute replacement of existing stock than net additions to stock.[16] Many of these replacement purchases will be "unplanned," in the sense that the household will replace whenever it becomes functionally necessary rather than on some predetermined schedule. Further, differences in mean income and asset level between young and old augur for a relatively weak plan-purchase relationship in the older groups. Many high-income households, particularly those with large assets, may not report "plans" to buy consumer durables because their budgetary position can absorb sizable expenditures without the necessity of their making explicit forward provision.

One of the most striking results in Table A-12 is the dominant importance of the anticipatory variables, especially buying intentions, in the explanation of differences in purchases among households. Table A-12 tends to understate the comparative importance of both anticipations and buying intentions relative to objective variables because the stepwise regression procedure does not permit estimation of the partial correlation between purchases and objective variables, holding the other variables constant, or purchases and anticipations, holding buying intentions constant. Even so, the cluster of intentions variables clearly accounts for the major share of total explained variance except in the 45–64 age groups, where the financial variables seem to be at least as important. In addition, the data suggest that, among anticipatory variables, a major share of the explained variance is due to "opinion about buying conditions" (O). This variable by itself contributes more than half of the total variance explained by anticipations, and interactions involving O are more important than any other single variable in this cluster.

---

[16] This line of reasoning seems to suggest that S' should be somewhat higher for older households—with relatively large and obsolescent stocks of durables—than for younger ones. I do not think the conclusion follows; a durable that "needs replacing" to a thirty-three-year-old suburbanite and his wife might be perfectly satisfactory to their parents; Table A-10 indicates that the average level of "replacement needs" is actually lower for older than for younger households.

Table A-13 summarizes the proportion of variance explained by selected groups of the four most important variables: standard intentions, contingent intentions, opinion about buying conditions, and family income ($\hat{P}$, $\hat{P}_c$, O, and Y). The proportion of total variance explained by all twenty-one independent variables is shown in the last row.

The results indicate clearly that: (1) Standard buying intentions are the most important single variable by a wide margin, even in the older age group where this variable is relatively less important than in the younger groups. (2) Opinion about buying conditions and income have about the same influence, on the average, but the former is generally

TABLE A-13

PROPORTION OF VARIANCE IN PURCHASES EXPLAINED BY SELECTED COMBINATIONS OF VARIABLES

R^2 or r^2 for	Subgroup:								
	A_1	B_1	C_1	A_2	B_2	C_2	A_3	B_3	C_3
$\hat{P}$	.089	.083	.144	.098	.092	.148	.035	.072	.102
$\hat{P}_c$	.010	.003	.003	.026	.002	.001	.011	.003	.000
O	.056	.009	.041	.015	.019	.019	.023	.019	.038
Y	.013	.027	.016	.012	.025	.022	.047	.044	.017
$\hat{P}, \hat{P}_c$	.101	.088	.152	.127	.095	.148	.051	.072	.103
$\hat{P}, O$	.126	.086	.161	.100	.100	.151	.050	.080	.116
$\hat{P}, Y$	.097	.102	.148	.101	.105	.162	.078	.102	.110
$\hat{P}, \hat{P}_c, O$	.137	.091	.171	.128	.103	.151	.065	.080	.118
$\hat{P}, \hat{P}_c, Y$	.106	.107	.156	.129	.108	.162	.089	.102	.111
$\hat{P}, O, Y$	.129	.104	.162	.103	.111	.164	.086	.107	.120
All 21 independent variables	.176	.150	.202	.154	.149	.185	.137	.150	.159

SOURCE: Basic data from Consumer Purchase Study, NBER.

more important for younger age groups; the latter, for older age groups. (3) Contingent buying intentions are most important for the A samples (due to the specifications of the intentions question), and also seem to be more important for the younger age groups generally. (4) The anticipatory variables account for a dominant share of the variance in purchases; the three best such variables account for between two-thirds and four-fifths of the total variance explained by all twenty-one independent variables.

Several points of interest should be noted. First, all three of the most important anticipatory variables have a common denominator—they represent essentially judgments about the net effect of a multitude of considerations on the likelihood of purchase. Standard and contingent buying intentions have been treated explicitly as judgments about purchase probability, necessarily involving considerations of current financial position, needs, future prospects, etc. Opinion about buying conditions is the same kind of variable, for it is a proxy for the net influence of factors such as income, assets, debt, expectations, etc. A priori, however, every household reporting intentions to buy should have a higher probability of purchase than every household not so reporting. In contrast, households having a favorable opinion about buying conditions—i.e., those who think the present is a good time to buy durables—need not on a priori grounds have a higher purchase probability than all those having unfavorable opinions. Owing to their durable goods stock position, some households with favorable opinions are unlikely to purchase; some with unfavorable ones, quite likely. But the opinion variable is clearly different from variables such as income expectations, asset level, or debt in that the respondent is (implicitly) asked to evaluate the bearing of the relevant factors on his current financial situation. Thus, many respondents with favorable income prospects would—if asked—have indicated that these prospects were irrelevant to their current durable goods buying decisions because they had no assets and were already overburdened with debt. But the opinion variable, as well as the two intentions variables, essentially asks the household to weigh the factors relevant to their own purchase decisions.[17] None of the other variables used in this analysis have the property that the respondent is (implicitly) asked to assign his (subjective estimate of) relative importance to a set of (unspecified) objective variables or expectations, and to indicate how all these considerations balance out.[18]

Below, I give a more detailed examination of the behavior of variables in each category. Where possible, regression coefficients for variables in each category are presented net of each other but gross of variables in other categories, then net of all variables in the full regression. On the whole I exclude variables representing interactions between intenders and nonintenders because these behave erratically and cause erratic movements in the coefficients of other variables.

---

[17] It was noted above in Chapter 7 that the *Reports of the Consultant Committees on Economic Statistics* (Joint Committee on the Economic Report, 84th Cong., 1st sess.), found that, in time series data (1) buying intentions were clearly a useful predictor of durable goods purchases; and (2) expectations and attitudes were, on the whole, not useful, with the exception of a variable denoted "opinion about buying conditions." This is the variable constructed from responses to a question asked on the Survey of Consumer Finances, in which a projective technique is used—is this a (good-bad-other) time for *people like yourselves* to buy durable goods? (See note 4, above, and text discussion.)

[18] This argument is developed more fully in Chapter 5, especially pp. 137–139.

OBJECTIVE VARIABLES

The first category comprises the seven objective variables in the model. Table A-14 presents regression coefficients for these variables net of each other (upper panel) and net of anticipations and buying intentions (lower panel). In the upper panel five of the objective variables are consistently related to purchases in all subgroups, although only normal income (Y), transitory income (ΔY_t), and stock adjustment (S') show consistently significant relationships. Y and S' are significant in all nine groups; ΔY_t, in three of the nine. There is some indication that ΔY_t is relatively more important for young households, although subgroups with significant relations between purchases and ΔY_t appear in each life-cycle group. Liquid-asset change (ΔL_{-1}) and income change (ΔY_{-1}) have positive

TABLE A-14
SUMMARY OF CORRELATION DATA FOR OBJECTIVE VARIABLES

Subgroup	R^2 for Group	Net Regression Coefficients						
		Y	ΔL_{-1}	ΔY_{-1}	ΔY_t	T	H	S'
		NET OF EACH OTHER ONLY						
A$_1$	032	$+.0046^a$	$+.137$	$+.000$	$+.354^a$	-146	-084	$+089^a$
B$_1$	087	$+.0056^a$	$+.124$	$+.127^a$	$+.123$	$+.012$	$+.009$	$+.206^a$
C$_1$	.043	$+.0047^a$	$+.074$	$-.002$	$+.297$	$+.039$	-022	$+.150^a$
A$_2$	.057	$+.0036^a$	$+.126$	$+.026$	$+.625^a$	$-.047$	$+025$	$+.166^a$
B$_2$	.072	$+.0040^a$	$+.072$	$-.064$	$+.055$	$+042$	$-.157$	$+.199^a$
C$_2$	.052	$+.0042^a$	$+.087$	$+.036$	$+.063$	$-.123$	$+.029$	$+.155^a$
A$_3$	.075	$+.0047^a$	$+.131$	$+.141$	$+.062$	$+.081$	$-.494^a$	$+100^a$
B$_3$	.082	$+.0051^a$	$+.063$	$+.071$	$+.408^a$	$+.016$	$-.196$	$+.179^a$
C$_3$	.055	$+.0040^a$	$+.003$	$+.140$	$+.390$	$-.329^a$	$+.308$	$+.148^a$
		NET OF ANTICIPATORY VARIABLES AND BUYING INTENTIONS						
A$_1$		$+.0021$	$+.012$	$-.043$	$+.309^a$	$-.137$	$-.021$	$+.002$
B$_1$		$+.0050^a$	$+.046$	$+.110^a$	$+.089$	$-.039$	$-.102$	$+135^a$
C$_1$		$+0017$	$-.016$	$-.076$	$+.353^a$	$-.046$	-040	$+.024$
A$_2$		$+.0014$	$+.076$	$-.024$	$+.592^a$	$+.031$	-075	$+.069^a$
B$_2$		$+.0028^a$	$-.057$	$-.090$	$+.038$	$+.063$	$-.083$	$+.131^a$
C$_2$		$+.0032^a$	$-.004$	$-.031$	$+.075$	$-.058$	$+.046$	$+.036$
A$_3$		$+.0039^a$	$+.098$	$+.082$	$+.096$	$+.157$	$-.496^a$	$+.033$
B$_3$		$+.0044^a$	$-.006$	$+.077$	$+.455^a$	$-.032$	$-.237$	$+.127^a$
C$_3$		$+.0028^a$	$-.136$	$+.042$	$+.325$	$-.330^a$	$+.225$	$+.020$

SOURCE: Tables A-1 through A-9.
^{a} = Significant at 0.05 level.

coefficients in nearly all groups, although they are hardly ever significant. The coefficients of the other two variables, education level of husband and home ownership, are essentially random numbers; the only significant relations involving these variables both have the wrong sign.

There is no evidence that the regression coefficients for objective variables are systematically different among life-cycle groups, although it has already been pointed out that current financial variables are more strongly related to behavior for older households. Neither is there any evidence that the variant intentions groups show anything other than random differences in regression coefficients or consistency of relationships. Given the sampling procedure, this finding is to be expected.

After accounting for the influence of anticipatory variables and buying intentions, only Y, ΔY_t, and S' consistently show a net influence on purchases. As noted above, the other four variables behave in a completely random fashion as to sign, and the only statistically significant relations are those for T and H in groups C_3 and A_3. However, both T and H have negative signs in these groups. The inclusion of the anticipations and buying-intentions variables strengthens the evidence that ΔY_t has a differential influence among life-cycle groups, and also indicates that the influence of Y is differential. ΔY_t is now significant (5 per cent level) in two of the three subgroups with the household head between twenty-five and thirty-four. On the other hand, Y is now significant in only one of the three groups in this life-cycle class, in two of three groups with head between thirty-five and forty-four, and in all three groups with head between forty-five and sixty-four years of age. The regression coefficients are also generally smaller for the younger groups than for the older ones. Thus normal income appears to be relatively more important for older households; transitory income, for younger households. Given that the correlation between wealth and current income is stronger for older households, these results are consistent with the proposition that wealth rather than current income is the important decision variable, with current income being strongly related to behavior only when it serves as a good proxy for wealth.

One of the most interesting results is the influence of buying intentions on the net relation between purchases and stock adjustment. In the upper panel, S' was significantly related to purchases in every group; in the lower panel, S' becomes nonsignificant (with one exception) unless the group was asked intentions question B. All the signs are still positive, but it seems clear that the net predictive value of S' can be substantially eliminated by substituting an adequate set of buying-intentions variables.

ANTICIPATORY VARIABLES

The upper panel of Table A-15 shows regression coefficients for anticipatory variables net of objective ones; the lower panel contains regression coefficients for the same variables net of both objective factors and intentions to buy. In the upper panel opinion about buying conditions (O) is

TABLE A-15
SUMMARY OF CORRELATION DATA FOR ANTICIPATORY VARIABLES

Subgroup	Incremental R^2 for Group	$\hat{E}$	$E - \hat{E}$	O	$\hat{E}_5$	$O\hat{E}_5$	$\hat{C}$
			Net Regression Coefficients				
		NET OF OBJECTIVE VARIABLES					
A_1	.054	$+.517$	$+.332$	$+.424^a$	$+.114$	$+.049$	$+.117$
B_1	.009	$-.013$	$-.010$	$+.248^a$	$+.090$	$-.121$	$-.085$
C_1	.055	$+.066$	$-.197$	$+.226^a$	$+.126$	$+.196^a$	$+.443^a$
A_2	.015	$-.252$	$+.254$	$+.196^a$	$-.016$	$+.062$	$+.215$
B_2	.022	$+.491$	$-.326$	$+.304^a$	$+.069$	$-.076$	$+.087$
C_2	.027	$+.720^a$	$-.005$	$+.151$	$+.054$	$+.124$	$+.050$
A_3	.030	$-.274$	$+.255$	$+.075$	$+.041$	$+.317^a$	$-.166$
B_3	.023	$+.311$	$+.690^a$	$+.249^a$	$-.052$	$+.019$	$+.100$
C_3	.034	$+.668$	$+.306$	$+.322^a$	$+.045$	$+.092$	$+.093$
		NET OF OBJECTIVE VARIABLES AND INTENTIONS TO BUY					
A_1		$+.580$	$+.265$	$+.326^a$	$+.002$	$+.059$	$+.010$
B_1		$-.013$	$-.008$	$+.187$	$+.073$	$-.114$	$-.131$
C_1		$+.165$	$-.021$	$+.114$	$+.063$	$+.204^a$	$+.376$
A_2		$-.111$	$+.348$	$+.083$	$-.043$	$-.006$	$+.131$
B_2		$+.392$	$-.292$	$+.225^a$	$+.040$	$-.070$	$+.047$
C_2		$+.461$	$-.034$	$+.032$	$+.081$	$+.092$	$+.016$
A_3		$-.341$	$+.233$	$+.027$	$-.012$	$+.311^a$	$-.148$
B_3		$+.171$	$+.653^a$	$+.182$	$-.046$	$-.018$	$-.006$
C_3		$+.736^a$	$+.140$	$+.180$	$-.038$	$+.123$	$+.004$

SOURCE: Tables A-1 through A-9.
^{a} = Significant at 0.05 level.

clearly the most powerful variable of the six, being statistically significant in the expected direction for seven of the nine subgroups. Moreover, where this variable is not itself significantly related to purchases, the reason is the presence of interaction between O and $\hat{E}_5$. The interaction term has the expected sign in seven of the nine groups, although it is statistically significant in only two groups.

Of the other variables in this category, $\hat{E}_5$ appears to have very little influence after allowing for interaction with O; prior to the introduction of interaction, $\hat{E}_5$ was consistently positive, although not very strong. The price expectations variable $(\hat{C})$ is positive in seven of the nine groups although significant in only one. The expectations index $(\hat{E})$ and the surprise index $(E - \hat{E})$ are the most erratic of the anticipatory variables.

The greater importance of anticipatory variables, as a group, for the relatively young is accounted for largely by the differential influence of O and $\hat{E}_5$. In this connection, it can readily be shown that even before allowing for the influence of intentions, O and $\hat{E}_5$ generally have more influence on behavior in younger households. The data in Table A-15 indicate that either O or $O\hat{E}_5$ is significantly related to purchases in every group, including all life-cycle classes. But the extent of the relationship is quite different, as shown by tabulation, below, of joint F ratios for the combined influence of O, $\hat{E}_5$, and $O\hat{E}_5$ on purchases.

	Life-Cycle Class		
Sample	(1)	(2)	(3)
A	15 9	3.1	5.3
B	1.9	4.4	2.9
C	14.1	4.1	5.4
Mean	10.4	3.9	4.5

BUYING INTENTIONS VARIABLES

The variables involved are standard intentions $(\hat{P})$, contingent intentions $(\hat{P}_c)$, and the interaction of the two. All three have the predicted signs in almost every case; $\hat{P}$ is significant in all groups; $\hat{P}_c$ in five of nine; and the interaction term, in two of nine groups (Table A-16). The relative importance of these variables is related both to life-cycle status and to the intentions question. For example, $\hat{P}_c$ for the B group is a rather weak variable, as is $\hat{P}\hat{P}_c$; the reason is that contingent intentions for the B samples is based on responses to an extremely long-range question about buying intentions. Roughly 80 per cent of all households responded affirmatively to this question, many for several items. The $\hat{P}_c$ variable for the C groups is almost as vague and long range. For the A groups, however, $\hat{P}_c$ is a much more restrictive question, involving a high-probability cut-off relative to the other $\hat{P}_c$ variants; hence, the influence of contingent intentions on purchases is quite strong in the A samples, as is the influence of the interaction term, $\hat{P}\hat{P}_c$. The standard intentions variable, on the other hand, seems to be somewhat more powerful in the C groups than in the other two. The probable reasons have been discussed above (Chapter 2) at some length.

As regards the life-cycle pattern, not only is the variance explained by $\hat{P}$ and $\hat{P}_c$ considerably larger for younger households, but the regression coefficient for both variables tends to be larger for the young. In addition, the interaction of $\hat{P}$ and $\hat{P}_c$ is stronger for the younger households. By any criteria intentions to buy are plainly more closely associated with subsequent purchases for relatively young households than older ones. The probable reasons have been discussed above—the weaker wealth–current income correlation for the young, the greater importance of unplanned replacement of existing stock for older households, and the less compelling necessity for financial budgeting among older households because their incomes and asset holdings are larger.

TABLE A-16

SUMMARY OF CORRELATION DATA FOR BUYING INTENTIONS VARIABLES

Subgroup	Incremental R^2 for Group	Net Regression Coefficients		
		$\hat{P}$	$\hat{P}_c$	$\hat{P}\hat{P}_c$
A_1	.088	+.520[a]	+.147[a]	−.095[a]
A_2	.088	+.452[a]	+.159[a]	−.041]
A_3	.030	+.179[a]	+.087[a]	+.014
B_1	.047	+.334[a]	+.055	−.015
B_2	.057	+.416[a]	+.062[a]	−.046[a]
B_3	.040	+.274[a]	−.004	−.036
C_1	.111	+.406[a]	+.136[a]	−.034
C_2	.104	+.336[a]	+.004	−.006
C_3	.065	+.297[a]	+.066	−.023

SOURCE: Tables A-1 to A-9.
[a] = Significant at 0.05 level.

Before leaving the buying-intentions variables, it is useful to take a somewhat closer look at the structure of these variables relative to each other, to purchases, and to the stock adjustment variable—replacement needs for durables. In the classification scheme used above, stock adjustment is an objective variable. It could be argued, however, that a household reporting a particular durable good "in need of replacement" is saying much the same as a household reporting that a particular durable will "possibly be purchased within a year." The closeness of these relations can be seen from the zero-order correlation matrix involving the intentions variables and S', the relevant parts of which are reproduced in Table A-17.

The interrelationships here are rather interesting. The $P,\hat{P}$ relationship is about the same in the A and B groups, stronger in C, and generally

TABLE A-17
ZERO-ORDER CORRELATIONS AMONG PURCHASES, STANDARD AND CONTINGENT
BUYING INTENTIONS, AND REPLACEMENT NEED

Subgroup	$P, \hat{P}$	$P, \hat{P}_c$	P, S'	$\hat{P}, S'$	$\hat{P}_c, S'$	$\hat{P}_c, \hat{P}$
A_1	.30	.10	.08	.19	.31	−.03
A_2	.31	.16	.17	.21	.26	−.03
A_3	.19	.10	.10	.25	.23	−.11
B_1	.29	.08	.22	.28	.19	−.01
B_2	.30	.04	.21	.27	.22	−.05
B_3	.27	−.05	.14	.24	.17	−.17
C_1	.38	.05	.12	.26	.20	−.10
C_2	.38	−.03	.15	.36	.18	−.06
C_3	.32	−.01	.13	.39	.13	−.12

SOURCE: Tables A-1 through A-9 and Consumer Purchase Study, NBER.

weaker for households in the oldest age class. The $P, \hat{P}_c$ relation is quite weak except for the A groups, and tends to be somewhat stronger for households in the younger age groups. The P, S' relation should be random among the A, B, and C groups; it turns out to be somewhat stronger in the B samples than elsewhere, although not significantly so, and also to be random among life-cycle groups. The $\hat{P}, S'$ relation is strongest for the C groups, weakest in the A samples, and generally stronger in the older age groups. On the other hand, $\hat{P}_c, S'$ is strongest for the A groups, about the same for the other two, and apparently weaker for the oldest age groups. Finally, $\hat{P}_c, \hat{P}$ is consistently negative but very weak throughout.[19]

[19] The reader should bear in mind that the intentions variables in A, B, and C simply represent alternative ways of dividing up the households into groups with different average levels of *ex ante* purchase probability during the forecast period. Thus variant B divides the sample into those with a high probability of purchasing, those with anything less than high down to very low, and those with practically zero probability—corresponding to those reporting $\hat{P}, \hat{P}_c$, or neither. On the other hand, variant C divides the sample into those with anything down to a moderately high probability, those from moderate to quite low, and those with less than that. Variant A contains the classification that originally seemed to be the most useful, dividing the sample into those with very high probability, those with probability ranging from very high to fairly high, and those below that level. The following diagram is a rough quantification of the above adjectival distinctions.

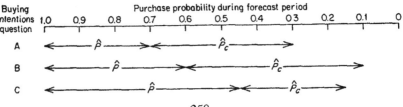

The way in which the replacement need, standard intentions, and contingent intentions variables typically interrelate for the variant samples is seen most clearly from the data for life-cycle class 1 in Table A-18. Net of all other objective and anticipatory variables, S' is significantly

TABLE A-18

INTERRELATION OF REPLACEMENT NEED, STANDARD INTENTIONS, AND CONTINGENT INTENTIONS FOR SUBSAMPLE GROUPS A_1, B_1, AND C_1

(standard errors shown in parentheses)

			Regression Coefficients		
	R^2	S'	$\hat{P}$	$\hat{P}_c$	$\hat{P}\hat{P}_c$
Group A_1					
$X_{1a}, \ldots \ldots, X_{13a}$	.084	.089 (.032)			
$X_{1a}, \ldots \ldots, X_{14a}$	.141	+.041 (.032)	+.334 (.048)		
$X_{1a}, \ldots \ldots, X_{15a}$	.149	+.009 (.034)	+.350 (.045)	+.085 (.030)	
$X_{1a}, \ldots, X_{16a}$	.165	+.002 (.034)	+.520 (.062)	+.147 (.034)	−.094 (.024)
Group B_1					
$X_{1a}, \ldots, X_{13a}$	.095	+.206 (.032)			
$X_{1a}, \ldots, X_{14a}$	.138	+.148 (.032)	+.279 (.043)		
$X_{1a}, \ldots, X_{15a}$	.141	+.137 (.033)	+.285 (.043)	+.042 (.026)	
$X_{1a}, \ldots, X_{16a}$	.142	+.135 (.033)	+.334 (.073)	+.055 (.030)	−.015 (.018)
Group C_1					
$X_{1a}, \ldots, X_{13a}$	.096	+.150 (.034)			
$X_{1a}, \ldots, X_{14a}$	.184	+.052 (.034)	+.326 (.035)		
$X_{1a}, \ldots, X_{15a}$	.192	+.032 (.035)	+.338 (.035)	+.082 (.030)	
$X_{1a}, \ldots, X_{16a}$	.196	+.024 (.035)	+.406 (.050)	+.136 (.040)	−.034 (.018)

SOURCE: Basic data from Consumer Purchase Study, NBER.

related to purchases in all three groups. The introduction of intentions reduces the coefficient of S' in all groups; S' is still significant only in group B. Adding $\hat{P}_c$ further reduces the coefficient of S', especially in group A; adding the interaction term increases both the $\hat{P}$ and $\hat{P}_c$ coefficients substantially while still further reducing that of S'. The net result is that S' seems to be completely redundant to the cluster of buying intentions variables ($\hat{P}, \hat{P}_c,$ and $\hat{P}\hat{P}_c$) except in group B.

INTERACTION VARIABLES

On the whole, the interactions make for little if any improvement in the performance of the model, with one—possibly two—exceptions. Neither ZY, ZS', nor $\hat{E}\hat{P}$ show any consistent relation to purchases. The explanation may be that the particular form chosen for these interaction terms is inappropriate—perhaps cross-product terms such as $\hat{P}Y$ and $\hat{P}S'$ would have provided a better fit. However, two cross-product terms involving $\hat{P}$ were already included in the regression, and the problem of separating out the net effect would presumably become quite formidable if two additional ones had been included.[20]

The other two interaction variables show some influence in the predicted direction. Opinion about buying conditions (O) appears to be somewhat more strongly related to purchases for nonintenders than for those reporting some intentions to buy. The coefficient of ZO has the predicted sign in only six of the nine groups, but it is statistically significant in three of these; all the significant coefficients have the predicted sign. This variable is more consistently related to purchases in the A and B groups, where households with standard intentions of zero are relatively numerous and presumably more heterogeneous with respect to *ex ante* purchase probability. The best illustration of the predicted relation occurs in the A_1 group. The relevant data are given in Table A-19.

In this group O is a very powerful variable when first introduced into the regression. The other two variables bearing on judgment about financial prospects—$\hat{E}_5$ and the interaction of O and $\hat{E}_5$—are positively related to purchases but have little influence on the O coefficient. When the buying-intentions variables ($\hat{P}$ and $\hat{P}_c$) are introduced, the influence of O declines somewhat; but it still retains a highly significant relation to purchases. However, when the ZO interaction is introduced, the net influence of O declines to a nonsignificant but positive number for intenders (where $Z = 0$). But for nonintenders (where $Z = 1$), the net influence of O is highly significant and is about as strong as when this variable was first introduced. Similar patterns are found in the B_1 and B_2 groups. As has been the case so frequently with expectational variables, the differ-

---

[20] Take the case of $\hat{P}\hat{P}_c$ and $\hat{P}S'$ for illustration. $\hat{P}_c$ and S' are highly correlated as cross-section data go; roughly 5 to 10 per cent of the variance in $\hat{P}_c$ is explained by S'. In every case where $\hat{P} = 0$, both cross-product terms would be zero, and where $\hat{P}_c$ is zero, S' would frequently be zero also; the result is bound to be a very high correlation between the two cross-product terms. These kinds of factors influenced the decision to use the ZS' and ZY interaction variables, although the results might possibly have been better if cross-product terms had been used throughout.

ential influence of O on the purchases of intenders and nonintenders is apparently much stronger the younger the age of the household head.

The final variable to be discussed is $Z_1\hat{P}_c$, where $Z_1 = 1$, when $E - \hat{E} = 2$, $Z_1 = 0$ when $E - \hat{E} < 2$. This variable is intended to measure the differential effect of contingent buying intentions on purchases for households with agreeable surprises, compared to those with either no surprises or disagreeable ones, along the lines discussed in Chapter 6. It was noted above that $\hat{P}_c$ is strongly related to purchases only in the A subgroups, where contingent intentions reflect "probable or possible

TABLE A-19

CONTRIBUTION OF SELECTED INTERACTION VARIABLES TO EXPLANATION OF
PURCHASES IN GROUP A_1
(standard errors shown in parentheses)

Variables Included in Regression	Incremental R^2 for Last Variable	Net Regression Coefficients					
		O	$\hat{E}_5$	$O\hat{E}_5$	$\hat{P}$	$\hat{P}_c$	ZO
$X_{1a}, \ldots, X_{10a}$	.043	$+.452$ (.072)					
$X_{1a}, \ldots, X_{11a}$	.005	$+.450$ (.072)	$+.156$ (.078)				
$X_{1a}, \ldots, X_{12a}$	.000	$+.410$ (.104)	$+.123$ (.099)	$+.049$ (.089)			
$X_{1a}, \ldots, X_{14a}$	.057	$+.353$ (.101)	$+.032$ (.096)	$+.039$ (.086)	$+.334$ (.045)		
$X_{1a}, \ldots, X_{15a}$	.008	$+.333$ (.101)	$+.017$ (.096)	$+.052$ (.086)	$+.350$ (.045)	$+.085$ (.030)	
$X_{1a}, \ldots, X_{20a}$	.005	$+135$ (.135)	$-.013$ (.095)	$+090$ (.086)	$+.526$ (.121)	$+.142$ (.034)	$+.286$ (.137)

SOURCE: Basic data from Consumer Purchase Study, NBER.

purchases over the next twelve months." The Z_1P_c coefficient is essentially a random number in other groups; and even in the A groups the relation is quite weak except in the youngest age group. Table A-20 summarizes these relations, presenting coefficients for the relevant variables in a stepwise regression.

Comparing the first two regressions shown for each subgroup, the coefficients of $\hat{P}_c$ decline slightly when $Z_1\hat{P}_c$ is introduced. The coefficients of $Z_1\hat{P}_c$ decline with age, moving from a significant positive relation to practically zero. Net of all independent variables, the coefficient of $Z_1\hat{P}_c$ is about the same as the coefficient net of only the intentions variables in the A_1 group, smaller in the other two groups. It should be kept in mind, as discussed in Chapter 6, that this interaction variable is constructed from the rather unsatisfactory makeshift used to measure surprise.

TABLE A-20
REGRESSION COEFFICIENTS SHOWING THE INTERACTION OF CONTINGENT
INTENTIONS AND SURPRISES
(standard errors shown in parentheses)

| | Regression Coefficients | | |
	$\hat{P}$	$\hat{P}_c$	$Z_1\hat{P}_c$
Group A₁			
$P = f(\hat{P},\hat{P}_c)$	+.397	+.095	
	(.042)	(.026)	
$P = f(\hat{P},\hat{P}_c,Z_1\hat{P}_c)$	+.398	+.086	+.143
	(.043)	(.029)	(.074)
$P = f(X_{1a}, \ldots ,X_{21a})$	+.521	+.132	+.153
	(.121)	(.034)	(.081)
Group A₂			
$P = f(\hat{P},\hat{P}_c)$	+.420	+.156	
	(.041)	(.027)	
$P = f(\hat{P},\hat{P}_c,Z_1\hat{P}_c)$	+.418	+.148	+.090
	(.042)	(.030)	(.070)
$P = f(X_{1a}, \ldots ,X_{21a})$	+.525	+.153	+.050
	(.129)	(.036)	(.078)
Group A₃			
$P = f(\hat{P},\hat{P}_c)$	+.246	+.112	
	(.049)	(.034)	
$P = f(\hat{P},\hat{P}_c,Z_1\hat{P}_c)$	+.246	+.112	+.006
	(.051)	(.038)	(.093)
$P = f(X_{1a}, \ldots ,X_{21a})$	+.367	+.092	−.058
	(138)	(.042)	(.102)

SOURCE: Basic data from Consumer Purchase Study, NBER.

In my judgment, therefore, the finding of any significant coefficients for $Z_1\hat{P}_c$ is encouraging, and may indicate that an adequate measure of income surprise is related to purchases along the hypothesized lines. The evidence is obviously rather weak, and much more work needs to be done on this problem.[21]

Summary

There seems little doubt that the most powerful forward-looking variables related to purchases of durable goods are (1) the household's subjective estimate of purchase probability, as reflected by intentions to buy ($\hat{P}$ and $\hat{P}_c$), and (2) the household's subjective estimate of whether its present and prospective financial position are good, bad, or indifferent from the viewpoint of durable goods purchases, as expressed by its opinion about buying conditions (O). These two variables, or interactions involving them,

[21] This general line of inquiry has a high priority on the research agenda of the Expectational Economics Center conducted by Albert G. Hart at Columbia University. The Columbia group will have the use of substantially more complete data on these same households.

account for over half the total explained variance in purchases. The reason seems clear enough. With one exception, all the other variables involve either fairly specific judgments about future events, statements of fact about financial circumstances, or statements of fact about recent changes in financial circumstances.[22] It has been argued above that the intentions variable is powerful in cross sections precisely because it enables households to be their own calculating machines, i.e., to reflect their own weighting of the idiosyncratic circumstances that lead to purchase decisions. The same argument holds for the opinion variable.

It also seems to be clearly established that both these anticipatory variables—and others in the same category—are more closely associated with the purchase decisions of relatively young households. Further, contingent buying intentions and opinion about buying conditions are both somewhat more closely associated with purchases for those households that do not report so-called standard intentions.

Other expectational variables that may prove useful for predicting purchases are long-range financial prospects ($\hat{E}_5$), especially for those with favorable opinions about buying conditions; the combination of income and business expectations ($\hat{E}$), especially for the very optimistic or very pessimistic; and the combination of unexpected income and unexpected business cycle developments ($E - \hat{E}$), especially for those with contingent buying intentions. The evidence here is a good deal weaker than for $\hat{P}$ or O, but in my judgment it is strong enough to warrant additional investigation.

---

[22] The exception is the stock adjustment variable (S'), which is strongly related to purchases by itself but appears to be largely redundant to an adequate set of buying-intentions variables.

Interrelations Among Intentions and Purchases for Individual Commodities

Introduction

THE problem of aggregating buying intentions for individual commodities is one of the most interesting in the analysis of these data. I have touched on one facet of the aggregation problem in Chapter 4 of the text, where I pointed out that aggregation of buying intentions is by no means a perfect substitute for aggregation of purchase probabilities because the probabilities associated with the same intentions question appear to differ among commodities. Other aspects of this problem deserve attention. First, is there any evidence that the characteristics of sample households are such that buying intentions tend to be associated with different probabilities for different groups of people? Evidence already presented suggests that this is not the case for households in different income, age, or education classes, since mean probability among intenders seemed to be essentially unrelated to these characteristics. But a serious "response" bias may nevertheless exist. One group of households may systematically answer intentions questions in terms of what they "wish they could" purchase, while another group may systematically interpret these questions as asking what they are "practically certain they will do" during the specified period. If so, it would be necessary to have some means of identifying these groups, since it would otherwise be impossible to make accurate estimates of mean purchase probability from surveys of buying intentions. The evidence examined above does not preclude the possibility of systematic differences of this sort; it simply suggests that such personality differences are not related to household characteristics such as income, age, or education.

Second, is the typical pattern of purchases within the durable goods complex one of substitution, complementarity, or no association; that is, are households that purchase commodity A more likely or less likely, other things equal, to purchase other durable commodities in addition to A? This problem relates to the analysis of consumer behavior proper rather than to the analysis of survey data as a predictor of behavior. Finally, if a household reports intentions to buy A and does not purchase, is it more likely or less likely, other things equal, to buy commodity B?

An Analysis of Response Bias

The first and second of these problems can be analyzed by an examination of interdependence between buying intentions and purchases for individual commodities. If the response problem is serious, some house-holds—perennial optimists—report a relatively large number of buying intentions but purchase neither more nor less than others with the same income, age, etc. Other households—perennial pessimists—report rela-tively few buying intentions but again purchase neither more nor less than others with the same economic status. The remaining households report a "normal" amount of buying intentions and make a "normal" amount of purchases. If such is the case, it can be shown that the sample as a whole will show a stronger degree of interdependence for buying intentions than for purchases. That is, those reporting intentions to buy A will be more likely, *ceteris paribus*, to report buying intentions for B,C, . . . , or N than will those purchasing A to report the purchase of B,C, . . . , or N as well.

The argument follows. Assume that data are available for a sample of households with the same income and demographic status but different interpretations of the buying intentions question; further assume that a per cent of the sample purchase commodity A and b per cent purchase B during the forecast period, that $\hat{a}$ and $\hat{b}$ per cent of the "normal" house-holds report buying intentions for A and B, and that $a = \hat{a}$, $b = \hat{b}$. Finally, assume that less than $\hat{a}(\hat{b})$ per cent of the perennial pessimists report buying intentions for A(B); more than $\hat{a}(\hat{b})$ per cent of the peren-nial optimists report intentions to buy A(B); but that both pessimists and optimists have the same purchase rates as "normal" households, i.e., equal to $a(b)$. To make the illustration concrete, it is specified that half as many pessimists and twice as many optimists report intentions as normal households, and that the three groups are of equal size. Given these assumptions, the following data would be obtained:

1. The number of households that report buying intentions for com-modity A—$\hat{P}_A$—aggregating across the three groups, would be

$$\Sigma \hat{P}_A = \hat{a}\frac{N}{3} + 0.5\hat{a}\frac{N}{3} + 2\hat{a}\frac{N}{3}$$
$$= 1.17\hat{a}N$$

Commodity B would show a similar pattern; hence,

$$\Sigma \hat{P}_B = 1.17\hat{b}N$$

2. The number of households reporting purchases of commodity A—P_A—again aggregating across the three groups, would be:

$$\Sigma P_A = a\frac{N}{3} + a\frac{N}{3} + a\frac{N}{3} = aN$$

For commodity B, similarly

$$\Sigma P_B = bN$$

If it is now assumed that buying intentions and purchases are both completely independent among households *within* each of the three response groups, the observed frequency of those purchasing or intending to buy both A and B, neither A nor B, A but not B, and B but not A would be the products of the respective probabilities, aggregated across groups.[1] Given the above assumptions about rates of buying intentions and purchases in the three groups, the observed frequencies would be those in the top panel of Table B-1. Testing for independence, the predicted frequencies of buying intentions or purchases for the sample as a whole work out as in the middle panel of Table B-1. The pattern predicted for the sample as a whole, in testing for independence among purchases, will be exactly the same as the observed pattern. But for buying intentions, the predicted pattern will differ from the observed pattern because of response bias.

Evidently, even complete independence between intentions to buy A and B *within* the three response groups will show up as some degree of interdependence in data for the sample as a whole. In this illustration, the differences between observed frequencies (based on the assumption *that each of the three groups is characterized by complete independence*) and predicted frequencies (testing the hypothesis that the sample as a whole is characterized by complete independence) are those in the bottom panel of Table B-1.

The observed pattern for buying intentions is one of positive interdependence; households reporting intentions to buy A will be more likely to report B intentions than others; those not reporting A, less likely to report B than others; and so forth. And the result is wholly due to the existence of response bias, because the observed pattern was based on the assumption of complete independence for both intentions and purchases *within* each of the three response groups.

If response bias does exist, buying intentions will always have a greater degree of interdependence than purchases, *ceteris paribus*. Note that the difference between the observed and predicted frequencies has the form:

$$(1.75 - 1.17^2)\hat{a}\hat{b}N$$

---

[1] For example, if a and b are the purchase rates for commodities A and B, respectively, the expected number of households purchasing both A and B (assuming independence) is abN, the expected number purchasing neither is $(1 - a)(1 - b)N$, the expected number purchasing A but not B is $a(1 - b)N$, and the expected number purchasing B but not A is $b(1 - a)N$.

TABLE B-1
Illustrative Distribution of Observed and Predicted Frequency of Joint Intentions and Purchases by Households Classified as Pessimistic, Optimistic, or Normal

Commodity Classification	Number of Households Reporting	
	Buying Intentions[a]	Purchases
	OBSERVED	
Both A and B	$1.75\hat{a}\hat{b}N$	abN
Neither A nor B	$(1 - 1.17\hat{a} - 1.17\hat{b} + 1.75\hat{a}\hat{b})N$	$[(1 - a - b) + (ab)]N$
A, not B	$(1.17\hat{a} - 1.75\hat{a}\hat{b})N$	$(a - ab)N$
B, not A	$(1.17\hat{b} - 1.75\hat{a}\hat{b})N$	$(b - ab)N$
Total	N	N
	PREDICTED	
Both A and B	$1.17^2\hat{a}\hat{b}N$	abN
Neither A nor B	$(1 - 1.17\hat{a} - 1.17\hat{b} + 1.17^2\hat{a}\hat{b})N$	$[(1 - a - b) + (ab)]N$
A, not B	$(1.17\hat{a} - 1.17^2\hat{a}\hat{b})N$	$(a - ab)N$
B, not A	$(1.17\hat{b} - 1.17^2\hat{a}\hat{b})N$	$(b - ab)N$
Total	N	N
	OBSERVED LESS PREDICTED	
Both A and B	$+(1.75 - 1.17^2)\hat{a}\hat{b}N$	No difference
Neither A nor B	$+(1.75 - 1.17^2)\hat{a}\hat{b}N$	No difference
A, not B	$-(1.75 - 1.17^2)\hat{a}\hat{b}N$	No difference
B, not A	$-(1.75 - 1.17^2)\hat{a}\hat{b}N$	No difference

Source: Basic data from Consumer Purchase Study, NBER.

[a] The calculation is as follows: The assumed intentions and purchases rates for commodities A and B in the three response groups are

	Buying Intentions		Purchases	
	A	B	A	B
Pessimists $(N/3)$	$0.5\hat{a}$	$0.5\hat{b}$	a	b
Normal $(N/3)$	$1.0\hat{a}$	$1.0\hat{b}$	a	b
Optimists $(N/3)$	$2.0\hat{a}$	$2.0\hat{b}$	a	b

For the pessimists, the frequency of intentions to buy and purchases are, assuming independence within each response group:

	Intentions	Purchases
Both A and B	$(0.5\hat{a})(0.5\hat{b})(N/3)$	$abN/3$
Neither A nor B	$(1.0 - 0.5\hat{a})(1.0 - 0.5\hat{b})(N/3)$	$(1 - a)(1 - b)(N/3)$
A, not B	$(0.5\hat{a})(1.0 - 0.5\hat{b})(N/3)$	$a(1 - b)(N/3)$
B, not A	$(0.5\hat{b})(1.0 - 0.5\hat{a})(N/3)$	$b(1 - a)(N/3)$

Multiplying, adding the comparable frequencies for the other two groups, and combining terms, aggregate intentions to buy both A and B are

$$0.25\hat{a}\hat{b}\frac{N}{3} + \hat{a}\hat{b}\frac{N}{3} + 4\hat{a}\hat{b}\frac{N}{3}, \text{ or } 1.75\hat{a}\hat{b}N,$$

the figure shown in the table.

The number 1.75 is simply the (weighted) mean value of the squares of rates assumed for buying intentions in the three response groups—normal, pessimistic, and optimistic households. That is,

$$1.75 = \left(1.0^2\frac{N}{3} + 0.5^2\frac{N}{3} + 2.0^2\frac{N}{3}\right) \div 3N$$

The number 1.17^2 is simply the square of the (weighted) mean intentions rates assumed for the three groups, that is,

$$1.17^2 = \left[\left(1.0\frac{N}{3} + 0.5\frac{N}{3} + 2.0\frac{N}{3}\right) \div 3N\right]^2$$

Thus, response bias will result in the observed intentions pattern showing a greater degree of interdependence than the observed purchase pattern whenever the rates of buying intentions in the response groups are such that the mean of the squared rates exceeds the square of the mean rate; more simply, whenever the intentions rates for the response groups vary from one another. This criterion seems to apply regardless of the relative sizes of the response groups in the sample. The illustration assumed equality of sample size, but the assumption is unnecessary. Further, this result follows regardless of the magnitudes of the differences in intentions rates for the response groups. In effect, a comparison of the interdependence patterns for buying intentions and purchases seems to be a definitive test of response bias, other things being the same.

EMPIRICAL FINDINGS ON RESPONSE BIAS

Several pairs of commodities were selected for the empirical analysis. These are, with the indicated designations,

$A_{1,2}$ = automobile, furniture
$A_{1,3}$ = automobile, room air conditioner
$A_{1,4}$ = automobile, high-fidelity equipment
$A_{3,5}$ = room air conditioner, clothes dryer
$A_{6,7}$ = range, refrigerator
$A_{8,9}$ = garbage disposal unit, dishwasher
$A_{4,10}$ = high-fidelity equipment, television set

The first four pairs have no apparent complementarity in either use or purchase; hence, it was anticipated that households purchasing one of these commodities would be about as likely as others to purchase the second commodity. On the other hand, it was anticipated that joint purchases of the two commodities in the fifth and sixth pairs would be more common than predicted on the assumption of independence, since purchase of both items in each pair frequently accompanies acquisition of a house or renovation of a kitchen. And in the last pair it was anticipated that joint purchases might be less common than predicted on the assumption of independence.

It seemed desirable to test data for more than one intentions question;

consequently, I selected one question with a relatively high probability cut-off point—definite intentions to buy within twelve months—and another with a much lower probability cut-off—probable or possible intentions to buy within twelve months. Chi-square is the appropriate test of independence. The observed frequencies in each of the four cells —purchased both A and B, purchased neither, . . . , etc.—are tabulated directly; the predicted frequencies, assuming independence, are abN, etc., as discussed above. The four groups were combined into two because both the predicted (and observed) frequencies in the abN or $\hat{a}\hat{b}N$ cells are generally very small (occasionally, less than one case), and the chi-square test loses validity with cells of this size. Hence the intended-to-buy (purchased) both and intended-to-buy (purchased) neither cells have been combined, as have the remaining two cells. No information is lost by this procedure, because any difference between observed and predicted frequencies necessarily has the same magnitude and sign in each of the combined cells.[2]

Chi-square statistics were computed for the sample as a whole, and for a subsample of relatively high- and relatively low-income households. Table B-2 summarizes the results for the seven pairs of commodities designated above as $A_{1,2}$, . . . ,$A_{4,10}$ for purchases and both definite and probable-possible buying intentions, and for both high- and low-income subgroups as well as for the total sample.

To determine whether there are systematic differences among households in the interpretation of buying intentions questions, the independence patterns for buying intentions and purchases must be compared.

---

[2] Chi-square for a 2 × 2 classification contains only one degree of freedom. Given the frequency of purchases or intentions to buy A and B and the sample size, tabulation of the observed frequency in any one of the four cells fixes the other three, as does computation of any one of the predicted frequencies. Suppose observed and predicted 2 × 2 tables are as follows, where 10 people report intentions to buy A, 20 report intentions to buy B, 5 report intentions to buy both, and the sample contains 100 people:

| | INTENTIONS TO BUY A | | | | | |
| INTENTIONS TO BUY B | *Observed Frequencies* | | | *Predicted Frequencies* | | |
	Yes	No	Total	Yes	No	Total
Yes	5	15	(20)	2	18	(20)
No	5	75	80	8	72	80
Total	(10)	90	(100)	(10)	90	(100)

The frequencies in parentheses are necessarily common to both parts of the table. The rest of the observed frequencies can be filled in once it is known that five people intended to buy both commodities; similarly, once $\hat{a}\hat{b}N = 2$—$0.20 \times 0.10 \times 100$— is computed, the rest of the predicted frequencies are determined. And the difference between predicted and actual in both sets of diagonal cells must be exactly the same in both magnitude and sign.

	Commodity Pairs						
	$A_{1,2}$	$A_{1,3}$	$A_{1,4}$	$A_{3,5}$	$A_{6,7}$	$A_{8,9}$	$A_{4,10}$
ALL HOUSEHOLDS $(N = 3157)$							
Purchases	0.0	0.0	0.0^a	0.1	47.5^b	28.2^b	0.8
Definite intentions to buy	3.0	0.4	0.8	0.7	34.2^b	15.3^b	1.2
Probable-possible intentions to buy	3.0	3.4	0.0	0.2	42.0^b	18.4^b	1.9
HOUSEHOLDS WITH FAMILY INCOME UNDER \$7,500 $(N = 1144)$							
Purchases	0.1	0.4^a	0.0	0.0	14.1^b	2.7	0.0
Definite intentions to buy	2.3	0.4	1.4	0.4	19.0^b	1.5	0.8
Probable-possible intentions to buy	2.6	1.1	0.6	0.2	25.1^b	2.5	0.3
HOUSEHOLDS WITH FAMILY INCOME OF \$10,000 OR MORE $(N = 1103)$							
Purchases	0.0^a	0.3	0.6^a	0.6	19.0^b	13.8^b	0.9
Definite intentions to buy	1.2	0.0	0.2	0.1	15.1^b	12.3^b	0.3
Probable-possible intentions to buy	1.9	2.0	0.0	0.0	8.9^b	9.9^b	0.1

Source: Basic data from Consumer Purchase Study, NBER.

Note: See accompanying text for durables designated by the subscripts. Chi-square is computed as the difference between the observed and predicted number of households reporting intentions to buy (purchases) for both or neither of the commodity pairs, and for one but not the other or the reverse. For example, commodity pair $A_{1,2}$ (automobile vis-à-vis furniture) showed the following observed and predicted combinations for purchases, using the sample as a whole.

	OBSERVED PURCHASES				PREDICTED PURCHASES		
		A_1				A_1	
A_2	Yes	No	Total	A_2	Yes	No	Total
Yes	133	515	648	Yes	131.8	516.2	648
No	509	2,000	2,509	No	510.2	1,998.8	2,509
Total	642	2,515	3,157	Total	642	2,515	3,157

Thus, the sums of purchases of both commodities or of neither are:

Observed	2,133
Predicted	2,130.6

The sums of the other cells are:

Observed	1,024
Predicted	1,026.4

Chi-square is computed as

$$\frac{(2.4)^2}{2,130.6} + \frac{(2.4)^2}{1,026.4}, \text{ or } 0.0$$

[a] The predicted frequency of intentions (purchases) for both commodities in the pair is greater than the observed frequency, indicating a pattern of negative interdependence. In all other cases, predicted frequency of intentions (purchases) for both commodities is less than the observed frequency.

[b] These show a significant degree of interdependence at the 0.01 level. The critical values of χ^2 with one degree of freedom are:

$$\text{.05 level, } \chi^2 \geq 3.84$$
$$\text{.01 level, } \chi^2 \geq 6.64$$

The observed pattern for purchases is affected by events that occur after the formulation of buying intentions, hence would not be observed in the intentions data because the event had not been foreseen. Many events of this kind occur between the date when buying intentions are reported and the end of the forecast period. For example, some households report intentions to buy a large number of durable goods because they expect to move to a new residence. Some of these households will move during the forecast period, purchasing a number of durables in the process; both their buying intentions and purchases will show a high degree of interdependence. Others of this group of intenders will not move during the period, and their buying intentions would presumably show more interdependence than their purchases because of this. But some households will move that had not anticipated a change in residence, and their purchases would presumably show a higher degree of interdependence than their buying intentions. On the whole, it seems reasonable to assume that the influence of such events, and of unanticipated events generally, will be random with respect to the observed pattern of independence among purchases, or if nonrandom, that there will be a corresponding influence on buying intentions.

The data do not support the proposition that response bias exists; more accurately, they do not support the proposition that a serious response bias characterizes the sample. In the two cases where the intentions data show statistically significant interdependence, purchases also show a statistically significant degree of interdependence. And in each of these cases both intentions questions—definite and probable-possible—show significant positive interdependence. In the other five cases, purchases show no significant deviation from a pattern of independence; and in all five cases, neither intentions question shows a significant deviation from independence.

The hypothesized negative interdependence between purchases of high-fidelity equipment and television sets is not apparent in the data. The only one of the seven commodity pairs in which observed joint purchases are fewer than predicted by the no-association hypothesis (automobiles and high-fidelity equipment) shows a chi-square value of less than 0.1. Although all possible combinations of commodity pairs were not tested, it seems probable that none would show a pattern of significant negative interdependence. The implication is that expenditures for durables typically tend to be substitutes for savings or for expenditures on nondurables rather than for other items in the durables category.

The results for subgroups of relatively low- and high-income households accord with those for the sample as a whole, although the evidence suggests that the patterns may be slightly different for households in the respective income classes. As before, all cases of statistically significant interdependence in purchases are matched by a corresponding pattern in the intentions data. But disregarding the question of statistical significance, both buying intentions questions compared to purchases tend to show a greater degree of positive interdependence for households in the relatively low-income group, while the reverse is true for households in the relatively high-income classes. In the middle panel of Table B-2, for example, six of the seven commodity pairs show higher chi-square values for both intentions variants than for purchases; among relatively high-income households, in contrast, five of seven commodity pairs show higher values of chi-square for purchases than for definite buying intentions; four of seven, higher chi-square values for purchases than for probable-possible intentions (bottom panel). None of these differences is statistically significant.

Additional evidence is provided by the analysis of data for more homogeneous subgroups. The sample was cross-classified into five income and three life-cycle groups, with sample sizes as shown in the tabulation below:

	Life-Cycle Class: Husband-Wife Households, Head Between		
Income Class	25–35	35–44	45–64
Under $5,000	131	55	56
$5,000–$7,499	460	266	176
$7,500–$9,999	383	338	189
$10,000–$14,999	206	342	209
$15,000 and over	66	133	147

Frequencies of purchases and of both definite and probable-possible intentions were computed for each commodity within each of the fifteen subgroups; predicted frequencies were calculated for the seven commodity pairs within each of the subgroups, and the corresponding actual frequencies tabulated. Both predicted and observed frequencies were converted to proportions, and t ratios were computed for the difference between predicted and observed proportions in the purchased (intended-to-buy) both-A-and-B cell.[3] All told, there were 105 t ratios for purchases, and the same number for both of the intentions questions—one

[3] Let p_A be the proportion of any given subgroup reporting purchases of commodity A; p_B, the proportion reporting purchases of commodity B. Then $p_A p_B$ is the proportion expected to purchase both A and B, assuming that purchases of A are independent of whether or not B was purchased, and vice versa. Designating $p_A p_B$, the predicted proportion of joint purchases, as f_p, and designating the observed proportion as f_o, the t ratio is $\dfrac{f_o - f_p}{\sigma(f_o - f_p)}$.

t ratio for each of the seven commodity pairs within each of the fifteen subgroups.

Table B-3 summarizes the joint distribution of these *t* ratios by purchases versus definite intentions to buy and purchases versus probable-possible intentions to buy. The *t* ratios are classified according to whether the observed frequency (f_o) is greater or less than the predicted frequency (f_p) and whether the *t* ratio is less than 1, between 1 and 2, or greater than 2. The data are arranged so that observations below the diagonal from upper left to lower right are cases where buying intentions show a stronger degree of interdependence (or a weaker degree of negative interdependence) than

TABLE B-3

TEST OF RESPONSE BIAS BY JOINT DISTRIBUTION OF *t* RATIOS

	t Ratios for Purchases						
	$f_o < f_p$			$f_o > f_p$			
	$t \geqq 2$	$2 < t \geqq 1$	$t < 1$	$t < 1$	$1 \leqq t > 2$	$t \geqq 2$	Total
t ratios for definite buying intentions							
$f_o < f_p$							
$t \geqq 2$	0	0	0	0	0	0	0
$2 < t \geqq 1$	0	0	1	0	0	0	1
$t < 1$	0	1	18	10	4	1	34
$f_o > f_p$							
$t < 1$	0	2	16	20	8	0	46
$1 \leqq t > 2$	0	0	3	5	10	3	21
$t \geqq 2$	0	0	1	0	1	1	3
Total	0	3	39	35	23	5	105
t ratios for probable-possible buying intentions							
$f_o < f_p$							
$t \geqq 2$	0	0	0	0	0	0	0
$2 < t \geqq 1$	0	0	2	0	1	0	3
$t < 1$	0	2	16	8	2	0	28
$f_o > f_p$							
$t < 1$	0	1	17	22	8	0	48
$1 \leqq t > 2$	0	0	4	4	10	3	21
$t \geqq 2$	0	0	0	1	2	2	5
Total	0	3	39	35	23	5	105

	SUMMARY		
	Upper Panel	Lower Panel	Total
Observations along diagonal	49	50	99
Observations above diagonal	27	24	51
Observations below diagonal	29	31	60
Total	105	105	210

SOURCE: Basic data from Consumer Purchase Study, NBER.
NOTE: See accompanying text for explanation.

purchases; observations above the diagonal, cases where purchases are more highly interdependent; and observations along the diagonal, cases where the degree of interdependence is approximately the same for both purchases and intentions.

These data provide evidence on several points. First, differences among households in the interpretation of buying-intentions questions do not appear to be a serious problem in this sample. Almost half the total observations fall along the diagonal; their t ratios for purchases and buying intentions are therefore approximately equal in magnitude, and $(f_o - f_p)$ has the same algebraic sign for both purchases and intentions. Further, only 20 of 210 observations fall more than one category away from the diagonal. Second, response bias among households does exist, and there is some indication that it is more serious for intentions variants with a relatively low probability cut-off. I infer this from the fact that more observations appear below the diagonal than above, and relatively more are below than above in the lower panel than in the upper one. Further, of the observations that are more than two categories removed from the diagonal, six of nine in the lower panel are below the diagonal while only six of eleven are below the diagonal in the upper one. Finally, it appears that the interdependence patterns for purchases are negative about as often as they are positive if commodity pairs with strong complementarity in use are excluded, such as the range-refrigerator or garbage disposal unit-dishwasher combinations. These two combinations comprise all the highly interdependent purchase patterns in Table B-3, although the t ratios are generally below 2 because of the small sample size. Excluding these cases, the remainder seem to be about evenly distributed around the dividing line where $f_o = f_p$. It may be that other combinations of commodities have a strong pattern of negative interdependence, but none of the ones used above seems to have this characteristic.

It should be noted that these conclusions may not apply to samples selected at random from the population. All of the analysis in this monograph is based on data for a thoroughly unrepresentative sample of households. In most cases, it is possible to check whether the results are sensitive to variations in such household characteristics as income, life-cycle status, or education—for which the Consumers Union sample is known to be atypical. If the results are not sensitive to such factors, it can be argued that they are likely to be applicable to the population generally. But in this chapter I have shown that differences in the degree of interdependence for purchases and buying intentions, though small, are apparently rather persistent for the lowest income groups in the sample, while no differences at all are apparent for the highest income groups. Hence, a random population sample might well be characterized by a much stronger degree of interdependence for buying intentions than for purchases.

An Analysis of Substitution Among Intenders

The third of the questions raised at the beginning of this appendix requires a rather different arrangement of the empirical data. The question here is whether a household reporting an intention to buy commodity A but not purchasing is more apt to purchase commodity B than a household neither reporting an intention to buy nor purchasing A. If this is the case it clearly makes more sense to combine the individual commodity buying intentions for each household into an aggregate, rather than to deal with them separately. If it is not, aggregation serves no particular point and may tend to muddy relationships that actually exist.

This problem is cumbersome for empirical analysis. It does no good to compare total purchases for a group of households that reported intentions to buy commodity A, but did not purchase, with total purchases for households that neither reported intentions to buy nor bought commodity A; it is also necessary to know the extent to which these respective groups of households had reported buying intentions for other commodities. Moreover, the analysis in Chapters 3 and 4 suggests that both affirmative and negative responses to buying-intentions questions reflect a continuous distribution of *ex ante* purchase probabilities rather than a dichotomous distribution of probabilities equal to unity and zero. The most efficient procedure seems to me to be a comparison of the relation between aggregate purchases and aggregate buying intentions for groups of households that, *ex post*, differ with respect to their reported intentions to buy or purchases of some particular commodity. For simplification I first make the extreme assumption (which I will later drop) that households reporting intentions to buy have purchase probabilities equal to unity; those not reporting intentions, probabilities of zero.

The analysis concerns aggregate intentions and purchases for households classified with respect to intentions and purchases relating to a specific commodity—any of the items for which data are available. Let P represent (weighted) aggregate purchases for all A, B, . . . ,N commodities, including the one used as the basis for classifying into groups; let $\hat{P}$ represent (weighted) aggregate intentions to buy, defined in the same way. Let P' represent aggregate purchases of all commodities *exclusive* of the one used as the basis for classification; let $\hat{P}'$ represent aggregate buying intentions, similarly defined. Then $P/\hat{P}$ or $P'/\hat{P}'$ are ratios of aggregate purchases to aggregate intentions. To denote the household's intentions and purchases of a given commodity A,B,C, . . . , or N, two subscripts are used; the first indicates whether or not the household intended to buy: $1 = \text{yes}$, $0 = \text{no}$; the second, whether or not they purchased: $1 = \text{yes}$, $0 = \text{no}$. Thus $(P/\hat{P})_{11}$ is the ratio of aggregate purchases to aggregate buying intentions, *including* those for the given commodity A,B,C, . . . , or N, for households that intended to buy and purchased A,B, . . . , or N during the forecast period. Similarly, $(P'/\hat{P}')_{01}$ is the ratio of aggregate purchases to aggregate buying intentions, *excluding* those involving commodity A,B,C, . . . , or N, for households that had not reported intentions to buy A,B,C, . . . , or N but had purchased during the forecast period. A leading subscript designates the commodity used as the basis for classification into intended to buy and bought, etc. Thus $_A(P/\hat{P})_{00}$ represents the ratio of aggregate purchases to aggregate buying intentions for households that had neither intended to buy nor purchased A during the forecast period.

The notation is further simplified by adopting the convention that $P/\hat{P}$ is Q, and that $P'/\hat{P}'$ is Q'. Hence, $_AQ_{01}$ represents the ratio of aggregate purchases to aggregate buying intentions, *including* those for commodity A, for households that purchased A but had not reported intentions to do so. $_BQ'_{10}$ represents the ratio of aggregate purchases to aggregate intentions, *excluding* those for commodity B, for households that reported buying intentions but had not purchased B during the forecast period.

The possible relationships can now be defined. There might be complete substitution: any household that reported intentions to buy A would either buy it or some equivalent item; any household that bought A without reporting an intention to buy would have reported intentions to buy an equivalent item that would not have been purchased. In short, the sum of intentions and purchases for all commodities would be the same regardless of whether the households had intended to buy and bought A, intended to buy and not bought A, etc. In the notation above,

$$_AQ_{11} = {}_AQ_{10} = {}_AQ_{01} = {}_AQ_{00};$$

and these ratios would all be equal to unity. The ratio of purchases to intentions excluding A would follow the reverse pattern from that of the classification with respect to A; that is, those who had intended to buy but had not purchased A would have made relatively more purchases of

B, C, . . . , N, etc.   In the above notation

$$_A Q'_{10} > {}_A Q'_{11} = {}_A Q'_{00} > {}_A Q'_{01}$$

A second possibility involves less than complete substitution.   Households intending to buy but not purchasing A would have purchased more B,C, . . . ,N, relative to intentions, than households intending to buy and buying A, but not enough more to compensate for the difference in purchases of A.   Similarly, households that had not intended to buy A but had purchased would have bought less B,C, . . . ,N, relative to intentions, than households that had neither intended to buy nor purchased; but, again, not enough less to compensate for the difference in purchases of A.   Those whose actions corresponded with their intentions would presumably have about the same ratio of P to $\hat{P}$.

In the notation used above,

$$_A Q_{01} > {}_A Q_{00} \gtreqless {}_A Q_{11} > {}_A Q_{10},$$

and

$$_A Q_{01} > {}_A Q_{10}.$$

Also,

$$_A Q'_{10} > {}_A Q'_{11} \gtreqless {}_A Q'_{00} > {}_A Q'_{01},$$

and

$$_A Q'_{10} > {}_A Q'_{01}.$$

In short, the pattern of the Q and Q' ratios would be exactly the reverse of each other.   Those reporting intentions to buy A but not purchasing would show relatively more purchases of B,C, . . . ,N but relatively fewer of A,B,C, . . . ,N than those reporting intentions and purchasing A.   On the other hand, households that had purchased A but had not reported intentions to buy would show relatively fewer purchases of B,C, . . . ,N but relatively more of A,B,C, . . . ,N than those reporting neither intentions nor purchases.

The third possibility is zero substitution.   In this case, intentions or purchases vis-à-vis A would have no effect on the relation between purchases and intentions vis-à-vis commodities B,C, . . . ,N.   The Q' ratios would be the same regardless of the A classification into which the household fell, while the Q ratios would depend on the A classification.   In sum, it would be found that:

$$_A Q_{01} > {}_A Q_{00} \gtreqless {}_A Q_{11} > {}_A Q_{10}; {}_A Q_{01} > {}_A Q_{10},$$

and

$$_A Q'_{11} = {}_A Q'_{10} = {}_A Q'_{01} = {}_A Q'_{00}$$

The remaining possibility may be thought of as negative substitution or complementarity. In this case, households intending to buy A but not purchasing would make relatively *fewer* purchases of B,C, . . . ,N than households that intended to buy and did so. Those that purchased A but had not reported intentions to do so would make relatively *more* purchases of B,C, . . . ,N than those that had neither bought nor intended to buy. By the same token, those that intended to buy but did not purchase A would make relatively *fewer* purchases of B,C, . . . ,N than those that had purchased A but had not reported intentions to buy. As before, the Q' ratios for those whose intentions coincided with their actions must be between the Q' ratios for the other groups. The Q ratios necessarily follow the same pattern except that the differences are bound to be greater. In the 01 group, for example, Q must be larger than Q' because the numerator must increase and the denominator does not change; in the 10 group Q must be smaller than Q', since the numerator does not change and the denominator necessarily increases.

In sum:

$$_AQ_{01} > {}_AQ_{00} \gtreqless {}_AQ_{11} > {}_AQ_{10}; \; {}_AQ_{01} > {}_AQ_{10},$$
$$_AQ'_{01} > {}_AQ'_{00} \gtreqless {}_AQ'_{11} > {}_AQ'_{10}; \; {}_AQ'_{01} > {}_AQ'_{10},$$
$$_AQ_{01} > {}_AQ'_{01}, \; {}_AQ_{10} < {}_AQ'_{10}$$

It should be noted that these tests may not show identical or even similar patterns for all the A,B,C, . . . ,N commodities. For example, it is perfectly conceivable that purchases of other items are completely unaffected by the purchase of a refrigerator, but are affected by the purchase of an automobile. On a priori grounds, a combination of positive substitution when A is the basis for classification and negative substitution when B is the classification basis appears less likely; yet there seems no necessary reason why this could not be the case.

The relation between Q and Q' ratios for the four possible cases outlined above, for the Nth commodity, is summarized as follows:

1. Complete substitution

$$_NQ_{11} = {}_NQ_{10} = {}_NQ_{01} = {}_NQ_{00},$$

and

$$_NQ'_{10} > {}_NQ'_{11} = {}_NQ'_{00} > {}_NQ'_{01}.$$

2. Some substitution, but less than complete,

$$_NQ_{01} > {}_NQ_{00} \gtreqless {}_NQ_{11} > {}_NQ_{10}; \; {}_NQ_{01} > {}_NQ_{10},$$
$$_NQ'_{10} > {}_NQ'_{11} \gtreqless {}_NQ'_{00} > {}_NQ'_{01}; \; {}_NQ'_{10} > {}_NQ'_{01}$$

3. Neither substitution nor complementarity

$$_NQ_{01} > {_NQ_{00}} \gtreqless {_NQ_{11}} > {_NQ_{10}}; {_NQ_{01}} > {_NQ_{10}},$$
$$_NQ'_{11} = {_NQ'_{10}} = {_NQ'_{01}} = {_NQ'_{00}}.$$

4. Negative substitution or complementarity

$$_NQ_{01} > {_NQ_{00}} \gtreqless {_NQ_{11}} > {_NQ_{10}}; {_NQ_{01}} > {_NQ_{10}},$$
$$_NQ'_{01} > {_NQ'_{00}} \gtreqless {_NQ'_{11}} > {_NQ'_{10}}; {_NQ'_{01}} > {_NQ'_{10}},$$
$$_NQ_{01} > {_NQ'_{01}}, {_NQ_{10}} < {_NQ'_{01}}$$

From this set of relationships it is clear that the Q ratios are a definitive test for complete substitution. If these ratios are all equal, there must be complete substitution; otherwise this cannot be the case. The Q ratios follow identical patterns if there is some, none, or negative substitution; hence, they cannot discriminate in these cases. But the pattern of the Q' ratios, if there is positive but less than complete substitution, is opposite to that for negative substitution or complementarity; and all the Q' ratios are equal if there is zero substitution.

At this point the assumption is dropped that households reporting intentions have perfect certainty about purchasing and, hence, *ex ante* purchase probabilities equal to one, as is the companion assumption that nonintenders have perfect certainty about not purchasing, i.e. *ex ante* purchase probabilities of zero. The analysis in the text makes it quite clear that these assumptions are unrealistic. If so, what is the affect on the Q and Q' ratios?

In the first place, the average Q ratio for the sample as a whole need no longer be equal to unity. Instead, the level of the Q ratio is determined by the characteristics of the buying intentions question. It will be recalled that Q is defined as the ratio of (weighted) aggregate purchases to aggregate intentions, that is, as $P/\hat{P}$. But P can be written as the product of the mean probability of purchase and the number of households in the sample, i.e., $\sum_{a}^{n} x'N$. Although x' cannot be observed, the fraction of the sample purchasing—x—is an unbiased estimate of x'. I have already shown that x is equal to $s + p(r - s)$, where s is the purchase rate for nonintenders; r, the purchase rate for intenders; and p, the proportion of intenders in the sample. It follows that:

$$P = \sum_{a}^{n} xN = \sum_{a}^{n} [s + p(r - s)]N$$

The denominator of the Q ratio $(\hat{P})$ is simply $\sum\limits_{a}^{n} pN$, where p is the proportion of the sample reporting intentions to buy each of the A,B, . . . ,N commodities and N is the sample size. Consequently,

$$Q = \frac{P}{\hat{P}} = \frac{\sum\limits_{a}^{n} [s + p(r - s)]}{\sum\limits_{a}^{n} p}$$

From this formula it is obvious that the Q ratio will equal unity only by chance. In general, the *level* of the ratio depends on p, which in turn depends on the characteristics of the intentions question. When p increases, previous discussion has shown that both $r - s$ and s will fall provided that x and p are relatively small. Since all the x and p terms are considerably less than 0.5, the Q ratio must fall as p increases, for the denominator must grow at a faster rate than the numerator.

However, the relative size of the Q ratios in the several classes of households is not indicated. I will now investigate these ratios for the 11 and 10 groups—those intending to buy and purchasing, and those intending to buy but not purchasing. If a household falls in group 11 (intended, purchased) for the Ath commodity, it would appear that the household's probability of purchasing B,C, . . . , or N should be less than if it had fallen in group 10 (intended, did not purchase). The expected value of total purchases for the ith household is the sum of its *ex ante* purchase probabilities for A,B,C, . . . ,N. If the ith household reported an intention to buy commodity A, it is known that one element in the sum of its purchase probabilities had a value somewhere between the cut-off point and unity. If the household purchased A, one of the elements in the sum of its purchases has a value of unity; while if the household did not purchase A, one of the elements in P has a value of zero. On the average, it seems to follow that intenders who purchased (group 11) must have lower Q' ratios than intenders who did not purchase (group 10), that is, $_{A}Q'_{11}$ must be less than $_{A}Q'_{10}$. The relation between $_{A}Q_{11}$ and $_{A}Q_{10}$ might be anything. *Ex ante*, $_{A}Q_{11}$ might have been equal to $_{A}Q_{10}$; but no necessary relation exists between the (observed) *ex post* $_{A}Q_{11}$ and $_{A}Q_{10}$ ratios. The reason is simply that I have classified by a variable (purchase or non-purchase of A) that necessarily involves the propositions that

$$(p_{A})_{11} > (\hat{p}_{A})_{11}$$

and
$$(p_A)_{10} < (\hat{p}_A)_{10}$$

where p_A represents observed purchases of commodity A; and $\hat{p}_A$, expected purchases.

However, further analysis indicates that this conclusion—$_AQ'_{11}$ is necessarily less than $_AQ'_{10}$—may not hold unless the distribution of purchase probabilities among those reporting intentions to buy A,B,C, . . . ,N is randomly associated with the distribution of purchases. But I do not think it reasonable to assume that, among a group of intenders, households that purchased had the same *ex ante* mean probability as households that did not purchase. Rather, I would have thought that *ex ante* mean probability was likely to have been higher among intenders who purchased than among intenders who did not purchase. If so, *ex ante* purchase probability for commodities B,C, . . . ,N might *also* be higher among A intenders who purchased than among those who did not purchase. This in itself would not be sufficient to change the above relation between $_AQ'_{11}$ and $_AQ'_{10}$, since any difference between these two groups in the mean probability of purchasing B,C, . . . ,N may show up as a difference in the average level of intentions to buy these commodities. However, part of any such difference in mean probability is also likely to show up as a higher mean probability among both intenders and nonintenders, as well as in a different distribution of the two. In short, if the probability of purchasing A is positively correlated with the probability of purchasing B,C, . . . ,N, holding constant intentions to buy B,C, . . . ,N as well as intentions to buy A, the observed Q' ratio among A intenders might be larger for the 11 group than for the 10 group; and this may be the case even if, substituting *ex ante* purchase probabilities for reported intentions to buy, $_AQ'_{11}$ is less than $_AQ'_{10}$.

The same line of argument can be used to show that the relation between the Q' ratios for groups 01 and 00 is also impossible to predict from the probability model. If probabilities for A nonintenders were randomly associated with purchases of A, or if purchase probabilities relating to B,C, . . . ,N were uncorrelated with purchase probabilities for A, holding intentions to buy constant, it would follow that

$$_AQ'_{01} < _AQ'_{00}$$

But if these assumptions do not hold, the observed relation might be $_AQ'_{01} > _AQ'_{00}$, although substituting *ex ante* probabilities, $_AQ'_{01} < _AQ'_{00}$.

The argument essentially proposes that classification of households into the above groups (11,10,01,00) is likely to introduce a consistent bias into the relation between the observed Q or Q' ratios and the "true" ratios—in which actual probabilities replace buying intentions. The observed ratios are defined as

$$_AQ_{11,10,01,00} = {_A(P/\hat{P})_{11,10,01,00}}$$
$$_AQ'_{11,10,01,00} = {_A(P'/\hat{P}')_{11,10,01,00}}$$

The P term is the sum of actual purchases, and is presumably an estimate of the sum of *ex ante* purchase probabilities for households in the respective classes. The $\hat{P}$ term is the total number of buying intentions reported by households in the respective classes, but will not be an estimate of the sum of probabilities except by happenstance. If the summation of (unknown) *ex ante* purchase probabilities for households in the respective 11, . . . ,00 groups is not randomly associated with $\hat{P}$ in these same classes, the relation among $_AQ_{11,10,01,00}$ or $_AQ'_{11,10,01,00}$ cannot be predicted with any confidence. This is especially the case if the (unknown) purchase probabilities for B,C, . . . ,N, holding constant intentions to buy B,C, . . . ,N, happen to be positively correlated with the (unknown) probability of purchasing A, holding constant intentions to buy A.

EMPIRICAL FINDINGS ON SUBSTITUTION

The net result is that the empirical findings based on the assumption of perfect certainty for both intenders and nonintenders become difficult if not impossible to interpret. The data (Table B-4) indicate that negative substitution or complementarity is the dominant pattern. In all but one case the Q' ratios show that

$$_AQ'_{01} > {_AQ'_{00}} \gtrless {_AQ'_{11}} > {_AQ'_{10}}; \; _AQ'_{01} > {_AQ'_{10}},$$
$$_BQ'_{01} > {_BQ'_{00}} \gtrless {_BQ'_{11}} > {_BQ'_{10}}; \; _BQ'_{01} > {_BQ'_{10}},$$

etc.; the same pattern is necessarily observed for the Q ratios. That is, households reporting intentions to buy a specific commodity and not purchasing are relatively likely to have reported buying intentions for other commodities that were also not purchased. Households purchasing a specific commodity without having reported buying intentions are apt to have purchased other items without having reported intentions to buy them either. And households whose intentions to buy (or not to buy) a specific commodity corresponded to their actions, show ratios between those for the other two groups.

These data would be inconsistent with the proposition that buying intentions reflect purchase probability if it could be assumed that the purchase probabilities for commodities B,C, . . . ,N, holding constant

TABLE B-4
Test of Substitution and Complementarity in Buying Intentions[a] and Purchases

Commodity by Which Classified	Household Types[b]							
	Q_{11}	Q_{10}	Q_{01}	Q_{00}	Q'_{11}	Q'_{10}	Q'_{01}	Q'_{00}
Room air conditioner	1.289	0.719	2.569	1.463	1.490	1.080	1.697	1.463
House air conditioner	1.048	0.607	2.250	1.702	1.069	0.843	1.818	1.702
Automobile	1.070	0.170	7.643	1.251	[c]	[c]	[c]	[c]
Movie camera	1.536	0.882	2.667	1.400	2.363	1.617	1.795	1.400
Carpets and rugs	1.219	0.529	3.176	1.649	1.331	0.756	2.171	1.649
Clothes dryer	1.211	0.552	3.007	1.793	1.289	0.776	2.184	1.793
Dishwasher	1.056	0.417	3.163	1.456	1.070	0.541	2.459	1.456
Food freezer	1.594	0.601	3.527	1.404	2.267	0.807	2.432	1.404
Furniture	1.240	0.485	3.531	1.468	1.387	0.781	2.297	1.468
Garbage disposal unit	1.067	0.388	2.586	1.516	1.083	0.509	2.040	1.516
High-fidelity equipment	1.287	0.533	3.146	1.827	1.625	0.875	2.013	1.827
Home heating system	0.944	0.300	2.260	1.444	0.927	0.404	1.661	1.444
Range	0.964	0.363	2.697	1.511	0.953	0.470	2.059	1.511
Refrigerator	0.996	0.387	2.946	1.625	0.994	0.514	2.155	1.625
Washing machine	1.301	0.500	2.863	1.496	1.460	0.713	1.973	1.496
Television set	1.097	0.514	2.686	1.453	1.161	0.782	1.814	1.453

Source: Basic data from Consumer Purchase Study, NBER.

[a] The question asked about intentions to buy within six months.

[b] Q_{11}; Ratio of total purchases to total buying intentions for households that intended to buy and bought the commodity listed in the stub, *including* purchases of and intentions to buy the commodity itself.

Q_{10}; Same as Q_{11}, for households that intended to buy but did not buy the commodity listed in the stub.

Q_{01}; Same as Q_{11}, for households that did not intend to buy but bought the commodity listed in the stub.

Q_{00}; Same as Q_{11}, for households that neither intended to buy nor bought the commodity listed.

Q'_{11}; Ratio of total purchases to total buying intentions for households that intended to buy and bought the commodity listed in the stub, *excluding* purchases of and intentions to buy the commodity itself.

Q'_{10}; Same as Q'_{11}, for households that intended to buy but did not buy the commodity listed.

Q'_{01}; Same as Q'_{11}, for households that did not intend to buy but bought the commodity listed.

Q'_{00}; Same as Q'_{11}, for households that neither planned to buy nor bought the commodity listed.

[c] The Q' ratios for automobiles could not be computed without price weights for the automobiles; since the weights could not be obtained for this tabulation, only Q ratios are shown.

intentions to buy B,C, . . . ,N, are not correlated with the probability of purchasing A, holding constant intentions to buy A. Since this assumption cannot be tested, the results are not inconsistent with the probability hypothesis. Moreover, within the framework of the probability model, the observed results can be explained by a combination of response bias, as discussed earlier in this chapter, and the influence of unforeseen events. Perennial optimists would tend to be found in the 10 category, and would depress the Q' ratio for that group, while perennial pessimists would gravitate to the 01 category, increasing the Q' ratio for that group. Similarly, households that experience favorable unforeseen events would consistently wind up in the 01 category, since they are apt to buy more than anticipated; those experiencing the reverse are apt to wind up in the 10 category, since they are apt to buy less than anticipated.

Although the Q or Q' ratios vary substantially when different commodities are used as the basis for classification, these variations do not appear to be related to any characteristic of the commodities—with the possible exception of home ownership. Items such as refrigerators behave much like dishwashers or garbage disposal units; consequently, the fraction of owners in the sample seems to make little difference to the substitution effect. However, items that would generally be purchased only by home owners—range, refrigerator, garbage disposal unit, dishwasher, etc.—show a stronger tendency toward complementarity than commodities that might be purchased by either owners or renters. For items that would be predominantly bought by owners the pattern in the Q' ratios is fairly consistent:

$$Q'_{11} \sim 1.0$$
$$Q'_{10} \sim 0.5$$
$$Q'_{01} \sim 2.0$$
$$Q'_{00} \sim 1.5$$

The explanation may be that intentions and purchases for these items are closely associated with house-buying intentions and purchases. A household intending to buy and buying a house or intending and carrying out kitchen modernization presumably reported intentions to buy and subsequently purchased a number of the individual commodities on the above list; this factor might explain the tendency of the Q'_{11} ratio to approach unity. Similarly, if a household intended to buy a house but did not purchase, its intentions to buy many household durables would not be fulfilled; classifying by one of these durables, households intending to buy some item but not purchasing would have reported intentions to buy many other items but would not have purchased them either. The reverse would be true for households that had not intended to buy a house but did so.[4]

[4] There is some evidence of a positive substitution effect *within* the classification scheme used in Table 22. Although households that both intended to buy and purchased a commodity are likely to show a ratio of aggregate purchases to intentions of

On the whole, the results seem to indicate that failure to fulfill a specific intention to buy (or not to buy) is less generally associated with a change in priority vis-à-vis particular items on the above commodity list than with a change in priority vis-à-vis the entire list relative to other categories of expenditure (or saving). The results thus suggest that households are apt to purchase household durable goods in clusters, and that factors leading to the purchase of one item will frequently result in the purchase of others at the same time.

---

about unity, they did not purchase every item they intended to. One can find substantial numbers of unintended purchases balanced by intentions that were not carried out. Consequently, another way of interpreting these results is that unintended purchases approximately balance unfulfilled intentions in the 11 group; unfulfilled intentions are much greater than unintended purchases in the 10 group; and the reverse is true for the 01 category. In the 00 group unintended purchases are customarily greater than unfulfilled intentions because of the characteristics of the intentions question.

Basic Data Sources

Background of the Consumers Union Panel

On most occasions, researchers design a field survey to provide data for the analysis of specific problems. The research design includes decisions on the sample size, the methods to be used in obtaining information from respondents, the questions to be asked, etc. On other occasions researchers are presented with an opportunity to obtain information subject, however, to certain limitations. A unique opportunity of this sort arose in 1958, when the Consumers Union Panel was initiated.

Mail questionnaire data from subscribers had been gathered for many years by Consumers Union of U.S. (CU), the product-testing and -rating organization. These questionnaires were of interest to economists largely because they contained data on intentions to buy major durable goods, as well as some rather crude supplementary data on income, expected and past changes in income, methods of financing purchases, and so on. Examinations of the CU buying intentions data over the postwar period showed that these data would have predicted changes in aggregate purchases of consumer durables by the United States population more accurately than intentions data obtained from consumers selected at random from among all United States households (as represented in the annual Survey of Consumer Finances conducted by the Survey Research Center at the University of Michigan).[1] The National Bureau of Economic Research consequently initiated a small-scale research program into the CU questionnaire data, most of which were still available.

It quickly became evident that the amount of economically useful data in these questionnaires to which durable goods purchases and buying intentions could be related was quite limited. Some alterations in the questionnaire format were suggested to Consumers Union prior to their regular annual survey in October 1957. These alterations included, among others, a change, from twelve months to six months, in the planning period contained in the buying intentions question. At the same time Consumers Union agreed to the inclusion in the October 1957 questionnaire of a request for volunteers for a special consumer survey; those who agreed to be surveyed were told that they would receive a more elaborate

---

[1] See Juster, "The Predictive Value of Consumers Union Spending-Intentions Data," *The Quality and Economic Significance of Anticipations Data*, Princeton for NBER, 1960.

questionnaire specifically designed for research on consumer purchases and financial decision-making generally.

The regular CU questionnaire had typically drawn about 120,000 responses from a total subscriber list of some 600,000. In October 1957 some 130,000 responses were received, of which just over 33,000 volunteered for membership in this special panel. The arrangement was that subscriber anonymity would be carefully preserved at all times. In April 1958, six months after the request for volunteers, a special questionnaire was mailed to the 33,000 households who had expressed willingness to participate. Along with information about levels of and changes in assets, debts, and income, data were requested on demographic characteristics, intentions to buy durables, attitudes, expectations, and ownership and recent purchases of durables. Because buying intentions were of special interest, the sample was split into five randomly selected subgroups, each of which was sent a differently structured question or combination of questions about intentions to buy. Very little detail was requested about income and assets because it was uncertain how such requests would affect the response rate; but one of the subgroups was sent a detailed asset question as an experiment. In addition all respondents were asked if they would object to receiving future questionnaires containing an identification number to enable reinterviewing, if that proved feasible and useful.

Close to 80 per cent of the April 1958 questionnaires were returned—just over 26,000 in all. Over 24,000 indicated no objection to answering future questionnaires containing an identification number; these households were assigned reference numbers in the order of their arrival. Different number blocks were used to designate the five subgroups into which the original volunteer group had been split. The response rate for the group sent a detailed asset question was the same as for the other groups.

A reinterview survey took place in October 1958, six months after the first special survey. Almost 20,000 returns were received from the 24,000 respondents who had agreed to answer identified questionnaires.[2] Apparently, then, the response rate for each successive survey in the panel was approximately 80 per cent of those answering the preceding one. It also

[2] The number was actually larger than 20,000. In the process of transferring information from the questionnaire schedules onto IBM punch cards, almost 1,000 questionnaires were apparently misplaced and not punched. (One box was presumably labeled "completed," although it had not been processed.) This error was not discovered until some time after the cards had been processed for the reinterview analysis; consequently, these 1,000 cases do not appear in the reinterview sample discussed in this report.

appears, incidentally, that this mail survey was much more successful in following up respondents who had moved than are most personal interview surveys. It is known that some 15 per cent of these households bought homes in the twelve months between October 1957 (when the first mailing address for panel members was received) and October 1958 (when the reinterview survey was mailed out). Thus, about 5,000 of the original 33,000 households moved during this period. The number of undeliverable (no such name, etc.) questionnaires returned unopened from *both* the April and October 1958 surveys was about 1,000; and some of these must have been returned because of undecipherable handwriting on the return envelopes from which the mailing list was compiled. Thus at least 80 per cent of the movers appear to have been followed.

Second and third reinterview surveys were subsequently taken under the auspices of the Expectational Economics Center at Columbia University, under the direction of Albert G. Hart. These surveys were mailed in April 1959 and April 1960. The response rate was in line with previous experience for April 1959 (about 16,000 returns) but not for April 1960 (about 8,500 returns). The explanation for the last is probably the degree of exhaustive detail contained in the questionnaire, which ran 50 per cent larger than previous ones and asked about dollar magnitudes for all variables.

The October 1958 Reinterview Sample

This monograph concentrates on the analysis of the special survey in April 1958 and the first reinterview, in October 1958. Some data from the April 1959 reinterview are included. My concern is with the factors associated with differences among households in purchases of durable goods, in particular, with the degree to which the intentions, attitudes, and expectations expressed in April 1958 are related to purchases over the subsequent six-month period. Consequently, two kinds of data problems must be settled. First, there is no assurance that households are "matched" in the two surveys: Identification numbers were assigned to April 1958 responses, and the same numbers were assigned to the October 1958 outgoing questionnaires. But there are numerous possibilities for error in the procedures used to ensure matching. The possibilities range from key-punch errors in transferring the identification numbers to punch cards to failure on the part of the mailing service to make sure that the outgoing October questionnaire (containing a reference number but no name, as agreed) was put into the proper envelope (containing a name but no number). The matching process was carefully supervised, with the original mailing list envelopes (containing both names and numbers) being checked with each insertion. But there are clearly widespread possibilities for errors, although not for a "run" of errors.[3]

The second problem arises because many questionnaires were incompletely filled out. Thus, some of the variables used in the analysis have unknown values for some respondents. There are three possible alternatives: exclusion of questionnaires with missing information, assignment of a neutral value for the missing variable, or estimation of the missing variable from other data on the same questionnaire.

For the first problem an elaborate matching procedure was instituted. Several pieces of information that should be either fairly stable or consistent were available from the two surveys: education of household head, age of household head, and family income and income change were used as the matching criteria. For the first two of these variables it was assumed that respondents were matched if the same category was checked in both cases, or if the category differed in a way that could be explained by normal "progress"—that is, people get somewhat older and might become more highly educated, but they can become neither younger nor less well educated. With respect to income, data were available for both April and October family income, actual and expected changes in income, and responses to a question about whether family income was unusually high or low in either April or October or both.

Based on these data, a certain number of cases were excluded because it seemed doubtful that the same family was represented. In borderline cases the respondent was eliminated from the sample on the grounds that it was far better to discard possibly accurate information than to try correlating the April buying intentions of one household with the April-October purchases of another. Altogether, about 5 per cent of the 20,000-odd October 1958 returns were eliminated because of doubt as to whether the same family was represented. About 60 per cent of this total comprised straight age or education differences that were in the wrong direction. Some of these cases undoubtedly consisted of the same household; but different people must have answered the two questionnaires, both considering themselves head of household. Others are doubtless either

---

[3] In this connection, the cost of obtaining information is clearly relevant, since additional resources will always enable a reduction of errors. I would estimate the total cost of obtaining some 24,000 April 1958 IBM punch cards from the returned questionnaires, plus some 20,000 October 1958 punch cards, as no more than $25,000. That is, the basic data cost roughly fifty cents per mail interview, including all costs of preparation, mailing, processing, and coding returns and of key punching. The cost is low partly because both the April and October 1958 questionnaires were completely precoded.

key-punch errors or the results of carelessness on the part of respondents. Incidentally, the number of age-bracket changes in the aging direction was close to what one would have predicted from the width of the bracket. An age bracket covering ages from thirty through thirty-four ought to lose about 10 per cent of its cases over a six-month period and ought to gain 10 per cent of the cases in the bracket covering ages from twenty-five through twenty-nine.

As regards the second problem—missing data on one or more variables —it was finally decided to exclude these households from the sample.[4] Many of these households had more than one piece of information missing, and estimating on the basis of information actually provided would have been hazardous in a large fraction of cases. Altogether about 13 per cent of the sample was lost for this reason, making a total of some 18 per cent excluded for either mismatched or missing data. Of the original 19,546 returns from the reinterview survey, a total of 15,810 were regarded as usable. Additional deletions were made at a late stage of the regression analysis. Households who reported that the expected change in their income or in general business conditions was "too uncertain to guess" were removed because it was impossible to know what a pleasant or unpleasant surprise would consist of for these people. About 10 per cent of the sample was lost here. Another substantial fraction was removed from one set of regressions (see Appendix A) because respondents in this group had either purchased houses during the forecast period or had reported intentions to buy houses at the beginning of the forecast period.

A complete tabulation of the numbers of responses to the various surveys, the numbers excluded, and the numbers utilized in the analysis is presented in Table C-1. Table C-2 shows the distribution of usable cases, classified according to age–marital status and the buying-intentions question.

Comparison of Consumers Union Panel with U.S. Population

As already noted, the Consumers Union sample was selected for analysis because of its availability and historical predictive value. Consumers

---

[4] Serious consideration was given to estimating missing values by using a regression technique. Two considerations led to rejection of the questionnaire rather than rectification by estimation. First, there was some reason to believe that the general quality of information contained on questionnaires with missing data was probably lower than average. Secondly, the sample was not randomly selected to begin with; consequently, population parameters were not being estimated in any case. Introducing a slight additional bias into an already strongly biased sample seemed a small loss to set against the substantial cost and time required to estimate values for cases with missing information.

TABLE C-1
Number of Households Responding to Surveys of Consumers Union Panel

	Basic Subsamples					
	A	B	C	D	E	Total
Original panel, formed Oct. 1957	7,069	7,069	7,068	7,069	5,000	33,275
Replies to April 1958 questionnaire						26,133
Did not volunteer for reinterview						1,831
Volunteered for reinterview	5,101	5,268	5,130	5,161	3,642	24,302
Replies to reinterview Oct. 1958[a]	4,205	4,287	3,987	4,226	2,841	19,546
Mismatched cases excluded	241	219	212	222	161	1,055
Cases with missing data excluded	601	594	569	519	398	2,681
Subtotal	3,363	3,474	3,206	3,485	2,282	15,810
Age-marital groups 4 and 5 (over 65 or unmarried) excluded	349	376	434			
Subtotal	3,014	3,098	2,772	b	b	
Cases with uncertain expectations excluded						
Age-marital 1 (married, 25–34)	103	103	100			
Age-marital 2 (married, 35–44)	98	125	100			
Age-marital 3 (married, 45–64)	109	112	107			
Total	310	340	307			
Subtotal in regression analysis[c]	2,704	2,758	2,465	b	b	
Cases with housing plans and/or purchases excluded						
Age-marital 1	229	176	206			
Age-marital 2	136	138	131			
Age-marital 3	65	64	53			
Total	430	378	390			
Subtotal in regression analysis[d]	2,274	2,380	2,075	b	b	

Source: Basic data from Consumer Purchase Study, NBER.
[a] Somewhat understated, for reasons discussed above, note 2.
[b] Samples excluded from regression analysis.
[c] These cases analyzed in Chapter 7.
[d] These cases analyzed in Appendix A.

Union subscribers are by no means representative of the United States population as a whole; and the sample of these subscribers that responds to questionnaires—which is the "universe" being sampled in this study—may not be at all representative of the total CU subscriber population. Further, the reinterview sample is not representative of CU subscribers that return questionnaires, and this is the sample whose behavior is actually examined in the monograph.

The following tables present some comparisons between the CU reinterview panel and the United States population. In most instances the population data consist of tabulations prepared for the Survey of Consumer Finances (SCF) conducted annually by the Survey Research Center at the University of Michigan. SCF data are based on a random sample of

TABLE C-2
DISTRIBUTION OF REGRESSION SAMPLES

Age-Marital Status	*Intentions-to-Buy Sample*		
	A	B	C
HOUSING ACTIVITY EXCLUDED			
Married; head-of-household age between:			
25–34	852	866	814
35–44	863	836	691
45–64	559	678	570
Total	2,274	2,380	2,075
HOUSING ACTIVITY INCLUDED			
Married; head-of-household age between:			
25–34	1,081	1,042	1,020
35–44	999	974	822
45–64	624	742	623
Total	2,704	2,758	2,465

SOURCE: Basic data from Consumer Purchase Study, NBER.

NOTE: Subsamples D and E and respondents who were either unmarried or over 65 years old were not included (cf. Table C-1).

all United States households. In cases where population and CU data are not available for the same year, the comparison is based on years that are as close together as possible. Since most of the distributions presented change slowly over time, any discrepancies in dates should not significantly affect the comparisons.

INCOME AND FINANCIAL CHARACTERISTICS

Probably the most striking difference between the CU sample and the population is the distribution by income and asset level (Table C-3). The CU median income is almost double that of the population. In 1958, more than half of the CU family units had an annual income over $7,500, whereas only 24 per cent of population families earned over that amount. Conversely, over one-quarter of the population earned under $3,000, compared to less than 2 per cent of the CU sample. These differences in income cannot be attributed to differences in the participation of wives in the labor force. The distribution of working wives by income class shows about the same degree of participation for the CU group and the population if full-time and part-time workers are aggregated. There are some differences in the distributions when the two are treated separately, but this may be due to differences in the definition of full-time work. There is some indication that the population may have a higher per-

TABLE C-3
FINANCIAL CHARACTERISTICS OF THE CONSUMERS UNION SAMPLE AND OF THE U.S. POPULATION

FAMILY INCOME	DISTRIBUTION OF FAMILY INCOME		EMPLOYMENT OF WIVES BY INCOME CLASS[a]					
	Population 1957	CU 1957	Full-Time		Part-Time		Full or Part-Time	
			Population 1956	CU 1960	Population 1956	CU 1960	Population 1956	CU 1960
	(proportion of sample)		(proportion of wives in income class who work)					
Less than $3000	.28	.02	.09	.09	.15	.15	.24	.24
$ 3,000–$3,999	.11	.04	.11	.05	.14	.13	.25	.18
$ 4,000–$4,999	.12	.08	.15	.08	.15	.20	.30	.28
$ 5,000–$7,499	.26	.28	.24	.08	.14	.19	.38	.27
$ 7,500–$9,999	.12	.23	.41	.14	.08	.19	.49	.33
$10,000 and over	.12	.33	.25	.19	.07	.16	.32	.35
N.R.[b]		.04						
Median	4,850	8,277						
Total			.19	.14	.13	.18	.32	.32

INCOME AND ASSETS

| Type of Financial-Asset Holdings: | Population 1957 | CU 1958 | Sources of Income:[c] | Population 1957 | CU 1957 | CU 1957 Main Source of Income |
	(proportion of sample)			(proportion of sample)		
Checking account	.55	.92	Wages and salaries	.82	.86	.82
Savings account	.50	.76	Own business or profession	.14	.20	.15
U.S. government savings bonds	.32	.49	Interest or dividends	.18	.14	.03
Other bonds	n.a.	.08	Rent or royalties	.09	.07	.02
Common or preferred stock	.11	.43	Other	.31	.14	.04
None of the above	.24	.02				
Amount of Assets						
Less than $2,000	.75	.43				
$2,000–$10,000	.17	.37				
Over $10,000	.07	.19				

SOURCE: Population data are based on the Survey of Consumer Finances as published in the *Federal Reserve Bulletin.* CU data are based on annual questionnaires.

[a] To make SCF data comparable to CU data the SCF published figures were adjusted to exclude households without a wife, without a husband, and those for whom marital status was not ascertained. Thus, 19 per cent of households that included both husband and wife had a full-time working wife, whereas only 13 per cent of all households had a full-time working wife.

[b] Not reported; SCF figure assigned, if not determined in interview.

[c] In the SCF data, royalties are included with "interest and dividends." Farm income for the SCF data is included in "other"; for the CU data, farm income is included with "own business or profession." The "other" category consists mainly of transfer payments (i.e., pensions, annuities, etc.).

n.a. = not available.

centage of working wives in the $5,000 to $10,000 income groups, as compared to the CU sample.

As would be expected for a high-income sample, the CU group has greater financial assets than the population: only 1.5 per cent of the CU sample reported having no liquid assets, compared to 24 per cent of the population; 19 per cent of the CU sample reported assets over $10,000, compared to 7 per cent of the population. A larger percentage of the CU sample than of the population holds each type of financial asset shown, the difference being especially large for common or preferred stock (43 per cent versus 11 per cent).

TABLE C-4

DEBT RELATIONSHIPS FOR THE CONSUMERS UNION SAMPLE AND THE U.S. POPULATION
(proportion of sample)

	Population 1956	CU 1957
TYPE OF CREDIT USED		
Did not buy anything on credit	.46	.44
Did buy on credit	.54	.56
Credit source[a]		
Instalment plan	.45	.16
Extended charge	n.a.	.09
Private source	n.a.	.04
Bank	.19	.25
Credit union	.04	.07
Finance company	.14	.04
Retail outlet	.23	n.a.
Car dealer	.01	n.a.
Other	.01	.01
Not reported	.02	.09
AMOUNT OF OUTSTANDING DEBT		
Under $500	.28	.20
$500–$999	.12	.14
$1,000 and over	.17	.18
No debt	.39	} .47
Not reported	.04	

SOURCE: Population data are based on the Survey of Consumer Finances as published in the *Federal Reserve Bulletin*. CU data are based on annual questionnaires.

[a] The distribution by credit source exceeds the proportion that "did buy on credit" because some households were in debt to more than one type of creditor. In the SCF data, 0.45 used instalment debt; and the distribution by credit source refers to instalment debt only (i.e., the distribution among credit sources other than instalment is a distribution of 0.45 but does not add to 0.45 because of the use of multiple credit sources). In the CU data the distribution by credit source includes both noninstalment and instalment debt. Because of ambiguities in the way the question was phrased, the "instalment" category for the CU data is less inclusive than that for the SCF data.

n.a. = not available.

CREDIT AND DEBT

Interestingly enough, the extent to which credit is used seems to be quite similar for the CU sample and the population: 56 per cent of the 1957 CU sample bought on credit compared to 54 per cent of the population (Table C-4). The distribution by credit source indicates some differences, but a detailed analysis is not possible because the categories are not sufficiently comparable: the distribution by credit source for the population is based on the use of instalment credit only, whereas the CU data are based on both instalment and noninstalment credit use. An "instalment plan"

TABLE C-5

OWNERSHIP OF DURABLE GOODS IN THE CONSUMERS UNION SAMPLE
AND IN THE U.S. POPULATION
(proportion of dwelling units)

	Population 1960	CU 1958
Household Durables[a]		
Air conditioner	0.12	0.22
Clothes dryer	0.17	0.33
Dishwasher	0.06	0.16
Food freezer	0.21	0.23
Range	0.96	1 00[b]
Refrigerator	0.94	1.00[b]
Television set	0.86	0.79
Washing machine[c]	0.41	0.75
Automobiles[d]		
One or more	0.73	0.96
One	0.61	0.68
Two or more	0.12	0.28
Do not own	0.27	0.04
Owner-Occupied Home[e]	0.54	0.70

SOURCE: Population data for household durables based on *Electrical Merchandising Week* data as published in *Statistical Abstract of the United States, 1960,* Bureau of the Census. Population data for automobiles from *Automobile Facts and Figures, 1957* and *1958.* Population data for home ownership from Survey of Consumer Finances as published in the *Federal Reserve Bulletin.* CU data are based on annual questionnaires.

[a] Population proportions were adjusted to include all occupied homes, both wired and unwired.

[b] The CU questionnaire asks the respondent if he owns a given appliance. If he lives in a rented dwelling in which the landlord supplies the appliance he would not report ownership. Only about 75 per cent of the CU sample reported ownership of a range and refrigerator for this reason, but it can be assumed that practically 100 per cent of the rented dwellings contain these appliances; 27 per cent of the CU sample lives in rented dwellings.

[c] Population figure is from 1960 *Census of Housing.*

[d] Data refer to 1956.

[e] Data refer to 1957.

category can be obtained from the CU data, but it is less comprehensive because of the way in which the question was phrased. Despite these problems, at least one general inference is possible: the population clearly relies more heavily on finance companies and less heavily on credit unions, relative to the CU sample. The distribution by amount of outstanding debt indicates that slightly fewer CU subscribers have debt outstanding; but those who do tend to have a larger amount outstanding than the population as a whole.

STOCK OF DURABLES

The differences between the CU sample and the population with regard to stocks of durable goods are consistent with the differences in income and financial assets (Table C-5). The CU sample has a higher percentage of ownership of every durable listed except television sets. For four of the durables (air conditioner, clothes dryers, dishwasher, and washing machine), the CU ownership rate is about double that of the population. For automobiles, the CU sample also has a higher percentage of ownership, with 96 per cent owning at least one car compared to 73 per cent for the population. Multiple car ownership is more than twice as frequent in the CU sample as in the population. The CU people also tend to own newer cars (Table C-6): 40 per cent of the CU car owners have a car less than two years old compared to 19 per cent of car owners in the population.

TABLE C-6

AGE OF AUTOMOBILES OWNED BY CONSUMERS UNION SAMPLE AND BY U.S. POPULATION

Age (years)	Proportion of Sample Population 1957	CU 1957	Cumulative Proportion of Sample Population 1957	CU 1957
Less than 1	.07	.21	0.07	.21
1–2	12	.19	0.19	.40
2–3	.13	.19	0.32	.59
3–4	.09	.11	0.41	.70
4–5	.11	.10	0.52	.80
5–6	.07	.05	0.59	.85
6–7	.10	.05	0.69	.90
7–8	.11	.05	0.80	.95
8–9	07	.02	0.87	.97
9–10	.04	.01	0.91	.98
10–11	.03	.005	0.94	.99
11–12	.02	.002	0.96	.99
Over 12	.04	.003	1.00	1.00

SOURCE: See Table C-5.

GENERAL CHARACTERISTICS

The CU sample has a slightly lower median age than the population, but the more notable difference is the very small portion of the CU sample under twenty-five or over sixty-five years of age (Table C-7). Only about 6 per cent of the CU sample fall into these categories, compared to 23 per cent of the population. The CU sample shows a much higher level of

TABLE C-7

SELECTED CHARACTERISTICS OF CONSUMERS UNION SAMPLE AND OF U.S. POPULATION
(proportion of sample)

	Population 1957	CU 1957
DISTRIBUTION BY AGE OF HOUSEHOLD HEAD		
Age		
Under 25	.09	.03
25–34	.20	.36
35–44	.23	.31
45–64	.33	.26
65 and over	.14	.03
Not reported	.02	
Median	43.7	38.5
DISTRIBUTION OF URBAN POPULATION BY CITY SIZE		
Population of city		
Over 1,000,000	.14	.16
100,000–1,000,000	.27	.29
25,000–100,000	.23	.22
2,500–25,000	.28	.25
Under 2,500	.08	.08
DISTRIBUTION BY EDUCATION OF HOUSEHOLD HEAD		
Education completed[a]		
None	.02	n.a.
Some elementary school	.22	n.a.
Elementary graduate	.18	n.a.
Some high school	.19	n.a.
High school graduate	.21	n.a.
Subtotal	.82	.21
Some college	.09	.21
College graduate	} .10 {	.24
Graduate school		.31
Other		.03

SOURCE: Population data for age distribution from Survey of Consumer Finances as published in the *Federal Reserve Bulletin*. Population data for education from 1960 *Census of Population*. Population data for city size based on 1960 *Census of Population* as published in 1961 *Statistical Abstract of the United States*, Bureau of the Census. CU data are based on annual questionnaires.

[a] The population distribution refers to the male population twenty-five years old and over, since head-of-household data are not available.

n.a. = not available

formal education, with over 50 per cent of its heads of household having graduated from college (in comparison to 10 per cent of the population) and with only 21 per cent having a high school education or less, compared to 82 per cent of the population. (The population figures in this instance refer to the male population twenty-five years old and over, because education data for heads of household are not available. There is no reason to assume that using the male population twenty-five years old and over instead of heads of household only would bias the comparison in any way.)

In regard to urban population distribution, the CU sample and the population are very similar. In housing status they differ, with the CU sample having a greater percentage of home owners.

An analysis has been made of magazine readership in 1955, comparing the CU sample and the population. For almost every magazine listed the level of readership was much higher for the CU sample, but the reading taste of this sample does not appear to differ substantially from that of the population. A rank correlation shows the following results: for the top thirty-eight magazines read by CU subscribers, rank r^2 between CU and the population was 0.80; for the top ten magazines, rank $r^2 = 0.61$.

A more up-to-date comparison—between 1962 CU subscribers and the population—has been published in the January 1963 issue of CU's *Consumer Reports*, pages 9–12.

Glossary of Symbols

B_r	Number of expected purchases by intenders in any given sample
B_s	Number of expected purchases by nonintenders in any given sample
C_i	Minimum purchase probability associated with the ith intentions question
$\hat{C}$	Expected change in durable goods prices
$\Delta\hat{B}$	Expected change in business conditions
ΔL_{-1}	Change in liquid asset holdings prior to the intentions survey
ΔY	Change in family income during the forecast period
ΔY_{-1}	Change in family income prior to the intentions survey
ΔY_t	Change in family income regarded to abnormal or unusual by the respondent
$\Delta\hat{Y}$	Expected change in family income
Δy	Difference between aggregate disposable income of the current period and disposable income four quarters earlier
Δy_{-1}	Lagged value of Δy
d	Weighted proportion of "don't know" households expected to purchase
E	Index of change in family income and general business conditions during the forecast period
$\hat{E}$	Index of household expectations about income and general business conditions
$\hat{E}_5$	Household expectations about their financial situation five years hence
H	Home ownership status of the respondent
$H_{11}, H_{10},$	Alternative classifications of respondents with respect to house-
H_{01}, H_{00}	buying intentions and housing purchases
N_i	Number of households in the ith sample
N_r	Number of intenders in any given sample
N_s	Number of nonintenders in any given sample
O	Household's opinion about whether "the present is a good or bad time to buy" durables
P	Weighted aggregate purchases of consumer durables by any given household
$\hat{P}$	Weighted aggregate buying intentions reported by any given household
$\hat{P}_c$	Weighted aggregate contingent buying intentions reported by any given household

p_i — Proportion of households in the ith sample reporting intention to buy

p' — Weighted proportion of "intending" households expected to purchase

Q — Purchase probability for any given household (throughout the manuscript, the symbol Q is used to represent purchase probability for any given respondent; In Appendix B, the same symbol is used to represent the ratio of aggregate purchases to aggregate buying intentions, i.e., $P/\hat{P}$)

r_i — Proportion of ith sample intenders who purchase during the forecast period

r'_i — Mean purchase probability for ith sample intenders

S — Stock of durable goods

S' — Stock of durable goods that the respondent reports "need to be replaced"

s_i — Proportion of ith sample nonintenders who purchase during the forecast period

s'_i — Mean purchase probability for ith sample nonintenders

T — Education level of household head

x_i — Proportion of households in the ith sample that purchase during forecast period

x'_i — Mean purchase probability for all households in the ith sample

Y — Normal family income

z — Weighted proportion of "nonintending" households expected to purchase

Index

Lightning Source UK Ltd.
Milton Keynes UK
UKOW06f0011131217
314372UK00003B/413/P

9 780691 624952